*Transport History*
*Volume 4*
*1971*

# Transport History
# Volume 4

Volume 4 of the journal *Transport History*

Editor: Baron F. Duckham
Reviews Editor: John R. Hume

 DAVID & CHARLES: NEWTON ABBOT

ISBN 0 7153 5469 8

COPYRIGHT NOTICE
© DAVID & CHARLES (PUBLISHERS) LIMITED 1972

All rights reserved. No part of this publication may be reproduced, stored in a retrieval system, or transmitted, in any form or by any means, electronic, mechanical, photocopying, recording or otherwise, without the prior permission of David & Charles (Publishers) Limited

*Set in Imprint
and printed in Great Britain
by Latimer Trend & Company Limited Plymouth
for David & Charles (Publishers) Limited
South Devon House   Newton Abbot   Devon*

Number 1

Volume 4 1971

March

# Contents

THE RAILWAYS AND STEAMBOAT COMPETITION IN EARLY VICTORIAN BRITAIN
*T. R. Gourvish* ... 1

FIFTY YEARS OF BUS SERVICES IN A HUNTINGDONSHIRE VILLAGE: THE CASE OF BUCKDEN
*F. H. W. Green* ... 23

JOHN PINKERTON AND THE BIRMINGHAM CANALS
*S. R. Broadbridge* ... 33

CONTINUOUS BRAKES—A VEXED QUESTION. HOW THE SCOTTISH RAILWAYS RESOLVED IT
*Campbell Highet* ... 50

BRISTOL'S SECOND OUTPORT: PORTISHEAD IN THE NINETEENTH CENTURY
*Bryan J. H. Brown* ... 80

BOOK REVIEWS ... 94

SHORTER REVIEWS ... 104

NOTES AND NEWS ... 109

Number 2                                                                                          July

# Contents

| | |
|---|---|
| BEVERLEY AND ITS BECK: BOROUGH FINANCE AND A TOWN NAVIGATION 1700–1835<br>*K. A. MacMahon* | 121 |
| THE BATTLE OF THE MANCHESTER RAILWAY JUNCTIONS<br>*F. C. Mather* | 144 |
| BANKS AND RAILWAY FINANCE: A NOTE ON THE SCOTTISH EXPERIENCE<br>*Wray Vamplew* | 166 |
| THE HULL & BARNSLEY AT SEA<br>*Michael Robbins* | 183 |
| BOOK REVIEWS | 189 |
| SHORTER REVIEWS | 205 |
| NOTES AND NEWS | 214 |

# Contents

| | |
|---|---|
| THE METROPOLIS ROADS COMMISSION: AN ATTEMPT AT TURNPIKE TRUST REFORM<br>*William Albert* | 225 |
| A FIELDWORK NOTE ON THE CONGLETON RAILWAY C 1807<br>*J. C. Hopkins* | 245 |
| THE NATURE AND GROWTH OF CROSS-CHANNEL TRAFFIC THROUGH CALAIS AND BOULOGNE 1840–70<br>*R. J. Croft* | 252 |
| TRANSPORT PROBLEMS OF GLASGOW WEST INDIA MERCHANTS DURING THE AMERICAN WAR OF INDEPENDENCE, 1775–83<br>*T. M. Devine* | 266 |
| BOOK REVIEWS | 305 |
| SHORTER REVIEWS | 315 |
| NOTES AND NEWS | 318 |
| INDEX | 329 |

T. R. GOURVISH

# The Railways and Steamboat Competition in Early Victorian Britain

IN THE EARLY STAGES of railway development in Britain, four companies (the London & Greenwich, London & Blackwall, Glasgow Paisley & Greenock, and Glasgow Paisley Kilmarnock & Ayr) met the sustained competition of a firmly established steamboat interest.[1] The railways quickly discovered that although steamboats were potentially a useful means of taking traffic beyond terminal stations, they posed a severe threat to profitable operation. This article will examine the initial experience of the companies concerned, and attempt to analyse the costs and benefits arising from their involvement in water transport.[2]

I

Steamboats were an important form of passenger transport in the London and Glasgow areas during the 1820s and 1830s. Although the omnibus retained control of the short-distance road traffic, it was unable to compete successfully with river transport. The steamboat, taking full advantage of the opportunities offered by the Thames and Clyde estuaries, enjoyed a virtual monopoly of pleasure traffic and a substantial share of commuter traffic. In London, there were by 1840 at least seven operators of local services from London Bridge to Greenwich, Woolwich, and Gravesend, and five companies sailing to the Kent Coast, northern England, Scotland, and the Continent.[3] In Glasgow, over thirty vessels were engaged in local routes in the 1830s, while about twenty coastal boats served the north-west of Scotland, Ireland, and Liverpool.[4] Services were naturally subject to seasonal fluctuation, especially on the Clyde, where many steamboats were withdrawn between November and February. Nevertheless, the annual traffic appears to have been larger than that commanded by other modes of transport. Although contemporary estimates should be regarded with suspicion, James Cleland claimed that there were 579,000 Clyde river passengers in 1834; in 1837, 692,000 passengers were said to be travelling by river from Glasgow to Greenock and beyond.[5] In London, the London–Gravesend traffic alone amounted to 119,000 as early as 1829–30, and five years later the number of passengers using Gravesend Pier was estimated to be 500,000.[6] Although competition between boat companies was keen, rates were often agreed in order to guarantee a satisfactory level of profit. Costs could be related to traffic returns by choosing large or small boats, and steamboats, unlike road and rail transport, were exempt from the government's tax on passengers carried.[7]

There is at first sight a degree of similarity in the position and experience of the railways affected by steamboat competition. All four companies were completed during the economic depression of 1837–42, and were conceived with urban and inter-urban traffic in mind. (See Table 1). Their traffic prospects were not identical, however.

TABLE I

CHIEF RAILWAY COMPANIES FIRST CONCERNED WITH STEAMBOAT COMPETITION

| Company | Initial Date of Authorisation | Date of Opening | Length in 1841 | Direct Population Served in 1841* |
|---|---|---|---|---|
| London & Greenwich | 1833 | 1836/8 | 3¾ miles | 391,158 |
| London & Blackwall | 1836 | 1840/1 | 3¾ miles | 446,436 |
| Glasgow Paisley & Greenock | 1837 | 1840/1 | 22½ miles | 382,119 |
| Glasgow Paisley Kilmarnock & Ayr | 1837 | 1839/40 | 40¼ miles | 395,023 |

The Glasgow companies shared the first seven miles of line, from Glasgow to Paisley. *Figures taken from the census of 1841. Those for the London companies comprise the population of districts immediately served by the railway: those for the Glasgow companies the population of Glasgow (city & suburbs) and towns directly served by the railway.

The London companies' lines were shorter than those in Glasgow, and this fact made the prospects of the Blackwall and Greenwich railways more dependent upon short-distance traffic, for which both steamboats and omnibuses competed. The Glasgow-based companies were fortunate in that they were also designed to serve a fairly substantial inland population, including the towns of Paisley, Johnstone, Ayr, and Kilmarnock. This distinction is not, however, useful if we are to consider the extent of railway involvement in steamboat operation. The London & Greenwich Railway, although competing with steamboats for the local traffic, was not directly linked with the Thames, and could not therefore consider the possibility of feeding into river and coastal services at Greenwich. The Glasgow & Ayr company did not depend upon taking traffic from the local river services on the Clyde. Although some boats did sail from Glasgow to Troon, Ayr, and Stranraer, the railway's advantage in speed became more critical over longer distances, and river competition did not hinder the company's progress. The management was more concerned with syphoning off the lucrative Scotland–England and Scotland–Ireland traffic by means of rail-connected services from Ardrossan and a working agreement with the Ardrossan Railway.[8] Both the Greenwich and Glasgow & Ayr companies, although affected by steamboat competition, did not find relations with their rivals to be a major preoccupation.

On the other hand, the initial prospects of the Blackwall and Greenock companies, which faced competition from both river and coastal boats, depended closely upon an ability to seize the steamboat traffic. The Blackwall Railway had been promoted with the specific intention of enabling passengers to avoid the congestion of London Pool: the Greenock Railway was intended to ease a similar situation on the Clyde. In each case, the railway's terminus was close enough to the river to facilitate interchange with steamboats, and it became a major policy to induce boats to sail to and from the 'railway pier' instead of the city centre. Superior speed, rather than cheapness or comfort, was emphasised in the railway prospectuses. The Blackwall company intended to cut the time taken by river by as much as one hour; the

Greenock company hoped to save passengers about one and a half hours. In this way, it was confidently expected that the railway would take the growing business and tourist traffic from the steamboats, and it was also recognised that receipts would be increased if 'feeder' services from the railway terminal were promoted. The opening of the two railways in 1840-1 was followed by a protracted struggle with the steamboat companies, and this struggle will be analysed in some detail.

## II

*The London & Blackwall Railway*

The company possessed an important advantage in its physical connection with the Thames at Blackwall, and prior to its opening in 1840 it rented Brunswick Wharf from the East & West India Dock Company, securing control of the rail-river interchange point.[9] From the start, therefore, the company's minimum objective was to ensure that the wharf was used by as many boats as possible. At the same time, it was considered essential to persuade steamboat operators to terminate there, in order to provide the railway with the entire London-Blackwall traffic. The directors' choice of policy was dictated by the relative importance of the the different traffics, and by the nature of inter-steamboat competition. The coastal steamboat companies did not on the whole cause the railway much inconvenience. The traffic was light and predominantly seasonal, and there was little competition among the boats.[10] In this situation, the railway could afford to be conciliatory, and the absence of steamboat rivalry enabled the directors to make limited agreements whereby boats sailing to the Kent coast and the Continent would make an additional stop at Blackwall, but would not terminate there.[11] The directors did, however, offer inducements, in the form of reduced landing charges ('wharfage') for boats which agreed to terminate at Blackwall. By 1842 this policy had succeeded in encouraging some Kent coast boats to do so.[12] The situation of limited co-operation brought a small number of passengers to the railway

# Railways and Steamboat Competition in Early Victorian Britain

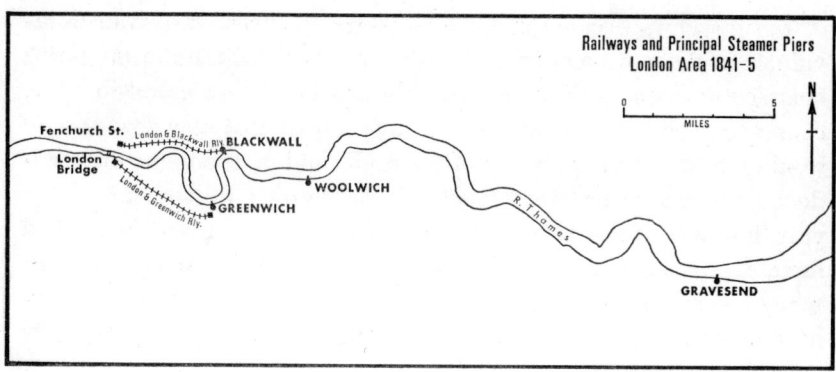

until London became connected by rail with Dover (in 1844) and with Margate and Ramsgate (in 1846).

The railway found it more difficult to deal with the local traffic to Greenwich, Woolwich, and Gravesend. This was not only potentially lucrative, but was also subject to the fiercest competition. The directors at first pursued a policy of negotiation, confident that at least half the local services would soon terminate at Blackwall.[13] The steamboat companies doubted the value of co-operation, however. Well-established concerns, such as the Woolwich and Diamond Steam Packet companies were certain that their ability to offer the passenger comfort, through travel, a direct communication with the city, and low fares would prevent the loss of traffic to the railway. Moreover, such was the nature of inter-steamboat rivalry that if one company expressed an interest in co-operating with the railway, it expected exclusive rights at the expense of others.[14] Differences in the level of operations, investment, and enterprise among the steamboat companies also hindered general agreement.[15]

The directors of the Blackwall Railway were thus forced to adopt new measures in order to ensure that the majority of local steamboat passengers transferred to the trains at Blackwall. Railways were not permitted to own steamboats directly, but it was possible for them to take alternative steps to ensure the same results. Accordingly, some of the directors decided at an early stage to invest as private individuals in the construction and operation of three steamboats. These boats commenced sailing between Blackwall and Gravesend in 1841, connecting with the trains, and it was hoped that the new service would take a substantial share of the traffic and persuade the independent operators to terminate boats at Blackwall.[16] By the end of the year, however, it was clear that the presence of the 'railway boats' had merely intensified competition for the Gravesend traffic. Although many steamboat companies included stops at Blackwall, they made little effort to connect with the trains, and the majority of passengers continued to travel through by boat.[17]

The Greenwich and Woolwich traffic was more easily brought to the railway. The boats of the Woolwich Steampacket and Waterman's companies began to use Brunswick Wharf as their terminal from 1841, and although rivalry persisted, in 1844 an agreement was eventually reached by which the traffic was divided between the two companies on an equal basis: provision was also made for through booking of passengers.[18] The short distance between rail-head and port of destination enabled the steamboat companies to make more intensive use of their boats. The Gravesend traffic, however, remained largely in independent steamboat hands throughout the 1840s. The directors made several attempts to persuade the shareholders to take a financial interest in the 'railway boats', but it soon became apparent that these were not a sound venture. In 1843 a special committee of investigation recommended that either a subsidiary company be formed to operate steamboats, or that the company's surplus capital be applied to the hire of boats.[19] The shareholders remained sceptical, however, and there seems little doubt that unfavourable criticism of the Blackwall company's policy in the railway press had exerted an influence.[20]

The directors, inexperienced in pricing matters, were frequently at a loss in their efforts to make both the trains and the 'railway boats' remunerative. It was difficult to decide whether the company should pursue a low fares policy or try to reach a settlement with its competitors on the basis of higher fares. The efficacy of applying discriminatory wharfage charges at Blackwall was also a matter of debate.[21] Indeed, it proved almost impossible to ensure that the independent steamboat companies quoted fares comparable with a combined rail-boat fare *and* made satisfactory connections with the trains at Blackwall. A differential of 6d between the London–Gravesend and the Blackwall–Gravesend fares was agreed in 1842, but the arrangement soon broke down. The directors employed several expedients: differential wharfage charges and outright competition by low fares were accompanied by promises of guaranteed working expenses, free railway passes, and greater shares in composite rail-boat fares for co-operating companies.[22] These did not, however, bring all the independent companies to heel. Animosity was caused by the railway's policy of allocating the most profitable landing times at Brunswick Wharf to the 'railway boats' and to friendly independents (such as the Star Company) which had agreed to terminate at Blackwall. This not only prolonged competition, but also encouraged companies such as the Diamond Steampacket Company to avoid the wharf altogether.[23]

By 1846 it was clear that the failure of the railway and the steamboats to reach agreement had damaged the interests of both. The Greenwich and Woolwich business, although subject to competition in 1845, was divided satisfactorily, and in 1847 the directors appeared satisfied with the results.[24] Difficulties with the Gravesend traffic remained, despite the willingness of both sides to negotiate, and the position did not alter until a direct rail link between London, Woolwich, and Gravesend was opened in 1849.[25]

The railway's steamboat policies had mixed results. Although most boats were induced to use the wharf (by 1844 eight vessels terminated there),[26] many companies continued to sail from London Bridge to Gravesend, and the action of the Diamond company in particular wrecked several attempts to stabilise fares at a higher level than that determined by direct competition.[27] By 1845 the railway's directors were more interested in improving land connections with other railways: plans were made to standardise the gauge and introduce locomotives in place of stationary engines, and in 1849 a branch connecting with the Eastern Counties Railway at Bow was opened.[28]

## The Glasgow Paisley & Greenock Railway

The Greenock company began preliminary negotiations with steamboat owners before the railway was constructed. In 1838 the directors declared that 'by starting steamers from Greenock on the arrival of each train to the numerous ports to which they now run, a great saving in time will be effected. . . . In this union of purpose, the Board is led to believe that many, if not all, the steam companies . . . will cordially join'.[29] But before the line was eventually opened to Greenock (in March 1841), the railway's management discovered that steamboat opposition to this plan would be stronger than anticipated. The railway was at a disadvantage in that its station at Greenock was some distance from the pier: its Glasgow terminus at Bridge Street was also a little further from the city centre than was the boats' landing place. This handicap was offset by the railway's superior speed and reliability over a relatively long journey (22½ miles) but, nevertheless, the steamboat owners had confidence that they would retain a substantial proportion of the traffic travelling beyond Greenock.

A distinction between the coastal and river traffics is again pertinent. The coastal traffic was certainly of more importance to the Greenock Railway than it was to the Blackwall company. The major route from Glasgow to England was via Liverpool or Fleetwood in the early 1840s, and there was also an important business traffic between Glasgow and Ireland (especially Dublin, Belfast, Sligo, and Londonderry). The importance of tapping this traffic was seen in 1840, when plans for a union of interest with an important steamboat company were considered.[30] However, the railway company failed to induce any boats to terminate at Greenock until 1845, although most coastal companies made a limited arrangement to connect with railway services by calling in at the port.[31] The issue does not appear to have been critical. From the opening of the railway in 1841, the advertisements inserted by coastal companies in the local newspapers included

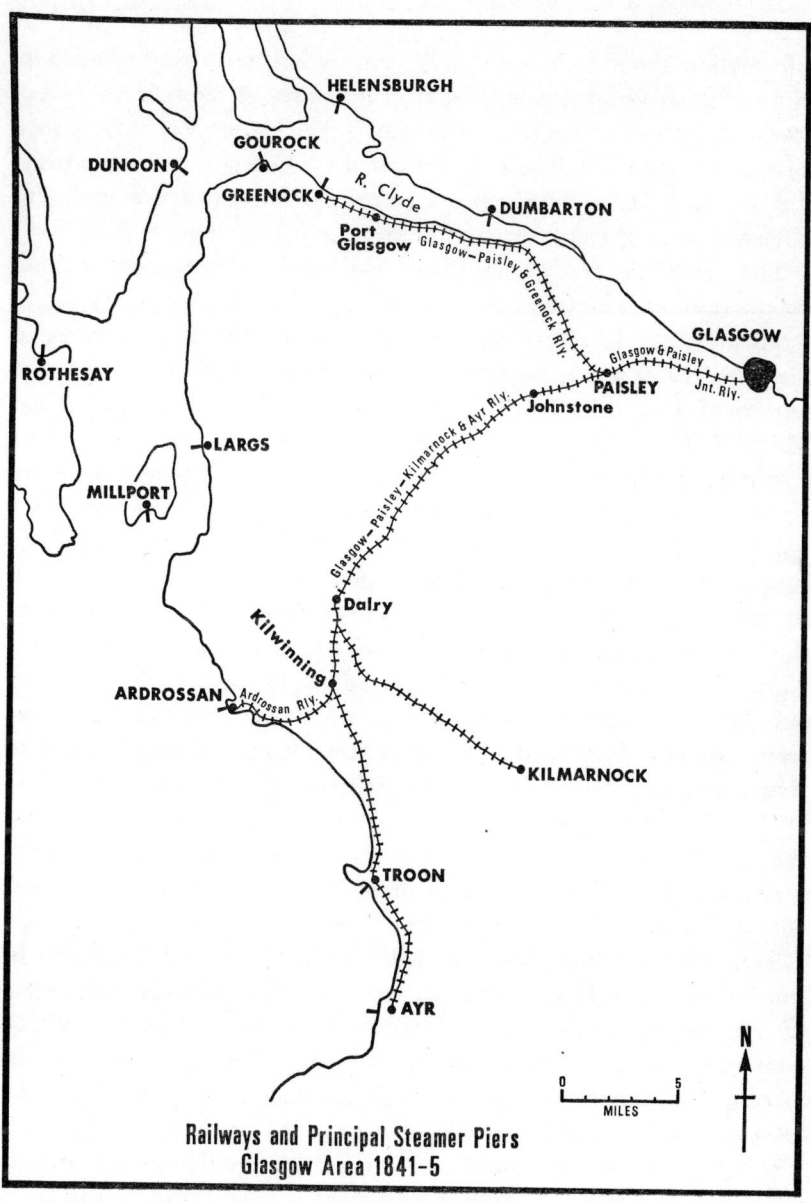

Railways and Principal Steamer Piers
Glasgow Area 1841-5

information about railway services, and invited intending passengers to interchange at Greenock.[32] In 1843 it was suggested that the Liverpool and Irish boats were landing most of their passengers at Greenock instead of Glasgow.[33] The competition of the Glasgow & Ayr Railway, and its efforts to persuade boats to use Ardrossan in preference to Greenock caused the Greenock Railway more concern.[34]

The size of the river traffic again made it an attractive proposition for the railway. The Greenock management was not only interested in acquiring the Glasgow–Greenock business: it also fully appreciated the potential of a summer traffic of about 400,000 passengers to the resorts of Gourock, Dunoon, Helensburgh, Rothesay, Largs, and Millport. The railway at first advocated negotiation with existing boat operators, but it soon became clear that substantial guarantees were necessary to ensure agreement. In 1841 the company was led into a policy of chartering boats to work exclusively for the railway. The sums agreed were designed to encourage boats to connect at Greenock by providing security against initial operational losses.[35] In this way, the railway gained the co-operation of the Bute Steampacket Company, the Dumbarton Steamboat Company, and a few smaller operators. The early fare schedules show, however, that through fares from Glasgow to the coastal resorts included 'allowances' made to these companies which cut into the railway's profit margin.[36]

Despite the generous nature of the railway's charter arrangements, the larger independent steamboat companies such as the Castle, Helensburgh & Gareloch, and Largs, Millport & Arran Steamboat companies refused to give up the Glasgow–Greenock traffic. These Glasgow-based companies intended to fight the railway by means of low fares and a refusal to connect with the trains at Greenock. Some of the companies which had offered boats for charter by the railway continued to sail to Glasgow and adjusted their landing times at Greenock to enable them to race the trains. In the period April–June 1841, the railway carried only 8 per cent of the traffic to the resorts.[37] The company was thus forced to adopt a more positive policy towards steamboat operation. A railway steamboat company, which had been considered as early as 1840, was formed in 1842. Directors and shareholders, acting in an individual capacity, raised capital to take control of the Bute Steampacket Company, and in May an agreement was made by which the 'Railway Steampacket Company' was to supply all the railway's requirements on the major routes.[38]

The involvement of Greenock Railway shareholders in steamboat enterprise was not successful in its quest to attract the majority of river passengers to the railway. Just as the Blackwall Railway found the opposition of the Diamond company, damaging, so the Greenock Railway faced the competition by low fares of powerful independents such as the Castle Steamboat Company.[39] Although the Railway Steampacket Company guaranteed a certain level of railway traffic (enabling the railway to cost its operations more effectively) and induced a number of smaller steamboat interests to co-operate, the challenge of the larger, Glasgow-based companies was stronger than anticipated, and receipts from the feeder services were disappointing. The railway was left with the alternative of abandoning the traffic, or of attempting to meet the pricing challenge of the Castle and other companies.[40] The directors chose the latter, but their efforts to attract cabin passengers by means of low third- and fourth-class fares in 1842 and 1843 were a failure. Although the low fares were justified in terms of low incremental costs, and extra traffic was generated, the patronage of river boats was not affected, and it appears that first- and second-class railway passengers were drawn to the cheaper accommodation.[41]

The strength of the independent boat companies lay in their ability to quote low fares, to offer passengers comfortable through travel, and to respond to changes in steamboat technology. The willingness of owners to invest in faster, more reliable boats reduced the railway's advantage and further calls on the shareholders were necessary to finance an extension of steamboat enterprise. A guarantee fund was created to provide the subsidiary company with new boats and to make up operational losses.[42] The Railway Steampacket Company was thereby able to keep pace with developments, and faster boats were introduced in 1844 and 1845. By this time, however, the whole traffic situation facing the Glasgow & Greenock was in the process of change. The promotion of the Caledonian Railway raised the strong possibility that Anglo-Scottish passengers would abandon the Greenock–Liverpool sea route. The Greenock management, having at first viewed the prospect with alarm, executed a remarkable *volte-face*: within two years of fierce opposition to the scheme, they welcomed it to the point of applying to Parliament for an amalgamation of the two companies.[43] Much of the river traffic was beyond the reach of any railway project, but the continued difficulty of steamboat opposition led the Greenock Railway, like the Blackwall, to seek the extension of traffic by means of connections with newly-promoted lines.[44] In 1847, the Railway Steampacket Company sold its boats to independent interests, and the railway ceased to exercise a direct influence over steamboat operation. Although it appears that the railway's policy from 1841 brought many passengers to the trains at Greenock, the profitability of its activities may be questioned. Here again, the operation of 'railway boats' was not only costly, but also antagonised the independent steamboat companies. Consequently, the railway's share of traffic beyond Greenock was severely limited.

## The Glasgow Paisley Kilmarnock & Ayr Railway

A few remarks on the policies of this railway may be pertinent. Although its viability was not threatened by steamboat competition, its experience of this traffic was remarkably similar to the two cases already cited. On the opening of the railway between Glasgow and Ardrossan (via the Ardrossan Railway) in August 1840, a steamboat service to Liverpool was introduced, forming part of the first rail-steamer link between Glasgow and London. Certain directors and shareholders contributed money to purchase the *Fire King* steamboat, a policy repeated by the Blackwall and Greenock railways. By February 1841, however, the economics of operation had been such that the boat was sold to J. & G. Burns, an independent coastal company.[45] The Glasgow & Ayr company was also interested in the Irish traffic. In 1841 negotiations for a Belfast service were conducted, and the steamboat owners were able to obtain £10 a day as guaranteed expenses, in addition to the profits on the traffic. The initial receipts again proved to be disappointing.[46] Thus the Ayr company, like the Greenock Railway, found that it was expensive to charter boats. It also quickly realised that to leave the services in the hands of independent operators could prejudice its interests. J. & G. Burns, having placed the *Fire King* on the Ardrossan–Fleetwood route, transferred the boat to the Belfast route, leaving the railway without its Anglo-Scottish service. The same boat was later hired by the Preston & Wyre Railway, also without success.[47] The Glasgow & Ayr was soon forced to consider, in conjunction with the Preston & Wyre, the direct provision of steamboats. A committee of 1843 paid close attention to the provision of boats for the Ardrossan–Fleetwood run, and its preoccupation with anticipated costs suggests that it was by no means certain that profits would result. Eventually, the shareholders of the two companies, acting in an individual capacity, purchased one boat each, and a new service commenced in 1844.[48] By this time, however, the future viability of the Fleetwood route was in doubt. Indeed, the chairman's prevarication over the scheme demonstrated that the management was torn between the provision of boats and the formation of an Anglo-Scottish route by rail.[49] The pattern of railway-steamboat relations was once more repeated.

The problem of negotiating with independent steamboat companies was further illustrated by the Glasgow & Ayr's relations with boats sailing to Stranraer, Belfast, and Londonderry. Not only was the company forced to agree to generous concessions which must have substantially reduced any profit arising from the traffic, but the management also acted as an agent in seeking loans for steamboat companies from the Union Bank.[50] Commissions of between 25 and 33 per cent were offered to companies co-operating on coastal routes south of Ayr.[51]

## III

How successful were the railways' early efforts in steamboat enterprise? Precise judgement is hindered by the lack of financial information, and even traffic statistics are hard to find. Not only did railways show extreme reluctance to provide the public with business details, but it must also be doubted whether the smaller companies possessed the accounting knowledge necessary for a full investigation of costs and receipts. However, the available evidence points to the unprofitability of the steamboat links promoted by railways. Losses appear to have arisen both in subsidiary companies and as a result of chartering vessels for railway use. It seems, therefore, that receipts did not cover the marginal operating costs of rail-boat services.

In London the Blackwall Railway's costs of handling traffic at the Brunswick Wharf appear to have been fully covered by the wharfage charged on passengers and goods:

TABLE II

COSTS AND RECEIPTS AT BRUNSWICK WHARF, BLACKWALL, 1841–7

| Date July–June | Total costs (includes rents, wharfage paid to E. & W. India Dock Co, wages and salaries) £ | Total direct receipts £ |
|---|---|---|
| 1841–2 | 3,628 | 3,743 |
| 1842–3 | 2,590 | 3,743 |
| 1843–4 | 2,594 | 4,169 |
| 1844–5 | 3,201 | 3,946 |
| 1845–6 | 3,224 | 5,819 |
| 1846–7 | 3,600 | 6,214 |

*Source:* L & B Reports & Accounts, RAC1/227A, L & B Cash Book, 1841–2, LBW23/10, L & B Revenue Ledger, 1840–2, BTHR.

Such an analysis is no guide to the profitability of traffic drawn to the railway by means of boat connections, and particularly, of passenger traffic. Indeed, a substantial proportion of the increased direct receipts at Brunswick Wharf came from goods traffic, which exhibited a fourfold increase in the five years to 1846-7. It would be a very difficult exercise to calculate the costs and benefits of traffic derived from steamboat feeder services, even if a full breakdown of receipts were available. In the absence of specific information, it is at least clear that the three boats built on the initiative of the Blackwall directors, although carrying a fairly large traffic to Gravesend, did not capture a proportion necessary to ensure profitable operation at low fares. The various negotiations with the steamboat operators suggest that the small profits gained at Brunswick Wharf were more than offset by the failure of the company to enforce relatively high rail-boat fares between London and Gravesend. There is ample evidence of the directors' anxiety that the shareholders should assume responsibility for the losses made by the 'railway boats', and of the shareholders' reluctance to undertake such a commitment. A net loss of £677 on the first three months of operation was declared, and the minutes clearly indicate that company monies were applied in 1841 to assist the enterprise.[52] By 1843, there was severe criticism in the railway press of the Blackwall's failure in steamboat operation, and eventually the boats reverted to independent control in the sense that the directors who had financed the project resigned on their failure to obtain a direct financial commitment by the railway company.[53] The low fares which the railway was forced to adopt for the through traffic to Gravesend forced receipts below the marginal cost of operation. This is emphasised by the recurring complaints of co-operating steamboat companies that they could not absorb the railway fare in agreed composite fares without losing money.[54] Between 1844 and 1847, there were several instances of conflict, and although the railway wished to raise fares it was forced to take a diminished share of through fares in order to maintain its agreements with co-operating companies.

The disappointing results of the Blackwall's steamboat policies were seen in the comparatively small share in total receipts which steamboat passengers represented. In 1842, the directors debated whether pricing policy should be determined by a traffic which formed only one-sixth of total receipts.[55] A detailed statement for 1847 and 1848 indicates that the position did not alter significantly despite the co-operation of several independent companies:

TABLE III

THE DISTRIBUTION OF GROSS PASSENGER RECEIPTS, LONDON & BLACKWALL RAILWAY

|  | Contribution to Receipts | | | |
| --- | --- | --- | --- | --- |
|  | Jan–June 1847 | | Jan–June 1848 | |
| Source of Receipts | £ | % of Total | £ | % of Total |
| Local Stations (railway) | 16,857 | 73·4 | 15,659 | 71·1 |
| Gravesend (steamboat) | 4,670 | 20·3 | 5,155 | 23·4 |
| Woolwich (steamboat) | 1,441 | 6·3 | 1,207 | 5·5 |
|  | 22,968 | 100 | 22,022 | 100 |

*Source:* L & B General Meeting, Directors' Report, 22 August 1848, RAC1/227A, BTHR.

The Greenock Railway at first pursued a policy of chartering boats. The boat companies were guaranteed sums ranging from £7 to £17 per day, and were also granted allowances out of composite rail-boat fares calculated on a zonal basis. For example, in 1841 the fares from Glasgow to Helensburgh (2s 6d first, 1s 6d second class) were the same as those charged from Glasgow to Greenock. Allowances varied from 15 to 45 per cent of the total fare. Both expedients to encourage co-operation were undoubtedly expensive, and early losses in 1841 were estimated to be £123 a week.[56] In the summer, small steamboat companies took advantage of the large seasonal traffic, quoting fares as low as 6d for the Glasgow–Rothesay and Glasgow–Dunoon trips (equivalent to 0·15d and 0·20d per mile), and depriving the railway and its subsidiary of a remunerative traffic to the resorts. The efforts of the Railway Steampacket Company involved considerable drains upon the railway's resources, particularly when capital equipment was required. The Greenock Railway's manager stated in 1844 that the shareholders had relinquished one and a half years' dividend to finance the steamboat subsidiary.[57]

Railway receipts had to cover not only the expenses of railway operation and the government's passenger tax, but also the cost of charter facilities and occasional guarantees against loss by feeder services. When the subsidiary company was formed, a similar system was extended to it, and allowances on through fares remained.[58] By 1844 the Greenock company was using its guarantee fund to cover the Railway Steampacket Company's working expenses: it was stated, for example, that the Rothesay boat required at least £40 per week to cover costs.[59] A survey conducted by the Glasgow & Ayr Railway estimated that the full weekly cost of operating an Ardrossan–Fleetwood boat (including provision for insurance, depreciation, and repairs) in 1843 was £163 10s.[60] Since the demand for transport was more responsive to the level of fares than to the speed of travel,[61] it was almost inevitable that the small profits made by the railways on their rail traffic were subsidising losses on steamboat feeder services, where pricing was affected by severe competitive constraints. Indeed, this experience was shared by many other railways which later became involved in steamboat operation. The Caledonian and Manchester, Sheffield & Lincolnshire railways in the 1850s and the Great Eastern Railway in the 1860s found profits on passenger services difficult to obtain. It was only on the South Coast routes to the Continent that the railway's early relationship with steamboats proved in any way successful. Otherwise, the frequent reversion of railway-controlled boats into private hands was characteristic.[62]

The experience of the companies which faced steamboat competition in the early Victorian period was thus identical in its lack of financial success. The railway was unable to exploit fully its potential advantages over a rival which had successfully adapted steam-power to water transport. The newcomer, intending to defeat rather than complement the steamboat, was forced into a relatively subordinate position until the logical implications of railway building produced a network capable of reaching most towns previously served by water transport.[63] The Blackwall and Greenock railways did not enjoy the expected fruits of their promotion, while the Greenwich company, although not directly interested in steamboat enterprise, found river competition damaging.[64] All three railways turned to land connections, and were soon involved in the affairs of other lines.

The implications of the case histories discussed in this paper are clear. The railway found it difficult to compete on equal terms with smaller concerns for the shorter distance traffic. Steamboats, with lower overheads, were able to exploit the seasonality of the passenger traffic by adjusting their capacities to fluctuating demand more promptly and precisely than could the railways. Demand, especially for excursion travel, was found to respond more readily to cheapness and comfort than to speed and reliability.[65] Certainly, co-operation between steamboat and railway would have avoided unnecessary duplication of facilities, and higher fares might have been introduced. But this could not occur while local steamboat operators found it uneconomic to supply feeder services without considerable guarantees. The coastal steamboat companies had been more willing to co-operate with railways precisely because the railway fare did not substantially reduce their tariffs. The railway companies were thus rather unwilling participators in steamboat operation, and the late 1840s saw a greater degree of co-operation between the two modes of transport. By this time, however, railway managements had abandoned ideas of securing all of the river traffic and were directing their attention to increasing revenue by means of connections with new railway companies. The high elasticity of demand for rail transport in London and Glasgow and the ability of steamboat companies to retain a large proportion of their established traffic ensured that the railways' early attempts to defeat steamboat competition and make profitable use of steamboat feeders were a failure.

*University of East Anglia*

## References

1. There were of course other minor examples such as the Hull & Selby Railway Company which met some steamer competition on the Ouse and Humber.
2. This is a much neglected field: see H. J. Dyos and D. H. Aldcroft, *British Transport*, Leicester (1969), 417. I should like to thank Dr J. R. Kellett and Messrs Thomas Hart and M. C. Reed for their comments on an earlier draft of this paper.
3. F. Burtt, *Cross-Channel and Coastal Paddle Steamers*, London (1934), 19–23; and F. Burtt, *Steamers of the Thames and Medway*, London (1949), 29; Select Committee on the Port of London, British Parliamentary Papers, 1836, XIV, Appdx 22.
4. W. M'Ilwraith, *The Glasgow & South Western Railway*, Glasgow (1880), 5; J. Cleland, *Statistical Facts descriptive of the Former and Present State of Glasgow*, Glasgow (1837), 14.
5. Cleland, op cit, 14; *Railway Magazine & Annals of Science*, IV (1838), 14.
6. Anon, *An Account of the Origin of Steam-boats ... and of their Introduction and Employment upon the River Thames between London and Gravesend*, London (1831), 73; T. C. Barker & R. M. Robbins, *A History of London Transport*, I, London (1963), 42.
7. The Kent Coast boats ranged from 140 to 230 tons, while the Woolwich and Greenwich boats were normally between 40 and 100 tons, SC on the Port of London, BPP, 1836, XIV, Appdx 17, 22, Accounts & Papers, BPP 1845, XLVII. The duty on passengers was, until 1842, ½d per passenger-mile, 2 & 3 Will IV, c 120.
8. *Glasgow Herald*, 17 August 1840; GPG Company Minutes, 9 September 1840; Glasgow Paisley Kilmarnock & Ayr (GPK) Traffic Committee Minutes, 1 April 1841, Scottish Record Office (SRO), BR/GPG/1/2, BR/GPK/1/7.
9. London & Blackwall (L & B) Company Minutes, 10 June 1840, LBW1/1, British Transport Historical Records (BTHR). The railway was opened in July 1840 between Blackwall and the Minories: an extension to Fenchurch Street was opened in August 1841.
10. This is suggested by the landing charges paid by coastal and river companies at Brunswick Wharf. Between January and June 1842 six coastal companies paid only £277, while the Woolwich Steam Packet Company paid £347, L & B Revenue Ledger, 1840–2, LBW23/14, BTHR.
11. L & B Directors' Report, 30 August 1842, RAC1/227A, BTHR.
12. L & B Directors' Report, 28 February 1842, RAC1/227A, BTHR.
13. L & B Minutes, 29 April 1840, LBW1/1, BTHR.
14. Eg, the Woolwich Steam Packet Company, L & B Minutes, 17 August and 18 November 1840, LBW1/2, BTHR.
15. See, for example, the conflict between the Star, Diamond, and Sons of the Thames companies, L & B Minutes, 14 December 1841, 24 March 1842, LBW1/2, BTHR. The Sons of the Thames boats were much smaller than those of the other two companies, thus affecting its attitude to acceptable fare levels, SC on the Port of London, BPP 1836, XIV, Appdx 17, 22, Accounts & Papers, BPP 1845, XLVII,
16. L & B Directors' Report, 26 February and 19 August 1841, RAC1/227A, BTHR.
17. The company's revenue ledger lists 15 companies paying wharfage, 1841–2. LBW23/14, BTHR.

18 L & B Minutes, 23 January 1841, 9 January 1844, LBW1/2, LBW1/6; L & B Directors' Report, 26 February 1841, 15 February 1844, RAC1/227A, BTHR.
19 L & B Committee of Investigation Report, 15 May 1843, RAC1/227A, BTHR.
20 See *Herapath's Railway Magazine*, 25 February, 15 April, 3/10/17 June 1843.
21 L & B Minutes, 9 November 1841, 4 January 1842, LBW1/2, BTHR.
22 L & B Minutes, 20 January, 15 March, 26 July 1842, 19 September and 3 October 1843, LBW1/2, BTHR.
23 L & B Minutes, 24 January, 12 December 1843, 12 March–23 April 1844, 18 March 1845, LBW1/2, LBW1/6, BTHR; *Herapath's Railway Magazine*, 15 April 1843. Competition did not end in 1842, as is suggested in Barker & Robbins, op cit, 49.
24 L & B Minutes, 8 April, 16 September, 7 October 1845, 23 March 1847, LBW1/6, LBW1/8; L & B Directors' Report, 17 August 1847, RAC1/227A, BTHR.
25 Barker & Robbins, op cit, 48.
26 L & B Directors' Report, 29 August 1844, RAC1/227A, BTHR.
27 L & B Minutes, 2–16 April 1844, 29 September–29 December 1846, LBW1/6-7, BTHR.
28 Jeffrey's comments at the general meeting, *Railway Times*, 31 August 1844; L & B Directors' Report, 19 August 1845, RAC1/227A, BTHR; Barker & Robbins, op cit, 50.
29 GPG Directors' Report, 18 December 1838, BR/GPG/1/2, SRO.
30 GPG Minutes, 9–25 September 1840, BR/GPG/1/2, SRO.
31 GPG Directors' Report, 15 September 1845, BR/GPG/1/3, SRO.
32 *Glasgow Herald*, 29 March 1841, et seq.
33 GPG Minutes, 22 November 1843, BR/GPG/1/3, SRO.
34 GPG Minutes, 17 September 1839, 14 August 1840, 21 July 1841, BR/GPG/1/2, SRO.
35 GPG Minutes, 5 March 1841, BR/GPG/1/2, SRO.
36 GPG Minutes, 12 March 1841, BR/GPG/1/2, SRO.
37 W. Harding's evidence, *Select Committee on Railways*, BPP 1844, XI, QQ 5434–5; GPG Miscellaneous & Special Ctee Minutes, 12 July 1841, BR/GPG/1/7, SRO. Difficulties of connection at Greenock are suggested in the railway's advertisements, eg, *Glasgow Herald*, 5 April 1841 and 25 April 1842.
38 GPG Miscellaneous & Special Ctee Minutes, 29 January 1840, 14 July 1841, BR/GPG/1/7; GPG Minutes, 20–7 April 1842, 27 December 1843, BR/GPG/1/3, SRO.
39 Eg, *Glasgow Herald*, 25 July 1842.
40 GPG Minutes, 20 May 1842; GPG Directors' Report, 6 January 1843, BR/GPG/1/3, SRO.
41 Ibid, and GPG Minutes, 9 November 1843, BR/GPG/1/3, SRO; Harding's evidence, *SC on Railways*, BPP 1844, XI, QQ 5347–57, and Harding's *Facts Regarding the Railway System* (1848), 8–9.
42 *Railway Times*, 7 January 1843; GPG Minutes, 14–27 December 1843, 16 October 1844 BR/GPG/1/3, SRO. 42 steamboats were built on the Clyde in the 1840s for the local passenger traffic, J. Williamson, *The Clyde Passenger Steamer; its rise and progress during the nineteenth century*, Glasgow (1904), 87.
43 GPG Minutes, 3 April 1844, GPG Directors' Report, 16 March 1846, BR/GPG/1/3, SRO.
44 Eg, the relations with the Clydesdale Junction, Edinburgh & Glasgow, and Glasgow

Barrhead & Neilston railways, GPG Directors' Report, 12 March and 15 September 1845, BR/GPG/1/3, SRO.
45  GPK Directors' Report, 17 February 1841, BR/GPK/1/1, SRO. It was suggested that the railway's management of the service had been responsible for its failure, *Railway Times*, 9 March 1844.
46  GPK Traffic Committee Minutes, 1–23 April, 5 June 1841, BR/GPK/1/7, SRO.
47  *Glasgow Herald*, 21 January 1842; *Railway Times*, 5 November 1842.
48  GPK Minutes, 15 March and 14 June 1843, 13 February 1844, BR/GPK/1/3, GPK Traffic Ctee Minutes, 6 January and (?) June 1843, BR/GPK/1/7, SRO; *Railway Times*, 3–31 December 1842, 9 November 1844.
49  *Railway Times*, 2–9 March 1844.
50  GPK Minutes, 7 February 1845, BR/GPK/1/3, SRO.
51  GPK Traffic Ctee Minutes, 6 June 1842, 6 January 1843, BR/GPK/1/7, SRO.
52  L & B Revenue Account, 31 May 1841, RAC1/227A, BTHR. A loan of £10,000 was used temporarily for steamboat purposes without the shareholders' knowledge, L & B Minutes, 12 October 1841, LBW1/2, BTHR.
53  *Herapath's Railway Magazine*, 3 June 1843; L & B Minutes, 20 February 1844, LBW1/6, BTHR.
54  L & B Minutes, 18 June 1844, 25 March 1845, 3 February 1846, LBW1/6, BTHR.
55  L & B Minutes, 7 June 1842, LBW1/2, BTHR.
56  Charter costs were put at £165 and receipts at £42, *Herapath's Railway Magazine*, 5 June 1841; an account of losses was presented to the directors in August 1841, GPG Minutes, 18 August 1841, BR/GPG/1/2, SRO.
57  Harding's evidence, *SC on Railways*, BPP 1844, XI, QQ 5366, 5423.
58  GPG Directors' Report, 5 January 1842, BR/GPG/1/2; GPG Finance Committee Minutes, 10 November 1842, 22 July and 16 October 1843, BR/GPG/1/5, SRO
59  GPG Finance Ctee Minutes, 10 February 1844, BR/GPG/1/5, SRO.
60  GPK Traffic Ctee Minutes, June 1843, BR/GPK/1/7, SRO. The estimate was for a boat of 300 tons, or three times the average size of a river boat. The capital costs were put at £14,000, depreciation and repairs at 10 per cent per annum each.
61  Harding, op cit, 8–9; *Herapath's Railway Magazine*, 8 April 1843.
62  A Late Shareholder, *Ought Railway Companies, in the Interests of the Public . . . to be Steamboat Proprietors?*, London (1871), 8–10; J. Williamson, op cit, 158–9; C. L. D. Duckworth and G. E. Langmuir, *Railway and Other Steamers*, Glasgow (1948), 48–9, 55; G. Dow, *Great Central*, London (1959–62), I, 175–6, II, 147–50.
63  Cf the over-simplified account in L. Girard, *The Cambridge Economic History of Europe*, VI, Cambridge (1965), 212, 243. My analysis is also applicable to steamboat services on the Yorkshire Ouse and Humber between York, Selby, Goole, and Hull. These (which dated from shortly after the Napoleonic Wars) contrived to fulfil a useful local function until their role was eliminated by the gradual completion of railway development in the Vale of York from the early 1870s. See Baron F. Duckham, *The Yorkshire Ouse: the History of a River Navigation*, Newton Abbot (1967), 83–5, 128; and W. W. Tomlinson, *The North Eastern Railway: its Rise and Development*, London and Newcastle (1914), 257.
64  A. R. Bennett, 'The First Railway in London', *Locomotive Magazine Souvenir*, XXI (1912), 46.
65  Despite the risks of explosion and the threat of bad weather, the steamboats were often preferred for their low fares, refreshment facilities, and the convenience of

landing-points. The unsatisfactory location of the Blackwall and Greenock railways' early termini was soon realised. Indeed, it could be claimed that steamboat competition was an important factor influencing the former company to seek a more central terminus in Fenchurch Street.

*For plate, provided by the editors,* see p 68

F. H. W. GREEN

# Fifty Years of Bus Services in a Huntingdonshire Village: the case of Buckden

MOTOR BUS SERVICES reached their peak of development in western Europe shortly after World War II. It has been shown, for example, by this writer, how the network of services then developed could be used as an excellent index to areas of community of interest.[1] That they still formed a reasonably good index, in spite of the enormous increase in the use of private cars, twenty years later, was demonstrated in 1966;[2] analysis of the somewhat attenuated network of rural services also showed then how areas of allegiance to local centres had in general changed very little. Study of local carriers' services back in the nineteenth century also reveals that, except in districts with great change in population distribution, those areas differ little from the present. There have, however, been few studies showing the changes over time in the provision of local public passenger transport. This essay shows what is revealed by examination of local services during the motor bus period in one village which happens to lie approximately at the boundary between the spheres of influence of two small towns in rural England, Huntingdon and St Neots. An intensive search has not been made for all records of former time-tabled services, but a sufficient number of old time-tables has been examined to show the interesting trends.

Buckden, a parish in Huntingdonshire, had a population of 998 at the 1921 census and 1,158 in 1961, and most of the inhabitants actually live in the village which lies on the Great North Road. It is notable for its possession of a former palace of the bishops of Lincoln, but otherwise its chief visual characteristic has been, and still is, its coaching house hotels, catering for long-distance traffic. We are concerned here, however, only with its local public passenger road transport over the last fifty years.

Buckden formerly had two railway stations. One lay a mile to the north of the village on the Midland Railway branch from Kettering to St Ives and Cambridge. Until this line was closed in 1959, it had for at least sixty years had only three trains each weekday in each direction. These were not timed to be of any use for commuting and were essentially cross-country connections to main-line trains at Kettering, Huntingdon and Cambridge. There was also a railway station two miles east of the village called Offord and Buckden, although it was in Offord Cluny. This station, on the main line from King's Cross, had a fairly frequent service, but it was too far from Buckden to be really suitable for routine journeys by residents of the village; it too was closed to passenger trains in 1959.

Although motor buses had been used more or less experimentally in various country districts before World War I, the great development took place in the years immediately following that war. Buckden certainly had a motor bus service in 1921, when F. J. Hinsby of St Neots was operating a bus on Thursdays and Saturdays between St Neots and Huntingdon;[3] in fact it ran twice each way on Thursdays and once on Saturdays. There is evidence from the same source that a bus ran through between Bedford and St Ives in that year, but it is quite clear that by April 1922 Buckden had a bus service for four days a week[4].

The service was basically one from St Neots to Huntingdon and Godmanchester, a journey which took 55 minutes for the nine miles. There were five buses each way on Saturdays and four on Thursdays. On Mondays there was one bus each way: a through service to and from St Ives, 30 minutes distant in time from Godmanchester. On Sundays there were two buses each way on the through route from St Neots to St Ives. It was clearly a market-day and week-end route and manifestly not for commuters, whether school children or adults. The commencement of Sunday operation is indicative of catering for holiday and social travel.

The operator was the National Omnibus and Transport Company Limited. This company had formerly been the National Steam Car Company and had operated paraffin-fuelled steam buses in London; when these proved no match for the petrol bus, the company started operating petrol buses from various centres in the Home Counties and later in the west of England. The service from St Neots was linked to its centre of operations in Bedford. The fare for the service provided in April 1922 is not known except that it was 7d from Godmanchester to St Ives. By December 1923 the through route from St Neots to St Ives had the route number 14, the service being almost the same as in April 1922.[5]

By September 1926 the service was a daily one with direct connections to and from Bedford at St Neots;[6] on Sundays one bus seems to have run right through from Bedford to St Ives. (The service between St Neots and Bedford was shared on weekdays with F. J. Hinsby, and this appears to have been the arrangement until Hinsby's vehicles were acquired in 1931.) There were now five buses each weekday and three on Sundays each way between St Ives and St Neots; and there was an additional one on Mondays from St Ives to St Neots which, unlike all the others, did not call at the Hemingfords. It is not clear whether the exact route taken was the same on each run, for the timetable shows various running times between Huntingdon and St Neots from 40 to 55 minutes, but all passed through Buckden.

The timings of first and last buses, given in the accompanying table, show that daily commuting was now possible.

### TIMES OF FIRST AND LAST BUSES
(Monday to Friday)

| Year | First Bus to St Neots | to Huntingdon | Last Bus arr from St Neots | arr from Huntingdon |
|---|---|---|---|---|
| 1926 | 0840 | 0730 | 1835 | 1815 (not Th) |
| 1928 | 0840 | 0730 | 1835 | 1815 |
| 1947 | 0743 | 0717 | 1823 | 1822 |
| 1953 | 0628 | 0712 | 2008 | 2252 |
| 1970 | 0629 | 0707 | 2025 | 2242 |

The single fare from Buckden to Huntingdon was now 6d and to St Neots it was the same. There is no mention of return tickets except on market days when a return ticket between Huntingdon and St Ives cost 1s 6d. In September 1928 the service was exactly the same as two years previously.[7]

In 1929, following legislation of the previous year which empowered the railway companies to operate bus services on the same basis as any other undertaking, arrangements were made with the National Omnibus and Transport Company to form joint companies. One of these, in which both the LMS and the LNER took shares, was the Eastern National Omnibus Company Limited; and so the time-table of September 1930 published by this new company shows route number 14 operating under this name, with a slightly increased service as compared with 1928.[8] The number of through buses was about the same, but the total number between St Neots and Huntingdon had been stepped up; and there now appeared the first short journeys between Buckden and Huntingdon only—two each way on Saturdays. These had, however, started by September 1929.[9]

By the summer of 1932 changes had been very slight, though there were now three short journeys between Buckden and Huntingdon on Saturdays.[10] Fares were still unchanged.

Generally speaking, bus services throughout the country slowly intensified between 1932 and the outbreak of World War II. The war brought special conditions, the journeys-to-work tending to predominate over other types of local journey, and special works' services became more common. Some of the changes survived the war. In the years immediately following, two trends in particular were now much in evidence: commuting services and journeys for pleasure and social reasons—for which there was a demand greater than the supply of vehicles available. The October 1947 time-table shows these.[11] The route through Buckden had now become Eastern National number 4A, route 4 having previously been the Bedford–St Neots route which had now become the purely local Bedford–Goldington service.

Route 4A now ran from Bedford to St Ives, all buses going via

## Fifty Years of Bus Services in a Huntingdonshire Village 27

Blunham and Tempsford, which had been served in 1932 only on Thursdays and Saturdays. There were now seven buses daily each way between St Neots and St Ives, all but three of which were through to and from Bedford. The exceptions were those shown in the table: a school service, which left St Neots for Huntingdon at 0800, passing through Buckden at 0717; and one from Huntingdon to Bedford passing through Buckden at 0743. These were the first buses of the day through Buckden. On Saturdays and Sundays the last buses in each direction through Buckden were rather more than an hour later than those shown in the table. The fares still had not changed and that this was economically possible was at least partly due to buses being generally more nearly full than before the war.

One result of the 1947 Transport Act was that the Tilling Group (which, together with the railways, controlled the Eastern National Omnibus Company) sold out to the government. The group had also controlled the United Counties Omnibus Company Limited, and, as a later consequence of this, it was decided to transfer the Midland section of Eastern National to that company in 1952. The transfer was effective as from 1 May that year. The March 1953 time-table of United Counties showed the route through Buckden as route number 150, which was essentially the same as the former 4A.[12] The through services from Bedford to St Ives had not changed much since 1947, but the number of short workings was increased. There were now eleven buses passing each way through Buckden on Mondays to Fridays, one each way being a Huntingdon school bus from and to Eynesbury Hardwicke, south of St Neots and just off the regular route. As shown in the table the first buses were now earlier, and the last buses later than before the war. The time taken between St Neots and Huntingdon was now usually 35 minutes, but one bus which omitted Grove Lane, Brampton, did the journey in 30 minutes.

In the February 1956 time-table, route number 150 was the same as in 1953, with the service much the same as three years previously.[13] As in 1953, fares were not quoted! Between then and 1967 the chief development was the amalgamation of route number 150 with route 141 (which had been Eastern National number 17 before the 1952 transfer, running between Bedford and Aylesbury about a dozen times a day, ie, about the same frequency as number 150).[14] Number 17 in 1922 had been the National service operating on Saturdays and Sundays only between Bedford and Woburn Sands or through to Leighton Buzzard. It appeared as a daily service by 1930, but shortly afterwards Eastern National had acquired some of the routes of the Aylesbury Bus Company and had thereupon extended route 17 to Aylesbury. By 1947 there were seven through services on Mondays to Fridays between Bedford and Aylesbury, but by 1953, as route number 141, there were thirteen through services.

There were by 1967 five buses through from St Ives to Aylesbury southwards on Mondays to Saturdays, six returning northwards, and four each way on Sundays. But quite a number of short workings existed on various sections of this long route. Through Buckden there were now fifteen buses southwards and twelve northwards on Mondays to Fridays; but asterisks and footnotes had multiplied in the time-table and are evidence that economy of operation necessitated diversions and short workings of various kinds. The reconstruction of the Great North Road compelled buses to take slightly different routes through the village, north and south, and incidentally also through Roxton, Blunham and Tempsford. The through buses from Aylesbury to St Ives do not make the diversion through Buckden village, but those in the opposite direction do so. One bus on Saturday night proceeds from Buckden to St Neots via Offord on the other side of the river. But apart from some later evening services, perhaps the biggest change in the route since 1956 is the diversion between Huntingdon and St Ives via Houghton and Wyton, instead of via Godmanchester and the Hemingfords, which are now served by a short local route. This is certainly in response to the considerable growth of Houghton and Wyton—which has a large RAF establishment—and also to the expansion of Hartford (which lies between them and Huntingdon). It is also probably due to a reduced number

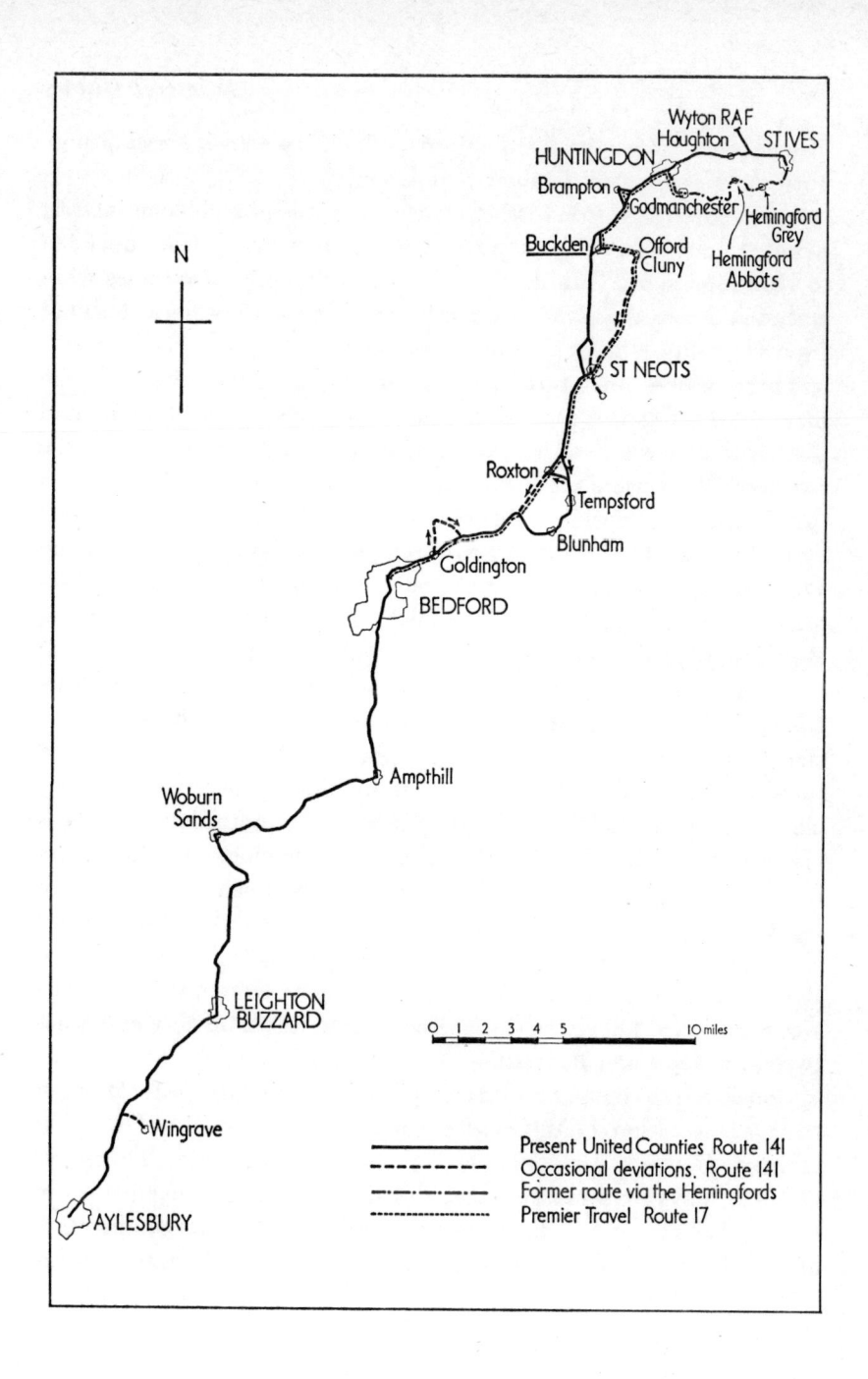

Wyton RAF
Houghton
ST IVES
HUNTINGDON
Brampton
Godmanchester
Hemingford Grey
Hemingford Abbots
Buckden
Offord Cluny
N
ST NEOTS
Roxton
Tempsford
Blunham
Goldington
BEDFORD
Ampthill
Woburn Sands
LEIGHTON BUZZARD
0 1 2 3 4 5 10 miles
Wingrave
AYLESBURY
Present United Counties Route 141
Occasional deviations, Route 141
Former route via the Hemingfords
Premier Travel Route 17

of passengers from the Hemingfords, which have an increasing proportion of car-owners in their population.

1970 shows very little further change; but it is of incidental interest to note than on Saturdays it is possible at 1118 to travel from Buckden to Huntingdon via Offord. The 1100 ex Huntingdon continues from Buckden across the river to Offord, where it then becomes the 1135 from Offord to Huntingdon on route 211.

There is one other bus service through Buckden which must be mentioned. It is the successor to some services in the Huntingdon district which were started by A. J. Gill at least as far back as the twenties. These were taken over in 1946 by Premier Travel Limited, a firm based in Cambridge. The route through Buckden was numbered 17 by Premier Travel, in whose time-table it is shown as operating on Wednesdays and Saturdays.[15] On both of these days a bus left Godmanchester at 1345, and proceeded via Huntingdon, Brampton, Buckden, Offord, St Neots, and then by the direct route to Bedford; it returned from Bedford at 1815, having offered there a connection from Birch Brothers' service from London. On Saturdays the bus started 15 minutes earlier from Hemingford Grey and it returned there in the evening. Wednesdays, it should be observed, are early closing days in Buckden as in Huntingdon. On Saturdays there was also a bus, which awaited the conclusion of the cinema performance, from Huntingdon as far as Great Paxton, between Offord and St Neots. By 1969 the Premier Travel service 17 was reduced to one bus each way on Saturdays only between Godmanchester, Huntingdon and Bedford;[16] the late journey was replaced by the United Counties service mentioned above. Few passengers now travel on service 17 between St Neots and Bedford.

Considerable changes have taken place in nearly fifty years. One can trace a succession of different predominant uses made of the bus services. Catering for shopping expeditions came early: Thursdays and Saturdays were market days. But the fact that in Buckden, as in many other places, Sunday soon became one of the days of operation of non-daily services, shows that the holiday and social traveller was also being catered for. Commuting by bus began to be possible only in the mid-twenties, but commuting by both workers and schoolchildren gradually came to constitute peak-hour traffic. The growth of industry in the district, which had been predominantly agricultural, and the coming of several Service establishments, provided the increased commuter traffic. Evening and Sunday traffic expanded after the war, but this has declined again with the increase in car ownership. (The county had until recently the highest number of cars, relative to the population, of any English county. In a family owning one car, the breadwinner may use it for work during the week and the younger members will commute by bus, but in the evenings and at weekends it is available for them.) Buckden, in contrast to many villages in East Anglia, has a better bus service than it had in the twenties. Although this may be partly accounted for by the factors mentioned in this paragraph and its considerable increase in population since the last census, it is probably even more due to its being on a traffic-generating cross-country route which passes through several towns and a considerable number of other big villages.

*Monks Wood Experimental Station*

## References

1. F. H. W. Green, 'Urban hinterlands in England & Wales; an analysis of bus services', *Geographical Journal* (September 1950), 116.
2. F. H. W. Green, 'Urban hinterlands; fifteen years on', a review of the British Bus Services map, compiled by J. C. Gillham, *Geographical Journal* (June 1966), 132.
3. *Motor Coach ABC*, No 3, August 1921. Published by the British Road Traffic Association, London.
4. *TBR* ('*Travel by Road*') *Guide and Time-Tables*, No 11, April 1922. Published by Rieu, Wiley & Company, London.
5. Ibid, No 31, December 1923.
6. National Omnibus and Transport Company Limited, Bedford and District Time-Table, September 1926.
7. Ibid, September 1928.
8. Eastern National Omnibus Company Limited, Bedford Area Time-Table, September 1930.

9 *Roadways Time-Table*, No 3, September 1929. Published by Roadways Time-Tables Limited, London.
10 Eastern National Omnibus Company Limited, Midland Section Time-Table, July/September 1932.
11 Ibid, October 1947.
12 United Counties Omnibus Company Limited, Eastern Area Time-Table, March 1953.
13 Ibid, February 1956
14 United Counties Omnibus Company Limited, Time-Table, April 1967.
15 Premier Travel Limited, Time-Table dated January 1963.
16 Premier Travel Limited, Time-Table dated 1969.

S. R. BROADBRIDGE

# John Pinkerton and the Birmingham Canals

IN SOME WAYS John Pinkerton, canal contractor, would seem to have a claim to be called the Thomas Brassey of canals. With his brother he worked on the Driffield Navigation (1768), Bishop Soil sluices (1770), Market Weighton Navigation & Drainage (1772), the Hedon Navigation (Hedon Haven) (1774), the Selby Canal (1775), on other parts of the Aire & Calder (1775–8), and the Calder & Hebble Navigation (1776–80). Alone he contracted for, amongst others, the Billingham embankment and drainage (1777), the Erewash Canal (1777–80), the Birmingham & Fazeley Canal (1783–9), the Dudley Canal tunnel (1785), the Basingstoke Canal (1788), the Gloucester & Berkeley (1793), the Lancaster Canal (1794), and the Barnsley Canal (1793–9). Closer investigation reveals, however, more differences than similarities, differences which, at root, are those between the situations of railways in the nineteenth century and of canals in the eighteenth.

Rarely did Pinkerton contract for the whole of any navigation, unless it was small. This was largely because, unlike his railway successors, he lacked financial resources and stability. He had no permanent nucleus of labour, relying almost entirely upon local manpower, and no equipment of his own, even of the simple forms required at the time. Above all, however, he was totally dependent upon the advances of money made to him, weekly or monthly, by his employers. As a result he was never able to take the whole responsibility for construction upon himself; he was always subject to supervision, even in minor details. Not surprisingly, therefore, considerable friction resulted, not unaided by his character, which seems to have been prickly and litigious beyond the normal. One result was a multiplication of documents which cast a flood of light upon the details of eighteenth-century contracting.

Amongst them those which illuminate his labours in the Birmingham area are particularly prolific.

His earlier work had been in Yorkshire and eastern England, and his first foray into the Midlands was to build the Broadwaters extension to the Birmingham Canal in 1783.[1] Six months later he was mentioned as 'engineer' to the Fazeley Canal, for which the Act had been obtained at the same time.[2] He certainly did not step off on the right foot with the staid John Houghton, clerk to the company, since before tendering

> he informed [Houghton] that, in some or most cases or places, it was customary for contractors to allow a per centage of . . . about four per cent. upon the amount of the contract to the principal agent of the Company . . . and requested [him] to inform him what was customary to be given . . . before he made his estimates, as the rate . . . must be taken into account.

Later Pinkerton claimed that this was a joke, based on an anecdote he had heard about the Leeds and Liverpool, but the damage was done. Houghton virtuously informed him that the Birmingham company did not allow their servants to take perquisites and, presumably, did not trust him thereafter.[3]

'Frequent disputes' between Pinkerton and Bough, the company's superintendent of works, over the Broadwaters extension, 'particularly respecting the cement to be used', were allegedly settled by the committee in Pinkerton's favour, but they were only an earnest of what was to come.[4] In particular, Pinkerton contended that,

> After the foundations were set out by the Company's Agents, they had, properly speaking, done with him, and ought not to have further interfered with him.[5]

But he could never achieve this degree of independence. Bough supervised his work to ensure that standards did not fall below those in the contract, and friction was certain to result. Nevertheless his work was presumably satisfactory, for he was immediately employed on the Fazeley canal, for which the Act had been obtained at the same time as Broadwaters.

As was apparently normal with the Birmingham company, although work started contracts were not signed, in part because Pinkerton's estimates did not agree with Bough's and they were submitted to 'some neutral Person' for a decision.[6] Surprisingly, both he and James Watt were asked to give an estimate of the cost of the canal prior to the advertisement for tenders, which would seem to put him in a privileged position.[7] In the event his tender arrived late, but he was awarded half the contract: that from Minworth to Fazeley, including the Curdworth Rocks and the Dunton Tunnel to be completed by midsummer 1787. The other section into Birmingham, which included the heaviest lockage, was given to Thomas Sheasby, later engineer to some South Wales canals.[8]

It was not until January 1787 that a contract was prepared, and at that time a covenant was added

> enabling the Committee (in case Mr Pinkerton should neglect to proceed in the execution agreeable to their expectations) to take the Works into their Hands and get the same executed . . . and to change the expence thereof to Mr Pinkerton's Account.[9]

Not surprisingly Pinkerton, who was by now deeply involved in the construction, raised objections: 'when I consider the power it is giving a superintendent over me, I cannot, consistent with my own safety, but make some objection to it'; but it was insisted upon because of 'the circumstances in which Mr Pinkerton then stood with the Dudley Company'.[10] The contract, though dated 25 July 1786, was not executed until 18 May 1787. It committed Pinkerton to complete the works by 24 June 1788 for a price of £11,563 8s 11¾d, to be paid as they progressed, with £500 retained for three years after completion, during which period he would keep the canal in repair.[11]

We must now turn to Pinkerton's circumstances with the Dudley Canal. In 1785 this company obtained an Act to extend to a junction with the Birmingham Canal at Tipton by means of a tunnel through the spine of the Black Country plateau. In August they advertised for a contractor for the tunnel:

> The said Tunnel to be executed by the Yard forwards, including the sinking of the Shafts, driving the Headway, widening the same to contain the Brick-

work . . . to be made nine Feet three Inches wide, five Feet six Inches deep in Water, and seven Feet high above Top Water, and to be continued from End to End in a straight Line; The Centers to be made three Inches higher than the above Dimensions to allow for sinking of the Arch, the bottom to be an inverted Arch of Culver Bricks of four and a half Inches, on sound Foundations, and nine Inches on springy Lands . . . the Side Walls and Top Arch to be nine Inches thick, and where it shall be found necessary, the Side Walls to be fourteen Inches thick, the Top of the Arch to be clayed four Inches thick, and Brick Ends or other sound Materials laid thereon, so as to conduct the Water in small Streams down the Outside of the Brick Work, thence through small Inlets into the Tunnel.

The lower arch was to be clay-lined, the mortar made with lime and boiling water with rough grit sand and the bricks beaten down with a mallet.[12] The contractor was to enter into a penal bond for £4,000. Notwithstanding his other commitments, and his apparent lack of experience in tunnel work, Pinkerton tendered and was accepted, with William Jessop as his surety. John Wildgoose was surveyor, to superintend the works under Thomas Dadford the engineer, with the assistance of Abraham Lees.[13]

By August 1786 it was found necessary to order Wildgoose and Lees to

pay strict Attention to the Execution of the Tunnel by Mr Pinkerton . . . and particularly that they do not suffer any soft or bad bricks to be made use of and in general to observe that the several Works are completed according to the Tenor of the Contract.

upon pain of dismissal for neglect.[14]

Less than a fortnight later a special committee meeting had to be called to authorise the treasurer to pay Pinkerton £500 on account over and above his agreed weekly payments, fixed at £150 in June, and he was ordered, in future, to pay out

such Sum of Money only, as Abraham Lees & John Wildgoose shall certify to be actually expended on the Course of such Week, and that Mr Thomas Fieldhouse Do see to the Application of such Money Weekly, in discharging Workmens Wages, and Bills for materials, and other necessary Matters, And that no Money be Issued or paid by the Treasurer but for those purposes.[15]

This was not the end of the problem, however, and three months later it had to be resolved 'that all orders enpowering Mr Ab. Hawkes the Treasurer to pay any Money to Mr John Pinkerton be and are hereby rescinded'.[16]

Pinkerton and Jessop were ordered to attend the next meeting, all goods and materials in his possession were taken over by the company, and legal opinion was sought as to whether they could enter his works without prejudice to his bond.[17] A meeting of representatives of the committee with Pinkerton and his attorney took place at Lord Dudley's London house on 11 May, at which the company refused to accept a suggestion that his contract be waived and the value of his completed works left to arbitration. They also refused an offer of £1,500, claiming at least £2,000, which they would accept in instalments, with interest, provided there was good security, 'as they have not the least Confidence in his personal Security alone'. Even so, they claimed they would lose upwards of £2,000 since 'many Applications made by Contractors [show] that the Tunnel may be compleated at the Price agreed for by Pinkerton'.[18]

No agreement was reached then but, under threat of legal proceedings, Pinkerton offered the necessary £2,000 for release from his contract, to be paid in four instalments, the last on 24 June 1790, with three securities. The company were to have all tools and materials and enter into the works immediately.[19] In the event proceedings had to be threatened to obtain the third instalment on time and actually commenced for the last. It was not until June 1792 that payment of £2,072 8s 6d including interest was finally completed.[20]

Pinkerton later claimed that his over-expenditure was

On account of the extreme hardness of the strata, and the immense quantity of water it made, a circumstance not apprehended from the information which had been collected from the most intelligent colliers in the neighbourhood.[21]

On their part the company complained that he left the care of the works to a nephew, 'who was a fine gentleman and neglected them' and added, for good measure, that they 'never wished to employ Mr Pinkerton again, having a very low opinion of him'.[22]

This was not Pinkerton's only other contract in the area at this time. When the Act for the Birmingham and Fazeley Canal had been passed in 1783, it had laid upon the company the obligation accepted by the original proposers in 1782, together with the Trent and Mersey Canal, of completing the Coventry Canal from Fazeley to Fradley. Early in 1784 a meeting of the four companies concerned agreed that, as a gesture of good faith, all should start the execution of their works, laying out £1,000 each. At the same time an Act should be sought to formalise the agreement. This Act (25 Geo III c 97) was passed in 1785 against considerable opposition from the Birmingham Canal, who did not want completion enforced until the route to Oxford was complete and who resented being made to pay half the costs of the Act. Nevertheless the Trent and Mersey had begun construction from their end in 1783 and Pinkerton had been appointed contractor in February 1784. By the time the Act had been passed he had completed four miles to Dennis Brook and the two companies agreed that he should continue as contractor for the remaining seven miles to Fazeley at a contract price of £8,716, the whole to be completed by Christmas Day 1786, and the two companies advancing £1,000 each in turn as the work progressed. The price included keeping the works in repair for three years, 'in order to prove that they are completed in an effectual and substantial manner,' £500 of the price being withheld for that period.[23]

It was not long before trouble arose. The Birmingham company had for some time been trying to ensure that the Broadwaters extension was completed properly, but even after Pinkerton had claimed to have repaired the defects it was reported 'left very incompleat' and the company refused to settle his account.[24] They also asked for a report on the Fradley/Fazeley works which, proving adverse, was sent to the Trent and Mersey, emphasising that

> The defects complained of are so various, and of such magnitude, as seem to call for the serious attention of both Committees, that the Undertakers may forthwith amend the imperfections of their past Works and avoid similar errors in their future proceedings.[25]

## John Pinkerton and the Birmingham Canals

A deputation from the Birmingham committee met the agent and engineer of the other canal and went over the section.

> They found that the part under execution by Mr Pinkerton was very incompleat injudiciously laid out and in many places very defectively executed . . . particularly in the direction of the Canal which . . . is curved in a very improper manner the pudling benching and many other particulars . . . seem to have met with equal inattention . . . and in General the defects are so notorious as not to require the Eye of an Engineer to discover them.

They recommended that no more be set out until Bough was present, 'having found that what he has heretofore done . . . has been approved and scarce ever alter'd by Mr Smeaton Watt and others who Survey'd it'—a eulogy they were surely to regret before many months were past.[26] It must be assumed in this context that Pinkerton, as the Trent and Mersey's original contractor, would inherit some of the animosity felt towards the other canal for promoting the amending Act and because they did not send committee members to meet this deputation.

Although Pinkerton agreed to go over the line with Bough and set it out again, next year it was once more reported that the works were 'very defectively executed and that considerable damage [was] likely to ensue unless great attention [was] paid thereto by the Engineer'. However, by July 1788 final accounts were ready for inspection, though Pinkerton did not announce the section as complete until December.[27]

Meanwhile work was proceeding on the Fazeley Canal, though it was held up because of delays in purchasing land, another common failing of the Birmingham company. Some of this was required for clay to make bricks, but some of it was land through which the canal had to pass, often urgently.[28]

At the end of 1786 Pinkerton reported that the levels were apparently wrong between Minworth and Fazeley and was allowed a resurvey by Bough in the presence of his nephew, George Pinkerton—apparently the 'fine gentleman' before mentioned. Their report showed an error of 'as much as four feet and eight inches' and possibly more between

Minworth and Birmingham; and Bull, the company's engineer, was ordered to resurvey the whole line completely, 'without having the least reference to the Field Books Notes or Calculations of Mr Bough'.[29] According to Pinkerton, Bough's reaction was: 'Damn it, I knew I was three feet wrong, but I'd not think it had been as much as it is.' George Pinkerton thought that this was what 'occasioned Mr Bough to become a great enemy to Mr Pinkerton'.[30]

Bull's report showed that Bough had represented the fall from Minworth to Fazeley as 77ft instead of 71½. Sheasby had estimated for this when tendering for the length, whereas Pinkerton had used his own, correct, section. The difference saved £1,400 on the estimate and made a whole lock unnecessary at Minworth.[31] Bough had even more to answer for, since Sheasby found that, as a result,

> he had lost the part of the line from Minworth to Fazeley. . . . For, by deducting the sum the mistake had added to his estimate, he found that his estimate was under Mr Pinkerton's and that, therefore, he was justly entitled to have the execution of the whole line from Birmingham to Fazeley.

He was reported to be 'mortified', but the company were to have more cause to be so than he.[32]

They felt progress was too slow and Pinkerton was told to make a weekly return of his proceedings while Bough (not, one would have thought, the best person for this) was ordered to make weekly returns 'by way of cheque to Mr Pinkerton's report'. He said not enough men were employed.[33] For his part Pinkerton admitted that 'the line has not the appearance . . . of being pushed on with that resolution that you may think necessary', but claimed this was because he had felt it necessary first to complete the canal from Fradley to Fazeley so that he could 'take the water after us till we get amongst the locks'.[34]

There were also complaints against Sheasby at this time, in particular for using poor materials, but he seems to have put these right and we hear of no further criticisms of his works. Those against Pinkerton, however, grew as time passed, and were eventually detailed in full when the differences between him and the company reached the stage of legal arbitration. It was alleged that, instead of puddling, gutters were filled with 'soil, gravel or sand', 'that such bad bricks were used they could scarce find enough for fronts' and 'that bricks were laid without mortar and mortar without bricks'. In the inverted arch of a culvert, 'the bricks were so loose that they might be picked out with one hand'.[35]

Similar evidence of the state of the works in October 1788, when Pinkerton was removed, was given by John Houghton and by William Hodgkiss, bricklayer, who 'refused to work for Mr P. because the materials were so bad' and affirmed that, at the fifth lock, 'when a boat went in and out, the whole face and back of the walls would move'.[36]

> There was such constant failures in the embankment, bridges, locks, &c that it never could be clearly ascertained when the canal was completed.

Many locks had to be taken down and rebuilt, and in some 'the mortar was as soft as when first laid'.[37] According to Bull, the brickwork in the Dunton tunnel was not in line and was 'daubed over ... with clay, in order, as he supposes, to prevent the joints being seen'. It fell in while building.[38]

Clearly, at this stage the company was trying to make out a case. Nevertheless, when in the 1960s Staffordshire County Council had occasion to take down one of his bridges for road widening, they found it only a half-brick thick on the arch,[39] and similar faults occurred on other contracts carried out by Pinkerton.[40]

Whatever the workmanship, in late 1788 he began to exceed his estimated price; money was cut off except by special decision and soon afterwards cut off entirely, pending 'a particular Acct of the nature of His Extra Works' because 'the Money he has already receiv'd greatly exceeds what ought to have been advanc'd, considering the quantity of Work yet remaining to be done'.[41]

Clearly the committee were tightening financial control. Shaw, the walling surveyor responsible for superintending the works, was dismissed for his 'connivance at the late transactions in the Works under [his] immediate inspection'. One must assume he had been receiving his share of the 4 per cent, for he was previously warned:

no one can doubt from the experience you have had that you must know it to be wrong yet you suffer such work to be done without the Committee hearing a word from you. . . . Your past conduct clearly shows you can but have little if any regard for the interests of your employers . . . let not the Undertaker . . . any more make you believe that Sand is Lime or that Clay unburn'd can be bricks.[42]

Notwithstanding all this, Pinkerton claimed in December that the canal would be open in six months, but in February 1789 he was told that, unless he could give 'sufficient and undeniable security' that he would complete in three months, he would be removed from the works, which would be carried on by the company at his expense. He 'declin'd looking out for any Security' and was allowed to appoint an agent, at his own expense, to keep an eye on the company's proceedings, though there is no evidence that he took advantage of this. Work continued and the first commercial boat passed on 11 August; the committee travelled over the line in their own boat six days previously.[43]

It might have been thought that all troubles were over, but in many respects they had only just begun. In December navigation was stopped by the failure of two of Pinkerton's locks at Curdworth. He was called back from the Basingstoke Canal to repair them and inspect the others 'to prevent as much as possible further damages of a similar kind'.[44] This was the beginning of a long history of collapses and repairs, which was not ended until thirty-five years later, when a report on repairs could at last state:

> As respects the Locks at Curdworth & Dunton which were built by the renowned Mr Pinkerton & which have in truth proved so costly to the Company it is proper to remark that the work necessary to put them in a tollerable state of security may now be considered as done.[45]

The financial problems were settled earlier, but required probably as much effort, at all events from senior officials and the committee. What was involved was the amount done by Pinkerton over and above his contract, for which he was owed by the company, and the amount carried out by the company in order to complete the canal, for which he owed them. It was not helped by the accounting system in use, which involved a detailed double-entry system but with no attempt to check on costs or even, as will appear, to find what lay behind the receipts given in return for expenditure.

After the canal was complete Bough was ordered to make accounts for settlement with both Sheasby and Pinkerton. The former was settled by August 1792, but Pinkerton refused even to see the committee to discuss the question. Relationships were presumably not improved when, faced with a demand from the Trent and Mersey for their share of the money withheld for three years from Pinkerton, which amounted to £287 10s, including interest, the company paid by a bill drawn on him on the grounds that he was 'considerably in the Company's debt'. Not surprisingly he refused to accept it and the account was not finally closed until all others were settled.

At length, in November 1794, legal proceedings were instituted, and Pinkerton eventually met the committee and agreed to comment on the accounts after going over the line with Bough. Nevertheless, it was not until December 1795, following more legal threats, that he sent his version of the accounts. They were referred to a sub-committee, which ordered a resurvey and called him in for consultations to reconcile the considerable differences between the two accounts.[47] Because of his other canal obligations these consultations took place at long intervals.

Pinkerton alleged that the accounts, by which the company claimed £5,870 11s 0¾d, were 'complicated'.

> The bills are in general without quantity or price and some of them, in one line, saying bricks, timber, &c so much money.[48]

Certainly the examples he gave seem to bear this out; it would be difficult, if not impossible, to see from them to what extent he had completed, or overfulfilled, his contract. He was allowed to see the originals (though we do not learn whether they were any more detailed) and presented his case. It was referred to a 'select committee' of three, who reported

> That he received from the Company much more indulgence than he was entitled to in deferring to take the completion of the canal into their Hands....

That when [they did] Mr Pinkerton had then receiv'd of the Company £12263 15s 6d being £700—6¼ [sic] more than the total of his contract

That from that time payments made by the Company . . . were correctly and minutely kept and clearly prove what Summs have been paid . . . in the completion of the Canal & in the repair thereof . . . [being] £5447 13 2½.

Pinkerton had claimed £3,051 2s 8½d as 'extras' which, if admitted, left him in debt to the company £3,096 10s 11¾d. According to Bull and Bough the 'extras' were only £1,337 13s 4½d. For his part Pinkerton claimed the company should have been able to complete the canal for £1,883 8s 8½d, but the sub-committee recommended that, as the company had an 'unquestionable right' to £3,096 10s 11¾d, Pinkerton ought to be 'required forthwith to make good that sum', while the account of extras went to arbitration.[49] As might be expected Pinkerton could not 'conform to the terms of the report . . . being fully convinced that there is a considerable balance due to me from the said Company'. He claimed £3,716 16s as extras, together with £1,380 caused by advance of prices due to delay in starting, making a total of £2,456 5s 3¼d due to him.[50]

When the suit came to an issue much argument took place about this matter of wage levels which served mainly to show that, whatever happened to wages and prices in general, the beginning of construction meant an increase in the prices of labour and materials in that locality. Thomas Dutton, a canal cutter working on sub-contract, said Pinkerton allowed him, at first, to draw 9s a week per man, then 10s and finally 12s as wages rose. Men on day work—which Pinkerton called 'a way no contractor can support'—received 1s 6d per day, later rising to 2s. When the company had tried to speed the work up by raising wages it

> did not produce the effect desired; for it was not given to the workmen generally but to the gangsmen. . . . These gangsmen gave the men under them no more wages than . . . before, so that the advances of prices did no more good, than that of adding to the pockets of the gangsmen, who were, in general, distinguished by the name of Bough's Darlings. . . . The foreman used, when he reckoned with them, to put down as many cube yards as would answer the wages he gave them.[52]

Whatever the true position, Pinkerton was not prepared to accept any of the figures put forward by the select committee and therefore it was not possible to agree on a reference to arbitration.

In any case Pinkerton wanted engineers as arbitrators, which the company refused, on grounds which are far from clear. Legal action was therefore commenced and, after several delays, looked like reaching an issue when the suit was withdrawn on Pinkerton's attorney agreeing to be bound by the decisions of three mutually chosen arbitrators.[51] Messrs George Humphreys, John Lawrence and Richard Poyton were agreed upon and Pinkerton entered into a £10,000 bond to abide by their award, which was to be completed by 23 January 1800. In fact, it was postponed five times and finally delivered on 10 September 1801.[53]

At the arbitration Pinkerton's main technical arguments were faults in the specifications and delay:

> It was impossible for him to begin till the Co's engineer had duly set out the line, and the line was not set out, so that he could begin, till eight months after the time in which everything should have been ready . . . the most material . . . parts of the line were not purchased . . . till eighteen months after the date of the agreement, even those very portions of land which he intended first to have begun upon.

As a result prices rose and he lost £2,750 15s 9d in increased costs of earthworks, buildings and 'agency' and in his own time and expenses.[54] However, his main fire, or that of his attorney, was reserved for the company's servants:

> nothing which, in the strictness of language, can be called blame attaches to either party . . . the Company . . . never in their collective capacity wished anything harsh, unjust or oppressive. . . .

The fault lay with

> falsehood and calumny, with which little, mean and envious individuals assaild his character, and poisoned the minds of the Company's Committee.[55]

The role of chief devil was reserved for Houghton:

> the man who could perform many of the labours of his occupation . . . unassisted and alone, and who, perhaps, never in his life, would have been laid

open to the inspection of the public, had not the Company, fortunately for themselves, contracted with the Defendant.

The rooted hatred which . . . this witness cherished against the Defendant, might be watered from many springs, but derived its chief strength from the character of the Defendant.

Such men as Bough . . . were . . . men at once vicious and needy, too ignorant to penetrate through a hypocritical disguise, and too low bred not to consider the head clerk . . . as a very great man.

Unfortunately . . . the Defendant came . . . and from his talents, and demeanour . . . was beginning to have considerable weight with the Committee . . . the head clerk . . . saw . . . that either the Defendant's character must be destroyed or his own consequence lost.[56]

Apart from the fact that the committee's minutes reveal no time at which Pinkerton was beginning to have considerable weight with them, the character of Houghton is not convincing. As revealed in his letters and memoranda, which are rather more wordy than pure business would necessitate, he seems rather likeable than otherwise, though a trifle pompous, and dedicated to the honest service of the company. Certainly there was no conspiracy by him about land purchases, as Pinkerton alleged; these were a perennial problem, caused mainly by the slackness of Meredith, at that time the company's solicitor. It is possible that Houghton was guilty of suppressing a rough account of extras submitted by Pinkerton in 1788 and found by accident by his attorney when looking, with permission, in the company's solicitor's box—probably to save himself the trouble of redrawing the accounts. However, it was of no import and the manner of its rediscovery does not suggest a deep-laid plot.[57]

Much argument raged round the question of responsibility for bad work. It has been suggested above, and this can be abundantly supported by entries in the committee's minutes at the time, that much of the blame must be placed upon Pinkerton. Some of it may have been caused by interference by the company's agents; Pinkerton makes a persuasive case that they adversely affected the mortar-mix. Nevertheless there seems no doubt that Pinkerton scamped his work, that there was little supervision of it by the company's servants on the spot, though much bickering, and that there was not adequate control of costs when he had gone. The episode is certainly revealing in the inadequacies of the men available for technical posts at a time when demand was fast outrunning supply and training.[58]

At the end of it all, the arbitrators ordered the company to pay Pinkerton £436 in full settlement, each side to pay its own costs. In the company's case these amounted to £334 5s 8d for solicitor's fees and £38 2s 4d for the arbitrators' expenses.[59]

The matter was not going to end this quietly, however. Immediately it was over Pinkerton published an account in full of the proceedings, accompanied by a preface in which he complained

> that this action was commenced against the Defendant for not cutting a Canal through land which the Prosecutors did not allow him to enter, for not using good workmanship and materials, in buildings they did not suffer him to erect, and for not coming to a settlement, when they never furnished him with an intelligible account of the expenditure they called on him to defray,

and accused the company of using forged documents from dead men. The publication was a

> vindication of his character, to explain how it came to pass that such an award was given, in a case so plain and clear, [as a result of which he] lost all his labour, and a considerable part of his property.

The company, however, had lost more, 'by employing such a miserable description of agents as those who have occasioned all this mischief'.[60]

Since this publication included all the attacks on Houghton which have been quoted, and many more, the latter took legal action, as a result of which the book was found 'a scandalous and malicious Libel', Pinkerton being fined £200 and imprisoned for a month. The general assembly of the company resolved that this action was 'highly proper', paid Houghton's costs and gave him £500.[61]

What happened to Pinkerton we do not know; certainly he does not appear to have executed any more contracts for a long time after the lawsuit.[62] In that sense it is quite clear who suffered most from the episode.

## References

1. British Transport Historical Records, minutes of committee of Birmingham and Birmingham and Fazeley Canal Navigations, BCN 1/4, 15 August 1783. (Submission of tender.)
2. Ibid, 2 February 1784.
3. J. Pinkerton, *An account of the cause lately arbitrated between the Birmingham Canal Navigation and J. Pinkerton* (1801), 314–15 (evidence of J. Houghton).
4. Ibid, 259 (Pinkerton's evidence, not borne out by committee minutes).
5. Ibid, 252 (Pinkerton's evidence).
6. BTHR/BCN 1/4, 23 April 1784.
7. BTHR/BCN 1/5, 11 February 1785.
8. Ibid, 2 January 1786, 22 April 1786. For Sheasby in South Wales cf C. Hadfield, *The Canals of South Wales and the Border*, passim.
9. Ibid, 12 January 1787, 26 January 1787.
10. Pinkerton, op cit, 130–1 (letter of 16 March 1787, 281).
11. BTHR/BCN 1/5, 18 May 1787.
12. *Aris's Birmingham Gazette*, 9 September 1785.
13. BTHR, minutes of the committee of the Dudley Canal DDC 1/3, 26 September 1785, 12 December 1785 (contract signed), 25 April 1786.
14. Ibid, 29 August 1786.
15. Ibid, 8 September 1786.
16. Ibid, 8 January 1787.
17. Ibid, 23 January 1787, 6 February 1787, 26 February 1787.
18. Ibid, 17 May 1787.
19. Ibid, 3 July 1787, 20 July 1787. Jessop was one of the securities.
20. Ibid, 12 February 1789, 20 June 1790 and minutes of assembly of Dudley Canal, BTHR/DDC 1/2, 25 June 1792.
21. Pinkerton, op cit, 232.
22. Ibid, 292.
23. BTHR/BCN 1/5, 28 October 1785.
24. Ibid, 4 May 1786, 19 May 1786, 24 July 1786.
25. Ibid, 30 August 1786.
26. Ibid, 13 October 1786.
27. Ibid, 3 November 1786, 3 August 1787, 10 November 1787, 11 July 1788, 12 December 1788.
28. Pinkerton, op cit, 87 (letter of 14 July 1786 from Pinkerton), 4, 84 (letter of 26 April 1787 from Pinkerton—the quotations on the two pages cited do not exactly tally).
29. BTHR/BCN 1/5, 8 December 1786, 22 December 1786.
30. Pinkerton, op cit, 234, 230.
31. BTHR/BCN 1/5, 5 January 1787.
32. Pinkerton, op cit, 234.
33. BTHR/BCN 1/5, 20 April 1787, 27 April 1787.
34. Pinkerton, op cit, 84 (letter of 26 April 1787 from Pinkerton).
35. Ibid, 8–9 (evidence of Lee, the company's solicitor and member of their committee).
36. Ibid, 29–30, 36–8.

37 Ibid, 17 (Lee), 39–40 (evidence of Blastus Hughes and John Taylor, bricklayers).
38 Ibid, 54–5.
39 Information from Mr Granville-Edge. It must be noted that it had, notwithstanding this, survived nearly 200 years.
40 Eg, within six weeks of opening the banks of the Basingstoke Canal collapsed twice (P. A. L. Vine, *London's Lost Route to Basingstoke*, 57) and the Greywell Tunnel on that canal seems to have been as badly built as that at Dunton (R. Harris, *Canals and their Architecture*, 112).
41 BTHR/BCN 1/6, 4 October 1788, 18 October 1788.
42 BTHR, Letter-book of the Birmingham Canal, BCN 4/371A, 4 October 1788, 23 September 1788 (Houghton to Shaw). Though catalogued in BTHR this is in private possession but can be obtained through Warley Public Library, to whom I am grateful for making it available.
43 BTHR/BCN 1/6, 26 December 1788, 13 February 1789, 17 February 1789, 5, 6 August 1789; Pinkerton, op cit, 17.
44 BTHR/BCN/371A, 19 December 1789 (Houghton to Pinkerton).
45 BTHR/BCN 1/11, 26 September 1823.
46 BTHR/BCN 1/6, 12 November 1790.
47 BTHR/BCN 1/7A, 21 November 1794, 5 December 1794, 23 January 1795, 27 February 1795, 18 December 1795, 26 February 1796, 9 September 1796.
48 Pinkerton, op cit, 565 (Letter of 1 November 1796 from Pinkerton).
49 BTHR/BCN 1/7A, 8 December 1796, 20 January 1796, 7 April 1797. It is to be noted that there are often minor arithmetical errors.
50 Pinkerton, op cit, 122, 124–5 (letters of 20 April 1797 from Pinkerton).
51 BTHR/BCN 1/7A, 1 April 1797, 30 June 1797, 6 June 1798; minutes of assembly of Birmingham Canal BCN 1/42, 28 September 1798, BCN 1/7B, 8 March 1799.
52 Pinkerton, op cit, 185–6, 304, 565.
53 BTHR/BCN 1/7B, 22 March 1799, 18 October 1799, 1 November 1799, 15 November 1799, 13 December 1799, 24 January 1800, 30 May 1800, 5 September 1800, 12 December 1800, 12 June 1801.
54 Pinkerton, op cit, 157, 549–50.
55 Ibid, 57–8.
56 Ibid, 527–9.
57 Ibid, 430–3.
58 Eg, 'A mistake having been made in fixing a mark for the top water line on the Fradley Canal, previous to it being cut, it occasioned the levels for the Birmingham Canal to be carried on, from the junction, upwards of nine inches too low' with a consequent need to raise all embankments and bridges as far as the first lock (ibid, 554).
59 BTHR/BCN 1/7B, 18 September 1801. It should be noted that a similar case, not completed until 1812, was the outcome of Pinkerton's association with the Barnsley Canal—cf W. N. Slatcher, 'The Barnsley Canal,' *Transport History*, I, no 1 (1968), 48–66.
60 Pinkerton, op cit, viii–x, xxv.
61 BTHR/BCN 1/42, 1 October 1802.
62 Someone of the same name was working under another contractor on the Thames and Medway and alone on the Yantlet Creek c 1823. If this was the same person he would have been about 80 at the time (Cf C. Hadfield: *The Canals of South and South-East England*, 92, 94n).

CAMPBELL HIGHET

# Continuous Brakes—A Vexed Question. How the Scottish Railways Resolved It

IN THE EARLY DAYS of railways such brakes as existed were worked by hand and usually operated on the wheels of only one vehicle in the train. There might also be a hand brake on the engine or its tender. As trains grew longer and heavier, and as speeds began to increase, there was a need for ever more brake power, not only to stop the trains at the appointed places, but (of equal importance) to enable them to be brought to a stand in the shortest time and distance in an emergency. This meant the inclusion of more braked vehicles in the composition of the train, and at the same time increased the number of personnel required to operate the brakes.

In 1840 the Railway Department of the Board of Trade was formed to afford some official guidance to, and supervision of, the railway companies in the exercise of the powers they obtained by their various Acts of Parliament. One of the department's early actions was to produce a formula governing the amount of brake power needed on trains. It was laid down that the last carriage, and at least every fourth vehicle in a passenger train, should be fitted with brakes. By 1856 the Board of Trade was beginning to appreciate the need for a change in this order, since by increasing the number of brake vans not only was the number of trainmen increased, but more vans were required than were necessary, thus adding unproductive weight and contributing still further to operating costs.[1]

Some better form of brake was obviously necessary as the lack of adequate brake power was continually figuring in reports on accidents. One such improved brake was that invented by Newall of the East Lancashire Railway. It could be applied by the guard and operated on all the vehicles in the train and was soon in use on several railways including the Highland. It is interesting to note that this brake afforded a means of communication between the driver and the guard, that this was recorded twenty years before the Newark trials, and that a further thirteen years were to pass before the government finally passed an Act making the fitting of continuous brakes compulsory. Nevertheless, in the 1862 edition of the Statutory Requirements for Railways a new section was included. This dealt with the precautions recommended as a result of accident inquiries, communications between guard and driver, and continuous brakes.[2]

The brakes on locomotives remained very primitive for many years. Except for early attempts at designing and fitting steam-operated brakes by Peter Robinson on the Glasgow, Paisley, Kilmarnock & Ayr Railway, and by William Paton on the Edinburgh & Glasgow, the only brakes provided were hand-operated on the tender. As many of the older tenders were four-wheeled and of light construction (in contrast to the six-wheeled tenders of later date), the retarding force which could be applied was limited and any assistance would require to be given by the guard.

It was usual to fit brake blocks to the trailing wheels of locomotives. This was not so bad in the case of 2-2-2 or 0-4-2 types, but when applied to a 2-4-0 a brake application could impose a severe strain on the crank pins. It was held by many engineers that to apply brake blocks to driving wheels would cause undue torsional stresses in crank axles. Yet this practice was gradually adopted as prejudice was overcome and design and materials improved. It was, of course, appreciated that the locomotive itself, by reason of its greater weight, was a powerful retarding force when equipped with brakes, and that if brakes were not fitted to it much of this effect would be squandered. As continuous brakes came to be increasingly used, the number of broken engine drawbars grew, and this quite serious factor, caused by the retarding force acting on the train while no such force was acting on the engine, resulted in the fitting of brake blocks to all coupled wheels becoming customary practice.[3]

In 1869 an American, George Westinghouse, successfully applied a brake operated by air pressure to a train in the USA. The year 1871 saw him in this country, visiting locomotive engineers and railway managements in an endeavour to interest them in his invention, and enhance the safety of the travelling public. The only Scottish company to show any real interest at this stage was the Caledonian. Benjamin Conner, the locomotive superintendent, went so far as to have an engine and train fitted with the Westinghouse Air Brake and, by permission of his employers, co-operated fully with the inventor, using the Wemyss Bay branch for tests and demonstrations. The first Caledonian engine to be equipped with this brake was no 92, a Conner 2-4-0 of 1865.[4]

During the early 1870s there was a series of disastrous accidents which caused considerable public outcry and vociferous demands for greater safety of rail travel. The government acted promptly by setting up a royal commission which took evidence from a number of persons, amongst them guards, drivers, and others, in addition to executive officers of the railway companies. From much of the evidence it became apparent that the commissioners had no satisfactory data regarding the performance of the various brakes, or the distances and times in which trains could be brought to rest. The recognition of this set the stage for the trials held on the Midland line between Newark and Nottingham in June 1875.

I

As is well known, brakes in use to a varying extent on different lines were tried, including the Westinghouse Automatic, fitted to a Midland train; Smith's Vacuum, on a Great Northern train; the Steel-McInnes Air Brake of the Caledonian; Fay's Mechanical Brake on a L & Y train and several others—not forgetting the pernicious Clark-Webb Chain Brake of the L & NWR. The honours of the day went to the first named, the Westinghouse Automatic. From a speed of 52mph a train weighing 203 tons 4cwt including engine, was brought to a stand in 913ft or 19 seconds on a dry rail. Under similar

## Continuous Brakes—a Vexed Question

conditions a train of 262 tons 7cwt was brought to a halt from $49\frac{1}{2}$mph by Smith's Vacuum Brake in 1,448ft, 29 seconds, while the Steel-McInnes brake required 1,603ft in which to bring to rest a train of only 197 tons 7cwt from $49\frac{1}{2}$mph. The time taken was $34\frac{1}{2}$ seconds, but the rail was wet. The L & NWR brake did a little better than this, 1,337ft or 29 seconds being required to stop a train of $241\frac{1}{2}$ tons on a dry rail.[5]

Following the trials, which as may be expected, were given wide publicity in the technical press, the Board of Trade sent out a questionnaire to all companies calling for information under eight heads, viz: (1) Whether any experiments with continuous brakes had been carried out; (2) If so, with what brakes; (3) Where and when; (4) What results were achieved; (5) Whether any further experimental work was contemplated; (6) The progress in fitting continuous brakes to their own stock; (7) On which trains was the fitted stock used; and (8) What steps had been taken for the interchange of information.

This was quite a formidable questionnaire; replies were received from a number of companies but in Scotland only the Caledonian, G & SW and North British replied.[6] This seems curious when it is remembered that at Drummond's trials on the NBR in December 1876 Cowan of the GNS was not only an interested spectator but was one of the panel of four locomotive engineers appointed to oversee the series. On this occasion the Highland was represented by Thomas Robertson, superintendent of the line. The information rendered to the Board of Trade by the three Scottish companies that did reply was interesting and indicative of a sound appreciation of the whole complex problem, and at the same time showed a unanimity of purpose strange when one considers the distrust and antipathy that existed between them.

The Caledonian said it had experimented with the Westinghouse, Steel-McInnes and Clark-Webb chain brakes. The first named had been thoroughly tested on the Wemyss Bay branch during the six preceding years, the Steel-McInnes on the Edinburgh–Glasgow line during the last two years, and in the previous year the Clark-Webb had been used on passenger trains between England and Scotland by both the Caledonian and L & NW companies. Until about the time of the questionnaire only the non-automatic form of the Westinghouse brake had been in use, but two trains were being fitted with the automatic form, and it was proposed also to equip a train with the Clark-Webb Chain Brake and to test them all in daily service. At that date the Westinghouse brake had been applied to two engines and thirteen carriages. No fewer than 125 Caledonian or West Coast Joint Stock vehicles were fitted wholly with the chain brake, or with chain connection only. Further tests were to be carried out on the same sections of the line as before, and the dissemination of information would be by personal inquiry, and by the public reading of records.

The G & SW was also going ahead but it was later in the field. Its reply showed that continuous brakes had been in use on this line since August 1876. It was the Westinghouse Automatic Brake and was used on the Glasgow–Carlisle main line. It was described as efficient in stopping, could be instantly applied by either guard or driver, was self-acting until all the air had been exhausted from the reservoirs, and was very easy to apply or release. There was not yet enough experience, however, to quote costing figures. Beyond ordinary working no further experiments were contemplated. Up until then twenty engines had been equipped and two more engines and twenty carriages were programmed for fitting.

By far the most valuable contribution was made by the North British and it is not difficult to see the hand of Dugald Drummond behind the pen. Experiments and competitive trials had been held under the direction of a committee of locomotive engineers from other railways. The brakes tested were the Westinghouse Automatic and the Smith's Simple Vacuum (on the NBR line between Glasgow and Edinburgh) on 22 December 1876. The Westinghouse was instantaneous in action, but Smith's was not and was not self-acting in the case of accident unless provided with exhausting pumps in the brake vans. The Westinghouse Automatic could be operated by driver or guard to control the speed to a nicety; Smith's brake, on the other hand, could be put on or off with perfect ease by the driver only, the guard having no control

# Continuous Brakes—a Vexed Question

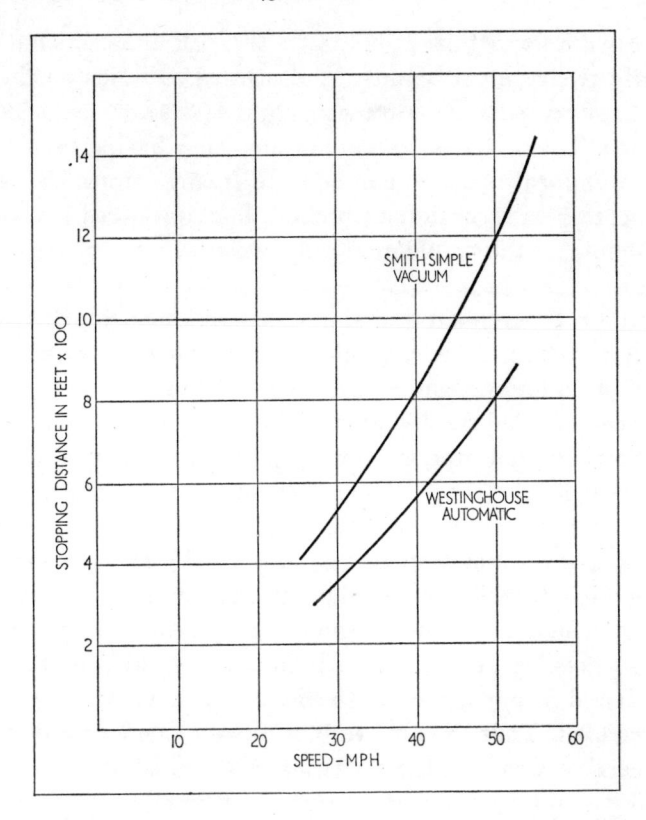

*Figure 1: North British Railway brake trials December 1876*

unless exhausting pumps were fitted in the brake van. When the brake had been operated by the guard by the application of an air pump, the train could not be re-started by the driver until the brake had been released by the guard. Intercommunication between the driver and guard was neither reliable nor safe. Up to the date of the report no maintenance costs were available. No further experiments were envisaged on the NBR as this company had decided on the Westinghouse as being the best yet devised.

The Westinghouse Automatic Brake had been in use on the through expresses with the Midland Railway between Edinburgh and Carlisle for nearly twelve months and was also fitted to trains on the Edinburgh–Glasgow, Glasgow–Helensburgh, and Glasgow–Balloch sections of the line. The NBR was unaware of any steps having been taken to have one uniform brake system adopted (many companies were still experimenting with continuous brakes), but considered it very desirable it should, as this would materially assist the interchange of coaching stock.

How near Drummond and the NB board came to achieving this desirable end! T. E. Harrison conducted his own series of trials on the North Eastern Railway and in a very concise but detailed report to his board recommended the adoption of the Westinghouse brake. On the Great Northern, however, there was a lack of unanimity at managerial level. The general manager, Henry Oakley, favoured the air brake for much the same reasons as did the two northern companies. Stirling preferred the vacuum system, probably having the question of expense in mind, for this was thought to be slightly cheaper in first cost at any rate, though as yet there were no really reliable figures to prove the issue. Possibly because of the influence of Watkin on the MS & L, the GN board favoured the Smith Simple Vacuum Brake and Oakley was overruled. Thus the opportunity to have one uniform brake for the three East Coast partners was lost and the additional expense of providing dual fittings on East Coast Joint Stock became necessary.[7]

In 1878 Parliament enacted the Railway Returns (Continuous Brakes) Act (41 & 42 Vict Cap 20) by which the companies were required to furnish particulars of their progress in fitting continuous brakes each year.[8] But there was still no legal obligation to fit continuous brakes to passenger trains. It was still only a recommendation that such a procedure was desirable. Not until the Regulation of Railways Act (52 & 53 Vict Cap 57) was passed in 1889 did this become compulsory, and then only after more alarming and serious accidents involving much loss of life and serious injury had occurred, culminating in the dreadful affair at Armagh on 12 June 1889.[9] Three years was set as the period in which compliance with the order should be completed, yet a number of companies, including the Highland and GNS, lagged behind. As late as 1894 a question was raised in the House of Commons concerning the dilatoriness of the Highland in this matter, to which the reply was made that the Board of Trade might have to take action against the company for non-compliance with the requirements of the Act. That there had been technical difficulties to overcome at the outset, especially as regards the reliability of the various brakes, cannot be denied. But once it was proven that there were at any rate two efficient and reliable brakes available there was little or no excuse for the companies to show such reluctance to provide so essential a safety measure, especially when their continued livelihood depended on the safe transit of their passengers.

## II

The foregoing is a brief account of the position in the 1880s and the events leading to it. However, what of the five individual railway companies themselves? On the North British nothing really effective had been done in the matter of continuous brakes by mid-1876. True, no 421, one of Wheatley's second class of 4-4-0s had been equipped with Westinghouse fittings, but this was for, and specially restricted to, the Anglo-Scottish trains run in conjunction with the Midland. This was the position when Dugald Drummond arrived at Cowlairs. His company's reply to the Board of Trade inquiry is clearly indicative of the forward thinking of this dynamic man. That he had come on the scene too late to have any art or part in the Newark trials probably did not bother him in the slightest. Like the MacTavishes at the flood, who had their own boat, he would run a series of brake trials of his own. The story of these trials has been well told by John Thomas in *The Springburn Story*. It is not intended to recapitulate the whole account here, but some details must be given.

Both the Smith brake and the Westinghouse were tested, and for the purpose two of Wheatley's '420' class were fitted; together with their trains they weighed 173 tons and 166 tons 10cwt respectively. On the vacuum-fitted train there were 31 pairs of wheels, 29 of which were braked. Its rival had 29 pairs with 25 pairs blocked, the proportions of braked weight to total weight being 86·55 per cent and 86·02 per cent respectively. The results of the trials on the Edinburgh–Glasgow section are shown on the graph (see p 55) in which the distance required to bring the trains to a stand after the application of the driver's brake valve has been plotted against the speed of the train when the application was made. Both brakes show an improvement on the performance at Newark.

To witness these trials a great galaxy of railway officers was present. In addition to those most directly concerned (the NB directors and chief officers, George Westinghouse and Smith's representative, a Mr Yeoman) there were James Smithells and George Brittain, general manager and locomotive superintendent of the Caledonian; James Mathieson and James Stirling, superintendent of the line and locomotive superintendent of the G & SW; Joseph Armstrong Jr from the Great Western; and many others, including representatives from Indian States. In order that there should be no chance that any accusation might be made that the tests were rigged in favour of one or the other of the brakes, Drummond formed a panel of four locomotive engineers to act as referees. This panel comprised William Cowan, GNS; James Stirling, G & SW; James Haswell, chief assistant to the locomotive superintendent of the NER; and Barton Wright, locomotive superintendent of the L & YR.

The NB board was favourably impressed by the manner in which the Westinghouse Automatic Brake functioned and at once declared its intention to adopt it as standard for the line. At the same time Drummond determined to carry out his obligations to the full, and ten engines and trains were fitted with each brake, to be tested in daily service for a period of six months. The violent reaction of Yeoman to this decision and the vituperative correspondence on the subject in the technical press show the wisdom of having had the four-man committee watching the trials.

At the end of the six-month period Drummond issued a statement

## Continuous Brakes—a Vexed Question

of the relative costs of the two systems. The equipment provided by the specialist firms cost £235 for the Westinghouse fittings against £180 for the Vacuum Brake Company's fittings. Materials supplied by the railway company cost £104 2s 5d and £64 15s 11d respectively, whilst labour costs were £154 15s 4d and £188 12s 1d, the totals thus being £493 17s 9d for Westinghouse and £433 8s for Vacuum. Maintenance during the period amounted to no more than £5 12s 3d and £8 5s 4d. In 1879 Drummond was able to report on the maintenance costs of Westinghouse fittings over the nine-month period from October 1878 to June 1879. The figures quoted below show that, so far as the locomotives were concerned, the cost was exceedingly slight per engine mile. Twenty-eight engines were included in the record:[10]

|  | Materials £ s d | Wages £ s d | Total £ s d |
|---|---|---|---|
| Locomotives | 7 1 9 | 8 13 10 | 15 15 7 |
| Coaching stock | 10 14 2 | 12 7 11 | 23 2 1 |
| Total | £17 15 11 | £21 1 9 | £38 17 8 |

In addition to all new passenger engines built by, or for, the company, a number of the older engines had the Westinghouse brake fittings put on, the classes varying from a Paton 0-4-2 of 1860 to a Wheatley 2-4-0 of 1869. Several of James Stirling's 4-4-0s on the G & SW had been fitted with Westinghouse brakes for the through trains between Glasgow and London. Stirling was not, however, going to accept all that was said in praise of the Westinghouse system without some experimentation of his own. In 1867 he fitted four engines and twenty carriages with the Smith non-automatic brake but kept them mainly to the Greenock road. In his annual report on rolling stock dated 1 July 1878 he stated that 'the Westinghouse brake had been fitted to 22 bogie engines and to other rolling stock. They are worked on the 10.15 am, 2.30pm, 5.00pm and 9.15pm Glasgow to Carlisle, and the 5.7am, 1.50pm, 6.25pm return and on the Pullman trains. Smith's vacuum brake has been fitted to six engines and they are running on the Greenock road on a year's trial from 1 April 1878'.

All the 2-4-0s of the '8' and '71' classes were equipped with Westinghouse equipment when they came out, as were Smellie's '157' class. Stirling's 4-4-0s were all fitted as were Smellie's '119' class when they were built. Some of the 0-4-2 tender and 0-4-2 tank engines were also fitted but in 1883 Matthew W. Thompson was elected chairman of the company. He was already chairman of the Midland and in that year that company forsook the Westinghouse in favour of the vacuum brake of Sanders' design as improved by T. G. Clayton, the carriage superintendent of the Midland. It should not therefore seem surprising that the Scottish company should change to the vacuum brake also, but by now, be it noted, that brake had been made automatic in its action.

The decision to make the change to the vacuum system was not taken without trial. Two of the '71' class 2-4-0s and two trains were equipped with the automatic vacuum brake in 1884. The engine fittings consisted of ejectors and application valves only. Later two of Smellie's 'wee bogies' were similarly fitted. All were allocated to Fairlie Pier.[11] In due course all the Westinghouse engines were fitted additionally with vacuum ejectors. From 1886 onwards all new passenger engines, except ten, were vacuum-fitted; the ten exceptions were also equipped with Westinghouse pumps and train pipes to enable them to work trains from the Caledonian, North British and North Eastern railways. All goods engines were fitted with vacuum brakes from 1892. In that year also the G & SW absorbed the Ayrshire & Wigtownshire, four of whose locomotives were 0-6-0s built by Neilson & Co in 1886 and were Westinghouse fitted. In the previous year, 1885, some of the elder Stirling's 0-4-2s which had been rebuilt as tank engines were given the vacuum brake for working the 'bus trains' —the suburban services on the City of Glasgow Union Railway; in Smellie's time all the '187' class had one or other of the two popular brakes and five of the '221' class were vacuum-fitted at the same time. Manson fitted thirty of this class in his turn.

The Caledonian had been the first Scottish railway to show any real interest in George Westinghouse's brake, yet it approached the whole question of continuous brakes with characteristic Scots canniness. The

## Continuous Brakes—a Vexed Question

experimental work done by Conner and Brittain with the Westinghouse and Steel-McInnes brakes has already been noted, but the former was restricted to the Wemyss Bay branch by order of the board in November 1877. The following August, Sharp, one of the directors of the Caledonian, had some communication with Provost Robertson of Dundee concerning a proposed trial of an improved form of the Steel-McInnes brake, and he was authorised to arrange for this to be carried out.

Almost a year later, Smithells, the general manager, was trying to reach agreement for the Westinghouse brake to be fitted but the proposal was declined. Then at a board meeting on 16 September 1880 it was resolved to fit the company's trains with continuous brakes (not specifying which brake), and a committee was formed to watch progress. By 9 November affairs were beginning to crystallise and Sharp was asked to collaborate with Smithells in the formation of an agreement with the Westinghouse company. Two weeks later agreement was reached and authorisation for 50 engines and 500 carriages to be fitted was given. In January 1882 the board decreed that an extension of the brake to all the company's stock should be delayed until all the brakes then on order were fitted, but in March it was agreed that 60 new carriages then under construction should be similarly fitted.[12] Thus, although the Clark-Webb Chain Brake continued to be used on the through trains between Scotland and England—and continued to be an operational hazard—and the Steel-McInnes brake was still fitted to some of the stock, the Westinghouse was taking precedence.

Two months before Drummond took charge at St Rollox, a board minute recorded that 754 vehicles had been fitted with Westinghouse equipment at a cost of £17,700, and a further £12,000 was budgeted for the fitting of 824 more. In November 1882 Drummond amended this estimate to £30,000 and asked for authority to spend £5,000 each half-year until the work was completed. The board agreed and in March 1885 a proposal to extend the fittings to other coaching stock was agreed.

Drummond's success on the neighbouring NB was bearing fruit in his new territory, and if any emphasis were needed for a fully operative, efficient, continuous brake, the accident at Lockerbie on 14 May 1883 provided it. This accident was a double collision involving two passenger and one goods trains. Seven lives were lost and twenty-three people were injured. A passenger train from Stranraer passed signals at danger when approaching Lockerbie and ran into a goods from Carlisle which was standing across the junction on the down main line. The 9.15pm Glasgow–Euston Mail was then about 360yd distant travelling at probably 50mph, according to the evidence obtained by Major Marindin who conducted the Board of Trade inquiry. The Mail was drawn by two of Conners' 8ft singles and was made up of fourteen vehicles. The leading engine had a hand brake only and the train engine had Westinghouse brakes on the driving, trailing and tender wheels. The train was fitted with the Clark-Webb Chain Brake, but in three sections, so that only the front three vehicles could be braked from the engine, and the rear four from the rear van. Of a total weight of 270 tons only 126 tons were braked, whilst the driver of the train engine (not the pilot) had control over 73 tons with two different kinds of brake! It is therefore small wonder that the train could not be brought to a stand clear of the obstruction. If the whole train had been Westinghouse fitted, and a stop had been made similar to those in the NB trials seven years before, speed would have been reduced to possibly 16mph from 50mph, or 29mph from 55mph assuming a 5 second lag from the initiation of the application.

Major Marindin's comments were caustic and his criticisms were directed against the L & NW and Sir Richard Moon's stubborn upholding of a proven inefficient brake: 'If he [the driver] had had at his command a quick-acting continuous brake throughout the whole train he might have done much to reduce speed before the collision took place.' Again,

> The Caledonian Company have adopted the Westinghouse continuous brake and are rapidly bringing it into use on their system. If the two West Coast Companies cannot agree on the same continuous brake, it is not too much to ask that the whole of the stock comprising these important trains should be

so fitted, so that passengers may have the protection of an efficient continuous brake, no matter which company's engines are attached.[13]

Arising from this accident, the Caledonian renewed its efforts to convert the recalcitrant L & NW. One result was that in due course the West Coast vehicles were all dual-fitted which became the case with the stock jointly owned and worked by the other Scottish companies and their English associates.

In the July following the Newark trials the Finance, Works & Traffic Committee of the GNS gave some consideration to a letter from Mr Cowan, presumably in the form of a report on the different systems of continuous brakes used in the experiments on the Midland Railway by the Royal Commission on Railway Accidents. At this time nothing seems to have been done towards the adoption of a standard brake for their own line, and no serious consideration seems to have been given at board level until February 1883 when the Works & Stores Committee, finding that the fitting of continuous brakes was desirable and being of the opinion 'that the Westinghouse Brake best meets the requirements of the Board of Trade,' recommended that the Westinghouse company be sounded regarding terms and conditions for supplying the necessary equipment.

By 7 March 1883 the estimated costs were laid before the committee for fitting certain of the locomotive and coaching stock, together with such new stock as was budgeted for during the ensuing two years. Of the 62 engines then owned by the company, 12 were to be fitted and 157 of the 286 carriages, vans and other coaching vehicles. The total cost was estimated at £4,446. New engines, 13 tender and 7 tank, and 22 new carriages and vans accounted for another £2,555, bringing the grand total to £7,001. In addition allowance was made for an inspector at 30s per week, but no account was taken of maintenance. The following day, 8 March 1883, the board ordered that the question of continuous brakes be deferred for one month, although no reason is given in the minutes. Meantime the passenger superintendent was to report on the number of trains to which the brake could be generally applied. On 30 May the same year, an agreement with Westinghouse was drawn up and a fortnight later it was signed by the chairman, deputy chairman and secretary.

This was certainly a move in the right direction though it had taken eight years to bring it about. It is interesting to note that of all the minutes relating to continuous brakes in the records of the Scottish railways, only that of the GNS dated 21 February 1883 (referred to above) makes any mention of the best means of complying with the requirements of the Board of Trade, and that, be it noted, six years before the Act of 1889 made continuous brakes on trains conveying passengers compulsory.

James Manson, who succeeded Cowan in 1883 carried on the good work and in October 1885 obtained official agreement to fit three or four engines and ten or fifteen carriages each half-year with the Westinghouse brake at a cost of £105 per engine and £32 10s per carriage.[14]

Like the Caledonian the Great North remained a Westinghouse company until the end of its separate existence. The G & SW changed to the vacuum brake in Matthew Thompson's chairmanship and the North British likewise changed similarly in the early 1920s.

Of the five major railways in Scotland the only one to select the vacuum brake as standard from the start was the Highland, the company which was different in so many respects. Two years after Newark the directors replied to a Board of Trade inquiry that the company would be prepared to adopt the brake found most suitable by the large companies in the south. In July 1880 the directors went so far as to ask the locomotive superintendent, David Jones, to report on the expense of fitting the Westinghouse brake to three trains between Inverness and Perth. Jones' report was read at a Stores Committee meeting on 3 August 1880 and at the same time another pebble was cast into the pool to send out ripples of another kind.

On the Highland board at this time was that active railway enthusiast and benefactor the Third Duke of Sutherland, who also added lustre to other railway boards including the L & NW. At the meeting on 3 August a letter from the duke was read. This recommended for

*An early aerial photograph of Portishead Dock c 1921. The low water level reveals the outline of the former tidal pill. (Courtesy: Port of Bristol Authority)*

See, Brown 'Bristol's Second Outport', pp 80–93

*Another aerial view of Portishead Dock c 1937 showing the new generating station. (Courtesy: Port of Bristol Authority)*

See, Brown 'Bristol's Second Outport', pp 80–93

*Portishead tide mill and mill wharf, from a painting of c 1800. (Courtesy: Miss Eve Wigan)*

*The original pier and hotel (now the Royal Hotel) at Portishead from a lithograph of c 1850. (Courtesy: Miss Eve Wigan)*

See, Brown 'Bristol's Second Outport', pp 80–93

*Portishead Pier c 1890. In the background can be seen the Admiralty training ship* Formidable *and tender. (Courtesy: Miss Eve Wigan)*

See, Brown 'Bristol's Second Outport', pp 80–93

*Greenock Pier with typical Clyde steamers c 1840. The elegant Custom House in the background still stands. (From Beattie's* Scotland*)*

See, Gourvish 'Railways and Steamboat Competition', pp 1–22

*Team waggon c 1918 and horses (made of polyurethane foam) set against a photomural background of dock warehouses, Liverpool. (Courtesy: City of Liverpool Museums)*

See, 'Notes and News', p 112

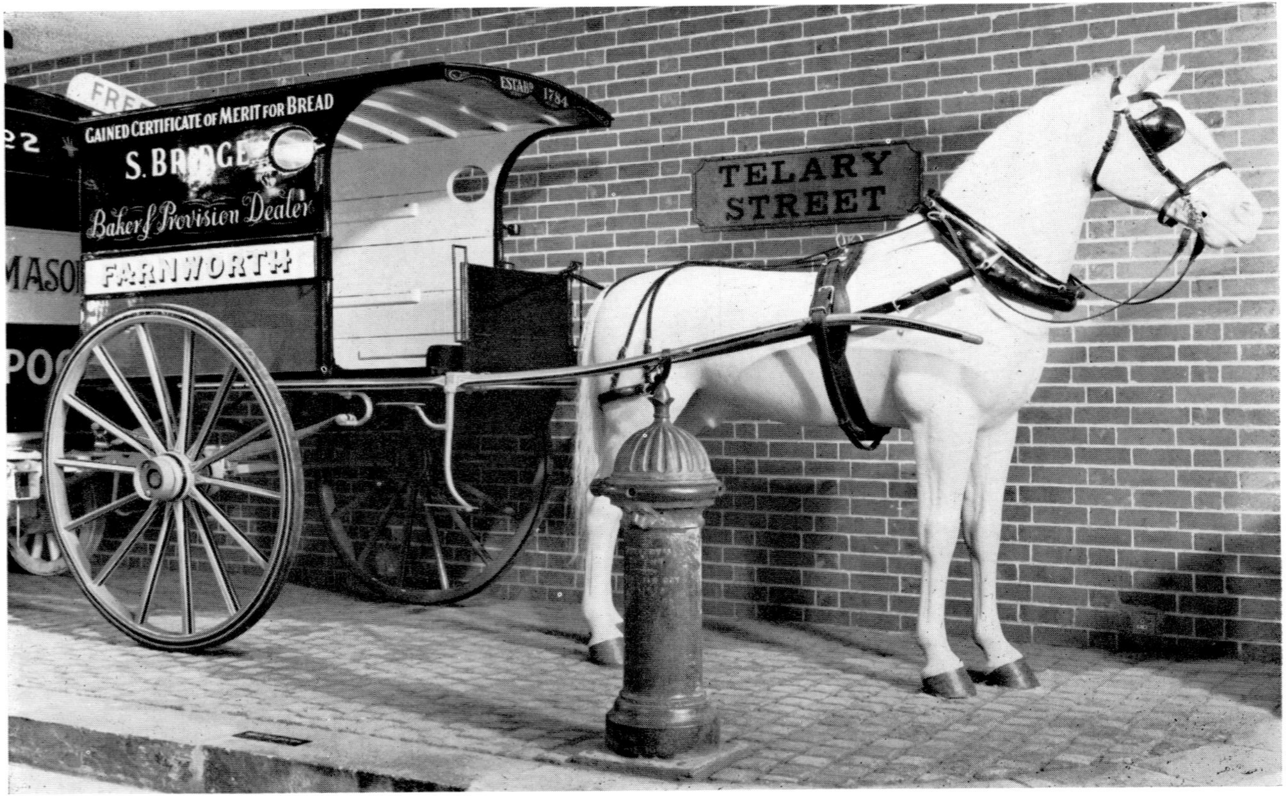

*A bread delivery van of about 1900 restored and displayed in the City of Liverpool Museum Transport Gallery. The street sign and drinking fountain are of cast iron. (Courtesy: City of Liverpool Museums)*

See, 'Notes and News', p 112

*The Liverpool & Manchester Railway's locomotive* Lion *with replica coaches. Another view in the Liverpool Museum Transport Gallery. (Courtesy: City of Liverpool Museum)*

*Ravenglass & Eskdale Railway* River Mite *backing on to a train at Ravenglass, May 1970*

See, 'Notes and News', p 112

*Entrance to the main harbour at Whitby. The West Pier on the right, lengthened under an Act of 1734, has Francis Pickernell's stone lighthouse of 1831. (Courtesy: J. Butt)*

*Whitby Bridge in the process of being opened by one of two electric motors. Designed by J. Mitchell Moncrieff, the bridge was built in 1909 by Keenan & Froude of Manchester. (Courtesy: J. Butt)*

See, 'Notes and News', pp 115–16

favourable consideration the chain brake in use on the L & NW. The matter was deferred until a full board meeting was held, and on 7 September that year the board resolved to request the loan of a train fitted with the Clark-Webb Chain Brake for a few weeks' trial. To this request there could be but one answer: was there not the possibility of further royalties being paid into the Clark-Webb coffers? The brake was tested on the Highland line during the winter of 1880-1. How it behaved is not recorded, but that it failed to line with the Moon-Webb eulogies is evident from a minute of 5 April 1881 when it was stated, and agreed, that 'the result of the trial of the Clark-Webb brake during several weeks last winter which was attached to an experimental train kindly lent by the London & North Western Company, and recommending that as the brake does not comply with the Board of Trade requirements the company should defer further consideration of it'.

There the matter seems to have rested until the following December when the whole question of continuous brakes was reopened by recapitulating all the correspondence and communications on the subject. It was unanimously resolved that the company could not, 'with propriety further delay the adoption of an efficient continuous brake for through passenger trains'. The use of the qualification 'through' ought to be noted. It was agreed that the brake to be adopted should comply with the requirements of the Board of Trade, and thirdly, that the Westinghouse brake having been adopted by the majority of the companies with which the Highland exchanged stock, was the best to adopt. As it 'was the only one which meets the requirements of the Board of Trade, it was accordingly agreed, failing a better brake being suggested, to dispose of the question finally at the January meeting'. Here was the only instance of frank admission that the fitting of continuous brakes could no longer be avoided, and that the Westinghouse brake was at that time the only one fully complying with the dictate of the Board of Trade.

At the January 1882 meeting a committee was formed to go into the whole question of the different kinds of brakes and David Jones was instructed to equip two trains, one with Westinghouse the other with

Smith's vacuum brakes, and test them on the 9.00am down Mail, Perth to Inverness, and the 1.30pm up train from Inverness to Perth.

By March 1882 the committee had visited Edinburgh, Newcastle, Doncaster, Crewe and Derby but were holding up their report until the home line's experiments were complete. At the same time it was decided to have the vacuum-brake train made automatic in action instead of simple vacuum as originally ordered. For a year and a half the business dragged on, until at the board meeting held on 7 October 1884 it was resolved to fit the engines with the automatic vacuum brake and to request the locomotive superintendent to prepare an estimate for the fitting of 300 fish wagons with pipes.

Again there was a long lapse of time. Fourteen months passed before there was any further mention of the vexed question. In February 1887 it was decided to fit the vacuum brake to the vehicles forming the 7.50am train from Perth and the 3.00pm from Inverness. The following month it was recorded that during the year ended 28 February fish wagons had been sent on the 3.00pm from Inverness on 275 occasions. It was therefore decided to fit all the company's fish and carriage trucks and horse boxes with vacuum pipes and it was not until 3 December 1889, following the Board of Trade circular of 24 October, that Jones was instructed to equip all passenger stock with the automatic vacuum brake or with pipes. In December 1892 an order was given to fit the Highland fish trucks with the Westinghouse brake, presumably because of their use over other lines on which that brake was standard.

Thus over the period from 1877 to 1889, the Highland Railway dallied with the question of continuous brakes; and although in the event the company did adopt a reliable brake it was not the one at first considered to be the only satisfactory answer to the promptings of government. How much the Duke of Sutherland had to do with the final decision has not been recorded, though it is relevant to remark that at the time of the decision to select the vacuum brake as the standard for the line, his other main interest (the L & NW) was still

## Continuous Brakes—a Vexed Question

employing the Clark-Webb monstrosity though in the course of changing over to the vacuum system.[15]

It is interesting to note the details contained in the Board of Trade return for the half year ended 30 June 1889. The particulars for the Scottish companies are as follows:

| Company | Westinghouse Brake Miles run | Faults | Vacuum Brake Miles run | Faults |
|---|---|---|---|---|
| Caledonian | 4,528,901 | 11 | 7,313 | 0 |
| Glasgow & South Western | 61,860 | 2 | 2,057,919 | 5 |
| Great North of Scotland | 788,729 | 13 | 174 | 0 |
| Highland | 904 | 0 | 816,482 | 4 |
| North British | 4,375,256 | 33 | 7,840 | 0 |
| Portpatrick & Wigtownshire |  |  | 30,161 | 0 |
| Total | 9,755,650 | 59 | 2,919,789 | 9 |

The miles run per fault were therefore, Westinghouse 165,350, and Vacuum 324,421. For the whole of Great Britain and Ireland the figures were: Westinghouse, 30,651,936 miles run with 241 faults, and Vacuum 71,215,230 miles run, 187 faults. The miles per fault were 127,186 and 380,830 respectively. It will be apparent that a slightly better mileage per failure figure was obtained with the Westinghouse brake in Scotland and the vacuum brake did not show up so well in the northern kingdom. The seemingly high incidence of failure with the Westinghouse brake was probably in some measure due to the difficulty, in those days, of finding a connecting hose which would stand up to the comparatively high pressures. Rubber and rubber composition techniques had not been sufficiently developed to produce a fully reliable article.

The chart on p 76, reproduced by the kindness of Messrs Gresham & Craven Ltd, indicates the development of the two brakes over the period from mid-1878 to mid-1889 as shown by the number of vehicles fitted with each brake at each half year. Also illustrated is the rapid decline in the use of mechanical brakes from 1883 onwards.

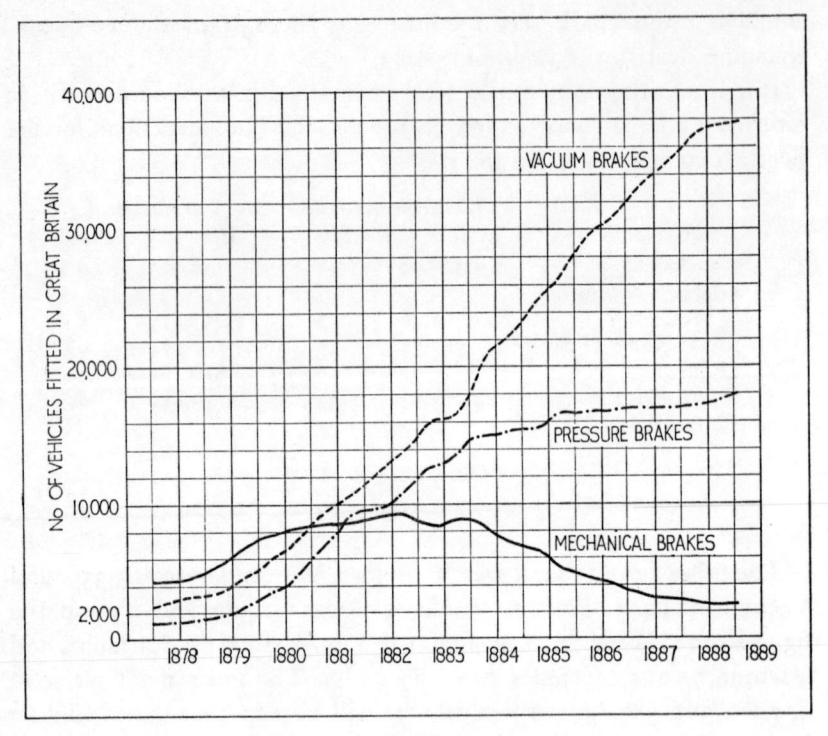

*Figure 2*

The use of two such different brakes as the Westinghouse and Vacuum systems on closely associated lines as, for example, the East Coast and West Coast partnerships, and their consequent interchange of stock, produced problems which emphasised the need for greater uniformity in practice, but such a blessing to the operating departments was denied to them.

In 1881 the North British, which like the North Eastern had adopted the Westinghouse brake, requested the Great Northern (which had espoused the Smith's vacuum brake) to fit all East Coast Joint Stock with the Westinghouse brake in addition to the vacuum brake. Until that year the ECJS vehicles had been only piped, thus the air brake could only be applied on any NB or NE vehicles in the train, but not to the Joint Stock vehicles which were fitted with vacuum brake only. 'If the latter were dual fitted the Westinghouse Brake could be applied throughout between Edinburgh or Glasgow and York, and the Vacuum Brake between that point and King's Cross. This would save considerable inconvenience and delay at present experienced at both Edinburgh and Glasgow in arranging carriages so as to derive the greatest possible benefit from the brake.' So wrote the NB. The GN management passed the letter to Patrick Stirling for his consideration and the request was promptly refused on the grounds of expense. A second similar request was made in 1887 and this time a reply in favourable terms was given. Thereafter ECJS vehicles were dual fitted.[16]

The two Scottish companies associated with the Midland operated a Midland-Scottish Joint Stock Agreement dating from 1 July 1879. By this arrangement the costs of providing and maintaining the stock operated on the through London services were apportioned between them. So long as all three companies used the same brake, the accounting had one common factor at least, but when the Midland and Glasgow & South Western changed over to the vacuum brake, leaving only the North British staunchly attached to the Westinghouse there was not a little confusion. Matters became somewhat simpler when the M & G & SW and M & NB arrangement was substituted for the MSJS Agreement in July 1899.[17]

With the development of the two principal brake systems assured, others such as the Steel-McInnes took second place.[18] The latter was a positive-pressure air brake in contra-distinction to the vacuum brake; that is to say, whereas in the vacuum system atmospheric pressure acting against a partial vacuum in the brake cylinders applied the brake, in the Steel-McInnes brake application was effected by means of an air pump after the manner of the Westinghouse. Brake cylinders on the carriages connected through levers with the brake blocks on the wheels. The cylinders were connected by a system of piping and the train pipes and reservoirs had to be filled with air at the required pressure on both sides of the brake pistons before the train could be moved. To apply the brakes, pressure was reduced on the underside of the pistons, and release was effected by building up the pressure once more. Thus both application and release caused a considerable wastage of air. Since all of this had to come from the pump on the engine the build up of pressure took time, particularly in the case of a long train. The great advantage of the system lay in the ease of graduation of an application. Against this were the loss of air pressure on application or release, which had to be made good before further movement could be made, and the further disadvantage that two train pipes were necessary between each vehicle. Some improvements were effected after the Newark trials but the adoption of the Westinghouse brake as standard in 1882 finally decided the fate of its only serious rival on this railway.

The Highland Railway's use of the Le Chatelier counter-pressure brake system was unique in Great Britain.[19] Several other companies had experimented with it, and discarded it, but the Highland in Scotland, the Snowdon Mountain Railway in Wales, and the Midland Great Western in Ireland were the only lines on which it became a standard fitting. The Le Chatelier brake worked on the principle that by reversing the valve gear of a locomotive while running, the valve events were also reversed so that the pistons worked against full boiler pressure during the latter part of the stroke instead of working expansively, after cut-off, as was normal. This method of working had the disadvantage of drawing smokebox gases into the cylinder with each stroke, and of course pumping them into the boiler with deleterious effects. To counteract this a jet of steam and water, controlled from the cab, was injected into the exhaust channel leading to the blast pipe. The retarding effect of this reverse working could be varied by altering the position of the reversing lever or screw.

The advantages claimed for the Le Chatelier counter-pressure brake were that the whole of the engine weight was available as a brake power, the absence of heating of the tyres by friction of the brake blocks on them (and consequent loosening of the tyres) and, since the wheels were not made to skid, rail-head wear was reduced and the liability to flats and rail-burn removed. The success of this brake on the Highland was probably in no small measure due to the long downhill runs from the several summits of the Grampians. Running may well have been smoother, particularly so far as the reciprocating engines were concerned, and after the fitting of Westinghouse or vacuum brakes to the engines, the life of the brake blocks would be quite considerably extended with consequent economies in stores.

*Wallasey*

## References

1. H. Parris, *Government and the Railways in the Nineteenth Century* (1965), 170.
2. Ibid, 201n.
3. E. L. Ahrons, *British Steam Railway Locomotive, 1825-1925*, Locomotive Publishing Co (1927), 105.
4. J. F. McEwan, 'Locomotives of the Caledonian Railway', *Locomotive Magazine*, 51 (1945), 7.
5. Ahrons, 230, 235.
6. *The Engineer*, 45 (15 June 1877).
7. F. A. S. Brown, *Great Northern Locomotive Engineers* (1966), vol 1, 234.
8. Parris, 208, 218n.
9. Ibid, 218.
10. *The Engineer*, 48 (18 July 1879).
11. Campbell Highet, *The Glasgow & South Western Railway* (1965), 51-2.
12. British Transport Historical Records (BTHR), Caledonian Railway Minute Books, 1876-1882.
13. *The Engineer*, 56 (1883), 31.
14. BTHR, Great North of Scotland Railway Minute Books, 1875-1883.
15. BTHR, Highland Railway Minute Books, 1877-1889.
16. Brown, 234.
17. BTHR, Glasgow & South Western Railway Minute Books, 1879-1899.
18. McEwan, 7.
19. Institution of Mechanical Engineers, Proceedings, vol 21, 1870.

BRYAN J. H. BROWN

# Bristol's Second Outport: Portishead in the Nineteenth Century

PORTISHEAD IS PART of the tripartite Bristol Docks system, which is under municipal ownership. It is some twelve kilometres from the city docks on which Bristol's wealth was originally founded (see Fig 1). The pressures for port development at Portishead were, however, not exclusively those of the increasing physical difficulties associated with the old inland river-port at the Frome and Avon confluence, for a significant part in the Portishead developments was played by leisure. Through most of its history Portishead had been concerned with the local coastal trade, mainly in agricultural products, and small quantities of coal from the Clapton mines exported to the Glamorgan coast for lime-burning.[1] In the eighteenth century it became an increasingly popular venue for day-trips run for the visitors at the Hotwells Spa, and was also visited by occasional groups of merchants and professional people from Bristol.[2] Such parties invariably arrived by boat, Portishead offering a suitable destination to the romantic sail down the Clifton gorge of the Avon; but the total numbers were small and did not encourage the provision of any special landing facilities until the early 1830s, when visitor numbers rose rapidly.

This rise in popularity stemmed directly from the activities of Bristol Corporation in attempting to create a seaside resort. The corporation had been extensive landowners in the parish since 1577, but until the enclosure of 1815–23 had shown little interest in the property.[3] Having seen the success of resort development at Weston-super-Mare, and the beginnings of such development at Clevedon, the decision to create a resort on their land was taken in 1827. An estate road was laid out, building plots surveyed, and a hotel (now the 'Royal Hotel') constructed. In addition a small masonry slipway (called a pier in contemporary accounts), 'by which water passengers will be enabled conveniently to land at any state of the tide', was completed in 1831. The slip underwent several major repairs (eg in 1836) and was rebuilt in 1849.[4]

These and other facilities quickly resulted in increased patronage for the resort, most of the visitors continuing to arrive by sea as road communications to Bristol were very poor. The slipway cannot have been very satisfactory, being suitable for use only by small craft, and in 1832 an earlier proposal by William C. Mylne, for a deep-water suspension pier was revived.[5] Nothing came of this suggestion, and the difficulties did not stop the establishment two years later of a regular steam packet service from Hotwells, on which run several boats were plying by the summer of 1838.[6] Passengers were landed both at the pier and on the Parish Wharf, the latter continuing to attract limited commercial use including the importation of building materials for the new seaside villas.

In 1838 a plan was put forward anonymously for a masonry pier running north-east from a point just west of the hotel (see Fig 2).[7] Having no landward communication proposals this can only have been intended for the landing of pleasure passengers, and would have been a replacement for the original landing-slip. No moves towards its construction were made. The following year saw the first signs of a later expansion by Bristol dock interests when a pier at Portishead figured as one of three suggestions made by I. K. Brunel to the Joint Dock Committee for solving the docking problems of the *Great Western*, launched two years earlier.[8] Brunel's plan (see Fig 3) envisaged two roads running from St Georges and Portbury to a pier on the eastern entrance to the Pill, with a further road from the pier to the hotel crossing the mouth of the Pill on a bridge.[9] Presumably this would have enabled the hotel to be used by embarking transatlantic passengers as well as enabling the pier to double as a leisure facility.

Also in 1839 another plan for a 'Great Western Steamship Pier' was produced by John (later Sir John) McNeill.[10] In his original scheme two piers were proposed (see Fig 5), one being a 210 metre 'suspension roadway' which led to a 180 metre masonry landing pier.[11] An Act was obtained for a reduced version of this scheme, but no construction work began due to 'defects in design and want of support',[12] so that only holidaying visitors arrived at Portishead, not engineers and navvies; but the former were not of sufficient numbers to warrant the construction of any new landing facilities. In 1845 there appeared a plan which brought hope of a renewed expansion in the Portishead leisure industry. This was Brunel's scheme for the Portbury Pier and Railway.[13] Similar in conception to his 1839 plan (but to overcome the docking problems of the *Great Britain*) this scheme substituted rail links for road, and included a branch across the Pill to a station near the hotel (see Fig 4). The railway was to be atmospheric, with an inclined plane taking the carriages up to connect with the then unfinished Clifton Suspension Bridge. The company perished in the collapse of the railway mania and was wound up in 1851 having commenced no actual construction work.[14]

The addition of a railway connection might have saved the Portishead leisure industry from decline, but it did not materialise. Weston-super-Mare was served by the Bristol & Exeter in 1841 (their branch to Clevedon opened in 1847), and as early as 1843 the comment that Portishead '. . . has attained the height of its celebrity and is fast retrogressing'[15] was heard. Any possible leisure investments were drawn away from the area, and there were no more plans concerned solely with the handling of the local leisure traffic. Nevertheless, leisure re-appears as an important factor in later developments.

A new and eventually more productive phase started in 1853, with dock proposals by C. F. Thomas and W. R. Neale. The Thomas plan was certainly the most ambitious ever conceived for the site, and the most uneconomic: two large breakwaters were to be constructed to make Portishead (Woodhill) Bay into a tidal harbour, and a 45 metre channel was to be cut through the hill (which rises to nearly 60 metres in height) to a large tidal basin. From this, two 20 hectare docks were to be entered through locks. Four large graving docks and a canal to the Avon at Pill were also included.[16] In view of the unnecessary complexity of this plan it is a wonder that Thomas ever set pen to paper, and his scheme was not seriously considered. What it did, however, was to create a climate of renewed interest in the Portishead site that alighted more favourably upon Neale's plan which appeared a few months later.[17] It was a derivative of this plan which was finally constructed at Portishead, but it took twenty-six years to reach fruition. The building of railway, pier and dock was the outcome of a complex series of rivalries between a number of Bristolians (many of them members of the corporation), and also of the difficulties experienced in the City Docks due to the increasing size of shipping.[18]

The Bristol & Portishead Pier & Railway Company was formed by the main opponents of the Bristol Port Railway & Pier Company in 1862 (the latter's object being the construction of a railway from Hotwells to a pier at Avonmouth, which opened in 1865). The Portishead company included among its leading members the Bristol aldermen, Ford and Robinson, together with M. Castle, R. Fry and Sir Greville Smyth. The company's first plan followed almost exactly the Portbury Pier plans of Brunel in 1839 and 1845.[19] Construction began in 1864, but in 1865 the plans were changed so that the main line was taken on a quay along the west bank of the Pill, terminating at a pier below the hotel (see Figs 6 and 7).[20] The scheme for the east bank was completely abandoned in this revised plan, the Act for which gave the company powers to provide 'basins, quays, entrances, gates etc, to the value of £80,000',[21] which was the first indication of its intention to expand into a dock undertaking.

The line, originally broad-gauge (which was worked by the Bristol & Exeter for 60 per cent of gross receipts) opened on 18 April 1867. Part of the pier was opened in 1868, and the whole system and pier were complete in April 1870.[22] The undertaking was quickly seen to be successful: 'Portishead Pier Success' ran one headline, 'now with the low water extension passengers to and from Ilfracombe stations exceed 180 daily, and on Saturday over 250 passengers landed and disembarked from these stations',[23] and a service to Cardiff was rapidly established.[24] Thus the commercial success was, perhaps a little unexpectedly, founded upon the seasonal and fluctuating leisure industry, rather than the southern Irish packet trade. However, whilst contemporary newspapers commenting on the opening of the railway still viewed Portishead as a resort and point of embarkation for other resorts,[25] and cheap day excursions were run there from Bristol,[26] the Pier & Railway Company was already considering plans for a floating harbour.

The Portishead Dock scheme, designed by Barnett and Gale of London, was announced in November 1870, in direct competition with the Avonmouth scheme.[27] The relationship of the proposed dock to Portishead Pill, showing the extent to which unnecessary excavations were avoided, is shown in Fig 8, and little subsequent alteration was made to this plan.[28] Some critics of the scheme voiced the opinion that the company 'hoped to avert the doom of Bristol by duplicating the machinery which was to ruin her,'[29] referring to the expected loss of trade in the City Docks which were then back in the hands of the corporation. After a prolonged debate, the corporation invested £100,000 of its Dock Estate Surplus in the Portishead scheme in 1873, in preference to similar investment terms in the Avonmouth concern.[30] The latter already had some backing from the Midland and Great Western railways, while in addition the possibilities of increasing the income from the corporation's Portishead estate were seen. This money could not, unfortunately, save the Portishead docks from several constructional delays, which meant that the opening, in June 1879, was some two years after trading had begun at Avonmouth (which opened in February 1877).

The Portishead Dock was constructed by widening and impounding the Pill, which was formed into a floating dock of about 6·4 hectares. It remains today in substantially the original condition except for the walling of the east side, as a timber wharf, early in the present century. Entrance to the dock is through the original single lock, of 132 metres × 19·8 metres, which is slightly smaller than the equivalent Avonmouth Dock entrance. Until recent years the pier continued to function for pleasure traffic, and although this has ceased the structure

### Bristol's Second Outport: Portishead in the Nineteenth Century 85

has been extensively reconstructed and continues to serve as an entrance breakwater.

The lack of major alterations since completion nearly one hundred years ago only serves to illustrate that the docks were never the desired success. Avonmouth captured most of the international trade, not only through earlier opening but because of its superior location. In addition, Bristol Corporation took over both outports in 1884, and, as witnessed by the opening of the much larger King Edward Dock in 1908, policy aimed at the greater development of Avonmouth. Despite the large twentieth-century additions to the Portishead dock landscape, in the form of two generating stations and the recently closed Albright & Wilson phosphorous plant, there has been no dramatic increase in the use of the docks to render inaccurate Wells' statement in 1909 that 'in the light of subsequent events, the making of Portishead Dock appears as a blunder'.[31]

With the strictly limited success of the docks in the nineteenth century the amount of urban development in Portishead was small, and in 1900 the village remained in appearance an essentially rural community. The topography served to isolate the dockside from the residential areas built in the earlier resort phase (before 1850), and consequently after regaining certain land rights in 1898 the corporation decided upon a new policy for the Portishead Estate aiming for the growth of a residential suburb. Early in the twentieth century more roads were laid out, but building development was slow until the inter-war and post-war periods.[32] Also, by the end of the nineteenth century the numbers of day-visitors arriving from Bristol began a rapid rise, which continued well into the next century, re-establishing Portishead as a resort despite the attempts at industrialisation between 1860 and 1900.[33]

Thus the port of Portishead was subject to considerable change during the nineteenth century, but for various reasons development was not entirely successful. Looking back upon the early career as a resort, it is clear that it had few advantages over its two close rivals; in particular it did not possess the landward communications which resulted in their very rapid growth. At Weston and Clevedon a substantial leisure industry was necessary before large investment in a pleasure landing pier was a practical financial proposition. Indeed even in such situations the financial returns were likely to be very low, and subject to severe fluctuations dependent upon both the weather and the state of the national and regional economy. The failure of the Portishead leisure industry to expand after 1840 can be largely attributed to the continuing poor transport facilities, and this failure meant that there was little chance of success for the proposed passenger landing piers, or schemes which would have placed great reliance upon such an income source.

The success, based in large measure on leisure traffic, of the pier and railway after 1869, must have encouraged the attempt to develop Portishead as a Bristol outport—the railway was already paying its way even without goods traffic in large quantity—but the dock project was not based upon purely economic motives, being a consequence of political divisions in Bristol (not, incidentally, upon strict party lines). The required optimism of committed individuals simply could not overcome the locational advantages of Avonmouth, and total trade was not great enough to support two large outports. Hence Portishead in the nineteenth century fell between two possible modes of development which were both strongly determined by external factors, the most important of which was transport. The early lack, and later creation of, a rail link to Bristol, created an awkward compromise of leisure and industry which has yet to be resolved. Two twentieth-century schemes for new developments on the land between the mouth of the Avon and Portishead, the Portbury Shipyard of 1914–18 and the Portbury Docks Scheme of the 1960s, have proved abortive. However, a revised West Dock Scheme is still under consideration so that the present century could well see a new impetus to industrial and commercial development in the area.

*Bath University of Technology*

## References

1. E. Wigan, *The Tale of Gordano*, Taunton (undated), 123–4.
2. V. Waite, *The Bristol Hotwell*, Historical Association (Bristol Branch), 11; *Bonner and Middleton's Bristol Journal*, 15 July 1786.
3. J. Latimer, *The Annals of Bristol in the 18th Century*, Bristol (1893). 31. The corporation's policy of development may be followed in more detail in the 'Surveyors and Land Stewards Reports', Vol 1 (1809–28), 197–254, and Vol 2 (1828–42), 4–84, Bristol Archives Office (BAO) 04301 (1–2), AA10.
4. BAO, ibid, 71; and Bond and Fardon, *The Portishead Guide and Visitors Handbook* (1855), 7.
5. J. Latimer, *The Annals of Bristol in the 19th Century*, Bristol (1887), 396. Mylne's original plan, in the Port of Bristol Authority Archives, is dated 1828.
6. *Matthews Directory of Bristol*, 1838.
7. Somerset Record Office (SRO), DP 141.
8. C. Wells, *A Short History of the Port of Bristol*, Bristol (1909), 75.
9. SRO, DP 152. This plan is not signed, but in the absence of any documentary evidence of other proposals at this time it is supposed that this plan must be based on Brunel's ideas.
10. Wells, op cit, 75–6.
11. SRO, DP 153 and DP 166.
12. Wells, op cit.
13. SRO, DP 180.
14. C. L. Mowat, 'The Bristol and Portishead Pier and Railway', *Railway Magazine*, June 1955, 371.
15. *The Westonian*, 1 April 1843.
16. Wells, op cit, 108.
17. Ibid, 109.
18. See R. A. Buchanan and N. Cossons, *The Industrial Archaeology of the Bristol Region*, Newton Abbot (1969), 32–7 and 55–7, for a recent summary of the problems.
19. SRO, DP 284.
20. SRO, DP 325.
21. Wells, op cit, 186.
22. The Society of Merchant Venturers contributed £1,500 towards completion of the pier's low water extension in 1868, their main interest being in the improvement of Irish communications. See Wells, op cit, 186.
23. *Weston Gazette*, 23 July 1870.
24. *Western Daily Press*, 5 June 1868.
25. *Bristol Times and Mirror*, 20 April 1867.
26. Ibid, 3 August 1867. The cheap return cost 7½p.
27. Latimer (nineteenth century) op cit, 221.
28. SRO, DP 353.
29. Latimer (nineteenth century) op cit, 397.
30. Wells, op cit, 187–92, describes this event in detail.
31. Ibid, 263.
32. BAO, 08560 (Bristol Plan 66).

33 The author is at present undertaking a quantitative analysis of transport to the coastal towns of north Somerset as part of a PhD thesis at Bath University of Technology.

*Acknowledgements*

My thanks are due to Mr John Mainwaring, who has drawn the maps and diagrams for this paper; to the Port of Bristol Authority, and especially Mr John Corin their Public Relations Officer, for providing the photographs of the Portishead Dock; and to Dr R. A. Buchanan of Bath University for reading the script and providing much encouragement.

*For plates, provided by the author,* see pp 65–8

*Appendix*
Figures 1–8, referred to in the article, begin opposite

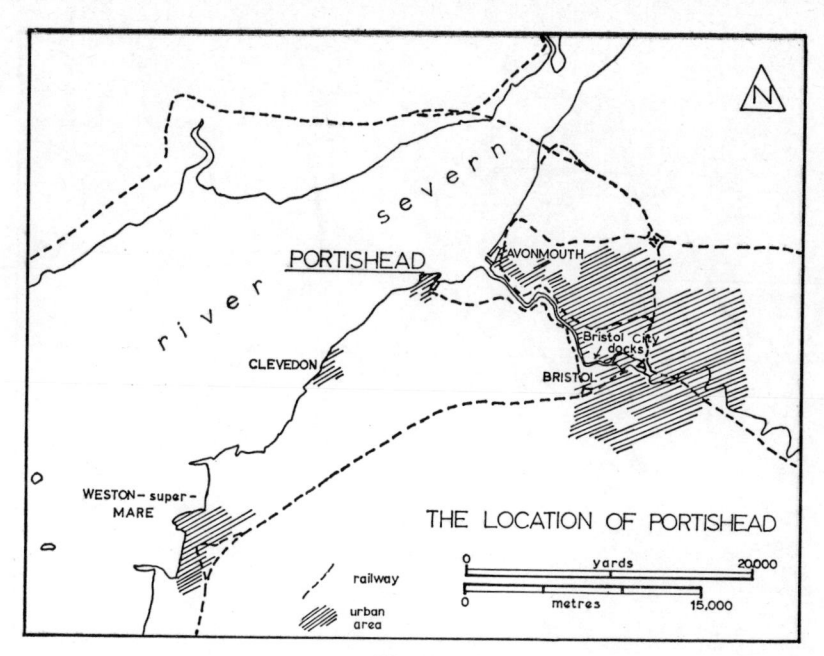

*Figure 1*

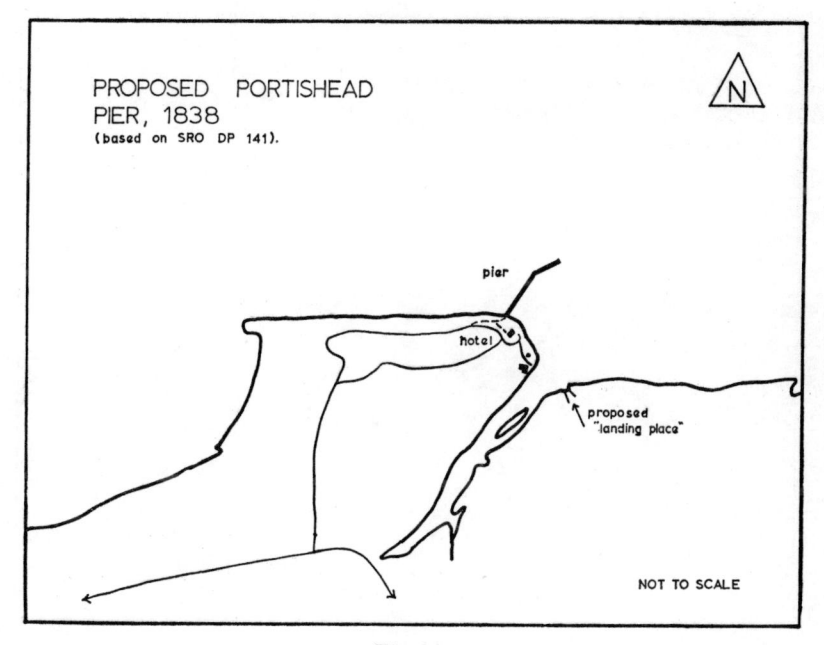

*Figure 2*

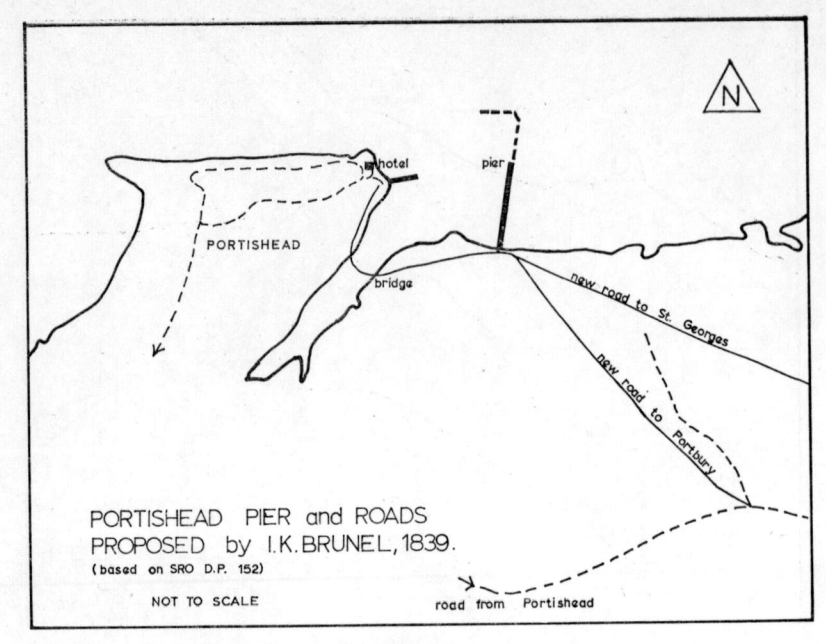

*Figure 3*

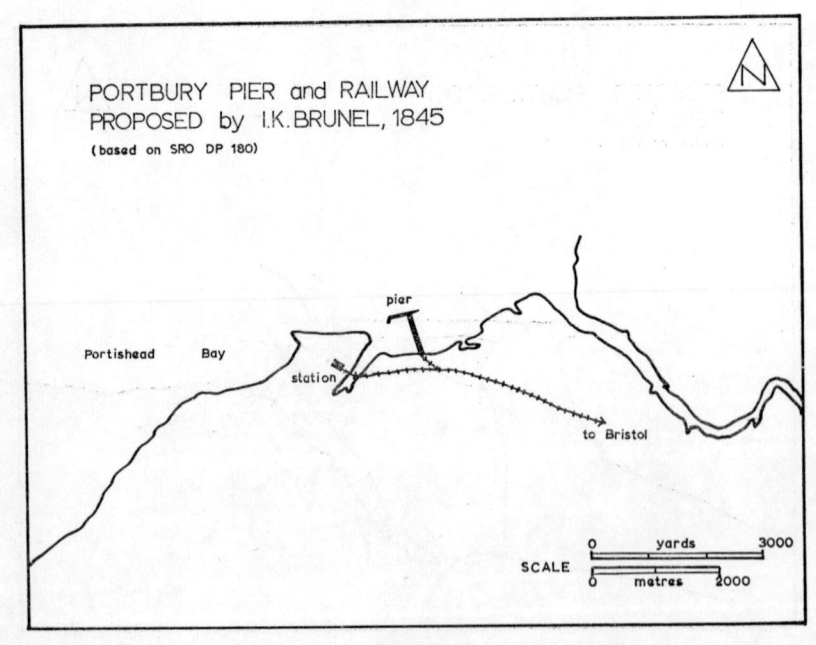

*Figure 4*

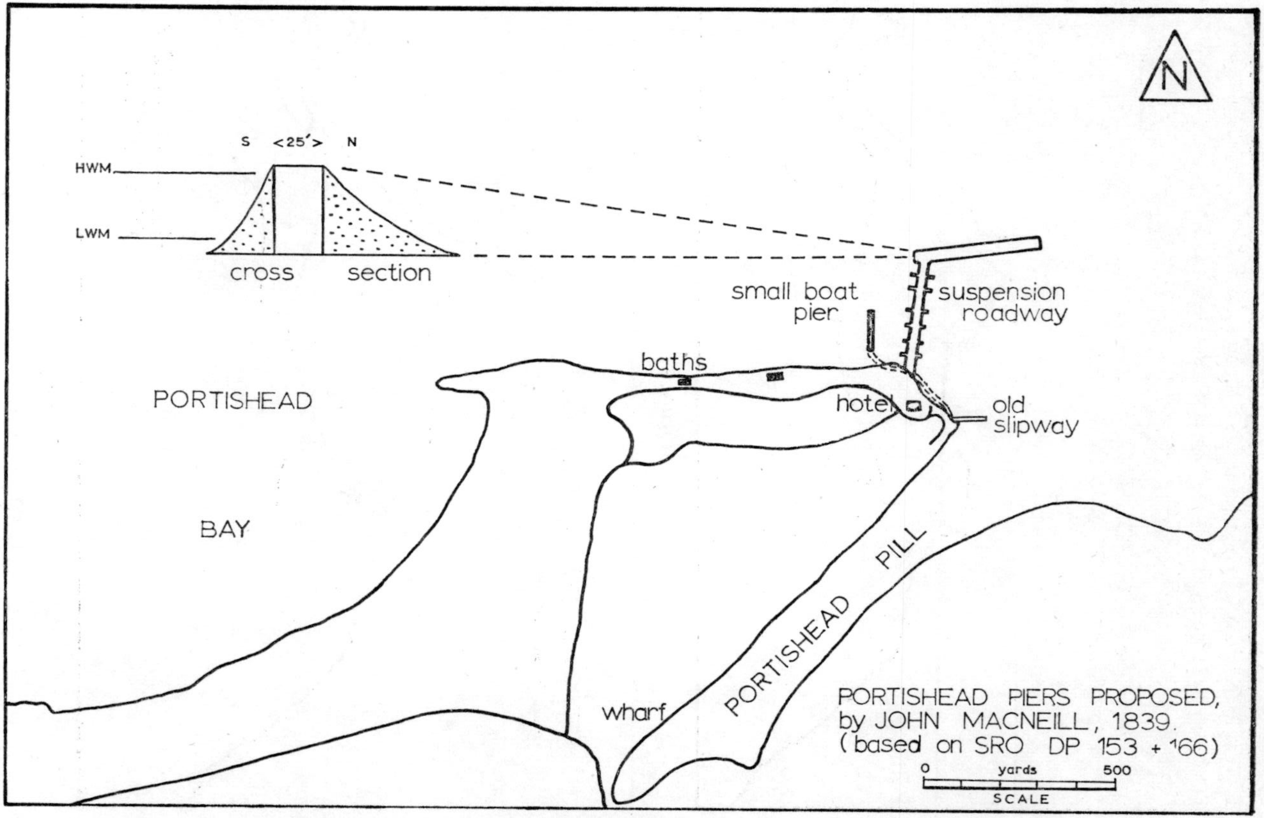

*Figure 5*

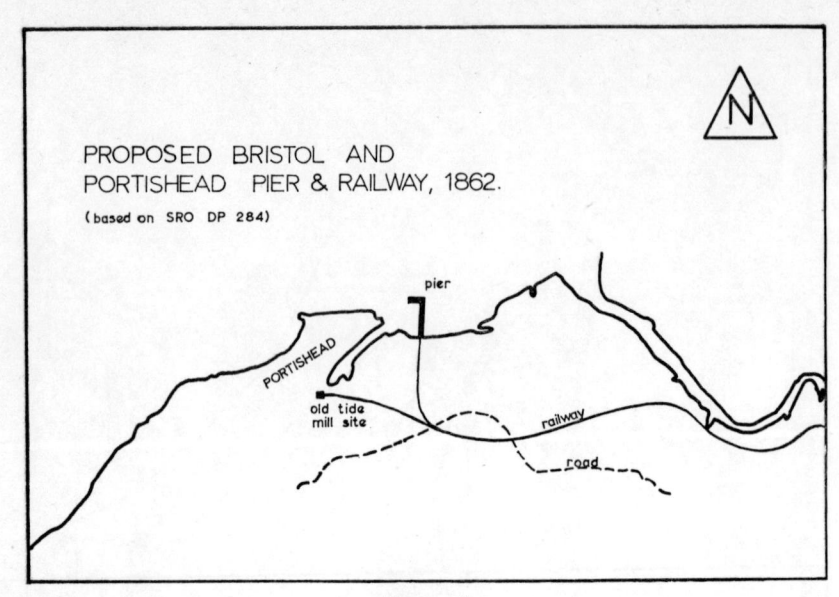

*Figure 6*

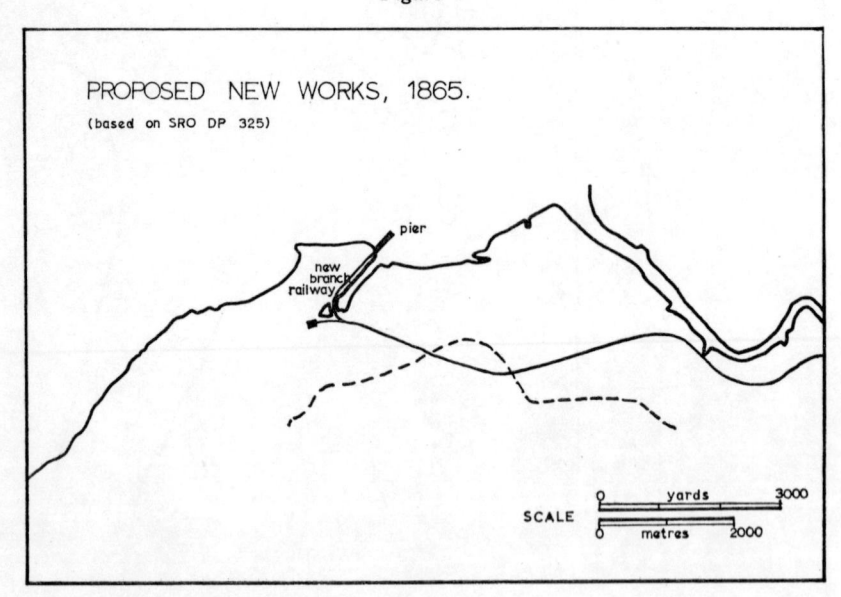

*Figure 7*

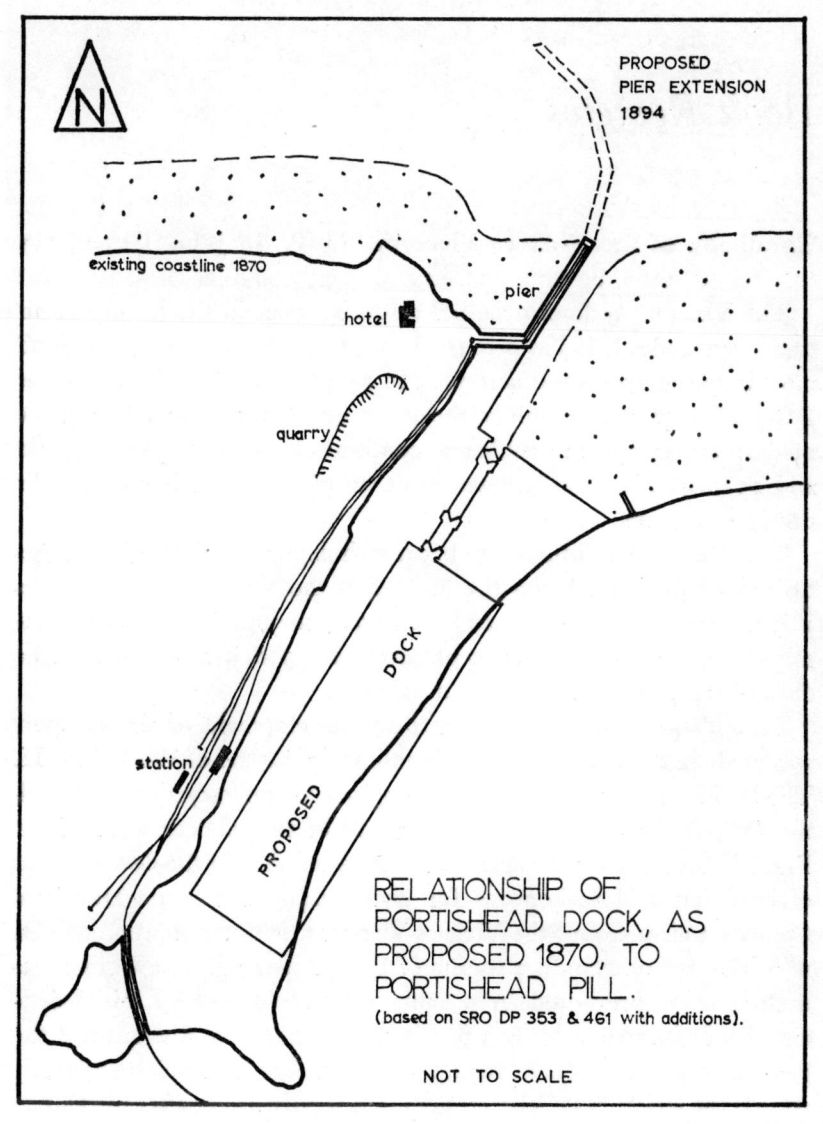

*Figure 8*

# Book Reviews

**Handbook of the Vickers Viscount,** by P. St. John Turner, IAN ALLAN, 1968, pp vi + 170, ill and diagrams.

The Viscount airliner occupies a special place in the history of air transport. Indeed, it has strong claims to recognition as the second most important transport aeroplane in history. The American Douglas DC-3 of 1936 was certainly the most important. The DC-3 made modern air transport possible and continues, even today 34 years later and 25 years after the last was built, to play its part in the world's transport system.

The Viscount is important because it inaugurated the era of gas turbine propulsion. From the day when the Viscount and its Rolls Royce turboprops were first experienced by the public on BEA's experimental services with the V630 prototype in 1950, it was clear that the days of the piston-engine were numbered.

Britain's greatest contribution to the development of air transport was made in the years immediately following the end of World War II. The lead in the development of jet engines for military aircraft, which the United Kingdom gained as a result of the pioneer work of Sir Frank Whittle, was put to good purpose after 1945 in the development of both jets and turboprops for civil purposes. The de Havilland Comet jet airliner and the Vickers Viscount, with turboprop engines, were the two outstanding results of this pioneering. The Comet was unfortunately prevented from achieving full success by initial deficiencies in its structure. But for these it might have inaugurated the general adoption of jets in 1952, six years before the Boeing 707 really started the jet era. The Viscount entered service a year after the Comet in 1953 but, unlike its less fortunate jet contemporary, was a complete technical success so that it sold in large numbers throughout the world. It thus established the turboprop as the prime propulsion unit for short-haul air transport, a role from which it is only now beginning to be ousted by the pure jet.

This book tells the story of the Viscount in considerable detail. It shows how the Viscount was conceived out of the recommendations of the government's wartime Brabazon committees, which forecast the various types of civil transport aircraft which would be required after the war. It then traces the technical development of the aeroplane and shows the important part played by the close collaboration between BEA and Vickers which turned the too-small and uneconomic V630 prototype into the highly successful V700 series. From the time when BEA's V701s were introduced into regular service on Europe's air routes and quickly established a complete competitive ascendancy over all other types of equipment, it was clear that, for the first time since the earliest days, Britain had produced a main line aeroplane which led the world in quality. Large export sales followed and it is startling now to remember that it was this British aeroplane which, in due course, introduced gas turbine operations to the United States and to almost all other parts of the western world.

The Viscount's success, which led to some 440 being sold, made a major contribution to Britain's balance of payments during the period 1953–64, while it remained in production. To this day, it continues to earn useful amounts of foreign currency in spares and support business. The Viscount is, indeed, an outstanding example of the type of product which Britain must continue to manufacture and export if it is to expand its economy and continue to improve its standard of living.

The Viscount's successor, the BAC One-Eleven short-haul jet airliner which has benefited enormously from the reputation the Viscount earned for its manufacturer, has come close to repeating its famous predecessor's success. As a result, it is playing a major part in the present record levels of British aerospace exports. The projected Three-Eleven replacement of the One-Eleven, the financing of whose development is now awaiting a government decision, is intended to continue this most successful line of business. It is to be hoped that

Britain will be able to benefit in the 1970s and 1980s from these technical and industrial progressions from the Viscount—an aeroplane which deserves to be remembered for the part it has played in showing that this country can hold its own in this technological century.

*London*                                                                             Peter W. Brooks

**The Worshipful Company of Wheelwrights of the City of London 1670–1970,** by Eric Bennett, DAVID & CHARLES, Newton Abbot, 1970, pp 171, ill, 50s.

The author quotes from a mid-eighteenth-century writer who argued that the craft of the wheelwright 'requires more Labour than Ingenuity'. Snobbish he may have been, but in essence he was right, for from the sixteenth century, when the dished wheel was introduced, wheelwrights met the growing demands of transport by the employment of rule-of-thumb methods, producing wheels of conventional size and construction, using patterns inherited from their forefathers and made originally by empirical methods. It was not until the late eighteenth century that they introduced the tyre: hitherto they had shod wheels with a number of separate 'strakes' and therefore did not ensure the thorough cramping of a spoked wheel which comes with the cooling of a hoop. It may be that this is one explanation of the dismal catalogue of wheel failures which accompanies the accounts of eighteenth-century coach travellers.

But if it did not call for initiative and inventiveness, the wheelwright's craft made heavy demands on, for example, the selection of wood, and above all on precision of workmanship. This being so it is surprising that the London wheelwrights were not finally incorporated until 1670. Mr Bennett traces their attempts to achieve this status back to 1630. A committee of inquiry then set up by the Court of Aldermen found that in both wheelwrighting and coach-building there was plenty of shoddy work, but apart from the suggestion that between then and the 1660s London was too occupied with graver matters, Mr Bennett has no explanation to offer for the delay in establishing a mechanism for control and supervision.

However, by 1671, the incorporation was in active existence, independent of the coachbuilders, and was very soon imposing fines (even upon past or future officers) for errors of construction, notably for overdoing the dishing; but as was usual with craft incorporations a lot of time was taken up in collecting fees and fining those who 'smooke Tobacco' at meetings. In fact they were firmly established in time for the great age of the wooden wheel and, as the eighteenth century went on, they came more and more into line with the pattern of the City companies: controlling their craft, looking after their sick and needy, safeguarding the interests of their members and entering—when occasion arose—into learned discussion on technical matters. Mr Bennett provides some extremely useful material on the General Turnpike Act of 1773—popularly the Broad Wheels Act—which triggered off a debate in which at least one Fellow of the Royal Society expressed learned opinions.

But by the early 1800s the writing was on the wall as newly admitted liverymen were drawn from a wide range of occupations—anything from umbrella-makers to pawnbrokers. In short as the incorporation grew in social prestige it lost touch with the shavings and sawdust, though enough loyalty survived to enable a majority to turn down a proposal to buy Great Northern Railway stock. Indeed it was not until 1872 that, in Mr Bennett's phrase, the company 'again turned its attention to the Trade'. This arose from a proposal that the livery companies should promote technical education. It was not until 1894 that anything worthwhile materialised and hereafter the company gave some support to a class for young wheelwrights down to World War II.

In short, then, Mr Bennett has produced an attractive book which will be of value to transport historians down to about the late eighteenth century. Thereafter, though its attractiveness in no way diminishes, it relates mainly to the social history of the City of London.

*University of Strathclyde*                                        S. G. E. Lythe

**Go Great Western: A History of GWR Publicity,** by Roger Burdett Wilson, DAVID & CHARLES, Newton Abbot, 1970, pp 198, plates and figures, 50s.

**Great Western London Suburban Services,** by Thomas B. Peacock (Locomotion Papers no 48), THE OAKWOOD PRESS, Lingfield, 1970, pp 105, maps, diags, ill, 21s.

Very many people not normally disposed to distinguish between one railway and another nevertheless felt a special affection and respect for the Great Western—at any rate, this is true of the twentieth century. There were many good features about the line, and quite a lot that were, for the traveller, less good—the stations, the secondary train services, and the catering. But public appreciation of the good points, and of the territory the railway served, was constantly stimulated by a stream of well-directed publicity. In 1886, under James Grierson, an advertising department was formed in the general manager's office, and from 1904 activity in all publicity fields was broadened and sustained. In the 1920s especially, under Felix Pole's general managership, the GWR published a stream of books and paperbacks of high quality at low prices, by Dr M. R. James, Sir Charles Oman, Maxwell Fraser, W. G. Chapman (a copy of whose original 1923 edition of *The 10.30 Limited* was given to this reviewer as a boy and is still cherished by him), W. Heath Robinson, and others. The books were good: *Holiday Haunts* was a sure-fire annual commercial success; the printed bills and leaflets, though rather conservative in their Winchester and Cheltenham types, were always recognisably GWR; the jig-saw puzzles, 44 of the them, were a fine series, some with 400 pieces; but the posters and the art work were generally rather unsatisfactory, without the professional finish that characterised Teasdale's publicity management on the LNER, or of course Frank Pick's on the Underground. The ill-conceived 'roundel' of 1931, with the letters GWR squashed uncomfortably into a circle, was a wretched successor to the coat of arms on those superb engines.

Mr Wilson has explored this unfamiliar aspect of railway management with intelligence and sympathy. As a bookseller he has an eye for some of the technicalities, bibliographical and typographical (though all my copies of the railway handbooks are set in Plantin Light with ligatured ct and st, not Garamond as he suggests), and he notes the printers. A good deal of research (particularly in the *GWR Magazine*) and the fruit of personal inquiry has gone into the book; the information that station garden competitions originated on the Bristol & Exeter Railway in 1865 is a prime example. One could wish that some more of the sponsored publications—Collie Knox's *The Un-Beaten Track* of 1944, the handsome *Railway Gazette* supplement of 1935, and, surely a company-financed booklet, *The Town and Works of Swindon, with a Brief History of the Broad Gauge* (Swindon 1892)— could have been mentioned; and the publishers must be begged to abandon the confusing and unhistorical quirk of translating nineteenth-century prices into 1971 decimal currency.

Mr Peacock's paperback studies a subject that shows how deep railway writers have now to dredge to produce another of the old style 'historical' works. It is an enlarged version of a 1948 booklet. Descriptions of train services written up from timetables make dull reading unless they are illuminated by some comment on the changing patterns of the traffics they were provided to serve or to promote— growth of settlement and economic activity in the area. There is little of such illumination here. But there is much detail on stations served, locomotives and rolling stock, slip carriages, horse and carriage traffic, the approaches to Paddington, with the 'Crystal Palace' line, Crimea sidings, Cape Horn tunnel, and all. The rail-cars and autotrains so characteristic of the GWR secondary lines (with their *Haltes*, halts, and platforms) are covered; so are the road motors. There are some nice period illustrations; but the text is printed by a process which apparently does not permit proof correction—otherwise we should not have had 20 May 1890 given as the date of Paddington's last broad-gauge train.

*London*                                                                 Michael Robbins

**The Midland Main Line, 1875–1922,** by E. G. Barnes, GEORGE ALLEN & UNWIN, London, 1970, ill, £2·75.

One had hoped that Barnes' Midland books were to form a trilogy, but here is his second volume coming straight up to the consequences of the Railways Act, 1921. So be it! Such curious things happened in Midland history since the days of James Allport and John Noble that they could have filled two more volumes.

There was a mystique about the Midland Railway. For that matter there had been mystiques about the Great Western, and the London and North Western, and many other railway companies. But that of the Midland was more than usually peculiar, with its roots in the integrity of Ellis balancing the curious business methods of Hudson. For long after those were dead, there seemed in the Midland to be a blending of the grand and the sinister that was almost Roman. One feels that Sir James Allport, and long after him Sir William Guy Granet, would have managed very well under either the Twelve Caesars or the Borgia popes if they had not been themselves imperial.

Grandeur was in the company's wealth; in its splendid express trains for which John Noble, not to mention the locomotive and carriage men, did so much; in the rich expanse of its cruciform system; in its elegantly old-fashioned stations. On the sinister side there was that deplorable succession of accidents to those beautiful expresses which not once, but again and again were not merely smashed up but burnt to ashes in bleak places at night, while the company cheerfully continued lighting them with compressed oil-gas and working its people, especially signalmen, over inordinate hours. There was something sinister, too, in the later domestic set-up, with periodic whiffs of palace intrigue.

As to the last, one supposes that more years must elapse before the full facts of such things as the Deeley row may be published without malice, loyalties and counter-loyalties, or recourse to hearsay. At the same time one wishes that the author could have devoted something substantial to the curious circumstances under which the London, Tilbury & Southend Railway, an obvious and long-established Great

Eastern protectorate, suddenly became part of the Midland system. From what your reviewer has learnt from unofficial sources, both were very strange episodes indeed, even to the extent of being historical dynamite, and the shade of that clever lawyer, Guy Granet, looms as a grey eminence behind both. Richard Deeley and Cecil Paget both became disappointed, even bitter men. Both were brilliant men.

Mr Barnes has written a fascinating history, and if it be a careful one, should not all written history be such?

*Petersfield*                                                                      Hamilton Ellis

**The Lancashire & Yorkshire Railway, Volume Two**, by John Marshall, DAVID & CHARLES, Newton Abbot, 1970, pp 327, ill, maps and diagrams, 63s.

John Marshall's description of the major constituent companies of the L & YR was given in volume one, which was reviewed in *Transport History*, vol 2, no 3, 1969.

In this present volume Mr Marshall continues his history of the company by devoting his first five chapters to the various extensions and improvements made by the company to the basic system in the later years of the nineteenth century. The construction of various new branches, the arrangements of running powers, and the organisation of joint lines are described in detail.

The successful development in electric traction made by the L & YR on the Liverpool–Southport and Manchester–Bury lines is fully documented, as is the account of the L & YR shipping services which extended its influence to ports in Ireland, France, Holland, and Denmark.

The final chapters give details of the Locomotive, Carriage and Wagon departments based at Horwich and elsewhere, of the workings of passenger and freight traffic throughout the system, and of the administration and organisation of the railway. In these chapters can be found biographies of men such as John Ramsbottom and J. A. F.

Aspinall, whose work made the L & YR the railway that it was. Appendices include a chronology of the L & YR, lists of its chief officers and constituent companies, and, unusually, a list of the parliamentary Acts relating to the company.

This second volume continues Mr Marshall's chronological method of writing a detailed factual account of the development of the various aspects of the railway in isolation. This method elucidates each of these developments in turn, but does not allow us to see how they affect the rest of the L & YR or the railway system in the rest of the country.

This method of writing without any discussion either of cause or effect seems to be the main failing of the book. The development of the railway in Lancashire and Yorkshire was a great factor, both as cause and effect, in the growth of towns and the prosperity of the new Industrial Age. For this reason the chapters on operation and administration, omitting all discussion of the hopes and policies of the company, form an anticlimax, and not, as one would hope, a climax to Mr Marshall's account.

Nevertheless, the account is clearly written and well presented. The maps and diagrams are amply supported by both a well-chosen selection of photographs and a collection of portraits of the men important in the history of the L & YR.

Thus the work provides a most useful reference standard for any interpretive study of the L & YR and its influence on the two counties' social and economic growth in the latter years of the nineteenth century.

*Coalville, Leics*                                                                   Paul T. L. Rees

# Our Contributors

DR T. R. GOURVISH, Lecturer in Economic History in the University of East Anglia, was until recently on the staff of Glasgow University. He is a contributor to several periodicals on such topics as early railway management and eighteenth- and nineteenth-century price history. His study of Mark Huish and the London & North Western Railway will shortly be forthcoming from Leicester University Press.

F. H. W. GREEN is head of the Geographical Sciences Branch of the Nature Conservancy (Natural Environment Research Council). Before this he was for a time on a university staff and has also worked for the then Ministry of Town and Country Planning. Mr Green has done pioneer work on 'hinterland' towns of Britain and has published a number of papers on the topic.

CAMPBELL HIGHET joined the Midland Railway in 1920 and after serving an apprenticeship in the locomotive works transferred to the motive power department. He retired from the post of assistant district motive power superintendent at Bank Hall, Liverpool, in 1964. His main interest centres on the Scottish railways.

S. R. BROADBRIDGE is a Manchester graduate who has recently completed a thesis on Birmingham canals between 1766 and 1800. He is chairman of Staffordshire Industrial Archaeology Society and a contributor to several learned periodicals. His present position is Principal Lecturer in the Department of Business Studies, North Staffordshire Polytechnic.

B. J. H. BROWN, a geography graduate of Portsmouth College of Technology, is now a SSRC research student at Bath University of Technology working on the history of leisure in the Bristol region.

# Shorter Reviews

**Inshore Craft of Britain in the Days of Sail and Oar**, 2 vols, by Edgar J. March, DAVID & CHARLES, Newton Abbot, in association with FISHING NEWS, London, and INTERNATIONAL MARINE PUBLISHING CO, Camden, Maine, USA, 1970, pp 276 and pp 309, ill, 63s (£3·15) each.

Mr March is well known for his work on sailing drifters and trawlers and on the spritsail barges of Thames and Medway. In these volumes he examines virtually every kind of British inshore craft. Though his primary interest is naturally the vessels, the author includes fascinating glimpses of the crews who manned them and the fisheries in which they were employed. The country is divided geographically. Volume one deals with the East Coast from Shetland to the Thames; volume two follows the coastline round from Kent to the West of Scotland and also contains two chapters on pilot craft. The excellent illustrations and line drawings add much to a readable text.

The author draws on oral evidence and extensive personal correspondence over many years with those who knew the vessels, as well as making use of relevant Blue Books and miscellaneous local sources. Although this reviewer recognises that the subject's serious literature is not particularly extensive, it is a pity that no bibliography of secondary works has been included. Despite this omission the book is a considerable achievement in which readers may quarry for technical information or simply browse.

Baron F. Duckham
*University of Strathclyde*

**The Industrial Archaeology of the Lake Counties**, by J. D. Marshall and M. Davies-Shiel, DAVID & CHARLES, Newton Abbot, 1969, pp 287, ill, maps and diagrams, 50s. (£2·50).

This book is an excellent addition to the regional *Industrial Archaeology* series published by David & Charles. Its authors have avoided the sometimes narrowly antiquarian approach to this subject, by taking a very broad view and relating surviving buildings and other remains to the general industrial and social development of the Lakeland counties. For this reason, anyone interested in the transport history of this area must, in order to obtain a proper appreciation of its significance, read the whole book and not merely Chapter VII which deals particularly with this topic. As the authors emphasise in reference to railways, to look at these 'purely in terms of engineering or architectural features is to take far too narrow a view': surviving structures must be 'imaginatively related' to the economic and social life of the surrounding communities. In some ways, indeed, this transport chapter, read in isolation, is perhaps the least satisfactory in the book, being confined mainly to a bare outline of how turnpikes, railways, and docks were built, and to their existing remains. But scattered throughout the book are numerous references to the vital relationships between transport developments and the growth, location, markets, size, and techniques of the wide variety of Lakeland industries. Particularly significant are, firstly, the small and scattered nature of early industrial undertakings reliant on limited markets provided by packhorse, road, and river transport; secondly, the importance of coastal shipping to the rise of the coal, iron-ore, and other extractive industries; and thirdly, the industrial revolution created by the railways and the associated development of the iron and steel and shipbuilding industries in West Cumberland and Furness.

A. E. Musson
*University of Manchester*

**Pictorial History of BOAC and Imperial Airways,** by Kenneth Munson, IAN ALLAN, London, 1970, pp 96, ill, maps, £3.

Kenneth Munson provides a readable narrative of the history of BOAC and its main predecessor, Imperial Airways. But readers familiar with civil aviation will find nothing new here; on the post-1945 period there are only just over 20 pages of text, or less than one-third of the total. This is surely a missed opportunity since there is a great need for a good history of civil aviation.

Obviously Mr Munson's aim is to produce for the 'pop' market, at least in content if not price. The book is lavishly illustrated—indeed there are nearly twice as many pages of plates as text—and there is a useful fleet list. In fact it takes longer to go through these items than the text. Financial, economic and managerial problems are not ignored but they do tend to get cursory and haphazard treatment, with the result that one's appetite is often whetted but never satisfied. For example, one would like to know far more about the managerial and structural reforms carried out by Sir Miles Thomas and Sir Giles Guthrie. The author might also have avoided some loose statements had he paid greater attention to these matters. To take but one example: the statement that Imperial Airways was financially well founded in the mid-1930s is very misleading indeed given the fact that the company would have made a substantial loss but for government subsidies.

Derek H. Aldcroft
*University of Leicester*

# Notes on Reprints, etc

**Holiday Cruising on the Thames**, by E. & P. W. Ball, DAVID & CHARLES, Newton Abbot, 1970, pp 149, maps, ill, 42s.

As the title suggests, this is basically a guide to sailing in hired or private craft on the Thames, between Teddington and Lechlade. Of its type it is a model, handsomely illustrated with line drawings as well as half-tone blocks. Also included is a fold-out map of the river from Richmond to Lechlade. Though there is little history in this volume, it is a good introduction to Britain's most popular navigable river.

**Canal Enthusiasts' Handbook, 1970–71**, Charles Hadfield (ed), DAVID & CHARLES, Newton Abbot, 1970, pp 200 (including advertisements), maps, ill, 35s.

Similar in conception to the same publisher's Railway Enthusiasts' Handbook, this is a valuable handbook to the waterways authorities, societies and boat clubs, museums and publications. There is a substantial section on foreign canals, with details of impressive engineering works such as the fine inclined plane at Ronquières on the Belgian Canal de Charleroi à Bruxelles. The publication of this volume is a welcome sign of the growing interest in inland waterways for recreational purposes.

**Railway Enthusiasts' Handbook 1970–71**, Geoffrey Body (ed), DAVID & CHARLES, Newton Abbot, 1970, pp 176 (including advertisements) + xvi pages of timetables, ill, 30s.

The third edition of this work is even better than the earlier ones and is an exceedingly comprehensive survey of both preservation and commercial railway operation. It can be recommended not only to railway enthusiasts but also to anyone wishing for a rapid survey of railways in Britain and Europe.

**Bicycling 1874: A Textbook for Early Riders**, Anon, DAVID & CHARLES REPRINTS, 1970, pp 79, ill, 30s.

This is a reprint of *Bicycling: its Rise and Development, a Text Book for Riders*, whose anonymous editor claimed that he was supplying 'an admitted want'. It deals with the technique of riding the ordinary or 'high' bicycle and with touring and racing. The route descriptions are useful in indicating the condition of roads when railways were supreme. Despite the claim in the 'blurb' that the book shows 'how rapidly the bicycle became a tool for social and economic change', it is very clear from the text that the early cyclists were middle-class, and that the appeal of cycling in the 1870s was as a sport rather than as a new means of transport.

## Notes on Reprints, etc

**Industrial Archaeology in Hertfordshire,** by W. Branch Johnson, DAVID & CHARLES, 1970, pp 206, maps, ill, 50s.

One of the publisher's Industrial Archaeology series, as usual this volume has a chapter on transport. This deals very competently with roads, canals, railways and postboxes, while there are appendices listing London Coal Duty Boundary Markers, Milestones, and Victorian Posting Boxes. A disappointing feature is the absence of footnotes. There are ten illustrations of transport sites, which include some interesting bridges.

**British Goods Wagons, from 1887 to the Present Day,** by R. J. Essery, D. P. Rowland and W. O. Steel, DAVID & CHARLES, Newton Abbot, 1970, pp 144, ill with photos and scale drawings, 63s.

As the authors state in their introduction, goods wagons have attracted relatively little interest, at least in print. They do not have the glamour of locomotives and coaches, but as this book clearly illustrates, they have a fascination of their own. While this is basically a technical treatise, written for those, such as modellers, who are interested in constructional details, there is much perceptive comment on the way wagons were developed for particular traffics, and all railway historians could read it with profit. On the technical side the work is a model of clarity, and can thoroughly be recommended.

**The Campbeltown and Machrihanish Railway,** by A. D. Farr, OAKWOOD PRESS, 1969, pp 48, maps, ill.

This, number forty-five in the publisher's Locomotion Papers series, is remarkably the first published pamphlet on Scotland's only steam-hauled passenger narrow-gauge railway. Unfortunately the writer adds little to Mr N. S. C. Macmillan's articles on the railway in the *Campbeltown Courier*, and makes a number of errors in details. However Mr Farr has managed to bring together an interesting collection of photographs of this most charming railway.

**The Turnpike Age,** Peter Smith, ed, LUTON MUSEUM AND ART GALLERY, Luton, 1970, pp 30, map, ill, no price stated.

**Roads before the Railways 1700–1851,** by J. M. Thomas, EVANS, London, 1970, pp 51, ill, 35s.

The availability of methods for reproducing documents cheaply and accurately has opened up a whole new field for educationists, and publishers. The archive teaching unit is one example of the use of historical documents to give children a positive identification with the past. Less common, less flexible, but perhaps more permanent are books of facsimile documents, such as the subjects of this note. *The Turnpike Age* is not particularly oriented to the teacher, and in fact aims to present to a wider public some of the items in the Luton Museum collection. Certainly the most immediately attractive illustrations are some beautiful drawings by W. H. Pyne showing all classes of road vehicle, and road making, in the first decade of the nineteenth century. As well as having considerable artistic merit, these handsomely reproduced drawings are a most valuable record of vehicle design and operation.

*The Turnpike Age* has a large format (10·5in by 16·75in), but *Roads before the*

*Railways* is even larger (12·25in by 17·75in). The second in the publisher's 'History at Source' series is as the title suggests specifically aimed at schools. It is a well-chosen collection of forty-three letters, posters, advertisements, invoices and other documents culled from a wide range of sources. There is a concise introduction, brief notes on the documents, and a page of guidance on the use of the series. The print is large enough to be read easily by quite small children, but given the page size, not out of proportion. While the book form is less flexible than the archive teaching unit, it certainly reduces the chance of loss of or damage to individual documents.

**Historic Submarines,** by Commander F. W. Lipscombe, HUGH EVELYN, London, 1970, pp 38, 16 colour plates, also half-tones and line drawings, 63s.

Though strictly outside our field, we were glad to receive a copy of this most interesting work. The early experiments by intrepid inventors are concisely described, and the importance of French enthusiasm and perseverance in the development of the modern submarine clearly emerges. The sixteen plates, by Malcolm McGregor, are up to the publisher's usual high standard, and illustrate both typical and unusual craft, including two pre-nuclear steam submarines, the only big gun submarine (the British MI with a 12in gun) and the merchant ship submarine *Deutschland* used as a blockade runner during World War I. Altogether this book is a pleasant treatment of an unusual topic.

**A Century of Locomotive Building by Robert Stephenson & Co 1823-1923,** by J. G. H. Warren, DAVID & CHARLES REPRINTS, Newton Abbot, 1970, pp 461, ill, 105s.

The reappearance of this classic work is greatly to be welcomed, as for some time copies have been scarce and costly. Originally published in 1923 to celebrate the centenary of Robert Stephenson & Co, it is still the definitive account of the earliest steam locomotives, particularly of the period 1825-50. The many half-tone and line illustrations are appositely chosen, and this reprint, with its handsome binding, should be on the shelves of anyone at all interested in the development of the steam locomotive.

**British Shipping (1914),** by A. W. Kirkaldy, DAVID & CHARLES REPRINTS, 1970, pp 655 + viii, map and folding graphs, 126s.

First published in 1914, this work was written as an account of the then supreme position of the British shipping industry, but it includes sections on the evolution of the ship and the development of trade routes. Even the 'contemporary' material now of course possesses historical interest, and this is probably where the main value of the book now lies.

# Notes and News

*Recent Pamphlets*

Some excellent pamphlets on various aspects of tramway operation and preservation have appeared in recent years, and the three to hand are particularly attractive. P. H. Abell's *British Tramways and Preserved Tramcars* is an account of the working tramways and the working and non-working tramway museums, with details of their rolling-stock. There is a brief history of each of the preserved cars, and useful bibliographical notes. The booklet is illustrated with fifty-six half-tone illustrations and is available (price 6s) from the author at 6 Farndon Road, North Reddish, Stockport, Cheshire, SK5 6LY.

*An English Country Tramway*, by R. B. Parr, is one of the Tramway Museum Society's publications, and may be had from TMS Sales, 3 Oak Tree Lane, Mansfield, Notts, price 6s. This short history of the Burton & Ashby Light Railway, one of the few railway-owned tramway systems in Britain, is illustrated by some beautiful contemporary photographs. The complete absence of motor cars from the street scenes is particularly refreshing.

A very different system is described in *London County Council Tramways Handbook*, by 'Kennington'. Published for the Tramway & Light Railway Society by C. S. Smeeton of Worthing, this pleasantly-produced booklet is obtainable from A. D. Packer, 11 Clarence Road, Bideley, Bromley, Kent, BR1 2DD, price 10s 6d post free. 'Kennington' is the pen-name of four members of the T & LRS, and they combine to describe the acquisition by the London County Council of independent tramway companies between 1896 and 1909, extension and modernisation, the routes and services operated, the tram-cars used, and the depots and works which served them. This pamphlet is comprehensively illustrated, and is a model of conciseness. A folding track plan is included.

Urban transport receives generous treatment, not only from amateurs, but also from operating authorities. A leader, both in quality and in quantity, is London Transport. *Seventy Years of the Central* is the latest of Charles E. Lee's fine series of anniversary booklets, and is similar in format and approach to the others. The Central London Railway was unusual among tube railways in being entirely British in conception, and had the distinction of running the first multiple unit trains in Great Britain (1903). The pamphlet costs 4s, and is available from the Publicity Officer, London Transport, Griffith House, 280 Old Marylebone Road, London, NW1. Also available (price 18s) is J. Graeme Bruce's *Steam to Silver*, a history of London Transport surface railway rolling stock. As in Mr Bruce's earlier work on tube stock, *Tube Trains Under London*, technical change is related to the general development of the railway system and to changing traffic patterns. Fittingly, the booklet is well illustrated with photographs and diagrams.

The prolific Industrial Railway Society has produced two more useful locomotive handbooks. *British Industrial Locomotives —National Coal Board Surface Systems 1967–1969*, edited by A. R. Etherington, is in the society's pocket-book series, and is a valuable handbook to much the most British important operator of industrial locomotives. As usual with the society's publications, it is handsomely produced and illustrated. It may be obtained from A. D. Semmens, 44 Hicks Avenue, Greenford, Middlesex, price 15s. The other handbook, *Preserved Locomotives in the British Isles*, is published jointly by the IRS and the Narrow Gauge Railway Society, and is the most comprehensive list of its type so far compiled. There are sixty-four representative photographs, and comprehensive indices of owners and operators, location of preservation sites, main-line locomotive numbers, and locomotive builders and serial numbers. Price 16s post free, this handbook is a must for all railway enthusiasts. Distribution is in the hands of the Publications Officer, Narrow Gauge Railway Society, 55 Thornhill Avenue, Pateham, Brighton, BN1 8RG.

*Periodicals*

In the July 1970 issue of *The Lock Gate*, the journal of the Great Ouse Restoration Society, the chairman voiced the hope that the reconstruction of Roxton lock and sluices would be started soon. The society's fund for this purpose now approaches £1,000. The quarterly journal is available to non-members of the society at 11s 6d, post free, from the editor, D. K. Cassels, River Cottage, Great Barford, Bedford.

The August 1970 number of *Industrial Railway Record* contains articles on the Heseper Peat Railway, a curious West German undertaking with a cableway to transport wagon bodies across the River Ems; on the Cowley Hill Glass Works, St Helens, and its Borrows well-tank locomotives; on the narrow-gauge locomotives of Rumania; on industrial locomotives of Denmark and Greenland; and one on the transformation of the 1-1-2-1-1 Larmanjat locomotives of the Lisbon Steam Tramway into 0-6-0STs of fairly conventional appearance. Subscription to the *Record* is 18s for six issues, and should be sent to R. V. Mulligan, 41 Egerton Road, Birkenhead, L43 1UJ.

The October issue of the *Record* was devoted to the Whittonstall Railway, a colliery line in Northumberland and Durham built in 1908 for electric locomotive haulage, which proved unsatisfactory. Main and tail rope haulage was substituted in two stages, and the line lasted until the closure in 1966 of the colliery it served.

In the September number of *Railway Philately* the principal features include the first part of an article on 'Danish Private Railway Stamps', another instalment of 'Travelling Post Offices of Great Britain', and articles on railway newspaper and parcels stamps issued by the state railways of South Africa before 1910, and carrier stamps of the British Isles. Price 6s (30p) post free, this number may be obtained from Roger Kirk, 59a Hartley Road, Kirkby-in-Ashfield, Nottingham NG17 8DS.

In *Industrial Archaeology in Wales*, Newsletter no 6 of CBA group 2, Douglas Hague, the indefatigable editor, bemoans the tragic destruction of the Britannia tubular bridge, and expresses the hope that the Conway bridge is protected by sprinklers, as it is the only surviving tubular bridge. Copies of the newsletter may be had free from Douglas Hague at Edleston House, Queen's Road, Aberyst-

# Notes and News

wyth on receipt of a stamped addressed envelope at least 6 × 8in in size.

## News from the Preservation Societies

### Festiniog Railway

The Festiniog Railway opened its 1970 season with four steam locomotives available for service. Double Fairlie *Earl of Merioneth* and former Penrhyn Quarry Railway 0-4-0T *Blanche* had both received routine maintenance during last winter, but *Blanche*'s sister *Linda* and the Alco 2-6-2T *Mountaineer* both returned to service after more extensive overhaul. *Linda* returned to service converted from an 0-4-0 to a 2-4-0, and fitted with a superheater, the first on the Festiniog Railway. *Mountaineer*, although fitted with a new smokebox, continues to provide the major headache. The considerable amount of attention given to her since arrival has now enabled her to handle a reasonable train, but she still uses prodigious amounts of coal in doing so, much of which is drawn through her somewhat large diameter tubes into the smokebox. Experiments have been conducted with tube restrictors and firebox arches; they reduce the coal consumption but also the production of steam. However, apart from an embarrassing failure of *Earl of Merioneth* on the day of the Festiniog Railway Society's AGM, the locomotives have given stalwart service this last year, in spite of being subjected to another season of very intensive use. Work progressed throughout the summer on the rebuilding of the second Double Fairlie *Merddin Emrys*, using the new boiler supplied by the Hunslet Engine Company.

Permanent way alterations at Dduallt were completed by last Easter to divert the top end of the run round loop on to the beginning of the spiral, which is the first stage of the new construction to by-pass the former line submerged by the CEGB's pumped storage scheme at Tan-y-Grisiau. During the summer permanent way was laid around the spiral as far as the site of the bridge which will take the new route over the existing one; this work has been done to enable the permanent beams of the bridge to be brought to the site by rail. Two 4 ton and 2 ton concrete beams which comprised a new bridge to carry the line over a minor road by Nazareth Chapel, Penrhyn were offloaded from bogie wagons and placed in position by a 15 ton road crane on 23 January 1970.

A colour light signalling scheme at Tan-y-Bwlch was put into operation on 16 May. It has been installed as an interim measure pending completion of the full signalling scheme. Three aspect signals are operated from a panel installed in the old station building and are interlocked with the ground frames. Provided the road is set correctly, pressing the appropriate button either at the panel or at the ground frame (where remote operation buttons are provided) gives either a green for normal line operation or yellow for 'wrong line' running. The passage of a train over a treadle automatically replaces the appropriate signal to danger. Major Oliver of the Railway Inspectorate, who visited the railway on 12 April, complimented the railway's S & T department on the work carried out. The ministry regards the installation as a temporary one giving enhanced operating safety necessary because of the intensive service now being operated.

At Penrhyn work is rapidly nearing completion on the conversion of the old station building and adjoining former shop into a hostel for Festiniog Railway volunteers.

The traffic carried last year was again at

a record level. The season got off to a good start, in spite of cold wet weather, but late May and early June gave very disappointing results. Thereafter the traffic figures climbed steadily with a substantial increase on 1969 totals.

*Ravenglass & Eskdale Railway*

The Ravenglass & Eskdale Railway Preservation Society has at last managed to pay for *River Mite*, the splendid 2-8-2 bought to supplement the railway's ageing *River Esk* and *River Irt* (see p 71). Support for the locomotive is still needed, however, and the New Locomotive Fund has become the River Mite Maintenance Fund. Over ten years the society has contributed £21,725 to the railway, as well as invaluable volunteer support. Owing to a fortunate coincidence of good weather with peak traffic periods, the number of passengers carried in 1970 is expected to be higher than in 1969. The latest additions to rolling stock include six new saloon coaches, delivered during the summer, and a 'scooter', built at Ravenglass in August to save using an engine for minor messages. A new tender for *River Irt* is being constructed this winter. We congratulate the society on its tenth anniversary, and wish it many more prosperous years.

*Scottish Railway Preservation Society*

The society has purchased Wemyss Private Railway no 20, a Barclay 0-6-0T built in 1939. The locomotive was completely overhauled in 1968, and became available on closure of the railway in May 1970. On 22 October she ran through from Methil to the society's Falkirk depot under steam. The society is negotiating with British Rail about the acquisition of the railway from Aviemore to Boat of Garten, to be operated as a tourist attraction. If agreement can be reached, services may start in 1972.

*From the Museums*

*Liverpool*

As promised in an earlier issue, we include in this number photographs of the new transport gallery at Liverpool City Museum (see pp 69–71). Attendance at the gallery is proving very satisfactory.

*Swindon*

Attendance at the Great Western Railway Museum appears to have reached a ceiling of about 40,000, and the annual report for 1969–70 suggests that any large increase in attendance can only come from extension to give room both for permanent display and for temporary exhibitions.

*National Maritime Museum*

The reading room at the National Maritime Museum is being converted to a reference room and an information room, so that research readers will be accommodated in the main library. The staff of the Picture Department are preparing catalogues of the paintings, drawings, prints and historic photographs in the museum collections, and as a result until March 1971 no orders for prints from the historic photographs collection can be accepted.

*A Historic Canadian Canal*

Strategic considerations have often been a determining factor in construction of canals, and an interesting minor example has recently been exposed as a result of excavations by the Canadian National Historic Sites Service. This is the fortified canal at Coteau du Lac on the St Lawrence River, built in 1779–80 to by-pass some rapids. Disused from 1851, the excavations took place in 1965–6, and a brief account, illustrated with photographs, is published in *Canadian Historic Sites*, the first of an occasional series of papers prepared by the National Historic Sites Service, Department of Indian Affairs and Northern Development. Copies may be had from the Department, Ottawa, Canada, price $1·50 (Canadian).

*Documents Useful to Transport Historians*

The following covers the period January 1969 to September 1970 and has been prepared from notes kindly sent by archivists and librarians to whom the editors are most grateful.

*Aberdeen:* While the University Library reports no deposits, a University Archivist, Mr Colin McLaren, has been appointed who will have charge of future acquisitions.

*Aberystwyth:* The annual reports of the National Library of Wales show that the library is becoming an increasingly important repository of transport records. In 1968–9 Mrs E. D. Jones of Aberystwyth deposited accounts of Captain William Morgan relating to the SS *Express* sailing between Great Britain and Ireland, and in 1969–70 Mr T. G. G. Herbert of Aberaeron and Cilcennin presented miscellaneous volumes, correspondence and papers relating to the ship *Grosvenor* (c 1767), and a printed copy of a report to the Trustees of the Kidwelly Trust on a proposed turnpike road from the River Loughor to Carmarthen (1829). Other desposits in 1969–70 were the surveyor of the highways' account book for the parish of Llandyfrydog (1838–41, from the Rev R. E. Jones, Rhos-y-bol); a plan of a proposed tramroad from Brynich to Parton's Cross near Hereford (1810, from Mrs Josephine Murray, Penpont, Brecon); assignments of shares to the Hay Railway (1843–5) and the Rumney Railway (1842–56), and mortgages of tolls of the Cambridge and Ely and the Downham and Ely turnpike trusts (1763, 1819–29) presented by Messrs Riders, Lincolns Inn, London.

*Caernarvonshire:* Bulletin No 3 of the Caernarvonshire Record Office (County Offices, Caernarvon), price 4s post free, includes photographs of the Dinorwic Quarries locomotive *Jerry M* and of loading slates into a schooner at Portmadoc c 1890, as well as a short account of a marine archaeological investigation of the wreck of the sloop *Lovely*, lost in 1807. This is an excellent publication, well worthy of imitation.

*Cornwall:* The Cornwall County Record Office at Truro reports the acquisition of photographs of Royal Albert Bridge and several Cornish railway stations; of documents related to Gorran harbour, plans of Truro harbour and river; and of the book of reference of the Devon & Cornwall Railway (1841).

*Cumberland & Westmorland:* Deposited at the Carlisle office of the Joint Archives Committee for these counties are Workington Harbour tonnage books 1773–1838 and ships ledger 1795–1838; Port Carlisle anchorage books 1828–67; and papers relating to the proposed mid-Cumberland light railway (Wigton–Penrith, 1896–8).

*Derbyshire:* Recent accessions to the Derbyshire Record Office at Matlock include minute books and plan of the Ashbourne-Leek turnpike (1762–70 and 1835–55) and minute books of the Ashbourne-Belper turnpike (1836–89); plans and sections of the Cromford & High Peak Railway (c 1825); plan of a proposed railway from Ashbourne to Wirksworth (1827), and photographs taken of the last run on the Little Eaton Tramway (1908); minute books and other material of the Rowsley branch of the National Union of Railwaymen (1918–64); a large deposit of the records of the Butterley Company, including accounts for making rails for several early railways; a further deposit of Cromford Canal permit books; pages from a ledger of the Shardlow Boat Company (1831); material relating to the Nutbrook and Erewash canals; and xerox copies of correspondence concerning the Trent Navigation.

*Dorset:* While there have been no important accessions to the Dorset Record Office, three copies of posters advertising the opening of stations (Upwey, the new Upwey station, and the Weymouth & Abbotsbury Railway) have been obtained.

*Durham:* The Durham County Record Office, Durham, reports several interesting accessions, including a Turkish ship's passport of 1867; accounts of 'coals led from the several pits at Harraton Outside Colliery to Fatfield Staith for the use of Ralph Milbank Esq.' (1784–90); plans of intended railways from Darlington, Croft and Piercebridge to the Auckland collieries (1819), of West Hartlepool (1861), of the River Wear from Newbridge to Sunderland (1737), of the River Wear from Biddick to the sea, by John Rennie (1823), and of Greta Old Bridge (c 1800).

*Glamorgan:* Recent additions to the Glamorgan County Record Office, Cardiff, are an undated plan of the Duffryn, Llynir & Porthcawl Railway; a section of a proposed connection to this line from Bryn colliery (1844); and registers of incoming vessels (1894–1916) and of arrivals and sailings (1873–8, 1886–96) from Porthcawl Harbour.

*Guildford:* The Borough Museum and Muniment Room has received further additions to the records of the Wey and Godalming navigations, and of William Stevens & Sons, barge-owners. The corporation has recently published a neat summary of West Surrey waterways, with notes on documentary sources, which is available from the museum at Castle Arch, Guildford, Surrey, price 1s post free.

*Herefordshire:* The Hereford County Record Office, Hereford, has acquired papers of Stephen Ballard, a Herefordshire engineer, including the Register of Calls and Preference Shares of the Herefordshire & Gloucestershire Canal (1839–42); a cash book of the Great Northern Railway (1847–9); and photographs of the Worcester and Hereford, London and Bedford, and Avon and Evesham railway lines.

*Leicestershire:* Though the Leicester County Record Office, Leicester, reports no additions, detailed cataloguing of some collections received earlier has brought to light, among others, an engineer's report and estimate of expense for the proposed Melton to Stamford Navigation (1786); a plan of a proposed extension of the Leics & Northants Union Canal to Buckby (1803); a broadsheet opposing the proposed River Derwent Navigation from Derby to the Trent (c 1700); broadsheets concerning the proposed ballast shore at Jarrowslike (1670); papers concerning the Trent & Mersey, Derby and Erewash canals and Trent Navigation (1699–1931), the Cromford and High Peak Railway (1823–30), and turnpike roads in Leicestershire and bordering counties (1762–nineteenth century); ledgers, accounts and other papers of the Belvoir Highways Board (1863–71); and eighteenth- and nineteenth-century accounts of the Surveyors of Highways.

*London:* The British Transport Historical Records Office in Porchester Road reports the following additions: architectural drawings of stations and bridges (LNW,

L & Y and Midland railways); land plans of the Settle & Carlisle Railway (c 1869); LNER locomotive stock registers (1871–1948); GWR wagon stock books (1924–38); and River Weaver Navigation records (from 1819). There have also been many smaller accessions.

*Somerset:* Though there have been no accessions of collections specifically on transport, the Somerset Record Office, Taunton, reports that the MSS of Lord Hylton of Ammerdown contain leases of land for colliery tramways in the Kilmersdon area, and reports and prospectuses of railways. The accounts and papers of the concerns of William John Jolliffe and Edward Banks include a contract with the Company of the Proprietors of the Strand Bridge (1812).

*East Sussex:* Recent additions to the East Sussex Record Office in Lewes include historical notes on the Newhaven and Dieppe ferry; records of the Rye Harbour Commissioners (1724–1935) transferred from the Kent Record Office; Southover Surveyors Rate Book (1806–14); Loxwood End, Wisborough Green Highway Assessment (1654); and Hastings and Flimwell Turnpike Records (1781–1821).

*Other Record Offices:* Cambridgeshire and Isle of Ely Record Office, Cambridge; Cathedral Archives and Library, Canterbury; Carmarthenshire County Record Office, Carmarthen; the Brynmor Jones Library, University of Hull; Liverpool Record Office; Department of Local History and Archives, Sheffield City Libraries; and the City Library, York, all report that no deposits of records concerning transport history have been made.

*An Historic Port*
J. Butt writes:
Whitby, an attractive seaside resort on the north-east coast of Yorkshire, still retains much of its eighteenth-century harbour, although changes are very likely in the next few years. Originally, the town developed as a Celtic ecclesiastical centre in the sixth and seventh centuries, and the abbey in its foundation charter (1075) was granted control over the port and its revenues. Before the sixteenth century, however, it was merely a fishing port with little in the way of coastal trade.

The beginning of the exploitation of local alum shale at the end of Elizabeth's reign led to the development of the port, since coal had to be brought from Newcastle to supply the alum kilns. Thus, coastal trade from the port was encouraged, and shipbuilding began on a relatively large scale. By the late seventeenth century, Whitby was a prosperous town with a population of about 4,000, most of whom depended upon the sea for their livelihood.

Industrial and commercial development was encouraged by the local lords of the manor, the Cholmleys, who were responsible in the seventeenth century for much improvement to the harbour. In addition, the growing importance of Whitby as a haven for the colliers in the coastal trade can be judged by the fact that Parliament in 1702 allowed the town to levy 'passing tolls' on coal shipped at Newcastle and other ports in the North East. This provision survived well into the nineteenth century.

Piers which had been built or improved in the seventeenth century were drastically altered in the eighteenth century. An Act of 1734 led to the lengthening of the West Pier, and about mid-century much reconstruction of East and West piers took place. Later, a new fish pier was built, and quays added. Throughout the nineteenth century piece-meal improvement of the port proceeded, and final pier extensions were added in 1913.

Two outstanding monuments of this period of port improvement survive virtually unchanged. The largest lighthouse was erected in stone by Francis Pickernell in 1831 'under the direction of Colonel Cholmley, Lord of the manor of Whitby & others, trustees of the piers & harbour of Whitby' (see p 72). Two smaller lights date from only slightly later. The bridge carrying the road over the River Esk at Whitby was widened in 1835 to allow larger vessels to enter the inner shipbuilding and repairing harbour and brand-new ships just off the stocks to leave. The present bridge, dating from 1909, was built by Keenan & Froude of Manchester to the design of J. Mitchell Moncrieff. Originally hand-operated, the bridge had to be raised and moved in two sections parallel to the quays to allow ships access to the inner harbour. However, after a change to hydraulic operation, the bridge in 1953 was fitted with two electric motors of 25hp each which are now responsible for moving the two bridge sections (see p 72).

The eighteenth century saw the beginning of the port's golden age. By 1776, 251 small merchant ships were Whitby-owned, and the port possessed some 50,000 tons of shipping. Whaling, as well as coastal shipping, stimulated the demand for Whitby seamen and vessels; in 1817, probably the best year for the Whitby whaling fleet, 1,850 tons of oil were produced from 76 whales. Harpooners' cottages, dating from the 1720s, still survive in Whitby's older streets. Deep-sea fishing was the best training-ground for naval personnel and the outstanding testing place for ships. William Scoresby Jr, a great Whitby skipper like his father before him, left us in his *Account of the Arctic Regions* (1820 and reprinted by David & Charles 1969) a memorable account of whaling.

Captain James Cook (1728–79), RN, FRS, the great explorer, began his maritime career in 1746 as an apprentice to a Whitby shipowner and for his first great naval voyage to Botany Bay (1768) selected a Whitby-built collier, *Endeavour*. The builder of this ship, T. Fishbourne, also built the ships, *Resolution* and *Adventure*, commanded by Cook on his second voyage (1772). *Resolution* and *Discovery* (the latter built at Whitby by G. & N. Langham) were Cook's vessels for his third voyage in 1776 which ended with his death in 1779 in Hawaii. On the West Cliff stands a recently erected statue to Cook, not far from Whale-bone Arch (given by Norwegian whalers). These are two memorials to Whitby's golden age of maritime adventure.

*Industrial Archaeology, Vol 8 No 1*

The February issue, uniform with *Transport History*, includes the following major articles: 'The Royal Potteries, Weston-super-Mare, 1836–1961' by Bryan J. H. Brown; 'Aids to Recording (7) Industrial Archaeology and Photography: An Account of a Course at Flatford Mill' by Brian Bracegirdle; 'Londonthorpe Mill' by Ian S. Beckwith; 'Some Notes on the Van mine, Llanidloes, Montgomery' by T. A. Morrison; 'Beehive Coke Ovens at Whinfield, County Durham' by Bernard McCall; 'Funtley Iron Mill, Fareham, Hants' by M. D. Freeman; 'Henry Cort at Funtley, Hampshire' by R. C. Riley; and 'A Mill Still Powered by Steam' by Geo L. Stamford-Nutt. Annual subscription £2·50 (single copies 65p). Available quarterly from David & Charles.

# RAILWAY AND CANAL HISTORICAL SOCIETY

*Founded 1954*

The Society exists to bring together all those interested in the history of railways and canals and offers a quarterly journal, a lively monthly bulletin, visits to places of interest and local group meetings.

*Details of membership from: Hon Secretary, 174 Station Road, Wylde Green, Sutton Coldfield, Warwickshire.*

The Society also offers the following publications for sale:

**A SHORT HISTORY OF THE LIVERPOOL & MANCHESTER RAILWAY,** by G. O. Holt, (2nd edn, price 7s 6d, post free).

**HOW FFESTINIOG GOT ITS RAILWAY,** by M. J. T. Lewis, (2nd edn, price 12s 6d, post free).

*Available from Hon Sales Officer, 'Macrae', Stubbs Wood, Amersham, Bucks.*

---

## ST JOHN THOMAS BOOKSELLERS LTD

Specialists in Books on Transport History, Industrial History, Social and Economic History. Catalogues of works on these subjects are now available.

**ST JOHN THOMAS BOOKSELLERS LTD**

**30 WOBURN PLACE, LONDON WC1H OJR**

Telephone 01 580–9449

---

## ALL FORMS OF TRANSPORT

We publish a long list of books on transport history and allied subjects.

Send for our Transport leaflet which gives details of all our titles on Canals and Waterways, Railways, Road, Steam, Naval and Maritime History.

**David & Charles
Newton Abbot
Devon**

## Railways and Economic Growth in England and Wales 1840-1870

### G. R. Hawke

In this investigation of a topic hitherto largely neglected in the United Kingdom, the author has produced a book that will interest all historians of nineteenth-century Britain and economists concerned with economic growth. In the search for dynamic links between the railways and growth in other industries the extent to which the South Wales iron industry supplied the rails, the pricing policy adopted by the railways, and their management receive attention. The reduction of transport costs effected by the railways is assessed; and account is taken of Fogel's work in the United States.
47 text-figures   £6

## Transport and Turbans

### A Comparative Study in Local Politics

### David Beetham

Should Sikh bus conductors be allowed to wear their traditional turbans instead of the regulation cap? David Beetham analyses the complex political struggles that sprang from that seemingly insignificant point, which took seven years to settle in Manchester, and in Wolverhampton were ended after two years of fierce controversy by threats of suicide. He provides a fascinating and at times amusing study of different cultures trying to reach accommodation, which illuminates important aspects of race relations.   Paper covers 18/–   *Institute of Race Relations*

**OXFORD UNIVERSITY PRESS**

## Two New Books

### THE DORSET AND SOMERSET CANAL

### An Illustrated History

*Kenneth R Clew*

The canal was authorised in 1796, but the scheme failed in the early 1800's. It was to link Bristol and Poole by way of Frome and Wincanton with a branch serving the Somerset collieries round Nettlebridge. No work was done on the main line but there is still much of interest to be seen on the branch that was built.   £2

(Inland Waterway History series)

---

### THE OMNIBUS

### Readings in the History of Road Passenger Transport

*Edited by John Hibbs*

A selection of papers by members of the Omnibus Society covering Edinburgh experimental vehicles, early omnibus services, extended tours by motor coach, 100 years of railway associated omnibus services, and much more.   £2·50

**DAVID & CHARLES
NEWTON ABBOT
DEVON**

# Transport Museums
## JACK SIMMONS

'Professor Simmons has written an absorbing book. In form a guide to the most important transport museums in Britain and Europe—and as such a perfect and indispensable guide-book—it serves as an introduction to the history of transport in all its forms during the past two centuries. This book, packed with information in a most appealing way that offers one constant pleasure and surprise, is still more valuable for the vistas that it opens to the historical imagination, the significant themes and new subjects it suggests.' *History Today*
'I have read it with astonishment and delight.' A. L. Rowse     £4

# The Last Steam Locomotive Engineer: R. A. Riddles CBE
## H. C. B. ROGERS, OBE

Riddles joined the Crewe Works of the old London & North Western Railway in the years before the First World War and rose to the very top of his profession with responsibility on British Railways for more locomotives than any previous Chief Mechanical Engineer. He was responsible for the design of the 'Austerity' locomotives of the Second World War and for British Railways' Standard locomotives. His 2-10-0 has strong claim to being the finest steam engine ever to run in the British Isles.     £2·50

# Rail, Steam and Speed
## O. S. NOCK

In his latest book O. S. Nock recalls in vivid details the days of the steam locomotive. He describes some of the great line-side spectacles of pre-grouping days; North Western 'Jumbos' in the northern fell country; Great Western 'Cities', Great Northern 'Atlantics' and South Western 'T9s'. Engines like *Hardwicke*, *City of Truro*, *Papyrus*, *Silver Link*—names in a railway history book—come to life again.     £2·55

# 'Auto'-Biography
## My Forty Years of Motoring
## ARTHUR KNOWLES

Arthur Knowles grew up with the motor car. This is his fascinating and nostalgic glance back to the days of the pioneers. It's a *must* for everyone who mourns the passing of the 'string and copper wire' era.     £2·25

# *George Allen & Unwin*

# HAMILTON BLUMER LTD

*Antiquarian Booksellers*

Are Specialists
in Scarce and Out-of-Print Works on the
History of Technology, Transport and Commerce

We issue Catalogues

109 SOUTHAMPTON ROW
LONDON, W.C., IB 4HH
01–636–1763

---

# Advertising and the motor-car
## Michael Frostick
**Prologue by Ashley Havinden**

Michael Frostick, leading historian of the motor-car, has combed the advertising archives of the great manufacturers in Britain, the USA, Germany, France and Italy, and the leading collections such as that at the Montagu Motor Museum at Beaulieu in order to present a systematic account of the way in which the motor-car has been presented, promoted and sold. What this research reveals, as it scans the period from the era of the wealthy enthusiast's toy to the dawn of the universal two-car household, provides a delightful excursion into the recent past for motoring enthusiast, professional advertising man, and student of social history alike. In a fascinating prologue, Ashley Havinden, for over forty years art director of a leading London advertising agency, recalls many of the advertising personalities from pioneering days and some of the great motor-car campaigns, and offers a personal evaluation of the panorama of graphic styles represented.

$11\frac{1}{2} \times 9\frac{1}{2}$ in., 160 pages
160 illustrations (80 in colour)
£6

**Lund Humphries**

K. A. MACMAHON

# Beverley and its Beck: Borough Finance and a Town Navigation 1700-1835

BEFORE THE AGE of the turnpike and the railway, the three-quarters of a mile of navigable waterway known as Beverley Beck played an important part in moulding the economic fortunes of the capital of the East Riding as an up-river port. Prior to the Reformation, the town's primary significance was ecclesiastical and until 1548, when the Collegiate Church of St John the Evangelist was dissolved and its properties sequestrated by the Crown under the Chantries Act of the previous year, the Beverley Minster chapter of secular canons was a wealthy ecclesiastical corporation exercising considerable patronage and influence in Beverley and eastern Yorkshire generally. The church they served, with its rights of chartered sanctuary traditionally dating from the days of King Aethelstan, and its jewel-studded shrine containing the wonder-working relics of St John of Beverley, vied with Canterbury and Durham in attracting king, pilgrim, merchant and criminal alike. Royal patronage and pilgrim pence helped to build the magnificent fabric which today, in all the splendour of Gothic elegance, dominates the town and the countryside around. But ecclesiastical importance was not all for, in its fourteenth-century heyday, Beverley was very much a medieval Bradford enjoying a deserved reputation for its famous coloured cloths.[1] The town's Beck, providing a link with the navigable River Hull almost a mile to the east and so with the Humber, was therefore a waterway of vital importance.

As its sinuous curving clearly indicates, Beverley Beck forms an early canalised section of a stream into which flowed some of the watercourses which, at an early stage in the town's history, helped to determine the serpentine character of Beverley's main streets. It is impossible to say when the progressive process of canalisation really began. The local tradition that such improvement was instigated by Archbishop Thurstan of York in the early years of the twelfth century may have a substratum of truth but is more likely to represent a pious attempt to give additional lustre to the name of an archbishop who, in his capacity as Lord of the Manor of Beverley, has some legitimate claim to recognition as one of the town's founding fathers.[2] The existence by the middle years of the twelfth century of a church (appropriately dedicated in honour of St Nicholas) in the immediate vicinity of the 'Bekhed' testifies both to the early development of a mercantile community there and to the significance of the Beck to the minster town in the immediate post-Conquest period. Geography dictated that Beverley's 'port' should be somewhat to the east of the town and its minster. From the head of the Beck along the early way known as Flemingate leading towards the town, there is a marked rise in levels.[3] A fall of water in the vicinity of the present Beck Head would naturally determine the limit of navigation westwards and also explain the references in medieval records to the head of the Beck as being *'ad Torrentem'*.[4]

At the western end of the Beck was Parson's Bridge, no doubt so called from the probable proximity of the Rectory House of St Nicholas on the edge of the nearby graveyard: after the sixteenth century it was referred to as the Low Bridge. Today despite the name there is no Low 'Bridge' as such, the whole having been incorporated into the widened roadway at the end of the Beck. Nevertheless, on the evidence of the wording of a fifteenth-century covenant for the scouring of the Beck, it is possible that the 'torrens' or fall of water with the change in level was yet unculverted and that the Beck may well have been 'open' somewhat farther to the west.[5] Some support is given to this theory for there are notes of payments for keeping and cleansing the 'clew' and 'grayte' at Parson's Bridge.[6] Such a grate was clearly a trap designed to collect debris brought down to the Beck at this point.

Approximately 80yd to the east was the High Bridge which was taken down in 1729, the materials being used for the repair of the Low Bridge.[7] This upper reach of the Beck between the bridges was no

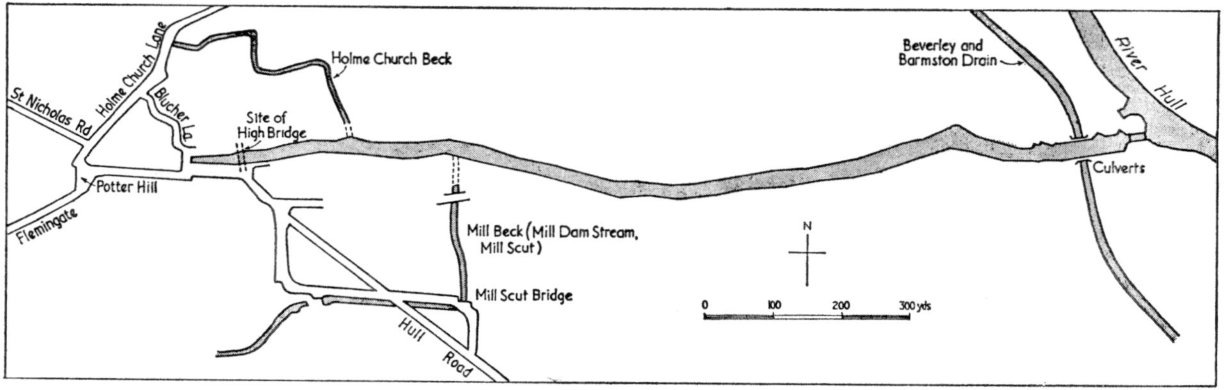

doubt the part referred to by Leland as 'the gut for the catchis': it was invariably given special attention when scouring was necessary.[8]

Ensuring a reasonable depth of water in the Beck was an ever-recurring problem. Tributary watercourses, many unculverted until the early years of the nineteenth century, flowed through the town and out into the valley of the River Hull to the Beck. These brought garbage and detritus which raised the level of the bed and encouraged the growth of weed. In the vicinity of the High Bridge the Holme Church Beck flowed in on the north side, and farther to the east on the south bank, the Mill Beck, draining the low-lying land of Beverley Parks south of the minster, brought its own tributary waters. Active inflow of water was too far removed from the head of the Beck and river tidal action was too sluggish to produce any effective sluicing action. The Beck was a tidal waterway until the building of the lock in 1802 at the confluence of the Beck and River Hull and riverine deposits additionally contributed to the problem of silting. The result was the necessity of periodic intensive 'bottom scourings', 'shavings' and 'dressings' of the Beck to maintain the navigation—projects which made considerable inroads on the town's financial resources. In 1454, for example, the governors of the town made such a Beck 'dressing' agreement with John Gargrave, a fuller. For 40 marks and with necessary sureties for due completion of the work, Gargrave engaged to scour and deepen the section between the two bridges and to cut the banks; the work was to be completed in a little over two months. He was also given authority to dam the Walker Beck, the main town tributary stream, the waters of which entered the Beck *via* the Mill Beck.[9]

When cleansing became necessary the considerable sums required were not easily found out of borough income and there was, therefore, inevitable recourse to the 'benevolence', the voluntary subscription, or, when necessary, to an assessment of the whole town community. In 1562 the 'benevolence of the severall wardes within the towne towards the beck skowringe' was £74 10s and the sale of 'stumpes or folon trees'—no doubt from the town pasture of Westwood—produced a

*Beverley and its Beck: Borough Finance and a Town Navigation* 125

further £90 8s 4d which enabled the corporation to meet the commitment of £77 18s for the cleansing operation plus a charge of £40 8s 3d for a new clough.[10] Such a project could not have been financed out of town income when, as the borough account roll for the year testifies, town receipts *in toto* were only £297 7s. In 1599 the town was again assessed for a 'ground scouringe' of the Beck and, at mayoral discretion, trees were to be felled in Westwood 'for the bankynge of the sayd Beck'.[11] The task was left incomplete and two years later there was a further levy to raise £20 'for scowringe forth the Becke ende unscowred and finishinge other things that is fitly to be donne about the sayd Becke'.[12] In 1638 another 'skooringe' assessment was laid and special Beck dues levied on 'unfreemen' of the borough. The new dues were apparently unpopular and, before the end of the year, legal action was ordered against those who had 'comed into Beverley Becke with there boates or keeles [and had] goane foorth of the same' without paying tolls.[13] A further major operation between 1649 and 1652, ordered to be carried out 'with all convenient speed', suggests an urgent attempt to remedy Civil War neglect.[14]

By the second half of the century increasing river trade intensified the problem of Beck maintenance. There are no details of the length of time the waterway was impeded during a cleansing operation and, in the absence of any worthwhile technical improvements to facilitate scouring, the two months allowed Gargrave in 1454 to cleanse the section between the bridges probably represents the average length of time necessary for that particular task—a major inconvenience to the shipman. In 1669 the corporation, having engaged themselves with a contractor in the sum of £130, were clearly getting concerned when completion to schedule appeared unlikely. Furthermore, scavenging costs were rising, the contract that year representing more than 40 per cent of the income deriving from the town's estates.[15]

The seriousness of the financial problem was heavily underlined in 1695 when another major operation became necessary: this came at a time when the corporation was finding it difficult to make ends meet. In February that year three aldermen and three chambermen were chosen by lot to collect subscriptions for the purpose—a proceeding in itself traditional but in this case probably indicating an understandable reluctance on the part of members of the conciliar body to undertake such a task at a time of economic stringency.[16] A more imaginative system of bottom-scouring the Beck was contemplated by organising some form of sluicing action by making a 'sufficient' clough in the Beck. But no evidence exists that such a scheme was implemented for William Ayre was subsequently given the task of carrying out a traditional scouring of the navigation throughout its whole length. Ayre's bill of £155 was met by loan and subscription—four members of the locally influential Warton family alone contributing £55.[17]

To this time few details are available about the method of scouring. Temporary cloughs were used to control the influx of tributary streams such as the Holme Church Beck and Mill Beck, and 'dambs' were placed in position in the Beck itself at low water to lock a section against the rising river tide or pen up water near the head of the navigation. The moveable 'barricade' referred to in 1752 was no doubt one of these.[18] With a much lowered water level the unpleasant task was presumably completed, section by section, by the use of scoop, shovel basket and cart. There can be little doubt that there must have been some damage in the town from flooding with the inevitable 'backing up' of tributary streams when 'dressing' and 'shaving' of the Beck was in progress.

After 1700 there is a suggestion, hinted at in 1695, of a change in method of approach to the whole problem of the maintenance of the navigation. In 1721 'a Dutch plough of about 25/-' was ordered from Holland: this was presumably a device for dragging along to tear up the bed in the hope and expectation that the combined effect of falling tide and tributary streams would remove the loosened deposit.[19] It is clear that the corporation was willing to listen to technical advice on the matter of this recurrent and expensive problem of 'dressing' the Beck even though there was an ultimate adherence to traditional methods; that such advice was forthcoming is indicative of the fact that serious thought was being given at this period to this and comparable problems. Nor could the corporation have been unaware of regional river improvement schemes. The Corporation of Doncaster together with the Sheffield Company of Cutlers and other parties had had a survey made of the River Don with a view to improving the river up to and beyond Doncaster and in 1725, after efforts a generation earlier had failed, York Corporation was taking energetic action to secure improvement of the navigation of the River Ouse.[20] Somewhat surprisingly, proposals for more effective maintenance of the Beck navigation came from John Warburton, *Somerset Herald*.

At this time, Warburton was preparing material for a projected *History of Yorkshire* and in connection with this had visited Hull in 1724.[21] Early the following year he was in Beverley and appears to have given the corporation considerable and much needed assistance over the matter of its records and property entitlements. For his 'indefatiguable industry and singular merit' he was presented with his freedom of the borough with excusal from the obligation of paying a fine and taking up office.[22] Warburton proposed the placing of a lock or floodgate near the High Bridge to collect water at high tide: at low tide the release of water from the reservoir thus created, he maintained, would have a scouring action and 'dissolve and wash away all that loose ousey matter that now cements together and obstructs the flux and reflux of the tide'. A second lock gate might be positioned at the head of the Beck near the Low Bridge, thus providing an additional reservoir which, in similar fashion, would help to clear the length between the bridges. An essential part of the plan, however, was to provide 'an engine boat like those in Flanders' for drawing up weeds and loosening mud prior to the actual scouring action being carried out. Further points in the Warburton plan included a proposed diversion of the Holme Church Beck to bring it in at the head of the Beck (instead of near the High Bridge) and the planting of willows along the banks to give stability. *Somerset Herald* estimated his scheme at £110 of which the major items would be the two pairs of lock gates costing £70. On the matter of raising necessary funds Warburton somewhat astutely suggested that subscriptions be invited with the inducement that the names of the chief benefactors and the sums individually given should be recorded on a tablet in the Guildhall for the benefit of posterity.[23]

Warburton's scheme incorporated his objections to a plan which had been proposed by a certain Mr P—. There can be little doubt that Mr P— was William Palmer who had been employed on the survey of the River Don between Sheffield and Doncaster in 1722 and who was at this time also concerned with plans for the improvement of the River Ouse. Francis Drake, the historian of York, claimed Palmer 'as an engineer of our own growth': an alternative possibility is that Mr P— was John Perry who had been consulted about works on the Ouse.[24]

Mr P—'s main objections to the Warburton plan were that because of the distance between Beverley and Hull, the narrowness of the River Hull, 'the free passage it hath many miles beyond Beverley Beck' and the slow ebb and flow of tide, 'the water would take a long time to rise to small plum height' and the consequent slowness of tidal fall could be of little effect in removing sludge. Furthermore, Mr P— asserted, Warburton's scheme for a reservoir could be criticised on the grounds that the distance between the two bridges was only one-eighteenth of the total length of the Beck and therefore, if three feet of water were 'pen'd up' in the lock proposed, the water released would only raise the whole level of the Beck by two inches: 'And if the water in the reservoir were raised two yards higher than the water in the Beck below, it would raise the other only four inches—and what' he asked 'can four inches of water do towards carrying away sludge?'[25]

A third opinion offered was that of William Lelham (or Lellam) who had been concerned with harbour works at Bridlington c 1717. Lelham's plan involved the use of a 'gin' in a lighter, the piling and paving of the banks, presumably to ensure greater precision in definition of the channel (and therefore easier flow) and the building of a three-arched bridge over the tributary Mill Beck or Mill Scut as it was sometimes termed. The reason for the last suggestion, no doubt, was to help speed up the scouring action of the Mill Beck as it entered the Beck. Lelham estimated his scheme would cost the corporation approximately £672. Unfortunately, the project is not given in sufficient detail to permit reasonable appraisal but, in any case, it would have been prohibitive on the ground of cost and would have involved an expenditure approximately twice the town's annual income.[26]

None of these plans apparently was acceptable but their soliciting or submission indicates corporation awareness of the necessity of resolving the constant problem of preserving the Beck navigation; it is clear too, that the tolls levied in 1704 on all Beck users (with non-freemen's rates double those of burgesses) were inadequate.[27] Furthermore, the importance of maintaining the navigation was being increasingly emphasised by the growth of nearby Hull, the shipping-crowded haven of which was reflecting the developing industrialisation of the West Riding and the Midlands and the increasing opportunities of the continental market.

Accordingly, in 1726, in order to raise the money required, the chamber decided to seek an Act of Parliament empowering the borough corporation to levy dues on all goods brought by water and landed within the town's liberties: the money so raised was to be used not only for the maintenance of the Beck but also for the repair of the roads leading down to the river. Sir Charles Hotham, one of the borough Members, took charge of the Bill in the Commons and royal assent was accorded in March 1727.[28] The Act cost the corporation nearly £150.[29] Under the Act, which stated penalties for fraud or non-compliance, persons in charge of any vessel were required before unloading (or, having shipped goods, before leaving) to declare in writing an account of cargo for assessment of toll and to pay accordingly. These tolls were to be additional to, and were in no wise to supplant the dues payable under the chamber order of 1704 referred to. The corporation was empowered to divert or dam any tributary streams as necessary during maintenance operations and pay compensation from the Beck revenues for any damage incurred. The substantial penalty of 20s was to be imposed on anyone depositing rubbish or filth in the Beck. The Act authorised Justices in Quarter Sessions assembled to levy a rate of up to 6d in the £ in any one year—and street cleaners were to be appointed to minimise the risk of street filth being washed down into the Beck 'which very much contributeth to the choaking up of the same'.[30] Furthermore, the Act allowed the corporation to deepen the River Hull as necessary. On the strength of the Act and the tolls sanctioned, the corporation raised an immediate loan of £200 at 4½ per cent pa to carry out a major cleansing operation.[31]

Hull showed no response to Beverley's concern with the River Hull, but it may be noted that the Hull Bench of Aldermen, in cynical opportunist fashion, sought the help of their two MPs to have a last-minute 'improvement' clause for Hull inserted in the Beverley Bill. Somewhat understandably the proposal got no further and Hull had to wait until 1755 for its first Improvement Act.[32]

Much of the subsequent discontent with the working of the Beverley Beck Act of 1727 and a major reason for its being superseded by a second in 1745 derived from the fact that income from tolls proved insufficient for the purposes intended and the schedule of tolls was found to be unsatisfactory in certain respects. This latter point was given emphasis when, at the committee stage on the second Bill in 1745, Alderman William Nelson of Beverley testified that some tolls granted under the 1727 Act were not proportionate to the value of the goods concerned.[33] After referring to the fact that the corporation had borrowed £1,050 which, together with the tolls collected had been used wholly for the purposes prescribed in the Act, Nelson pointed out, for example, that three hogsheads of sugar (approx 45cwt) attracted only 4d in toll whereas the duty on salt—comparable in bulk/weight—was 4d per ton.

Administratively, a further shortcoming of the earlier Act was that in certain cases toll was lost for clear lack of legal powers to examine the goods chargeable and to check weights. Under the Act of 1727 collectors were authorised to search vessels and 'take account of the lading of any ship', refusal involving a penalty of 20s. But a basic weakness of the relevant provisions of the Act lay in the drafting for, although the master of a vessel was compelled to declare his cargo

# Beverley and its Beck: Borough Finance and a Town Navigation

before landing or after stowing, the Act made no provision for collectors to carry out a check by weight on those goods on which toll was specified by weight.

A second Bill resolving these problems and costing the corporation £189—the equivalent of two years' tolls—received the royal assent in March 1745.[34] With effect from 1 May that year a whole series of additional dues became payable and in most cases these extra tolls ranged from 50 to 200 per cent above those specified in the earlier Act.[35] This second Act helped towards a solution of the recurrent financial problem of Beck maintenance. An increased income from tolls not only made more regular maintenance possible but also facilitated the raising of loans on the security of the tolls when a major cleansing operation became due. Henceforth the benevolence and the subscription were no longer necessary. The following table gives some appreciation of the improved financial position following the Act of 1745, not only in terms of toll and general income, but also in the increased expenditure on maintenance made possible.

### Table I
### BEVERLEY BECK TOLLS[36]

Income–Expenditure 1741–8 (to nearest £)

|  | 1741–2 | 1742–3 | 1743–4 | 1744–5 | 1745–6 | 1746–7 | 1747–8 |
|---|---|---|---|---|---|---|---|
| Toll Income | 78 | 81 | 75 | 82 | 137 | 117 | 104 |
| Total Receipts | 99 | 212(a) | 134 | 100 | 301(b) | 168 | 228(c) |
| Total Expenditure | 68 | 158 | 116 | 78 | 300 | 144 | 212 |
| Balance | 31 | 54 | 18 | 22 | 1 | 24 | 16 |

(a) Inclusive of £100 loan
(b) do £140 do
(c) do £ 50 do

After 1748 direct collection of tolls gave way to the practice of leasing, thus ensuring an agreed annual income without the administrative inconvenience and risks attendant on direct collection. In that year James Fenton of Rothwell (W Yorks) took a four-year lease of the tolls at £100 pa—financially advantageous to the corporation at the then level of total income as it meant an immediate saving of £20 pa on a collector's salary.[37]

Henceforth and throughout the rest of the period with which this survey is concerned, the corporation let the tolls to farm. The Beck dues thus leased out included those payable at nearby Grovehill and at Hull Bridge, the other two landing places within the borough liberties, but after 1761 the tolls at Hull Bridge were excluded:[38] in any case they were minimal. The list of Beck toll lessees together with a note of annual rents paid is summarised at Appendix I. Unfortunately, none of the lessees' account- or day-books appears to have survived and therefore after the financial year 1747-8 any assessment of actual toll income is impossible. Nevertheless, on the evidence of rents paid, a steady growth of the river trade is apparent throughout the second half of the eighteenth century and by 1791 the lease rent was almost double that paid in 1748: this, in a very real degree, reflected too the phenomenal growth of Hull's river trade in this period.[39] If the dramatic rise in rents from 1803 onwards is used as a criterion it is a tolerable certainty that, for some years, James Thompson must have found his lease of the Beck tolls profitably worthwhile.

The successive lessees do not appear to have had serious difficulties over the failure of keel captains to declare their cargoes and the incidence of attempts to defraud appears to have been small.[40] The penalty of £5 was sufficiently severe to prevent the possibility of the development of extensive malpractices and, as half the fine went to the informer, the risk of detection was heightened. Furthermore, as the lessees' financial interests were directly involved, surveillance would be close.

It is clear from the Beck accounts that, on the whole, after the Act of 1745 there was, with more money available, more regular maintenance than was possible before. Until 1775 no large-scale cleansing operation was carried out but in May that year George Savage, millwright of Hull, contracted to clear 3ft of sludge along the whole length of the Beck making 'the bottom of equal depth with the River Hull': this was completed by the end of August the same year.[41]

Savage agreed to do the work for £285 and Alderman John Hoggard, on whom conciliar pressure had to be brought to oblige him to fulfil his commitment, agreed, for £10, to remove all the soil and sludge thrown out in order to prevent it being 'washed down again by rain'. Some of the improvement to the Beck navigation can be explained by the fact that, in 1734, the corporation had bought a dredging boat and in 1777 one was specially built by Richard Hopwood of nearby Grovehill.[42] A description of this new boat as a 'dredging boat', and the fact that in 1782 the corporation was prepared to make it available for private use from time to time at nominal charge, suggests that it was technically more efficient than its predecessor and that its continued use on the Beck was considered unnecessary.

Although the basic purpose of the Beck Acts of 1727 and 1745 was to preserve and improve the navigation of the Beck, powers were acquired under both Acts to use any surplus funds for the improvement of the roads leading from the town to the Beck and the River Hull. But for some years the expense of obtaining the Acts, the necessity of raising loans on the security of the tolls and the costs of general improvements allowed little to be done in the matter of local road improvement. The provision of the dredging boat in 1734 already referred to and the building of a crane on which the Scarborough engineer, William Vincent, gave technical advice, represented substantial demands on limited resources.[43] In order to effect some measure of economy, seven parties, who *in toto* had loaned £900 at $4\frac{1}{2}$ per cent to the Beck Fund, were induced to accept 4 per cent in 1739.[44] In 1745–6, the year of the second Beck Act, with a loan of £140 from Anthony Pybus the year's accounts only showed a credit balance of 14s 5d on a total expenditure of £300. The usual device of borrowing from Peter to repay Paul followed: Pybus' loan was repaid by securing another from Alderman William Nelson in 1747–8.[45]

But the existence of a Beck Fund ancillary to, but entirely separate from that of the rest of the town's estates, helped to give a degree of resilience to borough finances which otherwise would not have been possible. When surpluses became apparent or could be 'organised' by deliberate neglect of maintenance, the Beck Fund was duly 'milked' but, for reasons already seen, this form of appropriation scarcely proved practicable until after 1762. From that year and with increasing frequency, sums were ordered by the chamber to be paid out of the Beck Fund to the town's receiver—not always being recorded as being required for improvement of the roads leading to the Beck and river as specified in the Beck Acts, nor, for that matter, being noted as loans. This amounted to a deliberate flouting of the relevant provisions of the Beck Acts. It is not merely coincidental that in 1761–2 when the project of a new guildhall was being considered, virtually nothing was spent on Beck maintenance:[46] a fairly substantial credit balance in the fund was thereby assured. The whole of this surplus of £105 was appropriated by the corporation with no particular use specified nor was it designated in the Beck accounts as a loan.[47] In 1765 the year's balance was again commandeered and in 1767 a further £50 was taken 'by order of the Chamber for the town's use'.[48] Loans totalling £260 to Ann Routh's Hospital in Beverley and £50 to the workhouse plus £200 'for town's use' were only made possible by deliberate economy on operation of the Beck and neglect of its maintenance. In the financial years ending in 1769 and 1770 total disbursements in respect of the Beck amounted to £30 and £26 respectively against a total income in each year of £239 and £326.

Such a policy of building up a fund made 'raiding' practicable and worthwhile, provided priorities were right and that a corporate willingness existed to disregard the provisions of the Beck Acts. But ultimately the price had to be paid and the major cleansing operation of 1775 was undoubtedly, in great part, the result of such 'planned' neglect. For this particular operation the credit balances of the previous three years were insufficient to meet costs and the result was the necessity of raising a loan of £100 from Thomas Wrightson, one of the Beck toll lessees. Such hand-to-mouth financial policy—if policy it were—was bad housekeeping, especially so when it is noted, for example, that the £260 loan to Ann Routh's Hospital between 1770 and 1773 was let out at 4 per cent while the corporation was paying 5 per cent to Wrightson.[49]

But at the same time the existence of a separate Beck Fund could be a very present help in trouble if the corporation were suddenly called upon to meet an unexpected major demand. The so-called Skidby Drainage Act of 1785 and the Enclosure Act of the same year which affected town lands at nearby Weel, resulted in a total assessment of £760 on the corporation by the respective commissioners.[50] Help towards meeting this sudden financial requirement was partially met by an increased charge for the purchase of freedoms, but a substantial contribution of £315 was only made possible by the existence of the Beck Fund.[51] This payment coupled with the allocation of £100 for unspecified street improvements resulted in a balance in the Beck Fund of £1 7s 8d at the end of the financial year 1785–6.[52]

But it was not only the corporation which found the Beck Fund of use from time to time. In 1757 Alderman Jonathan Midgely, presumably with the approval of his fellow aldermen, used the fund as a bank and borrowed £100 on short-term loan for his personal use. In 1784—the year of his mayoralty—Alderman John Hoggard took a personal loan of £350 paying 4½ per cent and offering part of his lands at Weel as security: the loan was repaid in 1789.[53] Such private loans naturally made money less readily available for improvement of either Beck or local roads, postponed intended improvements and, when sudden calls came, their effect had to be offset by raising loans. It may be noted in this context that the fairly substantial loan to Alderman Hoggard coincided with the demand by the commissioners of the Weel Enclosure and the Skidby Drainage.

On the credit side, however, it must be emphasised that sums were allocated for the purposes specified under the two Beck Acts, particularly from c 1780 onwards. In 1777 and again in 1783, and with increasing frequency thereafter, money was deliberately earmarked for streets and roads and after 1815 when the Beck Fund was in a comparatively flourishing state substantial sums were made available for such purposes. It is clear that a fair degree of street and road improvement within the town and its liberties was made possible by such availability of surplus moneys.

By the end of the century another type of problem with serious financial implications presented itself to the corporation. As early as 1344–5 an 'ingang' or entrance to the Beck had been made but until 1802 no record exists of any lock being built to maintain the level of water in the Beck on the fall of the river tide.[54] It was realised that regional drainage improvements would inevitably bring a lowering of the level of the water in the River Hull with a consequent effect on the depth of water in the Beck. In 1798 the Beverley and Barmston Drainage scheme, which was commenced under the authority of the drainage Act of that year, resulted in the cutting of the Beverley and Barmston Drain at a significantly lower level than the river.[55] This important land drain passed through brick-lined culverts under the bed of the Beck as it did in the case of the smaller Aike and Arram becks north of Beverley. With this development the fear that the maintenance of a satisfactory water level in the Beck was impossible without a lock was clearly justified. In May 1802, therefore, although borough finances had reached a critical level, the corporation decided that a lock should be made at the entrance to the Beck provided that the work could be done under the authority of the 1745 Beck Act and that a competent engineer considered such a scheme to be necessary.[56] William Chapman, who as engineer to the Beverley and Barmston Drainage Scheme was responsible for taking the new agricultural drain under the Beck, took the view that a lock was necessary to preserve the navigation, and Robert Osborne, the borough recorder, gave it as his opinion that the works envisaged came within the purview of the Beck Acts and as such were a justifiable charge on the Beck revenues.[57] The corporation thereupon went ahead with the scheme.

Thomas Dyson contracted to build the lock for £733 13s 6d according to the plans and sections he had submitted for approval, part of the contract specifying that if the mayor was dissatisfied with the work in progress he was at liberty to discharge Dyson, vacate the contract and make such payment as he thought fit and reasonable for the work already carried out—a precaution which scarcely suggests absolute confidence in the contractor's abilities. A loan of £1,000 at 5 per cent

### Beverley and its Beck: Borough Finance and a Town Navigation 137

was obtained from Miss Catherine Hewitt of Beverley on the security of the Beck tolls and certain loans were called in to help finance the project.[58] That this scheme should be carried out at a time of economic stringency deriving from wartime conditions is evidence of the corporation's realisation of the importance of the Beck and of a conciliar determination to preserve the navigation at all costs.

Under the general superintendence of Alderman William Middleton and John Prattman, Dyson (who was employed by the Driffield Navigation) satisfactorily completed the building of the lock in the late summer and early autumn of 1802.[59] But provision of a lock introduced an additional element of maintenance into Beck finance. Some considerable repair of the lock gates was necessary in 1814, and in 1819 over £100 had to be found for further repairs.[60] In 1828 new lock gates were needed and George Smith's bill for the work undertaken amounted to £236. Replacement of the gates necessarily brought interference with the navigation and, as the waters of the Beck had to be run off into the Barmston Drain, the opportunity was naturally taken to carry out a traditional scouring at further substantial charge. As a result there was a debit balance in the Beck Account in both 1827 and 1828 with no indication that the toll lessees—as was later the case—received any compensation for their losses during the period of such operations.

Explicably, the building of the lock made the Beck a stagnant waterway. This problem, exacerbated in the process of years by increasing industrial—and to some extent domestic—effluent, does not come within the purview of this survey. What is certain is that the early nineteenth-century borough senators in their understandable concern to preserve the navigation of their ancient and important waterway had unwittingly sown the seeds of a local public health problem of some consequence.

In the years following the building of the lock, the corporation made further considerable improvements to the Beck. The Low Bridge was rebuilt in 1806 and much 'pile and jetty work' was carried out the following year. John Rushworth, a well-known local mason, was paid nearly £100 for coping the Beck walls and in 1824–5 George Smith's account for fixing posts and rails along the banks of the Beck cost the corporation a further £200.[61]

Even if allowance is made in respect of the regular use of the Beck Fund for purposes of street improvements, the financial position became more serious in the early years of the nineteenth century and the accounts summarised in Appendix II scarcely give a true overall picture. A debit balance for example in 1807 of £1,063 was taken over by the town's receiver and does not figure in the Beck accounts for the following financial year. This substantial debt was apparently carried against a loan of £1,155 which Mayor John Lockwood, the Beverley attorney, advanced 'for the benefit of the town' in 1806.[62] Lockwood's helpfulness has to be measured against the fact that, in his mayoralty, there was heavy spending on the Beck, some of which, in view of the then current financial crisis, could have been spread over a longer period. Lockwood clearly found that a loan to the borough he served was an assured form of investment.

The loan of £1,000 from Miss Catherine Hewitt in 1802 substantially covered the cost of making the lock but added another £50 pa in interest in outgoings.[63] Repayment of the loan was effected by 1810 but additional financial cushioning was necessary. Accordingly, in 1809, there was recourse to the favourite contemporary device of selling annuities 'according to Dr Price's Tables'.[64] These enabled the last instalment of the Hewitt loan to be paid off and helped to ease matters financially for the next two or three years. In the long term, however, the sale of annuities proved financially disadvantageous to the corporation and the following table, compiled from the Beck accounts and associated records, illustrates how in a period of a little over twenty years nearly £2,000 was paid out to the purchasers and their executors against a total investment of £1,100; two of the four purchasers lived long enough to secure a return of more than double their original investment.

TABLE II
ANNUITIES ON THE BECK FUND 1809-32[65]

| Name | Date of Purchase | Date of Death | Purchase Price | Yield per annum | Total sums rec'd by purchaser/exor |
|---|---|---|---|---|---|
| Rev W. J. Wrightson | 6 Jan 1809 | 6 July 1832 | £ 300 | £ 30 | £ 683. 5.0 |
| Robert Spouncer | 6 Jan 1809 | 18 Oct 1816 | £ 300 | £ 45 | £ 317.12.0 |
| Sarah Thompson | 6 Jan 1809 | 27 July 1819 | £ 200 | £ 25 | £ 234.11.4 |
| Thos Wildon | 6 Feb 1809 | 15 Jan 1830 | £ 300 | £ 35.5.0 | £ 711.14.5 |
| Totals | | | £1,100 | £135.5.0 | £1,947. 2.9 |

Limitations of space preclude here any appraisal of Beverley's river trade made possible by the existence of this early navigation over which the town maintained such a careful and understandable watchfulness. But by the eighteenth century the picture is one of brown-sailed keel and river craft with names like *Prosperous* and *Speedwell, Hull Trader* and *Defiance, Hopewell* and *Friendship* nosing their way from the river into the Beck and down again with cargoes as various as those of John Masefield's dirty British coaster. The contribution which its Beck made in the pre-Railway Age to the economic well-being of Beverley can never be precisely assessed: today we can only have substantial assurance from limited statistics that it was both varied and considerable.

*University of Hull*

*References*

1. See eg Cal Close Rolls 1234-7 (301), 1253-4 (46).
2. In 1727 the Corporation of Beverley claimed the Beck as being 'formerly made from the said town to the River Hull'; *Journals of the House of Commons,* XX, 711 (Henceforth *JHC*). Archbishop Thurstan's charter (c 115-1128), the original of which is in Beverley Corporation archives, is printed with notes in W. Farrer (ed), *Early Yorkshire Charters,* vol 1 (1914), 90-1.

3 There is a rise in level from 20ft to 29ft 9in (Newlyn Datum) between Beckside and the minster (OS East Riding Sheet CCX, 12, 1927).
4 Historical Manuscripts Commission (henceforth HMC) Beverley (1900), 118, 121, 124, 126, 133, 135 and Town Ordinances 1467 which prohibited the repair of boats *super ripas magni torrentis Beverlaci* between Guchemere Lane and Parson's Bridge, A. F. Leach (ed), *Beverley Town Documents* (Selden Soc, vol 14 (1900), 57).
5 HMC Beverley, 11.
6 Ibid, 171, 174.
7 K. A. MacMahon (ed), *Beverley Corporation Minute Books 1707–1835* (Yorks Arch Soc, Rec Series, vol 122 (1958) (henceforth M), 14). The south side 'projection' of the bridge was not taken down until 1775 (Bev Corp Beck vouchers and receipts 1754–1777, 103) (henceforth BBVRB).
8 L. T. Smith (ed), *Leland's Itinerary in England and Wales* (1964 edn), vol 1, 46, would suggest this is the 'gut'; but see ibid LV 180 and V 39 where gut/cut apparently refers to the whole length of the Beck. On the analogy of the use of the term 'gut' for the narrow part of the river at Oxford, A. F. Leach (*Beverley Chapter Act Book*, II—Surtees Soc, 108 (1903), 745) considered that the 'Gut' was the upper part of the Beck.
9 HMC Beverley, 11.
10 Bev Corp Governors' Memorandum Book 1558–67 fo 48–9; and see HMC Beverley, 181.
11 Beverley Corporation Minute Book (henceforth BCMB) 1597–1660, 5(4).
12 Ibid, 14 (12).
13 Ibid, 69 (64).
14 Ibid, 91 (86), 92 (87), 97 (92).
15 J. Dennett (ed), *Beverley Borough Records 1575–1821* (Yorks Arch Rec Soc Series 84 (1933), 145 (henceforth D) ). In round figures, the total income from the town estates in 1668 was £304 (Beverley Roll of Account s/a).
16 D 184.
17 BM Lansdowne MSS 896, folio 167.
18 M 32, 33.
19 M 8.
20 T. S. Willan, *River Navigation in England 1600–1750* (1936), 29, 33–4, 41, 75, 80; Baron F. Duckham, *The Yorkshire Ouse: the History of a River Navigation* (1967), 61. The Sheffield Act for the Don was passed in 1726 and the Doncaster one in 1727. T. S. Willan, *The Early History of the Don Navigation* (1965), 17–24.
21 Hull Bench Book VIII, 724 (henceforth HBB); *Yorks Arch Soc Journal*, XV, 61; XXXV, 61; *Thoresby Soc Pubs*, XXVIII; *Misc*, ix.
22 M 11.
23 BM Lansdowne MSS, 896, folios 162, 164, 166 and 'Answers to Mr P—'s objections to Mr W's proposals', ibid folio 163.
24 J. D. Leader, *Records of the Burgery of Sheffield* (1897), 167, 350, 353; F. Drake, *Eboracum* (1736), 232; T. S. Willan, op cit, 84; A. W. Skempton, 'The engineers of the English River Navigations 1620–1760', *Trans Newcomen Soc*, XXIX (1953–5), 25 et seq.
25 BM Lansdowne MSS, 896 folio 163. Local topographical knowledge suggests that Mr P— was right so far, but if the convenience of shipping were excluded from consideration, Warburton's scheme, if put into operation would have had some effect at low water especially at the time of Spring tides.

26 For comment on these 'gins' see Willan op cit and C. Singer, E. J. Holmyard et al, *Hist of Technology* IV (1958), 628 et seq.
27 D 114.
28 *JHC*, XX, 711, 733, 740, 746, 768, 795, 812, 814.
29 The exact figure was £148 4s 5d, Bev Beck Acc Book 1726–1835 sa 1727–8 (henceforth BBAB).
30 13 Geo I c 4.
31 M 13. This £200 was, in fact, the sum bequeathed by Sir Ralph Warton in 1712 to set up the manufacture of 'coarse stockings', BBAB 1726–1835 (sa 1728–30), *vide* Reports of the Commissioners . . . Charities and Education of the Poor XXXVIII (1815–39), 694. The Charity Commissioners c 1822 were unable to ascertain how this money had been used as no manufacture of coarse stockings had ever been set up in the town.
32 HBB VIII, 742 (2 March 1727) and see the present writer in *Trans Georgian Soc for East Yorks*, V (1961) (henceforth *GSEY*).
33 *JHC* XXVII, 744.
34 £189 13s 10d, BBAB sa 1745–6.
35 For a complete schedule of tolls so obviating listing here, see Joseph Priestley, *Navigable Rivers and Canals* (reprinted Newton Abbot 1967), 66–7.
36 Compiled from BBAB 1726–1835.
37 M 29 East Riding County Record Office DDBC 26/Sect A/12 (henceforth ERCRO).
38 M 40.
39 On the economic development of nearby Hull see (additional to *Victoria County History—Hull*) W. G. East, 'The port of Kingston upon Hull during the Industrial Revolution', *Economica*, II (1931), and Gordon Jackson, 'Economic development of Hull in the Eighteenth century', (Unpub PhD thesis University of Hull, 1960).
40 Only half a dozen cases can be cited from the records.
41 M 55; BBAB (1774–5); BBVRB (1754–77), passim.
42 M 57 BBAC (sa).
43 BBAC (1734–5, 1737–8). William Vincent succeeded William Lelham (Lellam) as resident engineer to the Scarborough Harbour Commissioners; see D. Swann, 'The Engineers of English Port Improvements 1660–1830: Part 1', *Transport History*, I (1968), 158.
44 BBAB (1738–9).
45 M 26, but see BBAB sa which makes clear that the loan was £140.
46 See the present writer in *GSEY*, IV (1955), 68–81.
47 BBAB (1761–3). Taking figures to the nearest £, receipts in 1761–2 amounted to £124 and disbursements £19. Of this latter expenditure virtually nothing was spent on Beck maintenance.
48 Ibid sa. This type of misapplication of Beck funds was alluded to by the Municipal Corporations Inquiry Commissioners (Report, 1835, Beverley, 1462).
49 BBAB passim; M 50.
50 25 Geo III c 48 and 92; M 67–8; ERCRO, DDBC 3/125.
51 M 66, BBAB (1784–5).
52 BBAB sa.
53 Ibid, 1756–7; 1785–9.
54 Beverley Borough Account Roll, 1344–5.
55 38 Geo III c 63.

56 M 85.
57 ERCRO, DDBC/20/2.
58 ERCRO, DDBC 21/122, 31, 35.
59 BBVRB 1798–1802 sa.
60 BBAB sa.
61 There is a strong local tradition that the 'coping' at the sides is with stone taken from the nearby site of the former church of St Nicholas: there is slight documentary support for this view.
62 M 94.
63 M 85.
64 Richard Price, *Observations on Reversionary Payments* . . . (1771).
65 Compiled from BBAB and associated records.

*For plates, provided by the author*, see pp 169–71

## Appendix I

### BEVERLEY BECK: LEASES OF TOLLS 1748–1837

| Year | Lessee(s) | Annual Rent |
|---|---|---|
| 1748 | James Fenton | £100 |
| 1752 | Thomas Wrightson / Matthew Spenser | £110 |
| 1763 | Thomas Wrightson / Matthew Spenser | £110 |
| 1770 | Thomas Wrightson / Michael Farthing | £140 |
| 1780 | Richard Hutton | £180 |
| 1784 | Richard Hutton | £180 |
| 1786 | James Thompson | £180 |
| 1791 | James Thompson | £190 |
| 1803 | William Middleton / John Lee | £315 |
| 1807 | James Thompson | £372 |
| 1813 | James Thompson | £330 |
| 1819 | James Thompson | £380 |
| 1825 | John Webster / John Hodgson | £435 |
| 1831–7 | John Webster | £435 |

*Appendix II*

BEVERLEY BECK: INCOME AND EXPENDITURE AT
FIVE-YEARLY INTERVALS 1730–1835
(To nearest £)

| Financial Year beginning | Income (£) | Expenditure (£) |
|---|---|---|
| 1730 | 33 | 33* |
| 1735 | 119 | 69 |
| 1740 | 89 | 68 |
| 1745 | 301 | 300 |
| 1750 | 150 | 65 |
| 1755 | 160 | 66 |
| 1760 | 159 | 145 |
| 1765 | 138 | 114 |
| 1770 | 441 | 120 |
| 1775 | 154 | 150 |
| 1780 | 189 | 140 |
| 1785 | 216 | 215 |
| 1790 | 397 | 136 |
| 1795 | 329 | 280 |
| 1800 | 194 | 191 |
| 1805 | 441 | 158 |
| 1810 | 650 | 657 |
| 1815 | 395 | 301 |
| 1820 | 436 | 271 |
| 1825 | 770 | 411 |
| 1830 | 439 | 415 |
| 1835 | 661 | 623 |

\* Year incomplete (21 Nov 1730–1 May 1731).

F. C. MATHER

# The Battle of the Manchester Railway Junctions

THE BUILDING OF RAILWAYS into Victorian cities was a task beset by many difficulties. As Dr J. R. Kellett has shown, the process of penetration was two-phased.[1] At first lack of capital and influence, coupled with an understandable impatience to begin operations and see some return on heavy initial outlays, drove the companies to fix their stations on the outskirts of the built-up cores of towns. That was the position during the 1830s, when the foundations of the British railway system were being laid. By the forties, however, as the railroads gained in strength, and the potentialities of the new form of transport were more adequately grasped by both the public and the boards of directors, a movement had been launched to establish termini of a central character or at least to connect up lines converging on the cities from different quarters. Even then there was resistance and the purposes were by no means fully achieved. In 1846 a royal commission under Lord Canning's chairmanship examined nineteen schemes for drawing railways into the centre of London, and ended by rejecting them all. It did so on the ground that few of the passengers arriving by rail in London were through passengers, who would want to change from one train to another.[2]

Manchester was more fortunate. Though she did not obtain a truly central ter mnus,[3] by the middle of the century she possessed two connecting lines, running to the north and to the south of the town centre, and these linked the railways approaching from the south, east, and west. This was not achieved, however, without a struggle lasting for several years. With the aid of correspondence in the archives of the dukes of Shuterland, and of the minute books in the British Transport Historical Records, new light can be thrown upon the factors in the conflict. This paper is intended to do so, and thereby to augment our knowledge of the impediments to railroad construction within urban areas.

I

First, however, the pattern of events must be established. By 1840 the first stage in the making of railways into Manchester was complete. Five distinct railroads, all terminating on the perimeter of the city's built-up area, had been authorised or made. The Liverpool & Manchester line, opened in 1830, ran into a temporary station with makeshift accommodation at Liverpool Road, over on the western side of the town near the River Irwell, which separated Manchester from Salford. The Manchester & Bolton, completed in May 1838, ended at Irwell Street in Salford. On the eastern flank the Manchester & Leeds Railway, which had been sanctioned in 1836, and was already being constructed deep into the Pennines, had a station at St George's Street, Oldham Road. The other eastbound line, the Sheffield, Ashton-under-Lyne & Manchester Railway, had an agreement with the Manchester & Birmingham to share a common terminus at Store Street, London Road. The siting of these stations was unscientifically determined, being influenced markedly by the availability of land for present and future development.[4] Between them lay the town centre, a vast almost impenetrable barrier of houses and business premises, which would impede future attempts to link them up.

Matters could not be allowed to rest there. The urgency of constructing a rail junction through Manchester was greater perhaps than for many other cities of comparable size. Manchester was the collecting and distributing centre for a cluster of specialised manufacturing villages and towns in her vicinity. The French traveller Faucher described her in 1844 as 'a diligent spider... in the centre of the web'.[5] She was also the linchpin in the system of railway communications connecting the West Riding and towns like Stockport to the south and Rochdale to the north, with the port of Liverpool. In the interest of these localities no less than for her own welfare a connection was requisite between the lines which served them and the Liverpool & Manchester Railway.

In September 1836 the directors of the Liverpool & Manchester Railway Company considered a plan for linking their own line at Ordsall Lane, Salford, with the proposed Manchester & Cheshire Junction Railway, one of two main schemes current at the time for running into Manchester from Stockport and the south. The project included a branch through Salford to communicate with the Manchester, Bolton & Bury Railway. The board expressed itself favourably towards the scheme in general,[6] but when it came to examine the detailed plans on 9 January 1837, objected both to the branch to join the MB & B and to the mode of connecting with its own line—by an inclined plane of 1 in 50.[7] Notwithstanding the rebuff the promoters lodged their notices in the private Bill office in the following November.[8] By that time the rival southward schemes had been consolidated into the Manchester & Birmingham Railway, which was to build from Manchester (Store Street) to the Grand Junction Railway at Chebsey in Staffordshire, with branches to Crewe and Macclesfield. It was with that line that the proposed Manchester Connection Railway was now to connect in Manchester.

Strong opposition to the junction line was encountered from the trustees of the third Duke of Bridgewater, whose canal wharves at Castlefield the railway would intersect on its way from the L & M line to that of the M & B. These whipped up the Manchester Police Commissioners against the scheme, and an assurance was extracted from the law clerk of the proposing company that no application would be made to Parliament for a Bill during the remainder of that year.[9]

Eight months later, in July 1838, the directors of the L & M turned to encourage a connection of a different kind. The suggestion emanated from the Manchester & Leeds Railway Company, which proposed a link round the northern end of the town. The M & L would extend its own line from Oldham Road to a new and more centrally situated station at Hunts Bank on the River Irwell (the present Victoria station in fact), if the L & M would collaborate with the MB & B in constructing

## The Battle of the Manchester Railway Junctions 147

a link from the L & M main line near the engine shops west of Ordsall Lane through Salford to Hunts Bank. The M & L section was to be carried principally through a tunnel, whilst that apportioned to the L & M would make use of the existing MB & B line for a few hundred yards in the neighbourhood of the Irwell Street station, and would bridge the Irwell a little to the west of the Hunts Bank station. The new lines through Salford connecting with the MB & B would be built on arches so as to require the minimum interference with established property rights. This time the L & M board hastened to conclude. Within a week of the first communication's being received the treasurer was instructed to write to the chairman of the M & L stating that his directors 'were ready to enter upon the preliminary necessary arrangements'. Only one thing had to be cleared first. James Loch, the superintendent of the Bridgewater Trust, who was also an absentee director of the Liverpool & Manchester Railway, serving in the interest of the Duke of Sutherland, had to be approached for his approval. This he readily gave in a letter which was read to the board on 23 July.[10]

Somewhat surprisingly in view of their precipitancy in making the agreement, the L & M directors showed the greatest reluctance to carry it out. They went to Parliament for the necessary powers, obtaining them on 14 June 1839.[11] But for nearly three years afterwards they delayed acting upon them, driving their supposed partners, who quickly bought up land to complete their part of the bargain, to the extremes of desperation. The L & M board could give reasons for the apparent inconsistency. The Manchester, Bolton & Bury company had proved unco-operative. It began by asking in October 1838 that, in return for constructing the branch between the L & M line and its own, it should be permitted to charge more than its maximum toll on both by dubious calculations of distances.[12] Six months later it proposed that the L & M should itself make the entire junction, and pay to the MB & B 3d per passenger and 6d per ton of goods for traffic passing over the MB & B section.[13] The Liverpool directors also discovered that the Manchester & Leeds company had deceived them as to the amount of merchandise likely to flow along the junction line. After a full investigation, which included an interview with a director of the Leeds & Liverpool Canal, they concluded that the existing traffic, by canal, between Liverpool and Leeds and between Liverpool and intermediate places eastwards from Rochdale did not form a half of what it was estimated in the statements received from the M & L.[14]

Moreover, the directors were having difficulty in convincing some of their shareholders about the value of the junction with the Leeds line. On 19 March 1839 Isaac Crewdson, a Manchester Quaker, who claimed to have a great part of his investments in the L & M company, wrote to John Cropper, one of the directors, expressing want of confidence in the board and a desire to be assured that the latter would not undertake any great outlay on the line without acquainting the proprietors with their intention. Crewdson and his brothers had been encouraged in their opposition by William Garnett, a prominent Salford Tory.[15] The directors gave Garnett and Crewdson a 1½hr interview, and made them a promise that, if an Act of Parliament was got, every shareholder should 'have a circular with full notice of a general meeting to decide whether we shall proceed to make the junction'.[16] It may be doubted, however, whether this or any other of the factors mentioned so far did more than to strengthen an existing reluctance on the part of the directors to proceed with the line, for as early as September 1838 they declined to purchase land on the proposed route owing to 'the present uncertainty as to the junction line between the two railways'.[17]

It is clear that the doubts concerning the Hunts Bank junction were associated with a lingering predilection for a southern link. This project, which had been kept alive by the Manchester & Birmingham and Sheffield, Ashton-under-Lyne & Manchester companies, held out to the L & M the prospect of at least two important new connections, with the companies just named, perhaps even of three if an extension could be built from Store Street to the old M & L terminal at St George's Street; the Hunts Bank line promised only one, for with Bolton the L & M was already connected via the Bolton & Leigh line. Hopes of making the south junction had taken an unexpected leap forward in

April 1839, when James Loch revoked his earlier opposition, writing to the chairman of the L & M to express a preference for it over the line through Salford.[18]

On 16 December the board decided to shelve the Hunts Bank scheme, and instructed its 'junction' sub-committee to propose to the M & L and M & B companies the making of a connecting line to join together the three companies on the eastern side of the town 'at the united expense and for the mutual advantage of all'.[19] After some exploratory surveying by the company's engineer, Edward Woods, it was resolved to put to the M & L directors the possibility of a junction east of Store Street between the M & B terminus and the old M & L station,[20] this to be combined with a link between the L & M and the M & B. The proposal was made at a conference early in March 1840, but the representatives of the M & L stood firm by the Hunts Bank connection. As a gesture to the need for a more general railway communication through Manchester they suggested that a tunnel might be made under the centre of the city from Hunts Bank to the M & B line, but this was unacceptable to the L & M company,[21] presumably because its use would be dependent on the goodwill of the M & L, a company with an interest in blocking the exchange of traffic between the L & M and the SA & M.

For two years afterwards a stalemate existed in which neither of the two connecting lines was attempted. The main impediment to action was that the L & M board was divided internally over the merits of the two schemes. One party, having as its moving spirit George Loch, the son of James, strongly favoured the southern link. It was supported by William Garnett, whose election to the board in January 1840 the elder Loch's influence had procured.[22] The other, captained by John Moss, continued to press for the making of the Hunts Bank line, and opened negotiations for the purchase of the MB & B, which had previously been an impediment to the plan, but was in such poor financial straits by the spring of 1840 as to be willing to contemplate a sell-out to the L & M.[23] The two factions were about equally matched. George Loch claimed in the following November that there was 'a decided majority of the board favourable to going south rather than through Salford', but he added that his supporters were 'sadly wanting in the untiring and persevering singleness of view' of their opponents.[24] He could also have said that the latter included the chairman of the company, Charles Lawrence, and the deputy chairman, John Moss.

Not until early in 1842 was the *impasse* broken. At first it looked as if a solution was to be reached along lines diametrically opposite to what eventually happened. When the year opened, power in the L & M boardroom was slipping in favour of the southern link. First Joseph Sandars, then Lawrence and Moss, deserted to the southern camp.[25] Having ordered a survey of a route from their own main line through Castlefield to the M & B at Store Street, and on to the M & L station in St George's Street,[26] the L & M directors issued a fully documented address to their shareholders to prove that this line offered a shorter, more convenient, and less costly means of linking the M & L and M & B railways than the tunnel proposed by the M & L. They maintained that they could build an over-ground line from Oldham Road to Store Street, which would be not one third of the distance from St George's Street to Store Street via the tunnel, and would avoid 'the extraordinary mechanical anomaly of first taking the traffic down the inclined plane from St George's Road to Hunts Bank, equal to a perpendicular descent of 90 feet and then up again by means of a tunnel and lift to Store Street'. The directors also urged the superiority of Store Street as a 'general central station or *rendezvous*'. With the aid of a map of Manchester for 1794 they argued that the growth of the town in the intervening period had been away from Hunts Bank and in the direction of Store Street.[27]

The case was a much exaggerated one. As the map opposite shows, it was scarcely practicable to join Store Street and St George's Street except by a tunnel, which would have presented as many problems to the user as that to Hunts Bank, and would have rendered an exchange of through trade with the M & L all but impossible.[28] Moreover, from the viewpoint of travellers to and from Manchester, Hunts Bank and Store Street were about equidistant from the busy commercial centre

## The Battle of the Manchester Railway Junctions 151

of the town. On balance, however, the L & M company had more to gain from the Store Street than from the Hunts Bank link, and the shareholders, recognising this, endorsed the directors' proposals at a special meeting on 15 March.[29]

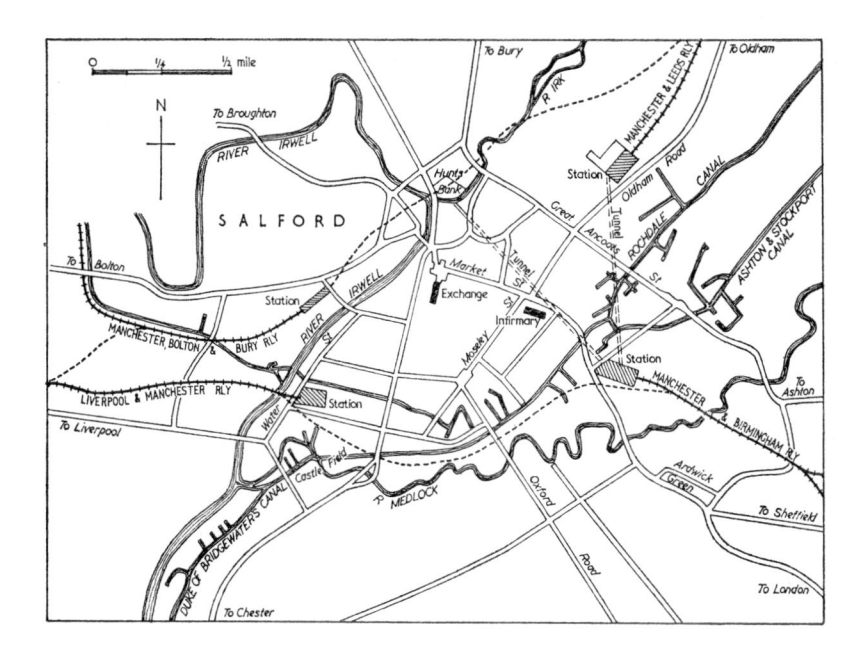

The triumph of the south junction party was short-lived. Even before it was attained Captain James Laws, the general manager of the M & L company, was scheming to subvert it. His company never wavered from its determination to have the Hunts Bank connection instead of the southern junction. With its directors the overriding objective was to procure a superior connecting line through Manchester for the Yorkshire to Liverpool trade to that which would be possessed by the SA & M. They may even have aimed at preventing the Sheffield company from obtaining any effective junction with the L & M line at all.[30] In Captain Laws the M & L company had a servant of indomitable will and immense astuteness. Cognisant that in order to disable an opponent it was first necessary to isolate him, he won over the Manchester & Birmingham company to his side. When, therefore, in January 1842, the L & M directors approached their counterparts of the M & B for a discussion of the southern junction, they were told politely but disconcertingly that the M & B company 'had yesterday concluded the basis of an agreement with the Manchester & Leeds Company to join their railway by means of a tunnel to Hunts Bank'.[31] Laws' masterstroke, however, was to conclude an alliance with the Mersey & Irwell Navigation during the following month for diverting the Yorkshire traffic to the water between Manchester and Liverpool. Arrangements were made for constructing a junction between the Leeds railway and the River Irwell at Hunts Bank,[32] and a discount of 5s per ton was offered to those private carriers on the M & L line who could prove that they conveyed by river between the two Lancashire cities.[33] At the same time he worked diligently to detach the L & M shareholders from the board of directors. In a pamphlet, which was circulated amongst them, he claimed that the directors had long subordinated the interests of the L & M company to those of the Grand Junction, in which they held large investments.[34] The M & L company also renewed an offer which it had mentioned earlier, to lease the whole L & M undertaking, paying the proprietors 10 per cent on their capital, provided that the Hunts Bank connection was made.

By the beginning of March several of the large Quaker shareholders in the L & M, notably one of the Crewdsons, were sufficiently disturbed to be pressing the board to consider the 10 per cent offer.[35] What had alarmed them most was the threat that the M & L company might rid itself of all dependence on the L & M by building a new line of railway through to Liverpool north of the existing one.[36] Nevertheless, as the outcome of the special meeting on 15 March showed, there was no general revolt of the shareholders against boardroom policies. The directors continued for a few more weeks to prepare for a southern junction line, but eventually they gave way. On 21 March, only six

## The Battle of the Manchester Railway Junctions

days after they had carried their proprietors with them for the Store Street link, they agreed to open top-level talks between their chairman and the chairman of the M & L to ascertain terms for going by Hunts Bank.[37] On 20 April they advised a further special general meeting of the shareholders to adopt the Hunts Bank line, on the grounds that neither the M & L nor the M & B company would assent to the southern connection.[38] The *volte face* within the board was produced principally by the reversion of John Moss to his earlier support of the north line and by the defection of Sandars and John Cropper, who were said to have been influenced by Moss, from the southern party.[39] An important permissive factor, however, was the collapse of the opposition leadership. George Loch stayed away from the crucial shareholders' meeting on 20 April, when the decision in favour of Hunts Bank was taken. His erstwhile followers, Theodore Rathbone, Robert Benson, Edward Cropper, David Hodgson and William Garnett, waited upon him prior to the meeting, and begged him to attend it. But he refused, not wishing to fetter his father's discretion. Joseph Langton, his fellow director in the Sutherland interest, abstained with him.[40]

From then events moved swiftly to their conclusion. The L & M company went to Parliament again for power to construct a line to Hunts Bank. The route differed slightly from that authorised in 1839. Leaving the L & M at Ordsall Lane Gate it ran through Salford close to the MB & B track but without actually joining it. The Bill received the royal assent on 30 July 1842,[41] and the new railway was opened on 4 May 1844. It connected with an imposing station in the Roman-Doric style, which the M & L company had brought into use at Hunts Bank four months earlier.[42] For the moment the southern junction was laid aside, but not for long. It was revived in January 1844 by the SA & M and M & B companies, which were anxious to share with the M & L the privilege of a continuous communication through Manchester with the L & M line. The link was to run from the L & M in Salford through Castlefield to the M & B line near Store Street. This proposal was later merged with one for a commuter line from Altrincham into Manchester, and the whole project was authorised to be carried out by the SA & M and M & B companies acting in conjunction with Lord Francis Egerton, the life tenant of the Bridgewater Trust. It was completed in 1849 as the Manchester, South Junction & Altrincham Railway.[43] Of the network discussed in the early 1840s only the link from Store Street to the M & L remained unmade at the close of the decade. But the proposal for a single central terminus of the Manchester railways had vanished. It was never seriously revived.

## II

It remains to unravel the factors in the struggle. The questions which stand most in need of an answer are three: why, in view of the manifest advantages of the south connecting line, did the L & M directors allow themselves to be diverted in the first place to Hunts Bank? Secondly, having obtained an Act of Parliament to build to Hunts Bank, why did they wait until their powers had almost expired before taking any action to construct the line? Thirdly, why did they change their course in March 1842 and make the northern link?

Charles Lawrence, the chairman of the L & M company, suggested an explanation which fits all these questions. He observed to James Loch: 'We went to Parliament for the act, not because we were anxious to make a communication with Leeds, but because we were afraid of the consequences of a North and rival line.'[44] The fear to which he alluded was that, if baulked in its intention to connect with the L & M through Hunts Bank, the M & L would build a competing line from Manchester to Liverpool north of the existing one. A brief *sortie* from Hunts Bank into Salford would take it to the MB & B line, which could then serve as the basis of a westward extension. The MB & B committee had already contemplated constructing a branch from Clifton to the north end of Liverpool in 1833.[45] It made sense, therefore, to forestall such a move by taking parliamentary powers to occupy the ground west of Hunts Bank. Having taken them, the L & M directors need feel no strong urge to act upon them, for the south junction line would serve their purposes better and there was something to be said for keeping

## The Battle of the Manchester Railway Junctions

the M & L and MB & B lines apart altogether. Nevertheless, as the 1839 Act approached expiry in 1842, the threat of a northern line to Liverpool revived, and worked to induce the shareholders and directors of the L & M to give way to pressure from the M & L.[46] A bargain was struck with the latter that neither company would promote a line in opposition to the other to the westward or eastward of Manchester respectively, and as a further guard against laying the foundation of a new railway to Liverpool the MB & B line was left out of the scheme.[47]

This was probably the main explanation of the course which events took. With certain directors, however, there were reinforcing considerations unconnected with the welfare of the L & M. George Loch maintained, with a consistency extending over several years, that the support given to the Hunts Bank line stemmed from such an origin. Writing to Lord Ellesmere in 1847, he referred to a serious struggle within the board between those directors who represented purely L & MR interests, and who therefore wanted a junction with as many other lines as possible, and those who were also members of the Grand Junction Railway board, and dreaded a connection to the south, 'lest a rival line to Birmingham or London might have thence arisen'.[48] It was his firm opinion that the acquisition of a direct link with the L & M would encourage the M & B company to extend southwards towards London to the detriment of the Grand Junction Railway Company, whose line would be by-passed. He spelled out his meaning in a letter to his father written in 1840:

> The discovery made on the opening of the Grand Junction railway that the travelling between London and Liverpool greatly exceeds that between London and Manchester is a discouragement to all lines of direct communication between the latter place and London. Having no other feeders of importance, a union of the Liverpool and Manchester and the Birmingham and Manchester by the South side of Manchester would afford very material aid to the resources of an extension line to Rugby. It would undoubtedly confer on them a share at least of the Liverpool travellers. It would thus be their interest to promote such a plan, and inasmuch as it would be stealing a march on the Grand Junction, we should have their feelings too in behalf of it, smarting as they now are under the imputation of having been done by Moss.[49]

In other words the making of the south junction would enable the L & B to compete for the Liverpool–London traffic, which would otherwise use the entire Grand Junction line between Earlestown and Birmingham. Once this was possible, the urge to create a shorter railway route from Manchester to London, avoiding the GJ between Crewe and Birmingham, would be reinforced.

George Loch's contention cannot be proved absolutely. It is a matter of suspicion rather than established fact. Nevertheless, although his division of the board into L & M and GJ factions is probably too clear-cut, there are indications that he was not wholly mistaken in imputing a Grand Junction motive to the advocacy of a northern link.

In 1839 the L & M railway board consisted of fifteen members—Charles Lawrence, John Moss, William Rotheram, Joseph Sandars, Hardman Earle, Joseph Hornby, John Cropper Jr, Robert Benson, David Hodgson, Thomas Sands, Theodore Woolman Rathbone, Nicholas Robinson, James Loch, George Loch, and Wallace Currie. Most of them were Liverpool merchants with little personal concern for the amenities of Manchester.[50] Apart from Cropper and Rathbone they had apparently only a small financial interest in the L & M railway—'altogether not a hundred shares', it was alleged by one large proprietor.[51] Of those listed above, however, the first seven were, or had recently been, directors of the GJ. John Moss, a banker from Liverpool, who was deputy chairman of the L & M, was also chairman of the GJ from its inception in 1833 down to 1841. Except for about five weeks in February–March 1842, when he bowed to the opinions of his colleagues, he was a consistent and determined advocate of the northern junction. Charles Lawrence, who succeeded him in the chair of the GJ in 1841, was chairman of the L & M. Though he once denied that he had 'ever been improperly biased in favour of' the GJ and against the L & M,[52] he too was a north-liner down to 14 February 1842 and again late in March that year.[53] He was in the chair at the meeting on 16 July 1838, when the Hunts Bank junction was first proposed by representatives of the M & L, and he hastened to express his approval of the idea of joining the two railways even before the matter had been properly discussed by the board.[54]

Other members of the Grand Junction party were more open-minded, but they were subject to Moss's influence. Of a meeting in November 1840 which resolved to open a fresh negotiation with the M & L company, George Loch wrote:

> The feeling of the Grand Junction portion of our directors is evidently and naturally towards the Hunts Bank junction. I should almost infer from the way in which Moss spoke of it this morning that something has occurred to render him particularly desirous to press it forward. It was obvious that his motives were not solely Liverpool and Manchester. The others do not go so far as he does, and would hesitate in taking such a step as to recommend the junction to the proprietary until they were satisfied they would obtain such a traffic as would pay 5 per cent on the outlay. Moss caught at this and asked whether they would be satisfied 'were 5 per cent guaranteed to them'. This would of course never do . . . but the question betrayed his anxiety on the subject.[55]

Moss was, indeed, the driving force behind the movement for the Hunts Bank junction, but his speeches did not reveal his real motives. It was he who tipped the scale in favour of it at the board meeting held on 21 March 1842. His method was to play on the fears of his fellow directors that resistance to the scheme would encourage the M & L company to resurrect the project of a north line to Liverpool,[56] but George Loch was convinced that he expressed more apprehension on that account than he seriously entertained.[57]

Down to the autumn of 1839 parties interested in the welfare of the Grand Junction Railway had obvious grounds to fear the growth of a rival to that concern in the London trade. In the mid-1830s no fewer than four schemes for making a rail connection between Manchester and London held the stage. One project, known as the Manchester & South Union Railway, formed by the amalgamation of two of these, would have eliminated the Grand Junction entirely from its proposed route by running on to Tamworth on the Birmingham & Derby line. The GJ directors, however, supported an alternative plan, the Manchester & Cheshire Junction Railway, for feeding into its own line at Crewe. Whilst this project flourished the Grand Junction element in the L & M board did not hesitate to encourage the notion of joining it to the company's railway by a south-connecting line round Manchester. One of their number, Hardman Earle, brought the proposition forward in September 1836.[58] In the following year the Manchester & Birmingham Railway was launched as a compromise between the conflicting schemes for railways running southwards from Manchester. This retained dangerous potentialities for the GJ, for it included the proposal for a line from Store Street to Chebsey near Stone in Staffordshire. The peril was much increased when in 1838 preparations were made to extend this from Stone to Rugby on the London & Birmingham line, thus threatening once again to by-pass the GJ altogether. A subsidiary company of the M & B was formed for the purpose, and an application was made to Parliament for the necessary powers on 11 February 1839.[59] The desire not to add to the project's importance by allowing it to promise an improved communication between Liverpool and London, as well as between Manchester and London, may well have induced Moss and his associates in the L & M board to play up the Hunts Bank connection at the expense of the southern link in 1838-9.

It is less easy to understand how this factor operated after October 1839, for in that month the GJ drove the M & B to terms which virtually required the abandonment by the latter of all but its Manchester to Crewe and Macclesfield sections. The Grand Junction, however, pursued its vendetta against the M & B by interfering with its right to run trains over the GJ line south of Crewe, and a violent quarrel broke out between the two concerns as the M & B line reached completion early in 1842.[60] Moss's endeavours to strangle the south junction and to substitute the Hunts Bank connection at that time may well have formed part of a plan to weaken the M & B by confining it to a purely local traffic. Moreover, the GJ was still not entirely free of the threat of an independent link with London and the south, for there was talk of making a Churnet Valley line in the winter of 1841-2.[61]

The Grand Junction Railway Company was not the only external factor in the L & M board to influence the struggle over the Manchester

### The Battle of the Manchester Railway Junctions 159

railways. Ever since the first Duke of Sutherland, then Marquess of Stafford and life tenant of the Bridgewater Trust, had bought into the L & M company there had been a community of interest between the Duke of Bridgewater's canal and the railway. This was sustained by the presence of three directors nominated by the Duke of Sutherland on the railway board. The connection was drawn closer in 1828, when as a condition of being allowed to bring their line over the Irwell into Manchester unopposed, the directors had promised Robert Haldane Bradshaw, then superintendent of the Bridgewater Trust, that they would not interfere with the water traffic to and from Yorkshire and that they did not purport extending their line beyond Manchester.[62] This undertaking, together with the Duke of Sutherland's extensive holdings in the railway company, explains why the directors displayed so much anxiety to consult James Loch, who was the duke's chief agent, as well as the head of the Bridgewater Trust, appointed in the interest of the second duke's brother, Lord Francis Egerton, before embarking upon any junction lines through Manchester.

James Loch at first used his influence to further the northern link, but he afterwards changed his mind, and in April 1839 came out openly in favour of the south junction.[63] In the following year the Bridgewater Trustees employed the civil engineer Cubitt to survey the ground for a southern line cutting across their wharves at Castlefield.[64]

Loch's authority, strengthened by the exertions of his son George within the railway board, was a factor of no mean importance in delaying the implementation of the Hunts Bank connection. Charles Lawrence observed in March 1842 that the line would by then have been made, had it not been for the hostility which the elder Loch had pressed against it.[65] This statement contains an element of exaggeration for the southern alternative possessed advantages which all could see. Nevertheless, it was true to a considerable extent. It would be unsafe, however, to assume that Loch's opposition stemmed from a desire to block all railroad communication through Manchester for the sake of the duke's canal. H. G. Lewin, the railway historian, believed that this was so. Alluding to the delay in making the Hunts Bank line he wrote:

'The real reason was probably the existence of some understanding with the canal companies, who anticipated a loss of traffic from canal to rail when a continuous line through Manchester was completed.'[66]

We have seen, however, that Loch was not opposed to every suggestion for a link through Manchester. What he wanted was the south junction, and that for the reason that it would pass through Castlefield. The object, as he explained to Lord Francis Egerton, was 'to make a great depot at Castlefield both for the sake of bringing your land into use and to afford the ready transhipment of goods from Canal to Railway and from Railway to Canal'.[67]

Moreover, it was not for canal reasons only that James Loch favoured the southern connection. He had to consider the Duke of Sutherland's holdings in the L & M railway no less than the welfare of the Bridgewater Trust. A letter to his son makes clear the part which both of his charges played in determining his initial opposition to the south line and his subsequent change of view:[68]

> I supported the Salford line originally for two reasons, first because I thought a continuous line through Manchester being one day inevitable, it was the best for the R.R. according to the information then in my possession. Secondly that it avoided Castlefield and thereby did least injury to the Canal. . . . Thirdly because I was advised that it was the best means of keeping off a North line. I altered this opinion in favour of the Castlefield line by the same principle that [if] a continuous line was inevitable, it occurred to me after more mature and deliberate thought that it was better to bring the land at Castlefield into the market, that by doing the R.R. and Canal business *well* at that place they could materially help each other, that it embraced all the R.R.s in place of one only, that if the Manchester and Birmingham or the Churnet Valley lines, should ever be extended to Birmingham or Derby . . . it would make the Liverpool and Manchester line the course from London etc. to Liverpool. Whereas it was strongly enforced on me by those who were likely to know the fact that if the Salford line was made and a bridge thrown across the Irwell at the place intended, it would become the foundation of a North line in place of keeping back that measure.

In an earlier letter, written to Charles Lawrence, he admitted that his doubts as to opposing the southern connection had been started by subordinates in the management of the Bridgewater Trust,[69] but there

## The Battle of the Manchester Railway Junctions

can be little doubt that he believed himself to be acting in the best interest of both concerns.

The ambivalence of Loch's position, as protector both of the canal and of the railway shares, must also be taken into account in explaining the sudden and dramatic collapse of resistance to the Hunts Bank scheme in March 1842. In his desire to overcome the opposition of the two Lochs Captain Laws had directed his fire as much against the Bridgewater Trust as against the L & M. In October 1841 he boasted that he would ruin the duke's canal unless the L & M board agreed to make the Hunts Bank line.[70] His subsequent compact with the Mersey & Irwell Navigation Company enabled him to issue in the following February a new scale of charges to carriers in the Liverpool to Leeds trade, which discriminated against those who preferred to make their own arrangements to carry by the Bridgewater Canal west of Manchester and in favour of those who accepted his terms to convey throughout by a mixture of river and railway. This unsettled the carriers on the 'Duke's', and Pickfords seem actually to have left the canal.[71] In the following month a report that the M & L had leased the Calder & Hebble Navigation raised the trustees' fears that the company might charge the full parliamentary toll on that waterway, thus crippling the through trade by canal between Liverpool and Hull, if the Hunts Bank connection was not built.[72]

It is difficult to believe that these considerations did not weigh with Loch, when he called off the opposition to the northern junction. His correspondence with his son suggests, however, that he was mainly influenced by the desire to avoid a further depreciation of the company's shares, which had already fallen £30 apiece as a result partly of the quarrel with the M & L and partly of a contest with the canals.[73] At that time the Duke of Sutherland was looking for an opportunity to sell at least a portion of his large holdings in the L & M, and it was imperative that nothing further should be done to shake confidence in the stock before the transaction was completed.[74]

## III

We may conclude that the impediments to building railway connections through Manchester were not just local obstacles. They also sprang from the cut and thrust of competition on the long-distance railway (and canal) routes of which Manchester was the hub—from London to Liverpool and from Yorkshire to Liverpool. Evidently the obstruction presented by this fierce rivalry to the smooth penetration of an urban area and the evolution of a convenient central station must be added to other known examples of the wastefulness of railroad competition. The damage, however, should not be overestimated. Within less than a decade of the ending of the struggle virtually all the overland rail connections planned at the time had been completed;[75] only the tunnels linking the M & L system to London Road continued unmade, and these were probably operationally impracticable. A more significant facet of the story is the light which is thrown on the limitations of competition. In the earliest years of railroad construction, when capital was scarce and risks were considerable, a strong promoting group like the Liverpool party was able to establish a foothold in more than one company, while the need to placate the canal interest brought the aristocratic navigation owner into the railway world. This tended to produce, here and there, an interlacing of power between concerns whose interests were not wholly at one. The Liverpool & Manchester Railway Company was a child of that era. Its directorate was not just a railway board but an exchange where divergent interests jostled one another for advantage. Even before the amalgamations of the middle forties introduced a fusion of a more institutional character the independence of the local railway company was sometimes more apparent than real.

*University of Southampton*

*The Battle of the Manchester Railway Junctions*     163

## References

1. J. R. Kellett, *The Impact of Railways on Victorian Cities* (1969), especially 4–14.
2. Hugh Douglas, *The Underground Story* (1963), 21–3.
3. The station called Central, opened in 1880, was in fact merely a butt-ended terminus for the Cheshire Lines Committee's rails approaching from the south and west.
4. Kellett, op cit, 164–5.
5. L. Faucher, *Manchester in 1844*, quoted from Kellett, op cit, 171.
6. British Transport Historical Records (BTHR), Minutes of the Liverpool & Manchester Railway Board, LVM 1/4, 26 September 1836 and 2 January 1837.
7. Ibid, 9 January 1837.
8. James Loch to Fereday Smith, 22 November 1837: Loch-Egerton Papers (LEP), Mertoun. For access to these and other papers at Mertoun I am indebted to His Grace the Duke of Sutherland.
9. Ibid, F. Smith to J. Loch, 24 and 30 November 1837.
10. BTHR, LVM 1/4, 16 and 23 July 1838.
11. *Journal of the House of Commons* (*JHC*), XCIV (1839), 343.
12. By reckoning the 1¼ miles of the branch from the L & M and of its own main line as 2 miles, and by charging for that supposed distance its maximum rates of 3d per ton per mile for goods, 2d per mile for first-class passengers and 1½d per mile for second-class passengers, BTHR, LVM 1/4, 8 October 1838.
13. BTHR, LVM 1/5, 8 April 1839.
14. Ibid, 9 and 16 December 1839.
15. Staffordshire County Record Office: I. Crewdson to J. Cropper, 19 March 1839, Sutherland Estate Papers (SEP), D593/K.
16. Ibid, W. W. Currie to J. Loch, 25 March 1839.
17. BTHR, LVM 1/4, 24 September 1838.
18. LEP, J. Loch to Charles Lawrence, 9 April 1839.
19. BTHR, LVM 1/5, 16 December 1839.
20. Ibid, 2 March 1840.
21. SEP, D593/K, J. Jellicoe to H. Booth, 17 March 1840 and H. Booth to J. Jellicoe, 9 March 1840.
22. Ibid, C. Lawrence to J. Loch, 26 March 1842 and W. Garnett to J. Loch, 14 January 1840.
23. Ibid, W. W. Currie to J. Loch, 28 May 1840.
24. Ibid, G. to J. Loch, 5 November 1840.
25. Ibid, G. to J. Loch, 14 February 1842.
26. BTHR, LVM 1/5, 21 January 1842; SEP D593/K, G. to J. Loch, 14 February 1842.
27. BTHR, RAC, 1/217, Liverpool & Manchester Railway Company Reports, 1824–45: Directors' Address, 28 February 1842; also Report to Special Meeting of Proprietors on 15 March 1842.
28. See also Kellett, op cit, 170.
29. BTHR, RAC 1/217, Printed Report of Special General Meeting of L & MR, 15 March 1842.
30. This at least was the impression formed by Boothby, an intermediary for the L & M, after a private interview with Houldsworth, the chairman of the Manchester & Leeds, in March 1842. Having heard Boothby's account, George Loch wrote to his father: 'Their ruling fear is what we believed, fear of the Sheffield line becoming

through our instrumentality a dangerous source of opposition to them.' SEP, D593/K, G. to J. Loch, 16 March 1842.
31 BTHR, LVM 1/5, 21 January 1842.
32 The agreement was reported to the M & I Navigation Committee as having been completed, on 18 February 1842. Manchester Ship Canal Company, Bridgewater Department, Mersey & Irwell Navigation Co Order Book, 1834–42, 18 February 1842.
33 SEP, D593/K, H. Booth to J. Loch, 7 February 1842.
34 BTHR, RAC 1/217, Printed Report of Proceedings at AGM of L & MR, 26 January 1842.
35 SEP, D593/K, G. to J. Loch, 2, 3 and 4 March 1842.
36 Ibid, J. Cropper to J. Loch, 5 March 1842.
37 Ibid, G. to J. Loch, 21 March 1842.
38 BTHR, RAC 1/217, Report of Board to Special General Meeting of Proprietors of L & MR, 20 April 1842.
39 SEP, D593/K, G. to J. Loch, 24 March 1842.
40 Ibid, G. to J. Loch, 20 April 1842.
41 *JHC*, XCVII (1842), 547.
42 *The Manchester Historical Recorder* (1875?), 125 and 128.
43 George Dow, *Great Central*, I (1959), 128–9.
44 SEP, D593/K, C. Lawrence to J. Loch, 26 March 1842.
45 BTHR, Minute of Manchester, Bolton & Bury Canal Navigation and Railway, Canal and Railway Committee, MBB 1/5, 21 October 1833.
46 Of the decision taken by the L & M board on 21 March 1842 to open a negotiation with the Leeds company for the Hunts Bank junction George Loch wrote: 'Moss brought this about by means of the most awful appeals to the fears of some of our directors in respect of a North line . . .', SEP, D593/K, G. to J. Loch, 21 March 1842.
47 According to George Loch it was because of this agreement with the Leeds company that the L & M took no part in making the Manchester, South Junction & Altrincham Railway in 1844. G. Loch to the Earl of Ellesmere, 15 March 1847. Duke of Sutherland's Private Collection, Mertoun, File 137, No 3538.
48 Ibid.
49 SEP, D593/K, G. to J. Loch, 5 November 1840.
50 The names of all the directors except the two Lochs appear in Gore's *Liverpool Directory* for either 1827 or 1841. The particulars of the composition of the two boards have been culled from printed reports of the companies in BTHR.
51 Alleged by Isaac Crewdson in a letter to John Cropper. Cropper in his reply was unable to contradict it. SEP, D593/K, I. Crewdson to J. Cropper, 19 March 1839; W. W. Currie to J. Loch, 22 March 1839.
52 Ibid, C. Lawrence to J. Loch, 26 March 1842.
53 The above impressions of the conduct of Moss and Lawrence are derived from various letters written to James Loch in the years 1839–42 mainly but not exclusively by his son.
54 BTHR, LVM 1/4, 16 July 1838.
55 SEP, D593/K, G. to J. Loch, 2 November 1840.
56 See above n 46.
57 SEP, D593/K, G. to J. Loch, 9 March 1842.
58 BTHR, LVM 1/4, 26 September 1836.
59 *JHC*, XCIV (1839), 18.

60  The details of the various railway schemes from Manchester to the Midlands are drawn from W. H. Chaloner, *The Social and Economic Development of Crewe, 1780–1923* (1950), 22–6. Particulars of the arrangement between the GJ and M & B companies in October 1839 are given in SEP, D593/K, R. C. Sharp to J. Loch, 13 November 1839, W. W. Currie to J. Loch, 26 October 1839 and G. to J. Loch, 27 October 1839.
61  LEP, J. to G. Loch, 6 December 1841. Correspondence About the Connexion Railway. See also SEP, D593/K, G. to J. Loch, 14 February 1842.
62  F. C. Mather, *After the Canal Duke* (1970), 53.
63  LEP, J. Loch to C. Lawrence, 9 April 1839.
64  BTHR, LVM 1/5, 10 February 1840.
65  SEP, D593/K, C. Lawrence to J. Loch, 26 March 1842.
66  H. G. Lewin, *Early British Railways: A Short History of their Origin and Development, 1801–44* (1925), 122.
67  Northamptonshire County Record Office, Ellesmere-Brackley Collection: J. Loch to Lord Francis Egerton, 7 February 1839.
68  LEP, J. to G. Loch, 6 December 1841: Correspondence About the Connexion Railway.
69  LEP, J. Loch to C. Lawrence, 9 April 1839.
70  LEP, J. M. Laws to J. Baxendale, 31 October and 14 November 1841: Correspondence About the Connexion Railway.
71  LEP, F. Smith to J. Loch, 10, 17 and 22 February 1842.
72  Ibid, F. Smith to J. Loch, 24 March 1843.
73  SEP, D593/K, C. Lawrence to J. Loch, 26 March 1842.
74  'The great object for the board to pursue is to make as good a bargain as possible, making the Bolton Junction as little liable to lead to bad consequences as may be. Our conduct must be to get the shares up again as high as possible and as soon as possible.' J. to G. Loch, 29 March 1842. See also J. to G. Loch, 25 March and 15 and 18 April 1842. Ibid.
75  Even the MB & B had gained some access for its trains to Victoria and the L & M line by October 1846. John Marshall, *The Lancashire and Yorkshire Railway*, I (1969), 58.

*Acknowledgements*

I am indebted to His Grace the Duke of Sutherland for permission to use the Loch-Egerton Papers, to the Staffordshire County Archivist, Mr F. B. Stitt, for access to the Sutherland Estate Papers, and to the Librarian of British Transport Historical Records and his staff for guidance in the use of the minute books of railway companies. Mr C. E. Makepeace, Local History Librarian, Central Library, Manchester, assisted me in the choice of illustrations. My thanks are also due to Dr W. H. Chaloner, Mr M. C. Reed, and Mr Charles Hadfield for help given in various ways.

*For plates, provided by the author*, see pp 172–5

WRAY VAMPLEW

# Banks and Railway Finance: A Note on the Scottish Experience[1]

IN THE INITIAL PHASE of railway promotion it was the shareholders who were important, since at least half the company's authorised capital had to be paid up before loans could be applied for; but once this stage had been reached other financiers achieved considerable significance as generally a quarter of authorised capital could be raised in the form of loans and mortgages. Lending money to railways became popular with the small capitalist because security of capital and stability of income was guaranteed, but these factors appealed also to financial institutions such as banks and insurance companies and it is they, rather than widows, spinsters and the like, who dominated the railway loan market. Yet despite their monetary significance, the literature of railway finance has paid relatively little attention to the role of these institutions, concentrating instead on the individuals who became shareholders and speculators. Recently, however, an article in the *Three Banks Review* looked at the relationship between the Royal Bank of Scotland and early Scottish railway development.[2] Unfortunately, it tended towards the antiquarian approach and contented itself with listing the railway companies with which the bank had dealings. The purpose of this note is to provide some analysis, enlarging the discussion to include Scottish banks in general and suggesting reasons why they behaved towards railways as they did. It must be stressed that the hypotheses advanced are tentative and more comprehensive research in both railway and bank archives will almost certainly reveal additional data on the companies' relationships with the banks.

A brief outline of the traditional view of Scottish banking is perhaps essential here in order to throw more light on the arguments presented. The general criticism of the lending policy of the established chartered

## Banks and Railway Finance: A Note on the Scottish Experience 167

banks and Edinburgh private banks was that inadequate funds were available to meet the growing demands of industry. The banks' cautious emphasis on stability had led to the largest part of their loanable funds being absorbed in discounting bills and in investment in government securities. Even the Commercial and National banks, founded in 1810 and 1825 respectively, despite their avowed national coverage and more liberal lending policies, proved themselves to be pseudo-revolutionaries and came within the fold of the older institutions by 1830. The reaction to this was a burst of new banking activity in the following decade, primarily in the west of Scotland. These new banks pursued an aggressive financial policy employing a large proportion of their resources in the discounting of ordinary trade bills, but there was still a general reluctance on the part of all the Scottish banks to participate in direct industrial financing.[3]

The banks were reluctant to aid fixed-capital formation by the purchase of railway shares (except for nominal subscriptions made on the grounds of prestige and goodwill) because of their need to possess liquid resources. No examples have been traced of banks taking significant share holdings in a railway company before the line was opened: ie, risk capital was not forthcoming from the banks. Where the banks did purchase railway shares it would seem that it was to obtain a return on their surplus funds. As these shares were in established railways they would be more marketable, especially as most of them bore guaranteed dividends and did not participate in the general fortunes of the railway company as did ordinary shares. Whether or not this flow of funds in and out of the railway share market had any direct impact on the finances of individual railway companies is open to question. Those railway directors who were also on the boards of banks could perhaps manipulate the banks' dealings in railway shares so as to influence the price of their own railway stock, but this would only be of importance to the railway at the time of floating new issues.

There is some evidence that one of the newer banks, the Clydesdale, was making share purchases throughout the 1840s, and that the Commercial was also involved in such operations before the railway mania; but, as far as can be ascertained, the general policy of most banks was to remain aloof from dealings in railway shares in the first half of the nineteenth century. Until the railway mania there was no stock exchange in either Edinburgh or Glasgow on which railway shares could be marketed; this would perhaps deter the Scottish banks in dealing in such investments. It might also explain why the Commercial Bank dealt in English and not Scottish railway shares. After the railway mania when achievements failed to match up to expectations an odium fell on railway shares for several years which must have dissuaded the banks from moving into this sphere of equity investment. It certainly dissuaded most types of investor, for the railway companies found it necessary to issue preference shares when they next went to the market for capital. With the development of the preference share and the gradual revival in the value of ordinary stock the railways eventually came to be acknowledged as stable financial units and, as railway stock grew in status, it entered more into the investment portfolios of the commercial banks. By May 1852 the directors of the Union Bank of Scotland had revised their previous opinions and accepted that it might be considered 'safe as well as advantageous to the Bank to employ a certain portion of their funds in such investments'.[4]

It has just been stated that the Scottish banks played only a minor role in the direct formation of fixed railway capital before 1850, but in fact they did aid capital formation indirectly by giving loans—which is tantamount to providing long-term capital if the loans were constantly renewed. As stated above, railways were entitled to borrow approximately a quarter of their authorised capital, and in Scotland a great proportion of the loans came from the banks, both from the newer, less conservative ones and from the older, established institutions. A reading of the minute books of the railway companies and of the banks makes it clear that loans from the banks to the railway companies were forthcoming throughout the century. The banks provided such accommodation for several reasons. First and foremost it was profitable. Secondly, it encouraged the circulation of their banknotes. Finally, it was a way of attracting railway company accounts which gave the bank

*A view of the head of Beverley Beck, looking eastward from Low Bridge*

*Another view of the upper reach, this time looking back to Low Bridge*
See MacMahon, 'Beverley and its Beck', pp 121-43

*A view immediately to the west of the lock. The River Hull lies just beyond the lock house*

*An open reach of the Beck. Formerly keels used their sails on this section when the wind served*
See MacMahon, 'Beverley and its Beck', pp 121–43

*A view of the culverts which take the Beverley and Barmston low-level drain (authorised in 1798) under the navigation*

*Barges discharging their cargoes near the head of the navigation*
See MacMahon, 'Beverley and its Beck', pp 121–43

*The bridge over Water Street, Liverpool Road Station, Manchester, presumably c 1830. (Courtesy: Manchester Public Libraries)*

See Mather, 'Manchester Railway Junctions', pp 144–65

*Platform and original Booking Office, Liverpool Road Station, Manchester. A photograph taken in 1955 (Courtesy: Manchester Public Libraries)*

See Mather, 'Manchester Railway Junctions', pp 144–65

*The Facade of Victoria Station, Hunts Bank, Manchester, 1845, by Tait. (Courtesy: Manchester Public Libraries)*

See Mather, 'Manchester Railway Junctions', pp 144–65

*Bridge over the River Irwell, Victoria Station, Manchester, 1845, also by Tait. (Courtesy: Manchester Public Libraries)*

See Mather, 'Manchester Railway Junctions', pp 144–65

*Stanier class 5 4-6-0 No 5025 at Keighley Station, Yorkshire, on 3 April 1971, heading a Worth Valley train*

See 'Notes and News', p 220

# Banks and Railway Finance: A Note on the Scottish Experience

use of the parliamentary deposit while the railway company's Bill was being discussed. Here it should be stressed that the banks did not make a general practice of lending to a railway company which had not begun operations. However, lending to established companies which were constructing additional main lines and branches was not unknown. Such were the benefits of being banker to a railway company that, in order to obtain accounts or safeguard those they already had, it seems to have been the banks' general policy to offer differential rates of interest on loans given to those railways which banked exclusively with the bank giving the loan and on loans to railways which banked elsewhere. The railway companies, well aware of their negotiating position, bargained with the banks over these differential rates, shopping around and trying to play off one against another.[5] The Arbroath & Forfar Railway, for example, originally had their account with the local bank, the Arbroath Banking Company, but transferred to the British Linen Company when further credit was refused, and whenever the 'Linen' was difficult they talked or wrote of the possibility of either going back to the Arbroath Bank, going to the Royal, or going to Sir W. Forbes & Company.[6]

Did this lending to the railways clash with the avowed policy of high liquidity advocated by some of the banks? It may be that the total amounts involved were slight in relation to other advances or deposits. It is virtually impossible to ascertain how much the banks were in fact lending to the various sectors of the economy, but considering the extent to which the railway companies were involved in bank loans the impression gained is that railway loans were not an insignificant proportion of total bank advances. It may be that the capital market was so saturated with demands that the banks allowed the railway companies to use them as a last resort, but there is no evidence of an ebb and flow in the railways' reliance on bank loans which might be expected from such a policy. It is also possible, of course, that the banks were never so reluctant to aid industry and commerce as has been made out by some authorities.[7] Walter Scott, writing in 1826, had no doubt that economic development 'had been produced by the facilities of procuring credit, which the Scottish banks held forth, both by discounting bills, and by granting cash accounts'.[8] Unfortunately he did not go into details.

However, the main reason why the banks were willing to loan money to the railway companies (and to other enterprises) was that it was virtually risk-free lending. The newer banks, shut out of certain lines of business by the established institutions, might have been more willing to expand in other directions and thus follow a less cautious lending policy than the older banks, but it is clear that neither were prepared to advance much, if any, risk capital. In fact they went to some lengths to minimise the risks involved in railway loans. Quite often loans were made only if stipulated conditions were followed as when the Great North of Scotland obtained £30,000 for six months from the North of Scotland Bank on the proviso that the remaining calls on preference shares were made within that six months.[9] The Wishaw & Coltness Railway had to promise to bring actions against defaulting shareholders before the Royal Bank of Scotland would lend them £20,000.[10] The Arbroath & Forfar, in debt to the British Linen Company, had to ask the permission of that bank when they wanted to pay a dividend.[11] Such interference with the financial policy of the railway companies was not uncommon, but the general method of ensuring relatively risk-free lending was to bind the railways' directors personally responsible as individuals for the repayment. Railway property was not a very marketable asset, and as such was an imperfect security with which to obtain a loan, but where the directors were willing to pledge themselves responsible for paying it back, a loan was much more likely. However, the directors usually made sure that they were relieved of their liabilities to the shareholders. The banks were well aware that this occurred—a memorandum from the North British to the Royal Bank gave 'no room for doubt that the Company is liable for and bound to relieve the directors of the sums advanced by the Bank for the Company's benefit'—but, as they had the directors' signatures on the loan contract, they knew that their money was secure.[12]

Even when the directors were willing to bind themselves a loan was not automatically forthcoming; the banks had to be sure that the railway concerned was a worthwhile project. Generally loans were made only to railways which were in operation. One exception to this was when the Royal Bank lent £20,000 to the Slamannan Railway while it was still being built, but as nearly £70,000 had already been spent on the line it was thought that every effort would be made to complete it, especially in view of the respectability of the shareholders.[13] As demands from the railway companies for loans increased in the 1840s, the Commercial Bank set up a committee specifically to deal with the question of such lending. The outcome of this was the laying down of certain general principles which, although never explicitly expounded by the other banks, seem to have been generally followed by them. Loans were to be granted only to trunk-line companies which were completed and in remunerative operation; the borrowings of these companies should be within their legal limitation; and the duration of the loan should not extend to any very lengthened period.[14]

This final regulation, if put into practice, would appear to conflict with the previously mentioned idea of continued loans being used to finance long-term fixed-capital projects. In fact it would seem that the renewal of a bank loan was by no means certain. The City of Glasgow Bank demanded a 'large' weekly payment to reduce the overdraft of the Edinburgh, Perth & Dundee Railway and the Clydesdale Bank declined to renew a £15,000 loan to the same company. When the Aberdeen Bank demanded the payment of interest and the balance owing, the Great North of Scotland Railway complied, but registered a formal decision to strike that bank from the list of the company's bankers.[15] Alternative sources of supply, often other banks, were usually found without much difficulty. This was not really a case of a second bank putting its capital at a distinct risk which a first bank had decided was too great, but more the conventions of banking at work. The banks simply did not regard themselves as providers of long-term loans and limited the renewals of their short- and medium-term loans accordingly.

The banks were understandably cautious in their dealings with railway companies. They were even more careful when individuals attempted to borrow money using railway shares as securities. The Clydesdale Bank had advanced up to 50 per cent of the value of such shares in 1839 but, as the railway mania developed in the mid-1840s and speculators in railway shares sought advances on the security of their stocks, the banks became more and more reluctant to give them accommodation.[16] Generally they were given only to established and valued clients and only when it was deemed 'necessary to keep the customers attached to the Bank'.[17] Even then strict precautions were made as to the maintenance of a wide (at least 25 per cent) margin between the value of the shares and the amount of the loan.[18]

A direct consequence of the failure of the banks to meet the extensive demands for personal loans during the railway mania was the rise of an institution peculiar to Scotland, the exchange company. The first, the Glasgow Commercial Exchange Company, came in May 1845, and by early 1846 there were six more in that city alone. Edinburgh had only one, the Exchange Bank of Scotland, although another was projected in late 1846. Farther north several companies developed around Dundee and Aberdeen.[19] The plan of these companies was to lend up to three-quarters of the market value of the stock taken as security. Funds were to be obtained partly from paid-up capital and partly from attracting deposits by offering high rates of interest.[20]

There was tremendous criticism of these companies by the normal commercial banks. Charles Boase of the Dundee Banking Company judged them 'a sort of society got up for promoting the mania of the day'.[21] They were ably defended by George Kinnear, manager of the Glasgow Commercial Exchange Company, who maintained that not only was the theory on which they were based sound, but that the commercial banks recognised this and were attempting to take away some of the exchanges' business by forming the British Trust Company to perform a similar function.[22] There was substance in his allegations for such a company was being promoted by the Royal Bank, the British Linen Company and the Bank of Scotland 'for the purpose of correcting the evils which have arisen to the banking interests of Scotland out of the operations of the existing Exchange Companies'.[23]

The banks were far better equipped to manage such business both in terms of financial reserves and commercial expertise. It was not they, but the exchange companies, that went bankrupt in the dismal financial aftermath of the railway mania. The exchange companies had stated that if the value of the shares they held as security fell by over 10 per cent the difference had to be repaid by the borrower or the stock was liable to be sold. However, when times changed and there was a general depression of railway property, they did not, or could not, take advantage of their declared policy. They had also taken the precaution of transferring many of the shares into their own hands (a policy which the banks wisely refused to follow) in order to have full control over their disposal should the occasion arise.[24] This proved to be their downfall as they were forced to pay the calls on the shares, it being impossible to sell them on the market because of the capital loss involved. In addition some of the companies appear to have actively participated in the speculation though, if the behaviour of the Northern Investment and Exchange Company is any guide, only to a limited extent.[25] Shareholders in this company received a dividend of 5 per cent in 1846 and 1847 but then nothing until March 1849, when they obtained 25 per cent of their capital back prior to the winding up of the company in 1851.[26] By 1853, like many of the railway mania speculations, all but one of the exchange companies had been liquidated. In contrast the commercial banks emerged relatively unscathed from the post-mania period to continue their policy of assisting established railway companies.

*University of Edinburgh*

## References

1. I am grateful to Professor S. G. Checkland for allowing me to make use of the transcripts of the minute books of the Scottish banks and to the directors of the banks concerned for permission to quote from these transcripts.
2. 'Early Scottish Railways', *Three Banks Review*, June 1967, 29-39.
3. R. H. Campbell, *Scotland Since 1707*, Oxford (1965), 139-42.
4. R. S. Rait, *The History of the Union Bank of Scotland*, Glasgow (1930), 295-6.
5. Minute Book of the Royal Bank of Scotland (MRB), 21 January 1846; Minute Book of the Commercial Bank of Scotland (MCB), 17 October 1844.
6. Scottish Record Office, Edinburgh (SRO), AFR 1/1 passim.
7. This is impossible to say without a detailed survey of the banks' minute books, but the impression gained from a random sample is that few long-term loans were forthcoming for business enterprises. It has not proved possible to verify how many of the shorter-term loans were renewed, but where a check could be made it seems that there was little renewing. However, the results of the check were biased by not knowing how many renewals were sought or how many of the businesses tried other banks.
8. Quoted in J. Reid, *Manual of Scottish Stocks*, Edinburgh (1841), 25.
9. SRO, GNS 1/1, 26 March 1854.
10. Report of the Wishaw and Coltness Railway, 30 June 1835 (Mitchell Library, Glasgow).
11. Minute Book of the British Linen Company, 1 June 1840.
12. SRO, NBR 1/5, 391. See also Select Committee on Borrowing Powers (1864), XI, 97-8.
13. MRB, 6 March 1839.
14. MCB, 17 October 1844.
15. SRO, EPD 1/3, 11, 109, 386; GNS 1/1, 436, 441.
16. Minute Book of the Clydesdale Bank, 22 February 1839.
17. MCB, 1 April 1845.
18. Ibid, also 16 December 1846.
19. A. W. Kerr, *History of Banking in Scotland* (1926), 215.
20. G. Kinnear, *Banks and Exchange Companies*, Glasgow (1947).
21. Quoted in W. H. Marwick, *Economic Developments in Victorian Scotland* (1936), 77.
22. Kinnear, loc cit.
23. MRB, 17 February 1847.
24. SRO, NBR 1/5, 86.
25. SRO, Account Book of the Northern Investment and Exchange Company.
26. Ibid.

MICHAEL ROBBINS

# The Hull & Barnsley at Sea

THIS INQUIRY BEGAN from reading some small print. The last sentence of a footnote to an article by Mr Baron F. Duckham on 'Railway Steamship Enterprise: the Lancashire and Yorkshire Railway's East Coast Fleet 1904–14'[1] stated that 'the Hull & Barnsley Railway also operated steamers for a time, but without much success'. I wondered what these steamers were; and what was in print about this venture. Mr Duckham, in response to an inquiry, wrote that his evidence for stating this was a minute of the Lancashire & Yorkshire East Coast Steamship Conference for 19 September 1907 which recorded the discontinuance of the Hull & Barnsley service. Dr G. D. Parkes's little book on the Hull & Barnsley[2] is silent on the subject, and so are the contemporary articles on the railway to which I had immediate access. Some closer investigation seemed to be called for, to determine whether this was what might be considered a normal extension of the Hull & Barnsley's business activities, or (as most of the railway's actions were) ultimately a move initiated by the Corporation of Hull to do some harm to the North Eastern Railway.[3]

The reasons for harbouring such a thought as this may need a few words of explanation. They are to be found, briefly and conveniently, in Dr G. D. Parkes's book just referred to, or at greater length in W. W. Tomlinson's great history of the North Eastern Railway. In short, the Corporation of Hull was intensely resentful and suspicious of the North Eastern, suspecting that the railway gave preference to the rival ports farther north; and the Hull Dock Company was an independent concern which failed to modernise its antiquated equipment. The corporation at length decided to support a rival railway-and-dock company, and it subscribed £100,000 to the Hull, Barnsley & West Riding Junction Railway & Dock Company (from 1905 the

Hull & Barnsley Railway) on its incorporation in 1880, and transferred certain lands to the new company, on terms which gave the corporation a virtual veto on the policies of the H & B. Two directors were nominated by the corporation; and every time the H & B in its unprosperous succeeding career attempted to make an arrangement with the North Eastern that was commercially sensible, Hull Corporation tried to prevent it. The joint dock Bill of 1899, though opposed by the corporation, was passed into law; but a proposed North Eastern–Hull & Barnsley working agreement was again frustrated by the corporation. Throughout its aim was to use the H & B as a lever to get the NER to do more for Hull than it wanted to. This is why one examines all the policies of the H & B as being those of its ultimate master, Hull Corporation.[4]

The first step in the process of operating, or becoming financially interested in the operation of, seagoing vessels was, for a British railway company, approval by Parliament of an application contained in a private Bill for such powers. This matter had not been absent from the minds of the Hull & Barnsley company when agreements with the North Eastern had been signed on 18 May 1900 and 5 June 1905; as the NER solicitor reported to his board in January 1906, they provided that neither company should oppose an application by the other for steamship powers to continental ports.[5] The Hull & Barnsley deposited a Bill accordingly for the parliamentary session of 1905–6. Charles Trotter, the chairman, tried to reassure the important Hull shipping firm of Thomas Wilson & Co in November 1905,[6] but was unsuccessful in removing their opposition at that stage. Wilson's, the Aire & Calder Navigation Co, and the London & North Western Railway petitioned against the Bill; Wilson's was the last petition to be withdrawn, but the Bill was unopposed by the time it reached the House of Lords' committee in April. Royal assent was pronounced on 20 July 1906.[7]

Explaining the application for steamship powers to the half-yearly meeting of the Hull & Barnsley proprietors on 13 February 1906, the chairman said: 'It does not necessarily mean that we have to start a

## The Hull & Barnsley at Sea

fleet of steamers, but we must have powers.' The Lancashire & Yorkshire, the Great Central, and the North Eastern, he pointed out, all had such powers already.[8] The GCR's predecessor, the Manchester, Sheffield & Lincolnshire, got steamship powers in 1864, the L & Y (for Humber ports) in 1904, and the NER in 1905. The NER operated through a half share (with Thomas Wilson) in the Hull & Netherlands Steamship Co. In an 'Illustrated Interview' with the Hull & Barnsley general manager, published in the *Railway Magazine* for November 1906 but presumably written on information supplied somewhat earlier in the year, Edward Watkin is reported as saying: 'They [the Hull & Barnsley] are now engaged in considering the best means and the direction in which such powers shall be exercised. In this development [of Humber–continental trade] the Hull & Barnsley Railway wish to play their part and to receive their proper share.'[9]

In fact, by the time this article appeared the Hull & Barnsley had decided to go into the steamship business by chartering two vessels to run on the Hull–Rotterdam route; Rotterdam was one of the seventeen ports, ranging from Dunkirk to Stockholm, specified in the Act of 1906. On 30 July the board had considered the possibility of sailings to Rotterdam. On 8 August W. A. Massey (of Brough, one of the directors nominated by the Corporation of Hull to the Hull & Barnsley board) reported that a Hull–Rotterdam service with sailings twice a week 'could probably be conducted without serious loss to the Company provided that arrangements could be made to secure sufficient Coal cargoes outward', and he suggested getting vessels on six-month charter. This recommendation was approved, in spite of its somewhat unenthusiastic commercial forecast, and on 27 November charters of the *Rosebank* and the *Louga* were reported, at £400 and £430 a month respectively.[10]

Two ships bearing the name *Rosebank* appear in *Lloyd's Register of Shipping* for 1906/7; one of them, built in 1901 at West Hartlepool, registered there, and owned by the Pyman Steam Ship Co, had a gross registered tonnage of 3,837. This was too big for the Humber short-sea liner trade—the average tonnage of the Lancashire & Yorkshire

Humber fleet in these years was under 1,000 tons.[11] The other *Rosebank* fills the bill: built 1906 at Glasgow by the Clyde Ship Building and Engineering Co, registered at Wick, and owned by the John O'Groat Steam Shipping Co (its only ship), with gross tonnage of 822 (corrected from 850 in *Lloyd's* later editions). The *Louga* was built in 1898 by Ramage & Ferguson, of Leith, owned by the Rasona Steam Ship Co, of Leith, and registered at Grangemouth, 952 gross registered tons.

Apart from Massey's reference to the prospects of coal traffic outwards, no reference to the type of cargo carried appears to have survived in the railway's records. The expenses incurred in running the steamers appear in the railway's half-yearly accounts as follows:

| | £ |
|---|---|
| Half year ended 31 Dec 1906 | 2,308 |
| ,,   ,,   ,,   30 June 1907 | 1,913 |
| ,,   ,,   ,,   31 Dec 1907 | 637 |

There are no further entries. Revenue derived from the steamer services is not separately shown; but, as the chartering cost itself was £830 a month, these must be net outgoings figures.[12]

At the half-yearly meeting on 12 February 1907, the chairman said that the steamship service to Rotterdam had been in operation too short a time to justify any criticism of the results.[13] Six months later, the chairman (W. S. Wright, who had succeeded Trotter), dealing with what he called the 'gross loss' of £1,913 on the steamers, said that two thirds of it was incurred in January and February, when the boats had to run light owing to the inland navigation on the other side being obstructed by the freezing of the Rhine. The apparent loss was, however, offset by the railway proportion of the traffic which they carried, the general net result being some little gain, which he had every reason to anticipate would be increased if the service was maintained. 'It is conceivable, however,' the chairman went on, 'that the special objects and interests of the Company, which the institution of the steamboat service was designed to promote, may be attained as effectually with a

## The Hull & Barnsley at Sea

less degree of responsibility by some well considered scheme of combination with other shipping companies.'[14]

What the chairman did not reveal was that negotiations had already begun in July with the North Eastern Railway, representing the Hull & Netherlands Steamship Co, with a view to the discontinuance of Hull & Barnsley sailings to Rotterdam if the Hull & Barnsley Co were to be assured of $27\frac{1}{2}$ per cent of imports, excluding North Eastern and Hull & Barnsley local traffic, from the Hull & Netherlands. Arrangements were concluded accordingly with the NER before the end of September.[15] So the item 'steamboat expenses' disappeared from the Hull & Barnsley's accounts. One expense was not shown: both C. W. B. Anderson, their dock superintendent, and James Barton, chief assistant to the accountant, on their way to Rotterdam on the company's business, were drowned when the Great Eastern Railway's steamer *Berlin* was wrecked off the Hook of Holland on 21 February 1907. The board awarded pensions to their widows.[16]

The carefully guarded expressions used on behalf of the Hull & Barnsley in relation to their steamship operations, and the extreme shortness of time during which actual charter operations were conducted—at a period in which the chairman described the increase in general railway traffic as 'phenomenal'[17]—suggest that the railway went to sea for tactical reasons. Its aim seems to have been to get a guaranteed share in the rail haulage of certain imported goods; and this it achieved, to the tune of $27\frac{1}{2}$ per cent of those not local to either of the railways directly serving Hull. The Hull & Netherlands Steamship Co improved its Rotterdam service; in July 1908 it began daily sailings between Hull and Rotterdam, with five ships named after Yorkshire abbeys—*Jervaulx*, *Kirkham*, *Rievaulx*, *Selby*, and *Whitby*. These continued until the outbreak of war in 1914.[18]

It looks very much as though the steamship venture was another minor but irritating skirmish in the long series of actions waged by the Corporation of Hull, through its instrument the Hull & Barnsley Railway, against the detested would-be monopolist, the North Eastern. Embarked on with no real expectation of commercial success, its result may have seemed worthwhile to the North Eastern's enemies in Hull. It was certainly another barb in its flesh.

London

## References

1. *Business History*, 10 (1968), 44–57; note 3 to p 49.
2. G. D. Parkes, *The Hull & Barnsley Railway* (Oakwood Press edns of 1946, 1948, 1959).
3. I am indebted to Mr W. J. MacDonald, Keeper of Records, BTHR, York, for assistance in my inquiries there, and for telling me of the *Berlin* connection; and to Mr V. W. Walker for help in investigations in London.
4. G. G. MacTurk, *History of the Hull Railways* (Hull 1879); Parkes, *Hull & Barnsley Railway*, 2–5; W. W. Tomlinson, *The North Eastern Railway: Its Rise and Development* (1914), 623–5, 663–4, 703–21.
5. NER, Solicitor's reports to Board, January 1906: British Transport Historical Records, York, NER 6/1.
6. BTHR, York, HBR 1/9 (cited as 'Board'), minute 2832, 29 November 1905.
7. Board min 2872, 27 February 1906; 2882, 27 March 1906; 2889, 24 April 1906; 2917, 30 July 1906.
8. BTHR, HBR 1/5, 13 February 1906.
9. *Railway Magazine*, 19 (1906), 405.
10. Board min 2918, 30 July 1906; 2931, 8 August 1906; 2965, 27 November 1906.
11. Duckham, article cited in note 1, 49.
12. H & BR Accounts, BTHR, RAC/Y1.
13. HBR 1/5, 12 February 1907.
14. *Railway Times*, 10 August 1907, 150 (without the last sentence); *Railway News*, 17 August 1907, 319, 349.
15. Board min 3058, 30 July 1907 (using the expression 'Hull and Holland Joint Committee'); 3075, 24 September 1907.
16. Board min 3009, 26 February 1907; 3020, 26 March 1907.
17. *Railway Times*, 10 August 1907, 150.
18. R. Bell, *Twenty-Five Years of the North Eastern Railway 1898–1922* (1951), 38.

# Book Reviews

**Railways and Economic Growth in England and Wales 1840–1870**, by G. R. Hawke, OXFORD UNIVERSITY PRESS, 1970, pp xiv + 421, diagrams, £6.

It is to be hoped that this important study will be welcomed more warmly than those from which it derives, the work of Fogel and others. One way of answering the question: 'what were the consequences of X?' is to use counterfactual analysis, ie, by asking 'what would have happened in the absence of X?' (sceptics might do worse than read J. D. Gould's lucid, persuasive and cautious article 'Hypothetical History' in the *Economic History Review*, 1969). G. R. Hawke has set himself the task of establishing the effects of railways on economic growth in England and Wales. He does this by assessing the 'social saving' (the difference between the cost of rail traffic and the cost which would have been incurred if railways had not been built) supplemented by linkages from the railways, such as the effects on particular industries, to see what other influences on economic growth there may have been. His main conclusion is that in 1865, the year selected for special examination, the railways contributed at least 10 per cent of the national income. The finding is important in itself, but the book's greatest significance is its meticulous demonstration of one way of tackling a problem, using the methods of quantitative economics.

This approach begins with a model and proceeds to an examination of the empirical material. The bulk of the book is devoted to the latter: a careful examination of the facts, using archival sources where possible, from which are produced series of figures. The author estimates, for example, series of ton-miles and passenger-mile statistics, establishes the cost by rail and also by the 'alternative' transport system. All the evidence is clearly set out; the reader can accept it, or he can reject or modify it if he has better information.

The two parts of the study—the model and the facts (essentially a series of arithmetical calculations)—can both be assessed for their validity. It is, I think, a pity that the model is not elaborated. In his introductory chapter the author evaluates the American work, an important contribution to the debate. But it would have been useful if he had set down the 'explicit assumptions and conditions' (p 30) which this technique demands. This lack is highlighted by chapter 14, 'externalities', where he briefly examines a number of ways in which the railways might have influenced economic growth beyond the direct use of rail transport (eg, by the diffusion of management techniques, and by the habit of investing). The problem here is this: what does one include? Precisely because the railways were such a major innovation, might they not have influenced all manner of relevant economic and social variables?

The empirical material similarly raises questions. Since the series he requires often do not exist he has to make estimates using the best available (including qualitative) information. This is straightforward enough for the discussion of rail transport. It is a different matter for the alternative transport system, especially when the sources are so meagre. For example, on the basis of the experience of two canal companies in the early nineteenth century he concludes, reasonably enough, that they operated under conditions of constant cost, and uses this as the basis for the later period. But would the canals have been able to carry the vastly expanded traffic with no increase in cost? Would not more canals have had to be built, or existing ones improved?

Clearly this is not an easy book; it has an intellectual rigour unusual in transport historiography. There is something daunting in the author's statement on p 284 that a sentence he quotes 'is best explained by exploring the algebra used to obtain it'. But the book is well written. There is precision in the use of words—perhaps a by-product of the requirements of this technique—and the author has an eye for the terse and cogent phrase. How succinct is his sentence on p 270: 'Railway companies treated their skilled employees with paternal firmness, and labourers were easy to replace.' It is indeed essential to state that this is more than an essay in the quantitative economics of the past. The blurb is right in saying that this approach is combined with 'the traditional methods of historians'. At the same time the latter can observe the ways of a different kind of methodology.

The publishing standard is high, but a few errors have crept in. On p 44 the figures of passenger costs are different from those in Table II.02. Footnote 2, p 399, should read 'cf., p. 348' not '384'. *Herapath* is wrongly spelt.

*Ruskin College, Oxford*                                                      Harold Pollins

**Early Wooden Railways,** by M. J. T. Lewis, ROUTLEDGE & KEGAN PAUL, pp xxiv + 436, ill, maps and diagrams, £8.

In his handling of what he rightly calls 'this comparatively unknown subject', Dr Lewis has undertaken a colossal task and has presented the results of his researches in a logical and readable way for which all students of the pre-history of railways must ever be grateful. This is not to say that the volume makes light reading, and indeed it is not intended to do so, but it is a work which no future writer on the subject can afford to ignore. This is the fruit of far more extensive and detailed scholarly research in this field than has been undertaken previously, as is exemplified by some 1,157 annotations in support of his statements.

Throughout, the word railway is used in its basic sense as being a prepared track which so guides the vehicles running upon it that they cannot leave the track, but the one limitation imposed by the title is that the rails are made of wood. This excludes the railways of the ancient world, as they were not wooden; the author also observes that 'they have no bearing at all on what came after'. The book thus sets out to cover the history of railways in Great Britain and Europe down to 1830, in so far as the rails were made of wood, and, for some centuries, these were used almost exclusively in the mining industry.

On the Continental side, Dr Lewis's work has been much more the discovery and collation of published material than delving into archives, but it should be emphasised that this does not mean relying on secondary sources, as most of such material consists either of contemporary descriptions printed at the time, or of subsequent publications of original manuscripts. The handling of this is in itself no mean task, as sources have been found in more than a dozen languages, and these, of course, not in their modern forms. German, Czech, and Hungarian records have produced some surprising details, and numerous remarkable illustrations. Among the latter, a military railway c 1430 from Munich, and a mining rail vehicle depicted on an altar triptych in the cathedral of Rosenau in Upper Hungary, are but representative of numerous treasures.

Happily, Dr Lewis has assumed that the reader is not a linguist and has translated into English all quotations, whatever the original language. The only exception to this rule is provided by the textual use of a few basic German technical terms which have no exact equivalent word in modern English. A nine-page glossary of both English and German mining terms is a valued feature. The problem of variations in place-names has been met by using those forms which appear most commonly in the mining documents, and cross-referencing the variants in the index. Local standards of weights and measures provide another hurdle, but the author has left them 'without any elaborate attempts at conversion'. With money, he has assumed that groschen and guilders mean nothing to most English readers, and has 'ventured to convert all German and Austrian monetary values into English terms appropriate to the period in question'.

Thus far we have been considering mainly the Continental side of the story, which occupies 85 pages, or approximately one-fifth of the whole work, but this is justified by the fact that it is covering mainly new ground, at any rate in the English language. In dealing with Great Britain, Dr Lewis tells us that he has relied far more on archives than on the printed word, and certainly his sources are widespread. Nevertheless, he shows a familiarity with most worthwhile printed works of reference up to a very recent date. As the immediate ancestor of the modern railway, the Newcastle waggonway is given the most detailed treatment that we have seen. Separate chapters deal with its early development; wayleaves and engineering; track; waggons; and operating and maintenance. Under the heading of 'the Shropshire railway', Dr Lewis elaborates on the distinctive features, to meet somewhat different needs, of the narrower-gauge lines in the Severn Valley.

Other historians will not necessarily agree with all the author's deductions from his new material, but difference as to the interpretation of facts is of the essence of historical study, and in no way diminishes our indebtedness to Dr Lewis for having discovered the facts. Both text and illustrations are so well produced as to make a really pleasant volume, and a 24 page index renders readily available the wealth of material contained in a noteworthy contribution to transport history.

*London* Charles E. Lee

**Railway Relics,** by Bryan Morgan, IAN ALLAN, London, 1969, pp 128, 40 plates, £2.10.

*Railway Relics* is a general introduction to the architectural and mechanical aspects of railway history, related specifically to surviving items, both 'preserved' and in use. It is welcome for treating architecture and civil engineering with the same enthusiasm as locomotives, though chronological, rather than subject, division of the chapters would have helped in relating different types of relic within their period. The space given to tramroads seems over-generous by comparison with the interest of their relics to the general reader.

The specialist might dispute the existence of a 'national tramway system', but will in any case find this book of little appeal. The author admits his dependence on secondary sources, acceptable in a book of this kind, though personal inquiry could, for example, have cleared up his doubts on the provenance of the section of 'Ticknall tramroad' track 'reported to be in place' at Ashby station (it came from a very different tramway, the electric Burton & Ashby Light Railways), and exorcised the concrete ghost of the wooden tramroad bridge at Preston. Checking and proof reading should also have removed errors like the references to the opening of Liverpool Lime Street in 1830, 'Great Chesterfield' near Cambridge, and 'Andrew Hankyside'.

The text is generally readable, though condensing seems in places to have led to confusion, as in the description of the stations at Ambergate, and language purists may view with alarm the 'conventionalisation' of the Bodmin & Wadebridge Railway. Some illustrations are of interest, though others are a little indistinct, or have lost vital portions in blockmaking.

More seriously, the book's usefulness is virtually destroyed by the astonishing omission of an index (apart from a list of engineers and architects), or even of any cross-references between text and gazetteer. If, also, more details had been given with each entry, the gazetteer might have resembled more closely the 'indispensable work of reference' the jacket claims it to be, and would have been a better guide to the 'hundred journeys of exploration' promised.

Altogether, it is more a book for the non-specialist visitor to the various preserved lines and museums, who may gain from it an idea of the relative historical importance of what he has seen. If he picks up some of the author's enthusiasm, all to the good, though Mr Morgan's hope that railway preservation may be publicly regarded in the same way as art and music seems unlikely to be realised.

*Romiley* J. A. Hall

**Shipping and the American War 1775–83: A Study of British Transport Organisation,** by David Syrett, THE ATHLONE PRESS, London, 1970, pp 274, £3.25.

Dr Syrett's monograph is an intensive discussion of the attempt to supply and maintain an army of 30,000 men in the American and West Indian colonies during the American War of Independence. The main title of the volume thus implies a broader investigation than the one which actually evolves: the reader who hopes to find a detailed case-study of the manifold problems of shipping and commerce during an eighteenth-century war will be disappointed. The difficulties inherent in merchant shipping during the American War are wholly incidental to the author's main task and any allusion to them owes an obvious debt to the researches of Professor Ralph Davis. Dr Syrett's aim is rather to uncover the means by which an eighteenth-century administration was able to transport a British army to the American continent and keep it relatively well supplied over seven years of war. As he emphasises, this was a logistics problem unique to modern history and probably not repeated for any other nation until the world wars of the twentieth century. Moreover, the authorities had to acquire the necessary vessels for this gigantic operation without the benefit of twentieth-century weapons of governmental control: they had to enter the market and hire ships through competitive bidding rather than by requisition. The ensuing examination of how this was done is strongly based on the abundant Admiralty and Colonial Office Papers in the PRO. The author's use of the former serves yet again to illustrate their value for historians of eighteenth-century British shipping. Each ship procured by the Navy Board for transporting troops had to be inspected, measured and fitted out wherever possible at a royal dockyard before entering government service, and the recorded examinations constitute an archive of great importance in the assessment of eighteenth-century merchant vessels.

Although primarily engaged in an exercise in administrative history, Dr Syrett has managed in two chapters to give, in some detail, the experiences of the Navy Board's transports and victuallers during the war. These should be of particular interest to transport historians if only for their evocative description of life on board ship. Again by concentrating on a relatively esoteric area of eighteenth-century history, the author has been able to throw interesting light on several important historiographical issues of the period. For example, he demonstrates convincingly that a major reason for the success of the

American rebellion was the British government's unwillingness to concentrate sufficiently on the transport and victualling services. Indeed, the evidence presented suggests that the system of supply was on the verge of collapse in 1782–3, clearly illustrating the yawning gap between government intention and action in the eighteenth century.

Though the approach is lucid and analytical, the author has a tendency to labour obvious points by illustrating them with several paragraphs of evidence and sometimes displays a fondness for the extreme, cut and dried generalisation. Thus British–American trade did not cease with the outbreak of hostilities (as Dr Syrett suggests, p 78); rather commerce did continue, though on a reduced scale, through Canada, Florida and British-held ports. Surely the government was not as unaware of the importance of the transport service as Dr Syrett implies? A more sympathetic appraisal (looking at the problem not simply through the eyes of the Navy Board) would probably have stressed the financial, administrative and political limitations on government action and that, given the scale and novelty of the problem involved, how well in the short run it was tackled.

*University of Strathclyde*                                  T. M. Devine

**Transport Studies: An Introduction,** by John Hibbs, JOHN BAKER, 1970, pp 120, ill, maps, £1.75.

The study of transport systems and the economics of their operation has grown rapidly in the last decade or so, not perhaps surprisingly in view of the enormous problems that transport has thrown up. A good introduction to the main issues is now badly needed but it can hardly be said that the present volume fills that gap. Despite the rather impressive-sounding blurb the book falls far short of expectations. It consists of six rather slim chapters four of which tell us very little indeed, while the remaining two on the function and control of transport do not get very far beyond the descriptive level. Even allowing for the fact that it is conceived as a fairly elementary text it will hardly provide very much for the student on which to sharpen his teeth. It is well written and easy to read and Mr Hibbs runs through most of the problems which face transport operators in Britain and the implications of these for consumers and the public at large. The main objection is that the treatment is so cursory, with little attempt being made to analyse the major economic and social issues such as investment allocation, pricing policies, cost-benefit analysis, congestion, subsidies etc. It is difficult to see quite what market the book will serve for even the intelligent layman will demand a little more than this limited treatment. It will scarcely serve the purposes set forth in the Foreword to the volume.

Nor is the volume terribly accurate. It is somewhat unfortunate that Mr Stebbings in his Foreword to the book suggests that the author 'never misleads the reader'. In fact there are many misleading, ambiguous or incorrect statements, some of which no doubt arise through lack of supporting evidence. To substantiate this criticism I shall note some of the points which call for correction, modification or elaboration. For example, it is very unlikely that British Railways were the first in the field with new financial techniques (p 24). Anyone who has read the evidence and memoranda relating to the First Report from the Select Committee on Nationalised Industries, 1967-8, would realise this was not correct. Despite the recently announced Weaver Junction–Glasgow scheme, I was surprised to find that 'officially the policy in Great Britain is to electrify the [railway] system' (p 34). No evidence is given to support the rather dubious statement (p 37) that on balance buses brought as much traffic to the railways as they took away. On pages 48 and 50 there are some very loose and meaningless statements about the effects of the repeal of the Navigation Laws on shipping and the slowness with which parliamentary control was extended to the railways. Surely the reverse is true in the latter case. Most of the independent airlines were absorbed by BEA in 1946–7 (p 52), while it is doubtful whether the independents could be regarded as effective in the 1930s. The figures on page 57 referring to private expenditure on travel appear quite nonsensical and the Geddes Report is quoted twice with the wrong date (p 36, n 3, and p 62). The opening sentence of the second paragraph on page 69 gives the reader a very ambiguous impression about the structure of airport ownership. On page 75 the author implies that the conference system in shipping was a substitute for mergers and the emergence of large firms. In fact both occurred simultaneously. Finally, on page 80 he assumes, on the basis of wage costs on the railways, that transport is generally labour intensive; in fact, compared with other industries capital intensity in transport is relatively very high.

With considerably more effort this could have been a useful book; as it stands I doubt whether it will serve as a suitable introduction to transport studies.

*University of Leicester*                                    Derek H. Aldcroft

**The Canals of North West England,** by Charles Hadfield and Gordon Biddle, DAVID & CHARLES, Newton Abbot, 1970, 2 vols, pp 236 & 260, ill, maps and diagrams, £2.50 each.

The canals of the North West have always attracted attention, largely because of their connection with the industrial development of the region, but their rise and decline have not hitherto been described for the region as a whole. In this latest addition to the well-known series 'The Canals of the British Isles', all the canals of the North West (except the Manchester Ship Canal) are dealt with, whether they be 5 furlongs or 100 miles in length. The result is a complex picture of promotion, construction, rivalry and decline. There is much of interest in this picture; for example, the amount of passenger traffic on the canals (64,414 passengers were carried on the Manchester, Bolton & Bury Canal in 1833–4, but four years later this traffic had been killed by the railways); or again the extent to which the canal companies themselves acted as carriers. There is some shattering of old myths, especially 'the myth that the Liverpool and Manchester Railway was a response to inefficiency and monopoly charges by the waterways'; here the examination of the 'three competing waterways' between Manchester and Liverpool makes it difficult to accept Jackman's account of the railway as a response to canal and river monopoly. Whether monopolistic or not, the canals lived by the carriage of goods, but here the evidence presented is fragmentary. It does show, however, the importance of corn, lime and limestone as well as of coal; unfortunately goods were often described simply as 'merchandise', and no breakdown of this seems possible. The role of the canals in bringing food and building materials to the growing industrial towns would merit fuller investigation.

This book gives the best and fullest account of the canals of the North West that has hitherto appeared, but it has all the merits and defects of the series to which it belongs. The merits are considerable: there is much new information based on the canal companies' own records, but a bibliography, at least of manuscript sources, would have been helpful; there are useful maps and pleasant and appropriate pictures. The defects are less easy to define, but the frequent absence of page references to books cited in the footnotes is an obvious example. Sometimes the detail seems excessive, especially in the discussion of abortive schemes; sometimes it is rather trivial as in the account of Queen Victoria's visit to the canal at Worsley in 1851. All facts are not born free and equal, and some of the detail might well have been sacrificed for a discussion of where the money for canals really came from. On this point the authors are largely silent, despite the present interest in capital formation and in the sources of investment. It would be an interesting experiment to write the history of canals, not from the usual standpoint of the canal enthusiast, but from the standpoint of the canal shareholder.

*University of Manchester*          T. S. Willan

**After the Canal Duke: A Study of the Industrial Estates administered by the Trustees of the Third Duke of Bridgewater in the Age of Railway Building, 1825–1872,** by F. C. Mather, CLARENDON PRESS: OXFORD UNIVERSITY PRESS, 1970, pp xx + 392, ill, £4.

The publication of Professor David Spring's pioneering studies opened the way to wide reassessments of the role of the landed families in nineteenth-century industrial development. Behind the aristocratic fronts there often lay considerable industrial empires: collieries and ironworks, canals and railways, harbours, markets and urban conglomerations vastly increased the rural wealth of many old dynasties. Among the foremost of such ventures was the canal and coal complex developed in South Lancashire by the 3rd and last Duke of Bridgewater and managed, after his death in 1803, by a distinguished trust on behalf of his carefully-nominated heirs.

Such writers as Messrs Bernard Falk, Charles Hadfield, Hugh Malet, Frank Mullineaux and V. I. Tomlinson have told us much about the unique 'Canal Duke' and his 'Bridgewater Millions'. In his latest book Dr Mather of Southampton University has traced the later history of the Bridgewater enterprises. And his long-awaited volume provides a uniquely detailed case-study of a major aristocratic industrial venture.

Dr Mather relates a very complicated story: the duke's 66 page will virtually ensured this. Bridgewater divided his extensive estates, leaving the Lancashire and Northamptonshire properties to his nephew, Lord Gower (who became 2nd Marquess of Stafford and 1st Duke of Sutherland). Stafford was to be succeeded by his second son, Lord Francis Leveson-Gower (who adopted the duke's surname of Egerton and was created Earl of Ellesmere). Such genealogical complexities led to practical considerations: for instance, Stafford took much care over balancing the prospective fortunes of his heirs, Earl Gower and Lord Francis.

Bridgewater went further, laying down not only the composition but also the detailed powers of the trust. The original administrators were his nephews-in-law, Sir Archibald Macdonald and E. V. Vernon-Harcourt (later Archbishop of York), together with the all-powerful superintendent, Robert Bradshaw. From 1803 to 1834 Bradshaw ruled with an iron hand, largely ignoring the wishes of the beneficiaries; and his nominated successor, James Sothern (who survived until 1837) was equally arrogant. Above all, the history was complicated by the fact that management of an important mineral and transport undertaking inevitably led the trustees into a morass of political, legal, social and transport alliances, strategies and plots.

Dr Mather's extensive researches among 'both very voluminous and very scattered' family and other papers allow him to lead the reader clearly through a tangled mass of details. He shows that able and ubiquitous Leveson-Gower agent James Loch, the organiser of the Sutherland clearances, manager of various aristocratic properties and liberal Whig intellectual, as the very capable Ellesmere superintendent from 1837. He examines in detail the canal's reactions to railway competition from the first talk of connecting Liverpool with Manchester and Birmingham in the 1820s. And he convincingly explains the long-continued mystery of Stafford's involvement with the L & M (which was designed to protect both of his sons).

The trust's operations are traced through many vicissitudes. There were difficulties over buying out Bradshaw and Sothern and replacing them with the dependable Loch. There was periodic rationalisation of management structure and operational plans, between years of enthusiastic expansion and worrying periods of consolidation. There were complicated negotiations over rates and routes with other undertakings. Dr Mather shows that the trustees were able 'on balance to hold their own' against the railways until the late forties. 'Historians of transport', he writes, 'have been too frequently content not to raise the question of causation in studying disputes between rail and water, tacitly assuming that railways were born with a "manifest destiny" to crush canals. There is a danger, however, of using too much hindsight in interpreting the motives both of railway directors and of canal proprietors. If conflicts came, it by no means follows that this was because the men in control planned several stages ahead that they should come.' But 'the Bridgewater people' (as Dr. Mather latterly calls them) were exceptional managers, with a large annual income and the security of vast aristocratic capital. They developed a network of local agents, expensively bought out such rivals as the Mersey & Irwell Navigation, learned how to deal with dishonest private carriers and defaulting allies and gradually became adept at balancing-out rival railways in a long-continued battle. Nevertheless, from 1844 the thought of an ultimate sale was implanted in the trustees' minds.

Railway development and amalgamations undoubtedly weakened 'the Duke's' position as a canal venture. It was one thing to play off competing local lines and waterways and another matter to take on the LNWR, the L & YR and the GWR. Yet 'what the Trust suffered from was not a dearth of ideas of how to come to terms with the railways, but a surfeit of them'. Loch, George Fereday Smith (the actual manager during 1837–87) and the Hon A. F. Egerton (Loch's successor as superintendent during 1855–91) skilfully negotiated strategic and tactical alliances with carriers, canals, railways and commercial interests. Few holds were barred in such contests. When, during an 1849 freight contest, the LNWR publicised the non-insurance of Mersey tideway goods, the trustees threatened to publish lists of the railway's passenger accidents. But eventually the trust accepted railway agencies, while diplomatically dividing the railway companies by masterly manoeuvres in the fifties. It was less easy to discipline the 'piratical' New Quay Company, which constantly defrauded the trust under an implicitly blackmailing Anti-Corn Law League directorate.

The GWR alliance proved disappointing; an alliance with the LNWR was logical, for geographic reasons, because of the company's independent position and perhaps, as Dr Mather hints, because the chairman, Lord Chandos (later 3rd Duke of Buckingham) sympathised with another venture controlled by a duke's son. But there was always a dual policy: the canals might be either sold or strengthened, and the trustees constantly considered both alternatives. At length the empire began to dissolve. The canal interests were sold in

1872; the land and the still developing Worsley collieries passed from the trustees to the 3rd Lord Ellesmere in 1903 and to a joint stock company in 1923; and the mines were nationalised in 1947.

It must be said that this is not a particularly easy book to read; one is inclined to become bemused by the intricacies of the narrative. But Dr Mather's volume was well worth waiting for. It is one of those rare books which are of importance to a wide spectrum of historians: it will be of interest to business historians, to those interested in the development of managerial techniques, to students of the landed interest and to all transport historians. The fact that Dr Mather obviously understands his chosen period in its entirety contributes to the virtues of a particularly distinguished book.

*University of Strathclyde* J. T. Ward

# Our Contributors

K. A. MACMAHON is Senior Lecturer in History in the University of Hull. His extensive publications on East Yorkshire history have included a number of booklets and papers on transport subjects and he is at present preparing books on early transport history and on Beverley. Mr MacMahon contributed to *Transport History* in July 1969.

F. C. MATHER, Senior Lecturer in History in the University of Southampton, is well known for his work on Chartism. His writings include *Public Order in the Age of the Chartists* (1959) and *After the Canal Duke* (1970).

DR WRAY VAMPLEW is Lecturer in Economic History in the University of Edinburgh. His doctoral thesis was on Scottish railway finance and he is author of several papers on related themes. Dr Vamplew previously contributed to *Transport History* in July 1970.

MICHAEL ROBBINS needs no introduction to transport historians. Of his many books, *The Railway Age* (1962), is probably the best known. Mr Robbins has been a member of London Transport Board since 1965 and was joint editor of the *Journal of Transport History* 1953–65. Besides his interest in transport he has done much to further the study and enjoyment of local history.

# Shorter Reviews

**Slow Boat through England,** by Frederic Doerflinger, ALLAN WINGATE, London, 1970, pp 253, ill, 35s (£1·75).

This is an attractive book, combining instruction in the rudiments of canal cruising with descriptions of many interesting cruising routes. Historical information is introduced where necessary, but the chief value of this volume is probably in its description of English canals at a crossroads in their history, with commercial traffic steadily declining, and canal cruising rapidly growing in popularity.

**Trams in Colour since 1945,** by J. Joyce, and **Buses and Trolleybuses 1919 to 1945,** by David Kay, BLANDFORD PRESS, London, 1970, pp 160 and 191, ill, 30s (£1·50) each.

Blandford have become well known as publishers of handsomely-illustrated handbooks on aircraft, road and rail vehicles. Each of these volumes has eighty pages of colour plates, with a general introduction and detailed notes on the subjects. Interesting features of both are the number of preserved vehicles included, and in the case of the tram volume, the number of early colour views.

**Traction Engines in the North,** and **Railways in the North,** by David Joy, DALESMAN PUBLISHING COMPANY LTD, Clapham, via Lancaster, 1970, pp 96, ill, 10s 6d (52½p) and 11s (55p).

Two new publications in the 'Dalesman' paperback series, the bulk of these volumes is taken up by photographs and details of rally traction engines, and of railway scenes. In the traction engine volume there is a short historical introduction illustrated by some fine early photographs, while in the railway book there are some really superb historic views.

**Fowler Steam Road Vehicles—Catalogues and Working Instructions,** edited by W. J. Hughes, DAVID & CHARLES, Newton Abbot, 1970, pp xvii + 134, ill, 35s (£1·75).

This is basically a reprint of three Fowler catalogues and the working instructions for road rollers and traction engines, while W. J. Hughes has added a neat nine-page history of John Fowler & Co's contribution to steam road-vehicle design. The company material is typical of the 1920s in layout and emphasis. It is good to have these scarce publications reprinted in a handy form.

**Industrial Steam Album,** by M. J. Fox and G. D. King, IAN ALLAN, London, 1970, pp 144, ill, 50s (£2·50).

One of the best books of its type and price the reviewer has seen, this is a superb collection of photographs of industrial locomotives in a wide variety of settings. The quality of the blocks is particularly good, making a pleasant change from some other recent albums. The enormous range of conditions under which industrial locomotives worked, and the many variations on the 0-4-0T and 0-6-0T are immediately apparent, as also is the aesthetic appeal of the steam locomotive at work.

### The GWR Stars, Castles & Kings, Part 2: 1930–1965, by O. S. Nock, DAVID & CHARLES, Newton Abbot, 1970, pp 160, ill, 60s (£3).

This is the latest in the David & Charles series of locomotive monographs, and is a worthy successor to the popular first part. A straightforward approach is adopted, the result being a very readable account of modifications to a sound basic design and their effects on performance. Particularly interesting is an artist's impression of the proposed *Pacific* of the war years. With domed boiler and 'King'-type bogie and cylinders, it looks like a 'Great Westernised' *Princess Royal*.

### The Fairlie Locomotive, by Rowland A. S. Abbott, DAVID & CHARLES, Newton Abbot, 1970, pp 103, ill, 50s (£2·50).

Mr Abbott, author of a series of articles in *The Engineer* on the same subject, deals comprehensively with perhaps the most fascinating of articulated locomotives. Ranging in size from the tiny locomotives on the Festiniog Railway to 138 ton monsters on the Mexican Railway, the Fairlie failed to achieve permanent success, though built in small numbers for many railways. Mr Abbott has succeeded in tracking down almost all reported Fairlie and Fairlie-type locomotives, and presents his findings concisely and clearly.

### Mediterranean Island Railways, by P. M. Kalla-Bishop, DAVID & CHARLES, Newton Abbot, 1970, pp 207, ill, maps, 50s (£2·50), and The Malta Railway, by B. L. Rigby, OAKWOOD PRESS, Lingfield, Surrey, 1970, pp 63, ill, maps and diagrams, 18s (90p).

By a curious coincidence, two books on the railways of Mediterranean islands have appeared almost simultaneously. Mr Kalla-Bishop's book deals comprehensively with all the islands which have or had rail systems, concentrating largely on Sicily and Sardinia. The successful modernisation of the Corsican system makes cheerful reading, and there is an interesting appendix on mineral railways. The Malta Railway only rates four pages, and no illustrations in an otherwise well-illustrated book, so Mr Rigby's booklet with its eight pages of illustrations, as well as maps and diagrams, is complementary to, rather than competitive with *Mediterranean Island Railways*. This was a curious line, which failed as a private railway, was taken over by the British Government, re-equipped and run at a profit until bus competition killed it off in 1931. The line had an underground terminus at Valletta, charming Beyer Peacock 2-6-2 tank locomotives, and rolling stock having affinities with both Irish and Welsh narrow-gauge prototypes.

### Railway Accidents of Great Britain and Europe, by Ascario Schneider and Armin Masé, translated from the German by E. L. Delloco, DAVID & CHARLES, Newton Abbot, 1970, pp 334, ill, maps and diagrams, 70s (£3·50).

A rather disconnected and sometimes inaccurate account of some of the more important European railway accidents, the work is valuable in drawing the attention of British readers to continental rail disasters, and has some interesting illustrations.

**Veteran and Vintage Cars, and Commercial Vehicles**, both by Cecil Gibson; **Older Locomotives (1900–42)**, by P. G. Gomm; and **Recent Locomotives (1947–70)**, by P. E. Randall, NELSON, London, 1970, pp 62 each, ill, 16s (80p) each.

The first in the publisher's Troy Model Club Series, each of these volumes has sixteen pages of beautiful coloured photographs of commercial models. Their appearance is symptomatic of the growing interest in collecting these items and because of their attractive format they should attract newcomers to the hobby.

**Handley Page: An Aircraft Album**, by Donald C. Clayton, IAN ALLAN, London, 1970, pp 126, ill, £1.50.

For this first monograph on the products of individual aircraft companies, the publishers have chosen Handley Page—a name that has figured prominently in the relatively short history of air transport. Unfortunately, since the book was written this great company has itself passed into history.

After an introduction outlining the history of Handley Page, the author mentions some of the valuable aerodynamic research carried out by the company, including the well-known leading-edge slat used to increase wing lift at low speed. Very much of the book is devoted to descriptions of each type of aircraft produced by Handley Page arranged in chronological order. Then follows a few words about some of the projects and proposals which did not fly and the author concludes with a complete type and production list of all the 150 Handley Page aircraft, real and projected.

Naturally, in a book of this size it is impossible to describe 150 aircraft in great detail. The technical information is limited and there are no three-view drawings, but almost every type which was built is illustrated and these photographs are outstanding. To have located photographs of some of the obscure types is a fine achievement, yet for the student of air transport the Handley Page airliners are naturally the most interesting subjects. The confusing period after World War I when Handley Page bombers were converted to airliners is clearly described and illustrated. Then follows the W8 through to the Herald and Jetstream including, of course, the ever-popular HP42 Hannibal.

*Royal Scottish Museum*     J. D. Storer

**The Midland & Great Northern Joint Railway**, by A. J. Wrottesley, DAVID & CHARLES, Newton Abbot, 1970, pp 221, 33 plates, maps and drawings, £2.50.

Any future historian of the Midland & Great Northern Joint Railway will have to acknowledge some degree of indebtedness to this study by A. J. Wrottesley. With praiseworthy thoroughness and accuracy, and in a manner that compels interest, the story of the system is recounted from the origins of the individual component companies to the final decline and closures under British Rail. Besides a chapter on rolling stock there are various sections, sometimes supplemented by line drawings, on equipment and other aspects of operation so that, overall, the treatment is sufficiently comprehensive to satisfy virtually all classes of reader. However, the cover's claim that this is a 'definitive' history requires some qualification: for to be so far more would be needed on the motivations and backgrounds of many of the proposals and developments, especially so the early ones, together with much more detailed discussion of financial aspects, and a keener awareness of the subtleties of the economic relationships between the railway and the areas it served.

This is, however, not to belittle Mr Wrottesley's work which has in fact encompassed a surprising amount within some 200 pages. Seven excellent local maps provide a valuable complement to the text, although the general map of the system would have gained substantially from a more forceful distinction between the M & GNR and other lines. The thirty-three plates are well produced, reasonably wide ranging in subject matter, and often of considerable historical interest, particularly the 1862 view of a train in Long Sutton station. The index is extensive and reliable and the appendices, comprising a table of opening dates, mileage tables, details of single-line sections, names and dates of directors and locomotive statistics, must serve to enhance the book in the eyes of any student. Finally, a word of mild complaint must be registered against the excessive number of sub-titles (for example, twenty-two in a chapter of seventeen pages); the practice may contribute to ease of reference but it is a grave hindrance to development of a smooth narrative and it tends to thrust relative trivialities into prominence. But this is perhaps a merely captious remark when so much has been achieved.

*Newport, Essex*            D. I. Gordon

**London Midland & Scottish: a Railway in Retrospect,** by C. H. Ellis, IAN ALLAN, London, 1970, pp 224, ill, £3.

As Mr Ellis notes in his introduction, this book is not presented as a history of its subject, and although the work has a loose chronological framework, there is no attempt to set the difficulties under which the LMS had to work in wider perspective. As might be expected, Mr Ellis's treatment leans heavily towards the mechanical and operational side, and there is undue emphasis (regrettably usual in works of this nature) on railway accidents. The finances of the company are barely mentioned, and there is no discussion of traffic figures or dividends. Although flashes of Mr Ellis's unmistakable style make this an easy book to read, the transport historian will, therefore, chiefly find interest in those sections where Mr Ellis has drawn on personal information which would not otherwise have survived. On this basis, it is to be hoped that few will be misled by Mr Ellis's complete reversal of the actual expectations and experience of the Liverpool & Manchester Railway in his statement about that company on p 115.

*University of Glasgow*     Malcolm Reed

**The Easingwold Railway,** by K. E. Hartley, THE OAKWOOD PRESS, Lingfield, 1970, pp 55, ill, 75p.

Oakwood's 46th 'Locomotion Paper' examines the 2½ mile Easingwold Railway, linking a north Yorkshire market town with the NER line at Alne. After periodic discussion from 1836, the local squire, Sir George Wombwell, secured an Act in 1887 and the line was enthusiastically opened in 1891. The little venture survived until 1957, carrying cereals, vegetables, coal, manures, wartime ammunition and declining numbers of passengers (in 1947 634 3rd class and one 1st class, the latter paying 8d). Profits were small and dividends negligible; but the Easingwold was a 'family' railway, backed by such real rail enthusiasts as the directing Smiths and the driving Paragreens. The most dramatic incident occurred in 1906, when four boys pushed-off wagons which careered over virtually the whole line; the saddest was the absence of the BR relief crew after the last proud journey. Mr Ken Hartley sensitively tells a good story of a brave little concern.

*University of Strathclyde*     J. T. Ward

## Notes on Reprints etc

**The Coal Viewer, and Engine Builder's Practical Companion,** by John Curr, CASS LIBRARY OF RAILWAY CLASSICS, 2nd edn, 1970, pp 96, plates, £3.15.

John Curr (1756–1823), probably a native of County Durham, was the viewer to the Duke of Norfolk's Sheffield Colliery from about 1780 until 1801. The present work, originally published in 1797, has long been used by historians of coal mining, the steam engine and early plateways. Its scarcity completely justifies this handsome reprint which effectively reproduces the engravings of the first edition. Charles E. Lee provides an introductory note summarising what is known of Curr's life. For the transport historian, the book's chief attraction lies in Curr's notes on cast-iron rail roads; but the student of the technological aspects of mining history has still more reason to be thankful for this reissue.

**The Horse-World of London (1893),** by W. J. Gordon, DAVID & CHARLES REPRINTS, 1971, pp 190, ill, £1.50.

This little work is essentially about the working horses of London rather than a detailed account of their various duties or a description of the vehicles they hauled. None the less there are many items which illustrate the extent to which urban transport in the nineteenth century depended on horse power and several approximate estimates of the capital locked up in horse flesh. According to Gordon there were some 300,000 horses keeping the wheels of the metropolis turning in 1893—representing a minimum direct investment of £7½ million, not counting of course the vehicles, harnesses, stables and so on. Possibly historians should develop yet further their awakening interest in horse breeding and sales as economic activities.

**Fall! Fall! Fall! öwerall. Berichte über den schleswig-holsteinischen Walfang am Beispiele der Stadt Elmshorn, 1817–1872,** by Emil G. Bai, CHRONIK DER SEEFAHRT, VERLAG EGON HEINEMANN, Hamburg-Garstedt, 1968, pp 112, ill, DM 19.80.

Elmshorn is one of those little towns of the lower Elbe with a surprisingly vigorous maritime past. In 1816 a group of burgesses formed a small company to take advantage of a subsidy offered by the King of Denmark and fitted out the *Flora* for the Greenland whale fishery. This vessel survived to the end of Elmshorn's participation in whaling, her last voyage in 1872 marking the demise of the whole enterprise. Herr Bai draws on ships' logs and secondary sources to give an interesting account of the exploits of the *Flora* and other vessels. In so doing he recaptures both the detail and spirit of Arctic whaling. Of especial interest are the excellent diagrams and sketches, while the clear photographs of superb scale-models (including close-ups of deck layout) are an important feature of the book. All these are Herr Bai's own work. One is not surprised to discover that it was the author who was responsible for the restoration of the ship models in the Hamburg Museum.

**The Merchant Sailing Ship: A Photographic History,** by Basil Greenhill and Ann Giffard, DAVID & CHARLES, Newton Abbot, 1970, pp 112, 127 photographs, £2.50.

Based on photographs in the care of the National Maritime Museum, the selection offered here depicts mainly nineteenth-century British- and American-built sailing vessels, from barge to steel barque. Coastal trading and fishing craft are well represented with perhaps only one exception. It is a pity that the game collier brig, once so characteristic a sight between Tyne and Thames especially, was not more photographed before its disappearance. The only one here, pictured appropriately enough in Whitby harbour, is obscured by lesser fry. However, this is a magnificent series of photographs which has been thoughtfully arranged to afford some fascinating glimpses into tiny shipyards and shipboard life as well as at the vessels themselves.

**The Thames Sailing Barge: her Gear and Rigging,** by Dennis J. Davis, DAVID & CHARLES, Newton Abbot, and INTERNATIONAL MARINE PUBLISHING COMPANY, Camden, Maine, USA, 1970, pp 94, many ill, £2.50.

This is another splendid photographic account of what is now virtually marine history. The Thames sailing barge developed from the open lighter of the seventeenth and eighteenth centuries, reaching its numerical peak as an esturine and coastal craft around 1900, when some 2,000 are said to have been registered. Today only the famous *Cambria* survives as a fully operational trading vessel. The photographs are accompanied by a facing text (rather than mere captions) and effectively show the rig, deck layout and other principal features of these handsome craft. Just one minor cavil: why is there no bibliography of previous literature on this subject?

**The Convict Ships 1787–1868,** by Charles Bateson, BROWN, SON & FERGUSON, Glasgow, 2nd edn 1969, pp xi + 421, ill, £3.75.

Mr Bateson's book, which first appeared in 1959, is a mine of information about life on board the convict ships during the eighty-one years that men were transported to Australia. Some 158,702 male and female prisoners were landed from Britain and Ireland, while many others, through disease or shipwreck, failed to see the continent of their banishment. This book, whose appendices and text have now been revised, tells their story. It is an account in terms of voyages, ships and men; but it is well documented and a useful quarry of information for those whose chief interests are administrative. Like most of this publisher's titles, the presentation is of a high standard.

**The Old East Indiamen,** by E. Keble Chatterton, reprint of the second edition of 1933, CONWAY MARITIME PRESS, 1971, pp 308, ill, £3.25.

This is a reasonably priced reprint of a classic narrative maritime history, easy to use. From a scholarly point of view it is unfortunate that sources are not normally indicated, but the book makes most enjoy-

# Shorter Reviews

able reading. The East Indiaman in war and in peace, conditions on board, and the risk of piracy are all dealt with in an engaging manner.

**The Rise of New York Port (1815–1860),** by Robert Greenhaugh Albion, reprint of the first edition of 1939, DAVID & CHARLES, Newton Abbot, 1970, pp xvi + 481, ill, £5.25.

In this fine study, the author analyses the importance of geographical advantage, port improvement, links with the hinterland and the development of American agriculture and manufactures on the growth of New York as a trading centre. There are some valuable trade and population tables included as appendices, and an excellent bibliography.

**The Art of Travel,** by Francis Galton, reprint of the fifth edition of 1872, DAVID & CHARLES, Newton Abbot, 1971, pp 17 + viii + 366, ill, £2.75.

Though not strictly transport history, this interesting volume illustrates the hazards of travel in undeveloped countries in the late nineteenth century and gives details of the expedients necessary to overcome them. Galton was a noted explorer, and it is worth bearing in mind that the fruits of his experience, embodied in this manual, may have helped the pioneers of road and rail development outside Europe and North America.

**A History of Modern Road Transport,** by A. A. C. Cardy, MACMILLAN, 1971, pp 64, ill, 35p.

One of the publishers' Signposts to History series, intended for use in schools, this is an accurate and pleasant introduction to road transport history. It consists of passages from contemporary literature linked by a well-written narrative. The writer is obviously an enthusiast for private transport, as trams, trolleybuses, motor buses and commercial vehicles together only rate eleven pages.

**British Electric Tramways,** by E. Jackson-Stevens, DAVID & CHARLES, Newton Abbot, 1971, pp 112, ill, £2.75.

Similar in format to the publishers' other picture books, this is a good introduction to a fascinating study. A wide range of sources has been tapped to provide illustrations which are, on the whole, of good quality. There is a useful appendix listing dates of opening and closing of British electric tramway systems, but no bibliography.

**A Treatise on the Steam Engine,** by John Farey, DAVID & CHARLES REPRINTS, Newton Abbot, 1971, pp 728 + 25 plates, additional diagrams in text, £8.40.

Farey's *Treatise*, first published in 1827, has long been a standard source for historians of the steam engine, and drawings from it have appeared in many books. This handsome reprint is therefore to be welcomed. Although not directly concerned with the application of steam power to transport, anyone interested in the background to that development can read the *Treatise* with profit.

**Railway Officials' Directory for 1922,** reprint, S.R. PUBLISHERS LTD, East Ardsley, Wakefield, Yorkshire, 1971, pp 116, ill, £1.50.

An attractive production, with laminated

card cover, this handbook lists railway officials in the year before grouping took effect. Additional information includes mileage open, dates of opening, and annual dividends, while the numerous advertisements are also interesting. Copies of this reprint may be obtained from booksellers.

**Great Western Railway Service Time Tables, Bristol to Exeter and branches, October 1886,** reprint, TOWN & COUNTRY PRESS, 42 Rectory Lane, Bracknell, Berks, 1971, pp 82, 65p.

Working timetables are always of interest to railway enthusiasts, and this GWR example is no exception, dealing as it does with the transition period from broad to narrow gauge. The reprint is attractively produced, with thin card covers.

**Talyllyn Adventure,** reprint of *Railway Adventure,* by L. T. C. Rolt, and *Talyllyn Century,* ed L. T. C. Rolt, DAVID & CHARLES, Newton Abbot, 1971, pp 289, ill, £2.50.

The Talyllyn Railway, the pioneer preserved railway, has been fortunate in its historians. L. T. C. Rolt's *Railway Adventure* is surely the best book yet written about the problems of amateur railway operation, while *Talyllyn Century,* consisting of a series of articles by members of the Talyllyn Preservation Society is a well-written, concise survey of the railway's history and of the activities of the society. The combined volume is well illustrated.

**Narrow Gauge Railways in Mid-Wales,** by J. I. C. Boyd, OAKWOOD PRESS, Tandridge Lane, Lingfield, Surrey, 1970, pp 300, ill, maps and line drawings, £3.75.

A second, much revised version of a book first published in 1965, this volume deserves a warm reception. Mr Boyd's careful scholarship and J. M. Lloyd's beautiful maps and drawings are well known to those interested in narrow-gauge railways in Britain. Here they are combined with numerous half-tone illustrations to bring the continuing story of a remarkable group of lines up to date. Mr Boyd also includes an interesting new section on mineral railways.

**Italian Railways,** by P. M. Kalla-Bishop, DAVID & CHARLES, Newton Abbot, 1971, pp 208, ill, maps, £2.50.

The Italian railway system has received relatively little attention from British railway enthusiasts, yet the complexity of its history, the longevity of its steam locomotives and its unusual use of three-phase electrification all make it of interest. Mr Kalla-Bishop is probably the greatest British expert on the Italian railways, and he deals ably with the history of the system, with locomotives and railcars and with operation. There are useful appendices giving details of main line and minor railways, locomotives and railcars, and a bibliography.

**The Picture History of the Somerset & Dorset Railway,** by Robin Atthill, DAVID & CHARLES, Newton Abbot, 1970, pp 112, ill, £2.50.

One of the latest volumes in the publishers' Picture History series, Mr Atthill's work is complementary to his history of the S & D, that most popular line. He has drawn on the fine photographic collection of Peters, as well as seeking out individual items from a wide range of sources. If your reviewer has a quibble, it is that too little attention is paid to structures, but otherwise the selection is well balanced.

## Shorter Reviews

**Railway History in Pictures: Wales and the Welsh Border Counties,** by H. C. Casserley, DAVID & CHARLES, Newton Abbot, 1970, pp 111, ill, £2.50.

Wales and the adjoining parts of England have been the setting for more varied railway activity than any other region in Britain, and Mr Casserley ably explores this marvellous variety by skilfully captioned photographs. His own fine collection is supplemented by a good selection of photographs from older sources and from other modern photographers. The quality of reproduction is high.

**Railway History in Pictures: Ireland, Volume 2,** by Alan McCutcheon, DAVID & CHARLES, Newton Abbot, 1970, pp 112, ill, £2.75.

This book complements Mr McCutcheon's first volume, bringing the story of Ireland's railways up to date, and following the same pattern. The author has unearthed a fine selection of photographs, many of excellent quality, to create a beautifully balanced book.

**The Lynton and Barnstaple Railway,** by G. A. Brown, J. D. C. Prideaux and H. G. Radcliffe, DAVID & CHARLES, Newton Abbot, 1971, pp 134, ill, maps and diagrams, £2.

A second edition of a volume published in 1964, this is a handsomely illustrated tribute to England's most popular narrow-gauge railway. Plans and elevations of buildings, as well as of locomotives and rolling stock, are included, while the sections on the promotion, construction and operation of the railway place it very firmly in its economic setting.

**The 10.30 Limited** and **Caerphilly Castle,** by W. G. Chapman, reprints, PATRICK STEPHENS LIMITED, 1970, pp 131 and 199, ill, £1.50 each.

These two volumes were originally published by the Great Western Railway as publicity for their Cornish Riviera express and the new Castle class locomotives which hauled it. Described as suitable 'for boys of all ages', they are concise, readable and accurate descriptions of railway operation on the GWR in 1923-4, well illustrated with diagrams and half-tone blocks. The reprints are nicely bound in cloth, unlike the original editions, and deserve wide circulation.

**The Railway Clearing House Handbook of Railway Stations (1904),** DAVID & CHARLES REPRINTS, Newton Abbot, 1970, pp 600, £6.30.

The 'Handbook' is a monumental volume both in size and in detail. The modesty of its title belies the scope of its coverage, as not only stations, but also private sidings of all types are included, as well as tabular information as to the facilities provided. A useful critical introduction by C. R. Clinker sets the 1904 issue in its context, pointing out that this edition contains references only to those railways party to the Railway Clearing House. This is a valuable source book, and its reprinting should widen appreciation of its merits.

# Notes and News

*The Postal Strike*

By now most readers will have forgotten the postal strike of January–March. Unfortunately its effects are now felt in this issue of *Transport History*, in the reduced review section, and also in 'Notes and News'. We hope that readers and publishers will bear with us.

*Recent Pamphlets*

F. K. Pearson, author of *Isle of Man Tramways*, a splendid technical history, has collaborated with W. G. S. Hyde in the preparation of the second edition of *Isle of Man Tramway Album*, published by the Douglas Cable Car Group. This is a beautifully illustrated fifty-two page brochure, with some fine early photographs, good modern views, and drawings of the Isle of Man's six tram systems. Copies are available from the group's treasurer at Woodlea, Clay Head Close, Baldrine, Isle of Man.

The Railway Philatelic Group is well known as a prolific publisher of finely produced literature, and its two latest publications are certainly up to its usual standard. *The Railway Theme—A Study of Railways on Stamps* is an examination of railway stamps and their subjects, and is illustrated with black and white reproductions of many of the stamps mentioned. This forty-six page pamphlet, with stiff card covers, is edited by C. A. Hart, and costs £1.10, as does the second edition of *The Railway Letter Posts of Great Britain—Part I*, by H. T. Jackson. First published in 1968, this is an excellent short historical account of the origin and evolution of railway postal services (as opposed to GPO mails carried by rail). There is an appendix listing railways, and their successors, known to have operated a railway letter service. Both these booklets may be obtained from the group's publication officer, A. J. Lowe, 'Rookwood', Bentinck Road, Altrincham, Cheshire, or from many stamp dealers.

*From John Hibbs, City of London Polytechnic*

Records of what services have been provided by bus companies at different times are generally well recorded, at least for the past twenty-five years (although the discontinuity of the world war has meant the loss of much data from the vital period of growth). In the face of rapid change, it is worth welcoming attempts to catalogue current services systematically, and especially in the case of the smaller operators. The publishers of the *Lincolnshire Transport Review* have done this for the small operators of north-east Lincs, and now comes a set of timetables of independent bus services in Northamptonshire (Midland Counties PSV Restoration Club, 11 Ashley Lane, Moulton, Northampton, price 7½p). Both are semi-commercial attempts to provide information for local use.

The second in a series of occasional publications of the Dore Village Society, *The Origins of the Sheffield and Chesterfield Railway*, by John Dunstan, is a thirty-two page card-covered pamphlet. Based on original research, this describes the battle between the Midland and the Sheffield, Chesterfield & Staffordshire Railway for the right to build a line from Sheffield to Chesterfield via Dore. The eventual victory of the Midland and the subsequent construction of the line are also discussed. Priced at 23p post free, copies are available from N. J. Dunstan, 14 Leyfield Road, Dore, Sheffield, S17 3EE.

Two interesting early railways form the subjects of recent Oakwood Press publications. *The Canterbury & Whitstable Railway*, the oldest steam-hauled passenger-carrying railway in southern England, is the subject of a thirty-five page booklet by Ivan Maxted, price 60p. This contains several interesting photographs, and a useful description of surviving engineering features and other relics, as well as a summary history of the line. Charles E. Lee's booklet *The Swansea & Mumbles Railway* was first published in 1942, a second edition appeared in 1954, and this third edition contains additional information bringing the history of the line up to date. Well illustrated with photographs and maps, this paper costs 90p.

*Poster*

The City of Lincoln Libraries, Museum and Art Gallery, have produced a most attractive reproduction of a poster advertising the *Favorite* paddle steamer on sailings from Lincoln to Boston c 1825. Printed in black on white cartridge paper, there is a woodcut of the vessel as a heading. Copies, price 15p, are available from The Museum, Broadgate, Lincoln.

*Periodicals*

*Sussex Industrial History* is a new periodical, published for the Sussex Industrial Archaeology Study Group by Phillimore & Co Ltd, Shopwyke Hall, Chichester, Sussex. It will appear twice-yearly, and the annual subscription is 75p. The Winter 1970–1 issue contains an excellent article on the Upper Ouse Navigation 1790–1868, by D. F. Gibbs (a recent contributor to *Transport History*) and J. H. Farrant.

The December 1970 issue of *Industrial Railway Record* contains articles on German and Pakistani industrial railways, and on steam locomotives for use in tunnels. M. J. T. Lewis contributes an article on the origin of an unusual geared locomotive *Mole*. Copies, price 15p, may be had from R. V. Mulligan, 41 Egerton Road, Birkenhead, L43 1UJ, while the subscription for six issues is 90p.

The Railway Philatelic Group's Journal *Railway Philately* continues to bring to light interesting items. In the December 1970 issue there is a note on the world's first adhesive postage stamps issued by the Stockton & Darlington Railway in 1835, and one on the Manx Electric Railway as a postal carrier, while the March 1971 number contains notes on forgeries, on Danish Private Railway Stamps and on minor railway stamps. The journal may be obtained from Roger A. Kirk, 59A Hartley Road, Kirkby-in-Ashfield, Nottingham, NG17 8DS, the annual subscription (for four issues) being £1.50, with an entrance fee of 25p.

Two further issues of *The Lock Gate*, the journal of the Great Ouse Restoration Society, have come to hand. The society is an active and lively one, and though its journal is mainly of local interest, readers involved in canal conservation should find it of value. The journal is issued quarterly, and costs 60p per annum. Subscriptions should be sent to D. K. Cassels, River Cottage, Great Barford, Bedford. *Double Nine*, the quarterly magazine of the lively

Pocklington Canal Amenity Society, also continues to appear regularly.

*A New Journal*

*Maritime History* made its debut in April under the promising editorship of Robert Craig, Lecturer in History at University College, London. It is concerned with merchant shipping in the broadest sense and the first number includes papers on Post Office steam packets on the Irish Sea, ship registry and Samuel Plimsoll, among others.

The journal, which is illustrated with maps and plates, also contains book reviews and Notes and News. It is published half-yearly by David & Charles at an annual subscription of £1.75. The next issue will appear in September.

*Record Office Note*

The Greater London Record Office, The County Hall, London SE1, reports the deposit of share certificates of the Grand Surrey Canal and the Southwark Bridge Company (1813-17).

*From the Museums*

From April 1971, Mr D. W. Waters, Secretary to the National Maritime Museum, will be promoted to Keeper. He succeeds Mr G. P. B. Naish, who will retire in June to take up a post as historical consultant to the director.

The Transport Trust has put forward a scheme to create a transport museum at Crystal Palace Low Level station. The plan has been worked out in collaboration with the Clapham Society and Sir Robert McAlpine & Sons to house the collection at present at Clapham, and is estimated to cost £515,000.

*Guild of Transport Teachers*

A meeting was held on 25 November 1970 in the City of London Polytechnic to discuss the formation of a body to link teachers of transport studies. A working party was set up to examine a proposed constitution. Anyone interested should write to John Hibbs at the City of London Polytechnic School of Business Studies, 84 Moorgate, London, EC2M 6SQ.

*Transport Books*

We note that the transport book business run formerly by Mr S. S. Stansfield of Inverness has now been taken over by Mrs Margaret Reed, 38 Glendaruel Avenue, Bearsden, Glasgow. Lists will be issued at regular intervals in response to postal inquiries.

*Wolverton*

Mr P. S. Richards has sent us the following: 'Wolverton, Buckinghamshire—a Bibliographical Note on a Railway Town'.

Wolverton grew up as the 'grand central station and depot' of the London & Birmingham Railway line, largely because it was half-way between the termini of that line. The necessary land was available and could be purchased at a reasonable price. An authoritative source has lamented the lack of studies on the following railway towns: Wolverton, Darlington, Earlstown, Ashford, Eastleigh and Horwich (introduction to Jackman, p xxvii). This statement is no longer entirely true, though it must be stated that some of the references are a little obscure and others have of course appeared since that book was revised. For example, Horwich has been the subject of an individual study (Turton, 1962) and general accounts of these towns have also appeared (Turton, 1961, 1967 and 1969).

Apart from contemporary guidebooks such as those by Roscoe, Chevins, Osborne and Head etc, (all of which are rather rare except Head which has recently been reissued), the earliest accounts of Wolverton appeared in the *Victoria County History of Buckinghamshire*. The references there, however, are very brief: in Volume II, published in 1908, there is a short paragraph on pages 126-7 and in Volume IV, completed in 1915 but not published until 1927, there are a few references on pages 505-9.

In 1945 Jellicoe and Barker described a plan for Wolverton Urban District; this contains a few references to the railway works. Three years later a book appeared by Hyde and Markham appropriately printed by a Wolverton firm, McCorquodale and Company. There is a brief account of railways and Wolverton on pages 166-8. In 1950 a book by Hyde alone was published containing a few references to the railways and in 1951 a further book, this time by Markham, dealt with the railways on pages 14-19, 28, 95-6, 122 and 146-7.

Using contemporary original manuscript sources, especially the minute books of the various committees of the London & Birmingham and later the London & North Western Railway Company, I was able (Richards, 1962) to describe the influence of the railway on the growth of that town. Later (Richards, 1967) a few notes were added to the original article. Subsequently an account appeared (Richards, 1969) of the way the railway company was able to help the Methodists in Wolverton to the mutual benefit of railway and church.

Once it was decided that Bletchley, Wolverton and Stony Stratford should form the new city of Milton Keynes, a spate of official reports appeared, mainly from the Ministry of Housing and Local Government. These reports have fortunately been summarised (Brown and Salt, 1969). Probably, however, the most detailed account appeared in 1968 and this is a thesis by Moira Courtman which can be consulted in the library of Queen Mary College, University of London.

The contents of this thesis, a substantia study in five chapters, may be briefly summarised: chapter I is a survey of the immediate locality before the coming of the railway and contains a reconstruction of the town and country relationships in the early 1830s; chapters II and IV trace in detail the physical extension of the town stage by stage from 1838, the growth of population and the process of acquisition of services and urban amenities; chapter III describes the present-day layout, land-use and the visual aspects of the town; and chapter V investigates the sphere of influence and delimits the area within which the rural population is served by or makes use of services and amenities available at Wolverton. Comparisons are also made with the first chapter and its findings and show how the railway town became a service centre in a locality formerly orientated towards older market towns. The conclusion contains a restatement of the town's problems and a discussion of the factors which gave rise to them. There is a resumé of the phases through which it has passed, up to the present when Milton Keynes, the Greater London overspill city which is planned for North Buckinghamshire, threatens its continuation as a separate community. There are eighty-three excellently produced maps and numerous photographs.

This list does not claim to be exhaustive. Much more still remains to be done even on one town, but it may help researchers in this field. In this note no account has been taken of contemporary newspaper resources which provide a valuable source of information, though one requiring a great deal of sifting. If approximate dates are known, then a great deal of trouble and labour is saved. *Acknowledgements:* Miss M. Courtman, of the Geography and Geology Library of the University of London, Senate House, Malet Street, London WC1; Dr D. G. Price, principal lecturer in the School of Commerce and Social Studies at the Polytechnic, Regent Street, London W1R 8AL. *References:* R. Bot, 'Milton Keynes: the first stage of the planning process', *Journal of the Town Planning Institute*, 54 (1968); E. H. Brown and John Salt, 'Plan for Milton Keynes', *Geographical Magazine*, August 1969; J. F. Cairnes, 'Wolverton Carriage Works: London and North Western Railway', *Railway Magazine*, 35 (1914); J. M. Campbell (Baron Campbell), 'Milton Keynes. London's latest new town', *Town and County Planning*, 36 (1968), 62-3; Moira Courtman, 'Wolverton: a study in urban geography' (MPhil thesis, University of London, 1968). A copy is also deposited in the library of Queen Mary College, Mile End Road, London E1; Sir Francis Head, *Stokers and Pokers on the London and North Western Railway*, David & Charles, 1969; F. E. Hyde and S. F. Markham, *A History of Stony Stratford*, McQuorquodale, Wolverton, 1948; F. E. Hyde, *Wolverton: A Short History of its Economic and Social Development*, Wolverton 1950; W. T. Jackman, *Development of Transportation in Modern Britain*, 2nd edn revised by W. H. Challoner, Cass, 1962; C. A. Jellicoe and A. Barker, 'A design for Wolverton Urban District, comprising the towns of Wolverton, New Bradwell and Stony Stratford, in the county of Buckingham', *Architect's Journal*, 18 October 1945; Charles E. Lee, 'The Wolverton and Stony Stratford Tramway', *Railway Magazine*, Vol 98, August 1952, 547-54; (The July 1970 issue of *Journal* in its column 'Why and Wherefore' contains a further feature on this line together with a photograph); S. F. Markham, *The Nineteen Hundreds in Stony Stratford and Wolverton*, Hillier, 1951; D. G. Price, 'A geographical study of retail distribution in Buckinghamshire, Berkshire and Oxfordshire with particular reference to market areas served by retail outlets' (PhD thesis, University of London, 1967) has a few references to Wolverton; Peter S. Richards, 'Influence of Railways on the growth of Wolverton', *Records of Buckinghamshire*, XVII, 1962, 115-26 (contains old OS maps of the district); 'Wolverton: some further notes', ibid, XVIII, 1967, 173-4; 'Methodists and the Railway: the story of Wolverton', *Proceedings of the Wesley Historical Society*, February 1969, 20-4; B. J. Turton, 'Geographical Aspects of the Railway Industry' (PhD thesis, University of Nottingham, 1961); 'The Railway Town: A Problem in Industrial Planning', *Town Planning Review*, Vol 32 No 2, July 1961, 97-115; 'Horwich: the historical geography of a Lancashire Town', *Trans of the Lancashire & Cheshire Antiquarian Society*, Vol 72 (1962), 141-50; 'The British Railway Engineering Industry: a study in economic geography', *Tijdschrift voor Economische en Sociale Geografie*, No 4 (1967), 193-202; 'The Railway Towns of Southern England', *Transport History*, II (1969), 105-19.

*News from the Preservation Societies*
*Festiniog Railway Notes*

The Festiniog Railway's 1970 season came to an end on Sunday, 20 December, after a weekend of Christmas Party trains on which 375 passengers (mostly local families and Sunday schools) travelled. Total passenger journeys for 1970 will be in the region of 355,000 (about 11 per cent up on the 1969 figures). A considerable boost to the total was given by the late autumn traffic which has shown a good increase.

For a few days right at the end of October the railway was in the unique position of having five steam engines available for service, but on 2 November work commenced on stripping *Earl of Merioneth* and *Blanche* for boiler examination, and it remains to be seen whether the happy occurrence will be repeated at a more useful stage of the 1971 season. *Merddin Emrys* has completed some initial test runs with its new boiler, which has proved highly satisfactory, both from the point of view of steaming and the economical consumption of coal and water. A considerable amount of work remains to be done to equip this engine for a five-year spell of heavy-duty service: inside motion, axleboxes and horns to be overhauled, wheel flanges welded up and profiles re-machined, and steam brake gear to be made and fitted, to mention just a few items. A full repaint is to be put in hand. The new longer boiler makes the tanks look smaller, but from most angles the parallel nature of the boiler is not too obvious. It is planned to provide new tanks more in proportion to the shape of the boiler when the existing ones require replacement, and in due course an overall cab with sloping top sides, of similar profile to the one on *Mountaineer*, will be fitted.

Laidlaw-Drew oil-firing equipment has been fitted to *Linda* and trials started early in November with both service and special trains, with steadily improving results. A decision will not be made on converting any other engines until it can be proved that the equipment can give satisfactory results. British Rail Engineering Ltd, Crewe, have been awarded a contract to construct fabricated cylinders with piston valves to Boston Lodge design for *Linda* and *Blanche*.

During the peak high summer service the remaining four-wheel passenger coaches were pressed into service on a diesel-hauled Tan-y-Bwlch–Dduallt shuttle service, provided to relieve the main trains of local traffic between these stations. The shuttle ran Mondays to Thursdays, leaving Tan-y-Bwlch immediately a main train arrived at Dduallt and running into the loop at Dduallt when the main train engine had run round its train. The shuttle would then follow the main train back to Tan-y-Bwlch, as soon as the main train had cleared section. By the time the shuttle ran into Tan-y-Bwlch the down main train would have vacated the down platform and the next up train would have taken water and be ready to leave for Dduallt, thus starting the cycle once more. The working timetable permitted a maximum of nine up shuttles and eight down, the balancing working being combined with a main train, giving a grand total of forty-three workings between Tan-y-Bwlch and Dduallt. The safe operation of such an intensive service demands efficient and stringent signalling, and it was only possible with the c.l.s. installation at Tan-y-Bwlch, a temporary signalling installation at Dduallt and the availability of trained and reliable staff.

Two of the four-wheel coaches employed on the shuttle (they date from the mid-1860s) deteriorated during 1970, and have been withdrawn from service for long-term rebuilds. As a replacement for these a prototype 'toastrack' bogie coach is to be built on a Hudson underframe. It will have all-welded steel body frame and side panels, steel floor, wooden half doors, wood slat profiled seats, ply ends and double-ply roof. It is essentially a utility, peak-season vehicle, cheap to build in money and time, but over a reasonably short distance it should give a comparatively comfortable ride.

The Narrow Gauge Railways of Wales Joint Marketing Panel (the publicity syndicate formed by the Festiniog, Talyllyn,

Snowdon Mountain, Vale of Rheidol, Welshpool & Llanfair and Fairbourne railways, using the 'Great Little Trains of Wales' theme) has been awarded the Wales Tourist Board's Festival of Wales Trophy 1970. The trophy has been awarded annually since 1958 (when the Commonwealth Games were held in Cardiff), to organisations which have given outstanding service to tourism in Wales.

\* \* \*

The Ravenglass & Eskdale Railway reports a modest increase in the number of passengers carried during the 1970 season. The new diesel shed at the north end of the station should be completed for the 1971 season, while the cafe at Dalegarth is being reorganised. Three more coaches are under construction at the works of Edmund Crow in Cleator Moor, and *River Mite* has had a major overhaul, including a repaint.

\* \* \*

The Great Western Society has a deservedly high reputation for the quality and the quantity of its locomotives and rolling stock. Recently the society has published a stock book to celebrate the tenth anniversary of its foundation. Priced at 25p, this publication is obtainable from the society at 196 Norwood Road, Southall, Middlesex. The list of locomotives is impressive—two Castles, two Halls, a Manor, a 2-6-0, two 2-6-2 tanks, an 0-4-2 tank, an 0-6-2 tank, three 0-6-0 tanks and four 0-4-0 tanks, including that mid-Victorian gem, *Shannon*, of the Wantage Tramway.

\* \* \*

The Scottish Railway Preservation Society has still not reached agreement with British Rail over the acquisition of the Aviemore to Boat of Garten section of the Highland Railway, but is continuing to acquire rolling stock. Latest items include a diesel shunter from the British Aluminium Company's Fort William factory and a woodenbodied hopper wagon from the Leith General Warehousing Company.

*The Yorkshire Derwent*

Readers will no doubt be interested to learn that a Yorkshire Derwent Trust has now been formed to try to rescue this delightful river for the inland navigator. We hope to be in a position to give the full relevant details in our next issue.

*Keighley & Worth Valley Railway*

It is encouraging to note that the enterprising Keighley & Worth Valley Railway continues to enjoy popular support. On a recent visit one of your editors travelled behind Mr W. E. C. Watkinson's beautifully restored Stanier Class 5 4-6-0 No 5025. The four-coach train, which included a buffet car, was well patronised (see p 176).

# RAILWAY AND CANAL HISTORICAL SOCIETY
*Founded 1954*

The Society exists to bring together all those interested in the history of railways and canals and offers a quarterly journal, a lively monthly bulletin, visits to places of interest and local group meetings.

*Details of membership from: Hon Secretary, 174 Station Road, Wylde Green, Sutton Coldfield, Warwickshire.*

The Society also offers the following publications for sale:

**A SHORT HISTORY OF THE LIVERPOOL & MANCHESTER RAILWAY**, by G. O. Holt, (2nd edn, price 38p, post free).

**HOW FFESTINIOG GOT ITS RAILWAY**, by M. J. T. Lewis, (2nd edn, price 63p, post free).

**MAP OF THE KINGTON, LEOMINSTER & STOURPORT CANAL** by R. J. Dean (30 in × 15 in) Scale 1 in to mile 30p.

*Available from Hon Sales Officer, 'Macrae', Stubbs Wood, Amersham, Bucks.*

---

# TRANSPORT HISTORY
Goose publications for industrial archaeologists and transport historians:

**MINOR RAILWAYS OF ENGLAND AND THEIR LOCOMOTIVES, 1900–1939** (new title)
George Woodcock 8¼″ × 5¼″ 188 pages, 77 illustrations
SBN 900404 06 X  £2.75

**A SHORT HISTORY OF THE MIDLAND AND GREAT NORTHERN JOINT RAILWAY**
Ronald H. Clark 9¾″ × 7¼″ 224 pages, 111 illustrations, pull-out map
SBN 900404 05 1  £3.75

**THE DEVELOPMENT OF THE ENGLISH STEAM WAGGON**
Ronald H. Clark 9¾″ × 7¼″ 256 pages, 314 illustrations
SBN 900404 02 7  £3.15

**THE OVERTYPE STEAM ROAD WAGGON** (new title)
M. A. Kelly 11″ × 8¼″ 144 pages, 180 illustrations
SBN 900404 07 8  £3.98

**THE VINTAGE YEARS AT BROOKLANDS**
Doctor Joseph Bayley 7¼″ × 9¾″ 272 pages, 136 illustrations
SBN 900404 00 0  £3.75

**BROUGH SUPERIOR**
The Rolls-Royce of Motor Cycles
Ronald H. Clark 8¼″ × 5¼″ 192 pages, 99 illustrations
SBN 900404 03 05  £2.38

**ALWAYS IN THE PICTURE** (new title)
the story of Veloce Limited, Motor-cycle Manufacturers
J. W. Clew and R. W. Burgess
9¾″ × 6″, 250 pages, 114 illustrations
SBN 900404 08 6  £4.50

*In Preparation*
**A TRACTION ENGINE MISCELLANY**
Ronald H. Clark    Publication late 1971
**THE RAILWAY FOUNDRY, LEEDS**
the history of a famous locomotive works by R. N. Redman
Publication late summer 1971
**THE AUTOMOBILES OF CHINA AND THE U.S.S.R.**
Maurice A. Kelly
Probable publication spring 1972
**THE UNDERTYPE STEAM ROAD WAGGON**
the second volume of M. A. Kelly's Complete History of Steam Road Waggon Builders
Publication spring 1972

*From your bookseller or* GOOSE & SON, *publishers, 23 Davey Place, Norwich NOR 38E, Norfolk   Tel: 0603 27241/2*

## ST JOHN THOMAS BOOKSELLERS

St John Thomas Booksellers is the retail shop in the David & Charles group and is situated at 30 Woburn Place, which is next door to the Tavistock Hotel, between Tavistock and Russell Squares, and within easy walking distance of Euston and the British Museum.

It specialises very much in history and artifacts and should therefore appeal especially to people like subscribers to this journal. All David & Charles books are stocked (as are current Readers Union titles—solely for inspection or purchase only by members producing identification) and you are welcome to browse here and then place an order with your regular bookseller.

If you already have a good bookseller, of course support him. Otherwise, try us. We're told we're prompt, courteous and we're certainly interested. We issue catalogues, welcome postal business, obtain mint copies of books on publication day, supply a growing number of university and other libraries at home and abroad. Get in touch with the manager, David Hounslow, and see what we can do for you.

## RU and D&C

RU stands for Readers Union, Britain's most respected group of book clubs. It has just been absorbed into the David & Charles group, will retain all its best features including a real appreciation of books, wonderful value for money, and fair dealing, but will be expanded with D&C energy and enthusiasm.

There are five clubs, plus numerous optional titles, including some that are bound to be of interest to the subscribers to this journal. You'll find an abundance of history, including occasional transport and maritime titles, books on artifacts and the countryside and natural history, all for below the publisher's prices and many at only a quarter of them.

It would cost you only a postcard and stamp to find out what RU plus D&C means . . . and you'll be surprised at the range and value of titles offered.

Send that card to Readers Union at PO Box 6, Newton Abbot TQ12 2DW.

## MARITIME HISTORY

A new journal published half-yearly in April and September
Papers in the first issue, April 1971 (120 pages), include:

The Post Office Steam Packets, 1821–36, & the Development of Shipping on the Irish Sea. PHILIP BAGWELL

Ship Registry – to 1707. RUPERT JARVIS

The Steamship *Bedlington*, 1841–54. STEPHEN B MARTIN & NORMAN MCCORD

Samuel Plimsoll & the Shipping Interest. GEOFFREY ALDERMAN

The Steamship *Great Britain* – Homecoming & Approach to Restoration. GRAHAME FARR

The National Maritime Museum's Exhibition of the Paintings of Reuben Chappell. BASIL GREENHILL

Book Reviews. Notes & News

> Edited by Robert Craig, BSc(Econ), Department of History, University College, London
> Annual subscription £1.75 including postage
> Single issues 90p

**DAVID & CHARLES**    NEWTON ABBOT DEVON

---

## HAMILTON BLUMER LTD

*Antiquarian Booksellers*

Are Specialists
in Scarce and Out-of-Print Works on the
History of Technology, Transport and Commerce

We issue Catalogues

**109 SOUTHAMPTON ROW
LONDON, W.C., IB 4HH**
01–636–1763

### Railways Round Exmoor

Robin Madge

64 pages    Fully Illustrated

53p    Post free

**The Exmoor Press
Dulverton, Somerset**

### Railway Enthusiasts' Handbook 1971-72

*Edited by*
GEOFFREY BODY

An essential work of reference and interest to all railway enthusiasts, its contents updating, expanding and complementing the information given in previous volumes.

£1.50

**David & Charles**
NEWTON ABBOT, DEVON

## Norman Smith
# A HISTORY OF DAMS

From 2800 BC until today; international coverage. A unique record.
296pp (9¼" × 6⅓") *with* 32pp *photographs,* 35 *maps and diagrams*
£3.75

## Geoffrey Hindley
# A HISTORY OF ROADS

Covering 4,000 years to 1970 of world-wide developments. Authoritative. Lively.
166pp (9¼" × 6⅓") *with* 16pp *photographs,* 7 *maps*
£2.75

## Peter Davies

WILLIAM ALBERT

# The Metropolis Roads Commission: an Attempt at Turnpike Trust Reform

## I

THE PARISHES were made officially responsible and accountable for the repair of their roads in 1555.[1] This system of road repair, based on an annual six days of compulsory labour from each parishioner, was notoriously ineffectual,[2] but in the mid-sixteenth century when wheeled traffic was infrequent and primarily local this may not have posed too serious a problem. In later years, however, as the number of vehicles and the volume of through traffic increased, some parishes, particularly those along the main roads, found that yearly statute labour was not enough to keep their roads in repair. The first turnpike authorities were set up in an attempt to provide temporary assistance for certain of these parishes.[3] Because the turnpikes imposed a new and unfamiliar tax they were actively resisted both locally and by Parliament. As the volume of road traffic continued to rise this resistance weakened, and the number of turnpike trusts began to increase. Only five trusts were established between 1663 and 1700, but from the early decades of the eighteenth century activity was stepped up. By 1750 a fairly extensive network of turnpiked main roads had been formed leading from London to almost every important provincial centre.[4] In the years that followed many more roads came under the control of turnpike trusts, and gradually they replaced the parishes as the agencies responsible for maintaining the main roads.

The turnpike trusts were generally more successful in maintaining the roads than the parishes had been.[5] This was true if only because they had more money to spend and were able to exercise unified control over stretches of road which might formerly have been repaired by many different parishes. However, the trusts were run by part-time volunteers, unskilled both in techniques of management and road repair, and while this is hardly surprising at a time when these skills were virtually unknown, it meant that the trusts themselves were plagued by numerous difficulties. Jobbery was frequent, knowledgeable road surveyors were almost impossible to find, and inexperienced administration often resulted in a precarious financial condition which made it difficult for some trusts to carry out their tasks adequately. As the amount of traffic on the roads increased, especially with the rapid rise of coaching from the 1760s,[6] these weaknesses became a more serious problem for the trusts and for the country.

During the eighteenth century Parliament had shown some concern with the problems of individual trusts,[7] and a number of general Acts were passed in an attempt to rationalise the trustees' powers and limit road use.[8] But, it was not until the end of the century that more systematic investigations, stemming largely from the interest shown by the Post Office and the Board of Agriculture, were conducted into the condition of the roads and the ways in which they could be improved. In 1796, 1798 and again in 1800, parliamentary committees reported on the working of the General Turnpike Act of 1776.[9] These reports were concerned primarily with the effects of weighing engines and wheel restrictions on trusts in the London area. In 1806 another committee, headed by Sir John Sinclair, chairman of the Board of Agriculture, reported on the use of 'Broad Wheels and other matters relating to the Preservation of the Turnpike Roads and Highways'.[10] These were the first of many committees set up over the next forty years which agonised over the affairs of the turnpike trusts and the parish roads.[11] The committees considered a great many questions—toll charges and collection, road repair, the advantages of certain types of wheels and waggons, etc—but we shall be concerned here only with the suggestions put forward for major structural alterations in the turnpike road system.

The first faint stirrings of reform came in 1808, when the 'Committee on the Highways of the Kingdom' suggested that a parliamentary committee be formed, financed by the trusts, to receive their accounts and possibly to set up a fund to underwrite experiments in road repair and carriage construction.[12] These quite limited proposals were not accepted. More ambitious recommendations were made by another committee in 1819. They suggested that general surveyors be hired, either by groups of trusts or by the quarter sessions, to provide professional supervision over road repairs, but more importantly, they urged the consolidation of all trusts within a ten-mile radius of London.[13] They argued that this would not only solve the great problems faced by the London trusts, but also would serve as a model which trusts in the rest of the country might follow. This resolution was a virtual repetition of the testimony presented to the committee by their principal witness John Loudon McAdam.[14]

McAdam, the talented and influential Scottish roadmaker, first came to the public's attention in 1810 when he presented his memorandum, *Observations on the Highways of the Kingdom*, to a parliamentary committee sitting in that year.[15] In 1816 he was appointed general surveyor to the large Bristol Trust, and it was here that he was first able to put his road repair theories into practice. He soon found out, however, that he was unable to do this without completely reorganising the trust's chaotic administrative structure.[16] This experience convinced him of the need for efficient administration, and from that time onward he was to concentrate his labours equally '... towards the introduction of a wise and well-regulated system of management for the roads as towards their mechanical construction'.[17] McAdam's firm belief that faulty administrative organisation was the underlying cause of badly repaired roads comes out clearly in his testimony of 1819. He claimed that the roads of the London trusts were in bad condition because the trustees were slow to adopt 'scientific' (ie his!) repair techniques and because of the extremely heavy traffic and the unavailability of suitable road materials.[18] He pointed out, however, that London was in an ideal position to receive materials by water: gravel from the Thames, flints by canal, beach pebbles from the Essex, Sussex and Kent coasts and granite chippings from Cornwall, Guernsey and Scotland which came to London as ships' ballast. Such undertakings had to be on a large scale, and this was precluded by the small size of the London trusts. Consolidation of the trusts would help solve this problem and also allow for a rationalisation of management and the application of more progressive repair techniques. If this testimony is compared with the 1819 committee's resolutions it is clear that McAdam was extremely influential. Nevertheless, there were other important factors underlying the move to promote trust reform, especially reform in London.

The population of London had almost doubled between 1780 and 1820[19] and the 'Coaching Age' was at its height in the early decades of the nineteenth century. This led to a great increase in the number and variety of vehicles on the city's roads[20] and in turn multiplied the repair problems faced by the London trusts as well as the inconveniences suffered by the road users. A major source of inconvenience was the great number of toll houses, toll-gates and side bars in and around the city. By 1827, there were fifty-six toll houses, forty-seven gates and forty-four bars on the roads controlled by the Metropolis Roads Commission.[21] 'XY' writing in *The Times* in 1816, voiced what was probably a widely felt grievance when he complained bitterly of the stops which had to be made almost every mile to pay a toll or show a ticket to 'men placed in a situation unfavourable to civilized manners, and who might be usefully employed in mending the roads, which they now obstruct in the most disagreeable manner'.[22] He urged that 'one general management' of the trusts in London would '... introduce improvements hitherto unthought of ...'. An outstanding example of the beneficial nature of such trust unification was provided two years later by the well-known consolidation of the North Wales portion of the Holyhead Road.

This trust's success was cited by yet another select committee which met in 1820 and reiterated the proposal for the consolidation of the London trusts.[23] Their reasons were essentially the same as those of the 1819 committee—a great deal of expense and inconvenience would be saved and the new unified trust would '... hold forth an example that cannot fail of being rapidly imitated in all parts of the country'.[24]

However, the London trusts were clearly unwilling to serve as an example for anyone, as is shown by their firm opposition in that year (1820) to a Bill which proposed to consolidate seventeen trusts controlling 277¼ miles of road both north and south of the Thames.[25] A committee of London trusts was formed, petitions against the Bill were submitted and it never received a second reading.[26] This committee was reactivated a year later to fight another attempt at consolidating the trusts. The committee argued that the roads were in good repair, under authorised administration, and that the Bill impugned the honesty of the trustees and would take control from those who best knew the local problems.[27] Even though the trusts organised a highly successful petition campaign, getting 116 petitions submitted against the Bill,[28] it was defeated by only a single vote.[29]

This narrow defeat must have encouraged the reformers for they continued to agitate. In 1825 they succeeded in getting a select committee to look into the question of the London trusts.[30] This committee was headed by Lord Lowther, an outspoken proponent of consolidation, and J. L. McAdam was once again the chief witness. It is, therefore, not surprising that the committee's findings simply provided more detailed confirmation of what previous committees had found. It was claimed that the roads were badly repaired, materials were unsuitable, administration lax, the financial position chaotic, and that the great number of toll-gates hindered the free flow of traffic.[31] They concluded:

> that a consolidation of all the trusts adjoining London is the only effectual method of introducing a proper and uniform system of management in the roads, economy in the funds, and of relieving the public from the present inconvenient situations and obnoxious multiplicity of turnpike gates, with which the inhabitants are now faced in every direction.[32]

These conclusions were essentially restatements of McAdam's testimony, and while it is difficult to question his opinion on the physical state of the roads there is some doubt as to whether the London trusts were in as adverse a financial condition as McAdam suggested.

A rough idea of the financial state of the London trusts can be gained by examining the accounts submitted by the trusts to Parliament in 1821.[33] For the county of Middlesex, in which most of the London trusts were found, the accounts show twenty trusts controlling 158 miles of road with mortgage debts of £296,625, arrears of interest of £6,182, and income and expenditure (both averaged over three years) of £95,475 and £86,050 respectively.[34] The very high level of mortgage debts would seem to confirm the view that the London trusts were in financial peril. However, a closer examination shows that this was not true. It must be remembered that, unlike the railways and the canals, the trusts were unable to issue shares in order to finance initial improvements, and as Pressnell has argued,[35] the trusts' mortgage debt should not, therefore, be considered as a debt *per se* (as the Webbs viewed it) but rather as a form of capital. If the trusts were consistently meeting their interest payments, ie if they did not have large arrears of interest and these payments did not account for a disproportionate share of expenditure, it can be claimed that the trustees were managing their finances with a reasonable degree of success.[36] Furthermore, if large interest payments were not being made, and assuming that the level of administrative expenses was about the same as in the 1830s (8·5 per cent of expenditure),[37] this meant that a high percentage of the trusts' income was being spent directly on the roads.[38]

A breakdown of the Middlesex accounts is given in column 1 of the table on page 232. This data does not, however, present a true picture of conditions prevailing in London, for a disproportionate share of both the debt and the arrears of interest are attributable to three small trusts. The Commercial, East India Docks Trust, formed in 1801,[39] had a mortgage debt of £169,050 (57 per cent of the county total), arrears of interest of £4,380 (71 per cent), while controlling only 4¼ miles of road. The other two trusts, the Archway-Kentish Town Trust (1811)[40] and the Poplar-Greenwich Ferry Trust (1812),[41] were responsible for a total of 3½ miles of road and had debts totalling £42,438. All these trusts were significantly different from the ordinary trusts. Owing to the high property values and the necessity of pur-

## The Metropolis Roads Commission

chasing and pulling down houses in order to widen the roads, the trustees were authorised to pay 5 per cent on loans (which were to be in the form of shares) while work was in progress and from 10 per cent to 12 per cent after the work had been completed.[42] The clerk of the Commercial, East India Docks Trust, testifying before a committee in 1833, contended that this trust was a form of private speculation similar to a canal company. He claimed that 'the only Distinction between it [sic the trust] and a Joint-Stock Company is that it is not perpetual'.[43] The special nature of these trusts and the fact that they were relatively new accounts for their high debts, and this makes it desirable to exclude them from our calculations. This is consistent with contemporary views on this question, for none of these trusts was included in any of the proposed Bills for consolidating the London trusts.

The omission of the above three trusts (column 2 of the table) provides a much more representative picture of conditions in London. Interest charges accounted for a small, manageable percentage of expenditure and compared extremely favourably with the average for all trusts (column 3). Only in Essex did the trusts pay out a smaller proportion of their funds in interest charges. The arrears of interest were negligible, and twelve of the seventeen trusts had no arrears at all. Finally, the income and expenditure per mile of the London trusts was higher than in any other part of the country and almost ten times the national average, while the debt per mile was only double that average.[46] This meant that the London trusts were able to spend the greatest part of their funds directly for road repair.

The preceding analysis suggests that although the trustees in London may not have been using the most up-to-date repair techniques, and while the multiplicity of toll-gates and toll-bars was a real and pressing inconvenience, nevertheless, they managed their financial affairs extremely well. These findings raise some doubts as to the validity of McAdam's damning criticisms of the trusts and also put the protests against consolidation into proper perspective. They suggest that the trustees who fought against the consolidation Bills were not

## TABLE
### (From 1821 accounts)[1]

|   |   | Middlesex trusts | Middlesex trusts (A)[2] | All counties |
|---|---|---|---|---|
| 1 | Number of trusts | 20 | 17 | 956 |
| 2 | Total mileage | 158 | 150 | 18,244 |
| 3 | Debt/mile[3] | £1,877 | £545.5 | £245.6 |
| 4 | Arrears of interest/mile | £39.1 | £8.5 | £28.75 |
| 5 | Income/mile[4] | £604.3 | £547.8 | £57.6 |
| 6 | Expenditure/mile | £544.6 | £537.4 | £54.8 |
| 7 | % of expenditure for interest payments[5] | 17·7% | 5% | 22·4% |
| 8 | % of expenditure available for repair expenses[6] | 72·3% | 85·0% | 67·6% |

*Notes*

1 Data from BPP, 1821 iv (247), and corrections in BPP, 1833 xv (703), 168–9.
2 This column excludes three trusts: Commercial and East India Docks Roads, the Archway Trust, and the Poplar–Greenwich Ferry Trust.
3 Debt includes floating debt and mortgage debts.
4 Income and expenditure are averaged over three years.
5 This is calculated by assuming that the trusts paid their interest obligations in full every year at a rate of 5 per cent. In fact, as the arrears of interest show, they did not do this, so we are probably overstating the actual amount paid out in interest. Also some trusts were able to pay lower rates of interest.
6 This figure is arrived at by taking the average amount spent by all trusts between 1834 and 1838 on administrative expenses (8·5 per cent)[44] adding 1·5 per cent as an allowance for legal costs (from 1831 all trusts had their authority renewed each year by a general Act,[45] and, therefore, legal expenses were somewhat lower in the 1830s than in the early 1820s), adding this total to the amount paid out as interest and subtracting this figure from 100 per cent.

all inefficient and incompetent men seeking to retain control of a lucrative local concession, but rather men who may have felt, with some justification, that they were doing a good job.

Following the report of the committee of 1825 the third attempt to consolidate the London trusts was made. The Bill introduced for this purpose differed substantially from previous ones in that it covered only about 133 miles of turnpike road run by fourteen trusts all north of the Thames, instead of the 277 miles of road both north and south of the river encompassed by the 1820 Bill.[47] The 1826 Bill did not include, as had former consolidation Bills, the large and influential New Cross Trust (40 miles), Southwark-Highgate Trust (61 miles) and Whitechapel-Shenfield Trust (34 miles). This had the effect of considerably weakening opposition, for evidence suggests that these trusts, especially the New Cross Trust, had been most active in organising campaigns against the 1820 and 1821 Bills.[48] In 1826 the amount of opposition was sharply reduced. The committee of London trusts was not formed, as had been done before, and less than thirty dissenting petitions were presented.[49] Critics claimed that this was due to the omission of the aforementioned trusts from the Bill and to the fact that it was rushed through Parliament. Writing in *The Times* in November 1826, the trustees of the Brentford Trust pointed out:

> Under the plea that the session was nearly at an end, and the public interests were suffering, those who solicited, or as it is technically called in modern language, 'worked the bill', used the greatest activity to forward it through its different stages. It was read a first time when there were hardly more than ten members present, and almost as soon as the usual forms would admit, a second time in nearly as thin a house. When, as the trustees learnt what was going forward, they solicited to be heard, that the calumnies which had been heaped upon them might be refuted, the only favour they could obtain was, that the bill should be sent to a committee upstairs; but they were informed . . . that it was too late to say anything against the principle of the bill, as that had been established by the second reading. . . .[50]

II

The trustees who opposed consolidation in London have been characterised by historians as somewhat dishonest incompetents seeking to retain control of the trusts as a source of '. . . lucrative posts for local people, and comfortable investment for local capital . . .'.[51] While there is probably some truth in these allegations there were far more significant reasons for their protests. The most important of these was the objection to the centralised control of what was seen as essentially a local prerogative—a central theme in the anti-Poor Law agitation of the 1830s. It was argued, 'that the institution of Turnpikes was viewed by our ancestors with great jealousy and alarm, and was only rendered palatable by the appointment of their fellow subjects resident in their immediate Neighbourhood to the management and Superintendence thereof'.[52] All the petitions presented against the Bill indicate that the trustees and local inhabitants feared that once power was centralised the authorities would then be less responsive to local problems.[53] This attitude was also reflected in a leading article in *The Times* which drew its readers' attention to the passage of the Metropolis Road Act and assured them

> that they are no longer liable to be way-laid or interrupted in their rides by the toll-bar keepers of local trustees; but are to have their tolls fixed by a little parliament, nominated without their consent and including even Irish and Scotch members.[54]

One of the most interesting aspects of the local versus central control controversy was set out in a petition from the trustees of the Kilburn Trust who saw quite clearly some of the more important possible consequences of the erosion of local authority. They argued

> that should the present Bill pass it will be a total departure from the considerate feelings, which the Legislature have always shown for Local Interests; that it will be a dangerous Precedent and may lead to Parliamentary Commissions interfering with the management of Towns, Schools and Charities, and the Interests of Parishes, Bridge Companies, . . . That your Petitioners cannot conclude without expressing their feelings in the present crisis, as Magistrates and Country Gentlemen, as they may be called upon to support the Laws and Government against the riotous proceedings of a Suffering Population, and to point out to your Lordships, that they have hitherto always found the repair of the Turnpike Roads, to be an important source of employment left in their hands, to ameliorate public distress and that to require of them the painful task of opposing and inflicting punishment upon the deluded, and at the same time to deprive them of the satisfaction of being able to administer to the necessities of the orderly and industrious, is to weaken the arm of Power, by lessening the influence—the higher ranks should ever endeavour to exercise over the lower orders by Kindness and liberality, and by which means the Government will best be enabled to preserve the peace of the Country and the goodwill of the People. The Labourous Classes ought not, and cannot long be supported by Charity however munificant it may be; work must be found them, and if there was no other argument against the Bill now before your Lordships, Your Petitioners contend that such an attempt to separate Local Interests from Local duties is alone a sufficient ground for their calling upon your Lordships to pause before you

pass a Law, the effect of which, must be to separate the People from the District and resident Authorities through whom alone they have been accustomed with respect and gratitude to look for employment and support in times of difficulty and distress.[55]

This petition, presented in May 1826, implies that 'riotous proceedings of a Suffering Population' were imminent. While this may have been simply to impress MPs, there were genuine grounds for concern. Following the collapse of the speculative boom in London in the autumn of 1825, which marked the end of five years of relative economic prosperity and domestic peace, economic conditions had continued to deteriorate. This undoubtedly revived memories of the violence and widespread unrest which had characterised the economically unsettled post-war years before Peterloo.[56]

Another question which was raised during the debate over consolidation was that of the relationship between the middle and the landed classes and the right to control the turnpike trusts. Writing in *The Times* in November 1826,[57] the trustees of the Brentford Trust claimed that by replacing local trustees mainly with MPs Parliament was discriminating against the middle classes. They saw this as an

> insinuation that men of business are least fit to conduct matters of business, or that in this highly commercial country as large a share of intelligence, integrity, and patriotic exertion does not exist amongst mercantile men, and in the middle as in any other class of society.

They also felt,

> for the indignity offered to the country at large, since it is a severe libel on a nation boasting of the first commercial men in the world, and pre-eminent for the public acts of those in the middle class, that a sufficient number could not be found out of the 1,400 elected from their class in the metropolitan county itself, to discharge with ability, or be entrusted with the guardianship of the turnpike roads.

Finally, they hinted darkly that this action would produce 'dire calamities, both private and public, by sowing the seeds of discord amongst the community which root deep into the minds of injured individuals, and by their growth tend gradually to dissolve the social compact'. This protest, which came at the beginning of the period of Reform agitation, had a certain validity generally, for in 1822 the qualifications required of a trustee were altered so as to exclude non-landowners.[58] The requisite estate values were raised and, except within ten miles of London, personal property was no longer to be considered as a sufficient qualification. James McAdam ascribed this change to

> the Circumstance of the Landed Interest not being sufficiently attended to at Turnpike Meetings and the other Parties, in Towns particularly, possessing considerable personal wealth, frequently attend those Meetings, not having that personal interest in the Road which Landed Proprietors must naturally possess.[59]

It was this assumption, that landed wealth was to be equated with the right and responsibility to govern, which the Reform movement sought to break down. Although the question of who was to control the turnpike roads was relatively insignificant when compared with such major considerations as currency reform or the Corn Laws, none the less it was practical local issues such as this which helped to demonstrate to the more conservative sectors of the urban merchant and manufacturing community the need for them to have proper representation in government; and it was the pressure which these groups brought to bear, coupled with that of the popular radicals, which was of such importance for the success of the struggle for Reform.[60]

Besides the general issues raised during the consolidation controversy there were also specific allegations made against the promoters of the legislation. These were directed against both Lord Lowther[61] and J. L. McAdam, but primarily against the latter, who it was claimed tried to consolidate the London trusts to suit his own ends. The Brentford trustees argued that[62] 'speculators' (meaning McAdam) saw consolidation of the London trusts as 'the best mine from which to enrich themselves . . .', and that, 'finding their gigantic schemes and ambitious views frustrated, unless the trustees of the metropolitan districts could be replaced, they had recourse to every calumny to

## The Metropolis Roads Commission

bring them into discredit'. The trustees of the Kilburn Bridge Trust were probably closer to the mark in suggesting that McAdam was motivated as much by the desire for power and prestige as for money.[63] While much of the criticism was overstated it must be remembered that the trustees were reacting against what they felt to be unfair attacks, led for the most part by McAdam, upon their ability and honesty. Considering the extremely sound financial condition of most of the London trusts, it would seem that they had good reason for feeling as they did.

Despite determined opposition, the Metropolis Roads Commission came into existence in July 1826.[64] It was hoped at the time that it would solve the problems on the London roads as well as providing a model which would be adopted by trusts throughout the country. The success of the commission was cited in 1833 by a House of Lords select committee as evidence that local trust consolidations were the only answer for the difficulties facing the turnpike system.[65] However, as with previous committees, which had made similar recommendations since 1819, no scheme was offered as to how these consolidations could be carried out. The first attempt to do this came two years later in a Bill to consolidate all the trusts in England.[66] The Bill proposed that a central board of commissioners be set up with the power to compel local trusts to consolidate. These trusts were to elect boards to manage the affairs of the new unified trust, but the central committee was to have control over appointments, salaries, all items of expense over £100, and any other aspect of management. These quite radical proposals were clearly modelled on the administrative provisions of the 1834 Poor Law Amendment Act, which provided for a central board with fairly wide powers over unions of local poor law authorities.[67] Indeed, as the Webbs have observed,[68] Edwin Chadwick, the author of this Act, and John McAdam held many similar views on the need for more professional administrators and for more central control of local government. However, forced unification and the extreme degree of centralisation advocated in the 1835 Bill went far beyond anything McAdam had ever proposed. He seems to have recommended voluntary consolidation and favoured only a limited degree of supervision, mainly in the form of a central audit of trust accounts.[69]

The 1835 Bill was dropped,[70] and in the following year a similar Bill was defeated after 157 petitions had been presented against it.[71] But the proposals contained in these Bills continued to be put forward. In 1836 a select committee recommended the formation of a central board in London to control the finances and management of the trusts;[72] in 1839 another select committee presented a detailed scheme for the formation of local trust unions;[73] and the 1840 House of Lords committee proposed yet another variant on the theme of trust consolidation.[74] None of these attempts was successful. It was not until 1849 that a rather weak Act 'to facilitate the Union of Turnpike Trusts' was passed,[75] and this simply provided a framework within which the trusts could, if they wished, consolidate with one another. This Act was too limited and came too late to help the turnpike trusts.

The more concerted efforts from the early 1830s to improve the turnpike system were part of a more widespread movement of reform undertaken by the Whig government, the most notable achievements of which were the New Poor Law (1834), the Municipal Corporations Act (1835)[76] and the reorganisation of the parish road system (1835).[77] Trust reform was, however, undoubtedly low on the list of government priorities and was probably pushed even lower as active opposition to any form of centralised control increased after the passage of the Poor Law Amendment Act. The Whigs saw their parliamentary majority steadily eroded from the early 1830s, and with the growing unrest throughout the country from 1836 they may have felt it was impolitic to weaken their support in local areas by another unpopular measure. The strong opposition to trust reform arose both because of the fear of centralised government control and because solvent trusts did not want to unite with trusts in financial distress.[78] Parliament was concerned with reform but seems to have been unable to reconcile this concern with their desire not to compromise the trusts' creditors. This remained a major obstacle to reform. All the above factors combined to

## The Metropolis Roads Commission

insure that the London experiment was not attempted in other parts of the country.

The Metropolis Roads Commission did not inspire imitators as its promoters had hoped, but did it fulfil its other stated objective? Did it do a better job than the trusts it replaced? It is difficult to provide a satisfactory answer to these questions for the kinds of demands made on the London roads changed so markedly over time, especially from the mid-1830s with the advent of the railways and the rapid increase in omnibus traffic.[79] However, certain aspects of the commission's performance do stand out. Firstly, it was able to rationalise and then steadily reduce the trusts' debts. When it assumed control of the roads in 1827 it inherited debts totalling £123,000, the bonded debt was held by 250 individuals, and the yearly payments to service the debt were £6,406 (8·5 per cent of income).[80] By 1832, despite the borrowing of an additional £20,000 to repair two new roads, the debt had been reduced to £100,000, there were now only two creditors, and interest payments were down to £4,607 (5·7 per cent of income).[81] A sinking fund of £5,000 was established and all debts were finally liquidated by the early 1850s.[82] The commission was also able to reduce salary expense, although the savings here were not very dramatic—only about £1,000 per year.[83]

The commission appears to have handled its finances extremely well, and under the supervision of J. L. McAdam's son, James, road repair was successfully carried out;[84] but a substantial reduction in the number of gates, one of the most important aims of the commission's supporters, was never realised. Some toll houses and gates were removed, but as the areas through which the roads ran became built up it was found that new gates and side bars had to be erected in order to prevent toll evasion.[85] The only way to get rid of the gates and bars was to turn the roads back to the parishes, and this the commission gradually did. Eight miles of road were given up in 1829;[86] three or four miles in 1845,[87] 51 miles in 1863,[88] and the remainder was kept under the commission's control until it was finally wound up in 1872.

## III

*Summary and Conclusion*

In the first decades of the nineteenth century there was growing concern with the condition of the turnpike trusts generally and with the mounting level of trust indebtedness in particular. An explanation of, and a possible solution for, this problem was offered by J. L. McAdam. He cited the small scale of trust operations as one of the main difficulties and suggested the consolidation of the trusts as the only way in which better-organised, more professional administrative procedures—the key to sound finances and well-repaired roads—could be introduced. McAdam's ideas strongly influenced the various committees which considered the question of the turnpike trusts, and he was instrumental in bringing about the London trust consolidation. This was done despite the determined opposition of the London trusts, and even though the Metropolis Roads Commission proved to be highly successful, further trust consolidation continued to be resisted throughout the rest of the country. It was not until after 1834 that detailed, comprehensive proposals for forcing the trusts to consolidate, modelled on the administrative provisions of Chadwick's Poor Law Amendment Act, were put forward. However, active local opposition and the government's need to concentrate its efforts on more urgent reforms combined to defeat all attempts to reorganise the turnpike system.

This brings us to a final question—would the turnpike trust system have been improved if consolidation had taken place throughout the country? Professor Pollard, referring to industry in the period, has said,

> It is by no means certain that larger size was always considered desirable or could even theoretically be defended as superior. On the contrary, organisation theory itself suggests that while there may be technical, financial or marketing advantages in growth, management difficulties tend to work in the opposite direction, towards a lower optimum size.[89]

This statement could also be applied to the turnpike trusts because the larger trusts (those controlling more than forty miles of road) do not seem to have been any more successful than the smaller trusts.[90] Also, although the general level of administrative competence was rising in the nineteenth century, the practice of large-scale management was still in its infancy, and McAdam's ideas on administrative reform were slow to gain acceptance.[91] It could be argued that more consolidations would have encouraged the spread of better management techniques, but this must remain conjectural. Finally, it must be remembered that the London experiment worked so well partly because the trusts taken over were in a relatively good financial condition, the roads were in reasonable repair, and the most debt-laden trusts in London were not included in the consolidation. In other parts of the country conditions were not so favourable. Many small trusts had low incomes and very large debts,[92] and their position became more desperate from the mid-1830s when competition from the railways began to be felt with devastating effect.[93] The stage-coaches could not compete, and as they disappeared from the roads so the trusts' incomes were reduced. In 1837, the trusts collected £1,510,000 in tolls,[94] and by 1849 receipts had fallen by about 26·5 per cent to £1,097,482. The magnitude of the problem had been completely altered, and it is unlikely that trust consolidation could have provided any more than the most marginal benefit to a turnpike system which, with the advent of the railways, soon became little more than an outmoded relic of the Industrial Revolution.

*University of East Anglia*

## References

1   2 & 3 Philip & Mary c 8.
2   S. and B. Webb, *English Local Government: The Story of the King's Highway* (1913), 27–50.
3   W. Albert, 'The Road Transport System in England, 1700–1839' (unpublished PhD thesis, University of London, 1968), 25–32.

4 Ibid, 46–76.
5 Ibid, 226–43.
6 W. T. Jackman, *The Development of Transportation in Modern England* (2nd edn, 1962), 310–15.
7 For example, there were three reports on the Kensington, Fulham and Chelsea Trust in 1731, 1751 and 1765. *Journals of the House of Commons (JHC)*, xxi, 837–8; xxix, 648; xxx, 429.
8 From the passage of the General Turnpike Act in 1773 to the next General Turnpike Act in 1822 there were fifteen amending Acts. See Albert, op cit, 130.
9 British Parliamentary Papers (BPP), 1796 (May) FS x 749, 1798 FS x 758, 1800 FS x 759.
10 BPP, 1806 (212) ii 241.
11 See Albert, op cit, 423–5.
12 BPP, 1808 (225) ii 333, 7–8.
13 BPP, 1809 (509) v 339, 4–6.
14 Ibid, 18–34. See also R. H. Spiro, 'John Loudon McAdam, Colossus of Roads' (unpublished PhD thesis, University of Edinburgh, 1950), 301–3.
15 BPP, 1810–11 (240) iii 855, 27–32.
16 Spiro, op cit, 236.
17 J. L. McAdam, *Remarks on the Present System of Roadmaking* (7th edn, 1823), vi.
18 BPP, 1819 (509) v 339, 26–30.
19 B. R. Mitchell and P. Deane, *Abstract of British Historical Statistics* (1962), 19; P. Deane and W. A. Cole, *British Economic Growth, 1688–1959* (2nd edn, 1967), 118.
20 T. C. Barker and M. Robbins, *A History of London Transport Passenger Travel and the Development of the Metropolis*, vol I (1963), 2–6.
21 First Report of the Commissioners of the Metropolis Turnpike Roads . . ., BPP, 1826–7 (339) vii 23, 31.
22 *The Times*, 8 February 1816, 4b.
23 BPP, 1820 (301) ii 301, 3.
24 Ibid, 3.
25 BPP, Public Bills 1820 i, 305–22.
26 Harrow TT Minute Book, 26 June 1820, LA/HW/TP 17, Greater London Council Record Office.
27 Ibid, 19 March 1821.
28 *JHC*, lxxvi, 183, 198, 203, 207, 216, 311, 321, 354, 356, 368–9.
29 S. and B. Webb, op cit, 177.
30 BPP, 1825 (355) v 167.
31 Ibid, 3–8.
32 Quoted in Jackman, op cit, 282.
33 BPP, 1821 (747) iv 343.
34 Mistakes in the 1821 data were corrected in 1833; BPP, 1833 (703) xv 409.
35 L. S. Pressnell, *Country Banking in the Industrial Revolution* (1956), 367–8.
36 See Albert, op cit, 141–5.
37 BPP, 1840 (256) xxvii 1, 9. Administrative charges included salaries and law costs.
38 See Albert, op cit, 141–5.
39 42 Geo III c 101.
40 51 Geo III c 156.
41 52 Geo III c 149.

## The Metropolis Roads Commission

42  See, for example, 42 Geo III c 101.
43  BPP, 1833 (703) xv 409, 43.
44  See note 37 above.
45  1 & 2 Wm IV c 6.
46  BPP, 1833 (703) xv 409, 168–9.
47  7 Geo IV c 142.
48  Albert, op cit, 110.
49  *JHC*, lxxxi, 223, 231, 234, 271, 296. Also *Index to the House of Lords Journals, 1820–1833*, 395.
50  *The Times*, 15 November 1826, 3e.
51  T. Fordish, 'History of the Metropolitan Roads', in *Report of the London Traffic Branch of the Board of Trade 1910, 1911* (cd 5472), xxxiv (27), 183.
52  'Petition from the Inhabitants of Clerkenwell against the Metropolis Road Bill', 12 May 1826 (629), House of Lords Record Office.
53  See, for example, 'Petition from Hampstead-Highgate trustees', 9 May 1826 (611), or 'Petition from Inhabitants of Isleworth', 12 May 1826 (629), House of Lords Record Office.
54  *The Times*, 10 November 1826, 2b.
55  'Petition from Kilburn Bridge-Sparrows Herne Trust', 9 May 1826 (611), House of Lords Record Office.
56  This is not to suggest that the unrest was purely attributable to conditions of trade.
57  *The Times*, 15 November 1826, 3e.
58  3 Geo IV c 126, art 62 and 63.
59  BPP, 1833 (703) xv 409, 96.
60  See Asa Briggs, *The Age of Improvement* (1959), 236–60.
61  *The Times*, 10 November 1826, 2b.
62  Ibid, 15 November 1826, 3e.
63  'Petition from Kilburn Trust . . .' (611), 9 May 1826. Spiro has characterised McAdam as '. . . cocky, vigorous, self-important', and that as a modern 'prophet' he could bear no criticism and was vain and imperious. Spiro, op cit, 272.
64  7 Geo IV c 142.
65  BPP, 1833 (703) xv 409, 3.
66  BPP (Public Bills), 1835 iv 539–45.
67  S. E. Finer, *The Life and Times of Edwin Chadwick*, 88–92.
68  Webbs, op cit, 174.
69  BPP, 1819 (509) v 339, 29.
70  *JHC*, xc, 489.
71  BPP (Public Bills), 1836 vi 427–40. Index to *JHC 1820–1837*, 1094.
72  BPP, 1836 (547) xix 335, iii.
73  BPP, 1839 (295) ix 369, iv. A Bill presented in the same year for creating trust unions was defeated.
74  BPP, 1840 (256) xxvii 1, 11.
75  12 & 13 Vic c 46.
76  Briggs, op cit, 275.
77  5 & 6 Wm IV c 50.
78  Albert, op cit, 114–15.
79  Barker and Robbins, op cit, 25–40.
80  'First Report of the Commissioners of the Metropolis Turnpike Roads . . .', 3–4.

81 'Sixth Report of the Commissioners of the Metropolis Turnpike Roads . . .', Bound Reports (MRC 51), 5, Greater London Council Record Office.
82 Ibid, Thirtieth Report.
83 Ibid, All Reports.
84 Ibid, All Reports.
85 'Report from the Select Committee on Metropolis Turnpike Roads', BPP, 1856 (8) xiv, 7.
86 10 Geo IV c 159.
87 BPP, 1856 (8) xiv, 4.
88 26 & 27 Vic c 78.
89 S. Pollard, *The Genesis of Modern Management. A Study of the Industrial Revolution in Great Britain* (1965), 10.
90 Albert, op cit, 145.
91 Ibid, 260.
92 See, for example, 'Abstract of the Statements of Income and Expenditure of the Turnpike Trusts . . . from January 1834 to 31 December 1834', BPP, 1836 (2) xlvii 297.
93 BPP, 1839 (295) ix 369, iii–iv.
94 BPP, 1872 (5) xviii, 4.

J. C. HOPKINS

# A Fieldwork Note on the Congleton Railway c 1807

I *Introduction*

IT APPEARS THAT LITTLE IS KNOWN generally of this early mineral railway and few references are known to the writer (see pp 250-1). The most relevant parts of a contemporary reference[1] are appended because of their possible importance in identifying a relic mentioned below.

Baxter's most helpful book[2] gives sufficient information for anyone starting to search for the route but makes the surprising statement that '... the Ordnance Maps of the district give no clues ... to traces of this elusive railway'. In fact, where not coincident with present road lines, or very close to them, the whole route is marked as public footpath on present-day maps of all scales from 1in to 25in, though is admittedly easily missed on the 1in version. There are still sufficient marks and clues on the ground to allow the route to be followed virtually throughout its length.

The lower terminus of the railway was at a point on Moss Road on the south-east edge of Congleton in Cheshire, at a height of about 428ft. The point is marked 'Coal Wharf' on Bryant's map,[3] a site which is now occupied by a private residence called 'Machine House'. The occupier's family have lived there for some generations and one is assured that marks in the garden show the position of the original (weighing or tipping?) machine. From this point the route ran roughly south over the nearby ridge of Mow Cop, at a maximum height of 980ft and down the other side a short distance to Stonetrough Colliery at 800ft, just inside the parish of Wolstanton in North Staffordshire. The line of the ridge approximates to the county boundary. The total route length is about 3·3 miles and the average gradients, as calculated, are 1 in 20 on the Cheshire side and 1 in 26 in Staffordshire.

The principal points of interest seem to be the vertical distances involved, the possibly short useful life, as noted by Farey, and the unusual cross-section of the rails. This last matter has become of increased interest recently as it appears possible that a fragment of the rail has been found, close to the lower terminus, which answers to the contemporary description (see the appendix and the plates on p 273).

There is uncertainty about the useful life of the tramroad. Farey, in the extract quoted in the appendix, says that it was 'almost or quite disused' in 1809 but Hansall,[4] writing apparently between 1817 and 1823, says that '. . . the town lies near to the Collieries, and to the Coal Wharf on Congleton Moss, it is well supplied with Coals at 14s. per ton'. This would seem to imply that the railway was still in everyday use.

II  *Detailed Description of the Route*

The Coal Wharf (SJ 8652–6126) on Moss Road is 1,900yd south, 15° east, of Congleton Town Hall and roads connect the two fairly directly. The wharf is now within 700yd of the Macclesfield Canal but, of course, this was not built till twenty years later, opening in 1831. The route, running south a short distance, joins a farm track in about 80yd which strikes off towards the ridge, though not climbing appreciably until passing Fairfields Farm and rising to Hillside Farm (SJ 8687–6029). The first slight ground markings are to be seen between these two farms and the straightness of the route on the map for 700yd in the vicinity of Hillside Farm is an early clue to the previous existence of a made-up track. The route continues up the bank through a wood and a low embankment is frequently clear just to the west of a stream. The first of the observed stone sleepers *in situ* can be seen in this stretch, if the state of the mud allows.

The number of sleepers, seen at various points along the route, total about a dozen and are all much the same. They are rough,

# A Fieldwork Note on the Congleton Railway c 1807

rectangular blocks measuring about 9in × 14in × 8in deep, usually with two rail-fixing holes about $\frac{3}{4}$–1in diameter, $2\frac{1}{4}$–$2\frac{5}{8}$in apart and 4–5in deep. Occasionally, it is found that only one hole is present in a block which is apparently unbroken. Unfortunately, no set of sleepers has yet been seen in position to indicate clearly the gauge of the track, though something in the range of 2 to 3ft is suggested by the dimensions of cuttings and embankments.

At the end of the straight portion above Hillside Farm, the route bends sharply south over a collapsed culvert and, in about 40yd, reaches the foot of an inclined cutting at SJ 8693–5998. This is still in excellent condition apart from a muddy track bed. It has a slightly sharper gradient at about 1 in 17, is 110yd long, possesses a width at base of about 10ft and a maximum depth of $9\frac{1}{2}$ft. Immediately at the foot of the cutting on the west side, there is a noticeable depression in the bank which, if contemporary, suggests that horses may have been led to and from the track here as a regular procedure, presumably for extra effort up the bank.

From the top of the cutting the line bends to the south-east to meet Mow Lane at SJ 9698–5958. It presumably crossed the lane by a low overbridge since the track is 12ft above the road level and it looks unlikely ever to have been much different. There are the remains of an approach embankment on the south side of the crossing but no other signs suggesting a bridge. At the crossing, a modern 'Public Footpath' notice now points to the southern portion only.

From the crossing a low embankment has been ploughed down in recent years and the track is not well defined for about 370yd, but it bears slightly to the south-east and climbs gently. At about the point SJ 8670–5916 the route is again seen clearly for some 280yd uphill as a track-bed running through what appear to be the remains of older, shallow diggings or quarries. About 130yd to the east of this area, there are later and much deeper (but perhaps similar) workings for ganister which were in use till about the 1940s. This portion of the route is now crossed by a motor-cycle scramble course and the resultant disturbance to the surface led to the finding of a sleeper in position at SJ 8671–5918 with what appeared to be the remains of a metal rail-chair still firmly in place (see plate, p 274).

Above this area the route continues across an arable field along a line marking a change in field gradient, below which no ploughing takes place. Another sleeper can be found here, having been rolled down the bank. Leaving this field at SJ 8656–5893, the route passes on to rough moorland, having reached a height of about 790ft, and bringing a clear view of the main ridge. The view to the west can, on rare occasions, encompass North and Central Wales. Within a few yards here can be seen upwards of a dozen sleepers still roughly in position and perhaps more would be revealed by quite shallow excavation. Those visible do not indicate what the gauge may have been but, as regards rail length, two pairs of sleepers suggest that it was around 3ft.

The line now swings south-east towards the ridge and is clearly seen for about 350yd on a low embankment with a well-preserved profile. At about SJ 8658–5887, a spur embankment is discernible on the down-hill side for about 40yd but which comes to an abrupt end when about 10ft high. It seems unlikely that it was merely a dump of unwanted material, as there are no cuttings in this region; but it is possible that it was used to convey coal to the 'Lime Kilns' (see plate, p 274) lower down the hill from this point, if they were working in the same period.

The line continues in a wide curve, rising gently, and becomes almost parallel to the ridge, but the signs become indistinct. In this region old quarries are marked on the larger-scale maps and could have been the source of the sleepers. The present ridge road is reached a few yards above Corda Well at SJ 8660–5838, at 910ft, and little height remains to be gained. Modern maps imply nothing other than that the line followed the ridge road for the next 630yd, but old maps and markings on the ground of shallow cuttings and low embankments show that it ran to the east of the road by distances up to about 30yd or so. The route appears to rejoin the present road at about SJ 8624–5774 and, in a further 130yd, reaches its maximum elevation

# A Fieldwork Note on the Congleton Railway c 1807

of about 980ft at the junction of Congleton Road and Tower Hill Road.

The line presumably turned into Tower Hill Road and dropped to Welsh Row Cottages in about 270yd. The road bears to the left here but the route continues almost in a straight line along the backs of the cottages and across more fields, being easily followed along hedge-lines and path-marks. It is interesting at SJ 8655-5697 to find the route crossed by another on the same level which clearly ran from Tower Hill Colliery to Mow Cop Colliery and the old lines which ran from this area to the Macclesfield Canal at Kent Green Wharf.

To digress briefly, this tramroad was of a heavier type as three sleepers can be seen on 36in centres of which the top face dimensions are 22in × 18in. The three are adjacent and bear two separate hole patterns. One set of holes appears on all three sleepers and comprises two holes 1⅝in diameter on 11in centres, whereas the other set appears only on alternate sleepers and comprises two holes 1in diameter on 3⅝in centres. Presumably a change of rail design occurred. Nearby, this route runs on an embankment 12ft wide and therefore the gauge was presumably in the range of 4 to 5ft. There are several deeds relating to this line in the Stafford Record Office, including the original indenture.

To continue on the route of main interest: the line still falls gently, crosses the road from Biddulph to Harriseahead on the level, crosses a small stream into the parish of Wolstanton and reaches the slag heaps of Stonetrough Colliery. These are, of course, trivial by modern standards and are soon skirted to enter the colliery yard at SJ 8671-5637, 800ft, where the position of the shaft can still be seen.

## III  A Fragment of Rail

The only significant relics known to the writer, except for various sleepers simply showing holes, are the sleeper *in situ* bearing the remains of a metal chair mentioned above, and the fragment of rail (see plates) found in 1967 by the writer near the Coal Wharf at SJ 8649-6115. Briefly, the piece is 16¾in long, bellied in form and apparently almost half of a rail which would have been about 3ft long and 2½in high. The top surface is half-round of ¾in radius and, with the taper of the 'belly', this gives the 'oval or egg-shape' quoted in the contemporary reference. The material seems to be soft cast iron. There is an integral cast foot with a load-bearing area of 2in × 4in and above this a half-round of about ⅜in in the horizontal plane, presumably to key into the next rail. The weight of this piece is 11¼lb, giving an approximate figure of 24lb per yard. The shape of the foot seems to be a good match to that of the chair found *in situ*, which could possibly be a foot from which the rail has broken away, and this suggests that the fragment is truly a piece of authentic rail.

IV   *Conclusion*

As previously noted, little appears to be known of this tramroad and documentary evidence is scanty. However, remains on the ground give a clear picture of the route over most of its length and much of it is now public footpath. On the Staffordshire side, the Stafford Record Office has interesting papers relating to activities in the district in the early nineteenth century but no documents of direct use have been found. Bryant's map shows little of the route on this side. On the Cheshire side, it seems clear that the land belonged to the Egertons of Oulton Park.[5] Unfortunately it may be that the documentary trail here was closed by the fire which destroyed Oulton Hall in 1926. However, searches of the Chester Record Office at intervals may yet yield results.

The writer will be grateful for any further information on these matters.

*Winsford, Cheshire*

*References*

1. John Farey, Senior, *General View of the Agriculture of Derbyshire*, 3 vols (1817), vol 3, 288 and 331 (extracts appended).
2. B. Baxter, *Stone Blocks and Iron Rails* (1966), 42, 96, 97.

# A Fieldwork Note on the Congleton Railway c 1807

3 Bryant's Map of Cheshire, 1831, 1¼in to the mile (portion shown on p 274).
4 J. H. Hansall, *History of the County Palatine of Chester*, Chester (1817–23).
5 Tithe Map for the Township of Newbold Astbury, 1839, Chester Record Office.
NB All position references are Ordnance Survey, quoted to 10m, and have been estimated from 25in maps. Altitudes are estimated from 6in and 25in maps.

*For plates, provided by the author*, see pp 273–4

## Appendix

Two extracts from John Farey, Senior, *General View of the Agriculture of Derbyshire*, vol 3 (1817), chapter XVI:

*Section 2, p 288:*

In the use of [these] wooden railways, the flanch or projecting nib for keeping the waggon on the railway was on the wheel: but now, the flanches of iron railways are almost universally cast on the bars and the wheels plain, by which they are fitted for being occasionally drawn off the rails on the common roads. I have heard it said that the earliest use of these flanched rails above ground (for they were first introduced in the underground Gates of Mines, it is said) was on the S. of the Wingerworth Furnace, leading to the ironstone pits by Mr. Joseph Butler about the year 1788.

I have observed however three instances in the district of flanched wheels being used on iron rails, viz. on a railway branch of the Ashby de la Zouch Canal, from Ilat Wharf in Measham constructed about 1799 wherein the pulley wheels ran on metal ribs cast on bars; another was on a separate railway near Congleton that will be mentioned in the next Section, whereon the bars were oval or egg-shaped according to Mr. Benjamin Wyatt's plan see *Repertory* NS Vol III 285 and XIX, 15 and the other on the Leicester Navigation Charnwood Forest Branch.

*Section 3, p 331:*

On the South East of Congleton in Cheshire, about 2 miles, at the N.W. corner of the Congleton Moss, a Coal-yard was established about the year 1807, for the supply of this Town (which is the 177th on the list with 4,616 inhabitants) and a railway was laid therefrom S, about 2 miles, to Stone Trough Colliery, in Woolstanton. It was laid with oval bars of iron, on the top of which the pulley-formed wheels of the trams ran, see p. 288 but when I saw this railway in July 1809, it seemed to be almost or quite disused, the reason of which I did not happen to hear.

R. J. CROFT

# The Nature and Growth of Cross-Channel Traffic through Calais and Boulogne 1840–70

THE LARGE EXPANSION in cross-Channel passenger traffic in the nineteenth century deserves more attention than it has so far received from transport historians. In 1840 the total number of passengers passing through the ports of Calais and Boulogne amounted to 73,100; by 1860 it had risen to 179,751 and in 1872 it was 273,081.[1] In trying to understand these developments there is, however, a double difficulty: to give reasons for the expansion, and to define the exact nature of this traffic.

*Possible Reasons for Growth*
By the mid-nineteenth century most of the shipping services on the short-sea routes between England and the Continent were in the hands of the railway companies, at first operated through subsidiaries and later directly. In the 1840s the South Eastern Railway established a regular run from Folkestone to Boulogne as well as supplementing the Dover–Calais packet service. In the following decade the London, Brighton & South Coast Railway with the Ouest Railway of France developed the route between Newhaven and Dieppe. Finally in 1861 the London, Chatham & Dover Railway Company took over the mail steamers for the Dover–Calais service and shortly after the South Eastern confined its services to the Folkestone–Boulogne route.[2] The traveller also had, it must be noted, the alternative of the older direct steamers from London to the French ports organised by the General Steam Navigation Company, a cheaper but slower service that seemed to lose ground to the railways' train-and-ship link to Europe.[3]

*The Nature and Growth of Cross-Channel Traffic*

The quickness and convenience of railway travel in reaching the ports on either side of the Channel probably played a large part in stimulating continental travel for the British. Once the travelling time between London and Paris had been reduced to half a day (and it became progressively less) the ease and attractiveness of a journey abroad increased considerably, and the spread of railways on the rest of the Continent of Europe must have provided a further stimulus. This aspect needs little further elaboration.

The question of price is more problematic. It is hard to know to what extent there was a reduction in the cost of a voyage across the Straits of Dover. The single first-class fare from London to Calais in 1836, before the railway came, was 28s;[4] in 1860 it was 30s.[5] For London to Dieppe in 1862 the ticket would cost 21s.[6] This would seem to suggest that for a relatively short journey, ie one accomplished in a matter of hours rather than days and for which the fare would only be a relatively small proportion of the total cost of a holiday, the extra shillings spent on saving minutes was acceptable to the public, particularly if it meant a quicker sea crossing. The fact that most travellers proceeding via Dover and Folkestone went first-class helped the three companies concerned in the exploitation of that route. The low-fare services of the Thames route that went with a very long voyage were a failure, but the Newhaven–Dieppe service with its moderately priced tickets and acceptable journey time was successful, particularly from the 1860s onwards. This may conceivably be an example of low price creating a demand in the way that the Dover or Folkestone services did not. Perhaps in continental as in internal railway travel the first-class passenger was becoming less dominant as the wider public realised the possibilities of a cheaper lower-class travel, a development for which the Ouest and London, Brighton & South Coast railways catered. However, the Dover and Folkestone routes probably owed their success generally to speed and not economy; this was also the opinion of the railway companies concerned.[7]

Basic fares could be modified and rendered more acceptable by return tickets at usually about one and a half times the single rate, and by excursions of various kinds which could be half a double ticket.[8] The advantages of returns applied equally to all routes, but excursions being brief—for a day or a weekend—were really only possible on the shorter sea routes. The South Eastern started them quite early. For instance, in 1848 they were advertising Easter weekend tickets for Boulogne from London, valid Thursday to Monday, for 27s first class and 20s second,[9] and in 1850 for Boulogne races the fares were 28s, 20s and 15s.[10] There were also excursions to Paris: in the spring of 1849 the Nord noted that 'plusieurs certaines d'anglais' had taken advantage of return fares from London at £3 and 44s.[11] Under the Continental Agreement of 1863 between the two Kent companies the issue of cheap tickets continued. In 1863 it was decided that the Chatham and South Eastern would charge 20s and 15s for weekend returns from London to Calais and 45s and 35s for monthly family tickets.[12] There was usually no third class, though the two companies did quote one for the 1867 Paris Exhibition.[13] The excursion system allowed the quality routes to be available on occasions to the less exclusive traveller and so helped to broaden the basis of the South Eastern and Chatham custom.

The fares quoted so far represented only one part of a possible journey abroad; if the traveller were to go farther afield and pay for his accommodation as well, the cost would naturally be greater. Little information is available on this facet of the cost of travel. A correspondent in *The Times* explained how a journey (time not specified) of 1,514 miles through Holland, Germany and France with 93lb of luggage cost him £10 18s 0d, but this was in 1847 before the European railway network was complete[14] and did not include hotels. Another example, also untypical, is the Englishman who travelled from May to September 1851 all over Europe by first-class hotel and train for £120.[15] A better instance is the description in the same year which claimed that 'a trip up and down the Rhine . . . may be done very jollily for £20'.[16] However, any estimates of the cost of foreign holidays are conjecture as it depended very much on the individual traveller.

The speed and convenience of rail travel, and, to a slighter extent, the special rates it offered, were stimuli to the propensity to travel

*The Nature and Growth of Cross-Channel Traffic*

which were exploited by the travel agent, who combined them with arrangements for cheap accommodation and a worry-free holiday which appealed to the less monied or perhaps less venturesome person. The role of the travel agent in the expansion of continental traffic may have been considerable, but it is difficult to assess in quantitative terms as no satisfactory histories have yet been written on that subject and there appears to be very little primary material available. Travel agents dealing with 'all-inclusive' tours abroad seem to have started operations in the 1840s, if one can judge from the advertisement columns of the national press. The Continental Railway Office in Regent's Circus, London in 1849 offered for £8 first-class travel to the French capital, full board and lodging for a week, and, beguilingly, a free entry to the principal places of public amusement and theatres 'under the guidance of intelligent cicerones speaking English'.[17] There was also the possibility of a 15 day excursion on the Rhine for 12 guineas and a tempting 'week of pleasure in Paris' for £10.[18]

It is not at all clear how large this trade was at this time or to what extent the South Eastern benefited from it. According to W. F. Rae, Thomas Cook (whose continental activities began in the next decade) chose not to use the South Eastern after they exacted such harsh terms for his excursion for 1,673 working men to Paris in 1861. Instead he approached the Brighton who were much impressed by arrangements in connection with the 1867 Exhibition, where he persuaded the railway to issue some return tickets at only 20s, and to provide trips of four days to Paris for working men at 34s. In 1873 after a dispute with the Great Eastern Railway he also signed an agreement with the Chatham.[19] Little evidence remains as to what extent the Folkestone route benefited from Cook's services, though in the Ouest archives it is recorded that the French company protested when in 1870 he offered his clients the choice of three routes to Paris, including the South Eastern.[20] The same documents also explain that henceforth Cook was to receive 6 per cent on all tickets he sold and not just on excursions.[21] If the South Eastern and the Chatham obtained fewer customers from the most famous travel agent of his day, it was perhaps because Cook catered for the more modest kind of tourist who would travel by the cheaper Newhaven route anyway, and was therefore no loss to the short-sea lines. Again, some of the persons crossing by Dover and Folkestone may have been on business as well as pleasure, a reflection if true, of the growing commerce with France.[22]

With the growth of European railways there developed amenities abroad that catered for the English visitors. The 1850s saw the expansion of the Riviera and its luxurious hotels and casinos at Monaco and elsewhere; France's annexation of the county of Nice in 1860 was a further stimulus.[23] All English travellers to French resorts, and until the Alpine tunnels most of those *en route* for Switzerland and Italy, would have passed by Calais, Boulogne and Dieppe. Germany and Belgium could be entered via Ostend or Flushing, though for the former port Dover was the place of embarkation and therefore the two southern companies earned money from that area of continental growth as well as from the others.

While the growing ease of travel in the nineteenth century is certain, and its manifestations in England and overseas palpable, if difficult to quantify, the innate propensity to travel is very hard to assess. Obviously rising spending power would come into the analysis. Perhaps the real cost of foreign holidays was falling both in relation to incomes, and to price levels generally. Travel was also stimulated by particular events. Every international exhibition, especially those abroad, led to increased traffic, both after as well as during the exhibition year. This surely suggests that the widening knowledge of the possibility of travel or the actual experience of it were very important, and that people who had gone to the Continent, perhaps as members of a tour for a special event, would acquire the taste for trips the following years as well. Falls in traffic can usually be explained by obvious events such as the French Revolution of 1848 or the Franco-Prussian war. Sometimes these deterrents were less dramatic and merely irksome, such as the passport restrictions of 1858,[24] or the cholera scare of 1866.[25] But in each case the decline was short-lived and the upward trend quickly resumed.

## The Nature of the Passenger Traffic

It is difficult to know precisely who the travellers were or even accurately where they were going, for the evidence is fragmentary and can only give hints here and there. As these hints are not at regular intervals it is by no means easy to tell if a difference between them indicates a trend or an isolated example. Class is perhaps the easiest subject for generalisation, though again hard to quantify exactly. The railways themselves considered the Dover and Folkestone services to be the first-class routes and the Newhaven second class.[26] It is not clear whether they meant the actual category of ticket, or the price and quality of service, as fares were lower for the less rapid Newhaven route. For British railways as a whole the higher-class tickets sold were a dwindling proportion of the total.

CLASS DIVISIONS IN BRITISH RAILWAY JOURNEYS
IN PERCENTAGE[27]

|      | first | second | third |
|------|-------|--------|-------|
| 1845 | 16·0  | 43·0   | 41·0  |
| 1860 | 12·31 | 31·53  | 56·16 |
| 1879 | 7·0   | 11·10  | 81·90 |
| 1890 | 3·70  | 7·70   | 88·60 |
| 1900 | 3·00  | 6·00   | 91·00 |
| 1905 | 3·04  | 4·38   | 92·58 |

It would appear that journeys on the cross-Channel steamers did not correspond to this trend, at least for travellers via Dover and Folkestone. This was obviously because third-class passengers were simply not catered for on boats or boat trains, except in exceptional circumstances, and because persons affluent enough to travel via Dover or Folkestone would probably be those travellers who would very likely go first- or second-class by train anyway. That is why the following figures for the second half of two exhibition years are not really typical, for on those occasions even third-class passengers could use the packets; nevertheless they show the importance of first- and second-class tickets.

### LONDON–PARIS PASSENGERS VIA FOLKESTONE/BOULOGNE BY PERCENTAGE[28]

| year | first | second | third |
|---|---|---|---|
| 1851 | 51·5 | 31·0 | 17·5 |
| 1856 | 51·0 | 31·5 | 17·0 |

The only other example available for a long period is for 1860 when there were no third-class passengers, and when it was noted that first-class passengers composed 88 per cent of those going via Calais and only 62 per cent of those travelling via Boulogne.[29] It is not clear if this is exceptional or whether the difference between the two ports was always as great. If so this is rather puzzling, as the Dover–Calais route from London to Paris was still slower than the other, although the actual sea crossing was somewhat quicker. However, a 70 per cent average on through first-class tickets still gives some indication of the possible nature of the short-sea route traffic. One further isolated instance is available, but as it is a statistic of an off-season month, it can hardly be regarded as typical: namely January 1850, when 78 per cent of passengers with through tickets travelling via Calais were first class.[30] As for the third class, even the Brighton–Ouest who catered for them found that in ordinary years only 10 per cent of their boat passengers were in that category and in 1865 they contemplated the abolition of that class.[31]

> Le comité est unanimement d'avis que presque tous les voyageurs de troisième classe prendraient des billets de deuxième si les troisièmes n'existaient pas.

This division of passengers into first- and second-class does not take into account excursions which would not necessarily all be included in the through tickets quoted above. In other words, although the great majority of those going from London to Paris via Calais or Boulogne were probably first class, many persons just crossing the Channel on a weekend or day excursion may have gone second. Furthermore, of those on first-class through fares from London to Paris, some may have

*The Nature and Growth of Cross-Channel Traffic*

been travelling on first-class excursion tickets whose costs were comparable with second-class ordinary ones. Again the problem is to quantify, for figures quoted in directors' reports may have been given because they were exceptionally good or bad. In 1850 it was said that of the 21,190 tickets from London to Paris for the second half of the year 7,276 were for excursions,[32] but there is no indication whether a third of all through tickets being excursionists was a constant proportion or not. Presumably at the times of exhibitions and other events reduced-rate passengers formed a larger group than at other times.

Calculations on the destinations of travellers are dependent largely on information on through tickets collected by the three companies concerned with the short-sea route. This can be misleading, for a traveller who is recorded as having a *billet direct* from London to Paris may, for example, have come from Manchester and be bound for Nice. Although landings and departures at Boulogne and Calais are not exactly equivalent to crossings to and from Folkestone and Boulogne, they give some idea of the number of people *not* going to Paris if figures for the latter are subtracted from them.

COMPARISON OF PASSENGERS LANDING AT FRENCH CHANNEL PORTS AND GOING FROM PARIS TO LONDON AND VICE VERSA[33]

| year | passengers through Calais and Boulogne | passengers with through tickets | percentage |
|---|---|---|---|
| 1860 | 172,970 | 105,180 | 61 |
| 1864 | 243,584 | 133,345 | 55 |
| 1865 | 252,085 | 132,562 | 52 |
| 1866 | 234,113 | 154,957 | 66 |
| 1867 | 346,253 | 268,312 | 77 |
| 1869 | 271,783 | 154,886 | 57 |

The figure for 1867 is of course explained by the International Exhibition in Paris. For that and other years it might be said that those passengers who disembarked at Calais or Boulogne and did not have a *billet direct* for Paris could be one of four categories. They might be excursionists just going across the Channel for a day or weekend trip with the intention of proceeding no farther. Alternatively they went to local destinations on or near the Channel coast where they landed. The Nord noted in 1860 that many English people liked to spend all or part of their holidays in this way.[34] Another possibility for people disembarking at Calais is that they were bound for destinations in Germany or Belgium. An early isolated example is January 1850: of the 365 fares from London via Calais 21 went to Brussels and 49 to Cologne.[35] In 1860 of the (approximately) 76,000 passengers through Calais 14,720 were to or from Belgium and Germany (or 8·6 per cent of the total at the two major Channel ports).[36] By 1868 39,547 were booked for Belgium or Germany (or 14·5 per cent).[37] Finally it was of course possible for some people, for unknown reasons, to book locally after they disembarked instead of buying through tickets at London Bridge or Victoria; 16,680 were in this category in 1868 (or just over 6 per cent for that year).[38] Returning to 1860, which is the only year in this period for which more detail is available, it is interesting to note that not all *billets directs* were London–Paris returns, but that quite a few were singles.

THROUGH TICKETS AT BOULOGNE AND CALAIS 1860[39]

| *single tickets* | *via Boulogne* | *via Calais* | *Totals* |
|---|---|---|---|
| between Paris and London and vice versa | 25,490 | 16,841 | 42,331 |
| between Paris and Folkestone and vice versa | 4,501 | | 4,501 |
| between Boulogne and Calais and London and vice versa | 1,245 | | 1,245 |
| passengers to and from Belgium and Germany | | 14,720 | 14,720 |
| *returns* Paris–London sold in Paris | 4,434 | 3,864 | 8,298 |
| *returns* Paris–London sold in London | 14,086 | 8,352 | 22,438 |
| Totals | 49,756 | 43,777 | 93,533 |
| NB There were also passengers by the Thames route | 9,509 | 2,142 | 11,651 |
| Totals | 59,255 | 45,919 | 105,164 |

*The Nature and Growth of Cross-Channel Traffic*

There were, therefore, more singles in 1860 than returns for the Paris–London run; but of course the latter should be doubled to produce 61,472 which added to the singles makes a total of 103,803 passenger units, of which 29 per cent were return journeys. One may suppose that the single tickets fell into several possible categories, such as people going abroad for a period longer than the validity of a return ticket (usually two months). They might also be permanent migrants or persons going very much farther afield—to India, for example, as many took a short cut across the Continent to the P & O liners in the Mediterranean. Alternatively they were travellers who came home by another route, such as Ostend. It should be emphasised that any conclusions can only be tentative as they are based on statistics that have happened to survive by chance and, as we have seen, there is no way of ascertaining how typical they are. However, it may be fairly safely suggested that most cross-Channel travellers went farther than Calais or Boulogne and that of these the majority went to Paris and beyond, for it must not be forgotten that the Paris figures quoted above include tickets for people *en route* for Italy, Switzerland and elsewhere who passed through the French capital.

Seasonal differences in travel also form a matter of surmise for the most part, for again little information is available. The following data exist, but are restricted both for date and for place as well as for the kind of traffic.

If in these three meagre examples any trend at all can be discerned it is perhaps a greater bunching in the months of July, August and September, which may indicate a diffusion of continental travel among people who were beginning to take annual holidays, and that travel was no longer the exclusive domain of the long grand tour, but related to a lesser stay in a resort. It is hardly surprising that most crossings took place in the summer and the least in winter if the purpose of most journeys was pleasure. Winter sports did not start till much later. Variations in March and April probably reflect Easter excursions.

The nationality of the cross-Channel traveller is one of those matters that is so 'obvious' that it is never mentioned. Official records for entry

## MONTHLY RETURNS OF PASSENGERS THROUGH CALAIS[40]

| 1865 | all passengers from England | % | 1856 | only passengers by mail packet | % | 1834 | only passengers from Dover | % |
|---|---|---|---|---|---|---|---|---|
| Jan | 6,857 | 5·1 | | 2,791 | 6·4 | | 2,080 | 6·1 |
| Feb | 6,071 | 4·5 | | 3,138 | 7·2 | | 2,283 | 7·0 |
| March | 7,483 | 5·6 | | 3,412 | 7·8 | | 3,178 | 9·7 |
| April | 10,185 | 7·6 | | 2,971 | 6·7 | | 2,545 | 7·6 |
| May | 10,045 | 7·6 | | 2,962 | 6·8 | | 2,610 | 8·0 |
| June | 13,366 | 9·9 | | 3,535 | 8·1 | | 2,649 | 8·1 |
| July | 16,130 | 12·0 ⎫ | | 3,756 | 8·6 ⎫ | | 3,730 | 11·3 ⎫ |
| Aug | 18,947 | 14·0 ⎬ 40·5 | | 7,108 | 16·2 ⎬ 35·3 | | 3,296 | 10·0 ⎬ 33·0 |
| Sept | 19,296 | 14·5 ⎭ | | 4,549 | 10·5 ⎭ | | 3,833 | 11·7 ⎭ |
| Oct | 10,519 | 7·8 | | 4,054 | 9·1 | | 2,946 | 9·0 |
| Nov | 7,425 | 5·6 | | 2,925 | 6·6 | | 2,091 | 6·2 |
| Dec | 7,789 | 5·8 | | 2,378 | 5·5 | | 2,127 | 6·5 |
| Total | 134,113 | 100 | | 43,579 | 100 | | 32,924 | 100 |

of aliens into the United Kingdom did not start until the end of the nineteenth century, and in the documents perused so far no regular runs of statistics on this question have been found, though it is quite likely that they may have survived in some French records.[41] The implicit assumption is always that most passengers were British, but unfortunately the only consular report on this (for 1862) is not a typical year, for the International Exhibition in London must have attracted a larger than average number of foreigners. In that year British subjects formed 63 per cent of the passengers passing through Calais, the French 18 per cent, Americans 4 per cent and the Italians 4 per cent.[42] According to the information already cited on return tickets for London to Paris and vice versa, about three-quarters of all return tickets in 1860 were bought in London and only one-quarter in Paris, which suggests a higher proportion of British travellers. The reasons for this lack of reciprocal balance and business travel lie as much in French social history as in British, and are therefore outside the scope of this study. However, there is a possibility that a lack of facilities was one reason for the low number of foreigners coming to Dover and Folkestone. The *Railway Times*, commenting on the stimulus given by the Cobden-Chevalier Treaty being in one direction only, said that one reason why so few Frenchmen came to England was that 'such things as excursion and pleasure trains are unknown to the North of France'.[43]

*Canterbury Technical College*

*References*

1 See appendix.
2 C. Graseman and G. W. P. McLachlan, *English Channel Packet Boats* (1939), passim.
3 Evidence to SC on South Eastern Railway Packet Bill, 1853, House of Lords Record Office, states that of an estimated 167,094 passengers in 1852 between England and the Channel ports only 35,094 went direct by sea all the way from London.
4 Evidence to SC on SER Bill, 1836, HLRO, states that the cross-Channel fare would be 10s and the coach from Dover to London 18s.
5 Evidence to London, Chatham & Dover Railway (Metropolitan Extensions) Bill, 1860, HLRO, says the rail fare was 22s, and the SC on Railway Powers, PP 1864 (XI) q 1148, gives the boat ticket as 8s.
6 Evidence to SC on London, Brighton & South Coast (Enlargement of Stations) Bill, 1862, HLRO.
7 Collection Chemin de Fer du Nord, 48 AQ *liasse* 3628, Archives de France, Memo to board of 7 Aug 1851 states 'les voyageurs passant par Calais et Douvres et payant un prix double de ceux perçus par Dieppe, forment une clientèle qui nous est acquise, et qui se developperait peu en baissant le prix'.
8 SC on Railway Powers, op cit, q 1155.
9 *The Times*, 18 April 1848.
10 Ibid, 14 August 1850.
11 AF, Nord 10, Mins I 280, 25 March 1849.
12 Mins of joint committee of SER and LC & DR, 22 June 1863, British Transport Historical Records, SER 1/90.
13 Ibid, 10 January 1867.
14 *The Times*, 24 July 1847.
15 Anon, 'The Roving Englishman', *Household Words*, 1853, 358.
16 Ibid.
17 *The Times*, 25 July 1849.
18 Ibid, 20 September 1849.
19 W. F. Rae, *The Business of Travel* (1891), Chapter V, passim.

20 SNCF Armement Naval, Paris, Mins of Continental Conferences between Ouest and LB & SC at London, 14 July 1870.
21 SNCF Arm Nav Ouest-LB & SC Mins, at London, 10 February 1870.
22 *South Eastern Gazette*, 18 June 1864, remarked 'The number of commercial travellers to and from the continent is stated never to have been so large as at the present time'.
23 See H. K. Cook, *Over the Hills and Far Away* (1947), especially 116–20, and J. R. Pimlott, *The Englishman's Holiday* (1947), 200ff.
24 George Measom, *Guide to the South Eastern Railway* (1859).
25 Report of HM Consul at Calais, PP, 1867, LXVIII, 16.
26 Evidence to LB & SC (Enlargement of Stations etc) Bill, 6 March 1862, HLRO. The LB & SC traffic manager stated, 'The South Eastern traffic is essentially a first class traffic. Our traffic to France may be considered a second class traffic.'
27 Charles L. Raper, *Railway Transportation*, New York (1912), 33.
28 BTHR, SER Gen Mins, 21 February 1856.
29 AF, Nord 3629, Memo from chief engineer to board, 5 October 1861.
30 AF, Nord 3628, Statement of through tickets sent by SER, February 1850.
31 SNCF Arm Nav, Mins of conference at Newhaven between LB & SC and Ouest, June 1865.
32 *The Times*, 5 March 1851.
33 Figures for 1860 from AF, Nord 3628, Memo of 29 July 1861; for 1864 and 1865 from Nord 15, board mins VI 137, 8 February 1866; for 1866 and 1867 from Nord Directors' reports for 1867; for 1869 from Capt Tyler, *Report on Channel Passage* (1870), 245.
34 AF, Nord 3628, Memo from chief engineer to board, 29 July 1861.
35 AF, Nord 3628, SER statement sent to Paris Office, February 1850, op cit.
36 AF, Nord 3628, Memo of 29 July 1861, op cit.
37 Tyler, op cit, 245.
38 Ibid.
39 Based on Nord memo of 29 July 1861, op cit.
40 Figures for 1834 from SC on SER Bill 1836; for 1856 from SC on Packet Contracts 1859; for 1865 from Consular Report.
41 The limited time and money available for research in France precluded research in this direction.
42 Report of HM Consul at Calais for 1862, PP 1864, LXI, 38.
43 *Railway Times*, XXXII, 206, 27 February 1869.

*Appendix*
PASSENGERS THROUGH MAJOR CONTINENTAL PORTS 1840–73

| Year | Boulogne | Calais | Dieppe | Ostend | Comment |
|---|---|---|---|---|---|
| 1840 | 52,807 | 20,293 | ? | 13,694 | |
| 1841 | 47,953 | 21,019 | ? | 14,066 | |
| 1842 | 48,493 | 20,921 | 3,199 | 13,780 | |
| 1843 | 56,864 | 19,146 | 5,631 | 13,857 | Railway reaches Dover and Folkestone |
| 1844 | 75,790 | 18,663 | 9,323 | 22,473 | |
| 1845 | 70,709 | 15,664 | 11,761 | 28,744 | |
| 1846 | 72,150 | 18,463 | 13,151 | 35,748 | |
| 1847 | 78,273 | 16,637 | 4,905 | 35,581 | |
| 1848 | 69,909 | 17,956 | 957 | 23,951 | Railway reaches Boulogne French Revolution |
| 1849 | 64,997 | 36,376 | 2,751 | 22,661 | Railway reaches Calais |
| 1850 | 86,411 | 54,030 | 2,096 | 26,359 | |
| 1851 | 108,544 | 95,606 | 25,515 | 41,151 | London Exhibition |
| 1852 | 87,820 | 56,466 | 13,025 | 21,184 | |
| 1853 | 95,236 | 65,594 | 16,208 | 21,039 | |
| 1854 | 99,181 | 64,687 | 18,613 | 20,627 | |
| 1855 | 136,321 | 80,393 | 39,311 | 17,998 | Paris Exhibition |
| 1856 | 99,034 | 84,653 | 34,651 | 21,501 | |
| 1857 | 96,777 | 78,698 | 38,939 | 19,190 | |
| 1858 | 87,409 | 68,045 | 31,947 | 20,585 | |
| 1859 | 86,579 | 68,853 | 35,931 | 17,538 | |
| 1860 | 103,829 | 75,922 | 39,719 | 18,794 | |
| 1861 | 120,838 | 75,177 | 43,044 | 19,367 | |
| 1862 | 161,658 | 131,050 | 55,592 | 33,127 | London Exhibition |
| 1863 | 122,756 | 123,573 | 40,800 | 20,510 | |
| 1864 | 134,546 | 120,534 | 45,487 | 20,821 | |
| 1865 | 136,104 | 134,227 | 47,876 | 20,087 | |
| 1866 | 113,948 | 125,992 | 38,707 | 15,997 | |
| 1867 | 152,931 | 200,156 | 84,668 | 19,717 | Paris Exhibition |
| 1868 | 109,325 | 142,221 | 35,577 | 19,320 | |
| 1869 | 116,441 | 156,353 | 50,992 | 20,933 | |
| 1870 | 76,608 | 108,184 | 35,558 | 45,510 | |
| 1871 | 63,772 | 117,919 | 48,285 | 75,544 | Franco-Prussian War |
| 1872 | 104,978 | 168,103 | 50,941 | 55,906 | |
| 1873 | 106,638 | 183,994 | 52,551 | 40,346 | |

Source: Anon, *Le Port de Boulogne*, Boulogne (1903), 101.

T. M. DEVINE

# Transport Problems of Glasgow West India Merchants during the American War of Independence, 1775–83

THE BASIC TRANSPORT PROBLEM which confronted any merchant involved in the eighteenth-century colonial trades was how to carry the exotic produce, imported from the Americas, safely, speedily and cheaply to his home port in the United Kingdom. Such a problem encompassed far greater difficulties than a similar operation today. For instance, the rigid limitations of time enforced on West India traders by hurricane seasons, maturation of the sugar crop and the necessity of arriving at market at an opportune moment, had to be tackled by a transport medium overwhelmingly dependent on the whims of the weather. This difficulty was immensely exacerbated by war. To the natural enemies of calm, hurricane and storm were added, during four conflicts throughout the eighteenth century, the human adversaries of privateer and man-of-war.

This paper attempts to elucidate some of the major obstacles which the colonial merchants of one British port had to surmount during the American War of Independence (1775–83) in their endeavour to bring their cargoes of West India sugar, rum and cotton safely to an attractive market within the British Isles. Some effort will also be made to indicate the most common methods used to circumvent these difficulties and to assess the role of increased operating costs in the secular expansion of the Clyde–West Indies trade.

I

When Thomas Tucker, Cromwell's Commissioner for Customs and Excise, surveyed the ports of the Clyde in 1656 he was quick to point to Glasgow's emergence as 'one of the most considerablest burghs of Scotland', yet was equally certain that the town's ventures into the West India trade had, by and large, proved abortive.[1] However, even before the Treaty of Union in 1707 which gave Scottish traders official entry into the monopolies of the English Navigation Acts, this somewhat gloomy picture had been considerably modified. Even while Scottish colonial ambitions were being smashed in the 'Darien Disaster', Glasgow merchants were vigorously, if less dramatically, forging the links between the Clyde and the Caribbean which were to act as the essential bases for the expansion of the city's eighteenth-century sugar-importing trade.[2] The visible sign of this late seventeenth-century growth was the establishment of a sugar-processing industry by a classic coalescence of West India merchant capital and Dutch or German technical and entrepreneurial skill.[3] Quite clearly, therefore, although Glasgow hagiographical tradition dates the growth of the Clyde–West Indies trade from the emergence of the important firm of James Milliken & Co in the 1720s, the commercial contacts had been gained long before.[4]

It is none the less true that the importation of West India sugar was subordinate in the city's external commerce to the importation of tobacco from the North American colonies of Virginia, Maryland and Carolina, at least until the outbreak of the American War in 1775. The decade before this date had seen a substantial expansion in the West Indies trade and for several reasons the collapse of the tobacco trade in 1775–6 was certain to lead to a still further exploitation of this sector.[5] For one thing a switch from the one area to the other was, on balance, a relatively simple matter for Glasgow merchants. To a very large extent it was merely a switch of emphasis for many of them, a more forceful intervention in a trade in which they had an existing interest, albeit one over which American commerce had taken precedence.[6] For those with more marginal interests in the trade, entry was made easier by movement into a copartnery with extensive connections with the Caribbean. Thus William Cunninghame, one of the wealthiest 'tobacco lords', became a partner in Robert Dunmore & Co.[7] To these personal links there might be added Glasgow's advantage of having much experience in supplying the equipment needs of a plantation economy, her existing potential for increased sugar importation as an important sugar-processing centre, her proximity to the herring fisheries of the Clyde and the West Coast (cured and dried fish was the major element in the diet of the West Indian slaves), and the developing demand for 'sea-island' cotton by the West of Scotland textile industry. An augmented supply of Scots factors had also appeared in the Caribbean since 1775, many of the loyalist Scots in colonial America having fled there when the rebellion occurred.[8] Finally, during the war the West Indies had an irresistible attraction for former tobacco merchants: through neutral ports in the Caribbean tobacco might continue to flow, although in much reduced quantities, from the rebellious American colonies.[9]

The stage thus seemed set for a full-scale development of Clyde–West India commerce: that such a spectacular expansion did not ensue during the period of hostilities itself is partly due to the transport difficulties which merchants had to contend with and which will be examined here.[10]

In the public eye the most striking problem was the seeming ubiquity of American privateers from the very early months of the war. Danger to their shipping from enemy attack was a relatively novel phenomenon for Glasgow West India merchants: Professor Jacob Price has pointed out how it was not until the latter stages of the Seven Years' War in the early 1760s that French privateers had penetrated the northern sea-lanes in force.[11] Glasgow's commerce had increased immeasurably from that date and the American rebels, in particular, would have personal knowledge of the rich pickings likely to be made from it. As early as the autumn of 1775, the colonials began to fit out privateers (always the weapon of the weaker naval power in time of war) at Philadelphia, Boston and other ports. In the first two years of hostilities it has been estimated that the Americans had over 170 such vessels at sea.[12] No time was wasted in deploying them in all parts of the Atlantic and 'very soon they swarmed round every one of the West Indian islands'.[13]

The convoy system was, of course, established to protect merchant shipping, but apart from the imperfections of the system itself,[14] Glasgow ships were vulnerable and almost unprotected in two critical areas—in the Clyde Estuary and Irish Sea and around the islands of the West Indies. The harbour of Cork on the south-east coast of Ireland was at once the main assembly point for convoys proceeding to the Caribbean and a major provision base for the plantations there.[15] From the outbreak of war until the winter of 1778 no official naval escort was supplied for the voyage from the Clyde to this port.[16] In 1776-7 the necessity of transporting an army to North America and provisioning it once there had left only ten naval frigates in home waters, of which six, it has been estimated, were being repaired.[17] In addition, the Admiralty's traditional desire for financial retrenchment during years of peace meant that trade tended to suffer severely in the early years of war and in the economy drives the smaller ships, the type well adapted for convoy duty, were the main sufferers.[18] The appeals of Glasgow merchants, the petitions of town council and Convention of Royal Burghs could do little to shift the Royal Navy's concentration on its major rôle of supplying the army in America, a task which exhausted much of the energies of a service notoriously dilatory in awakening from its peacetime somnolence.[19] The only crumb of comfort for Glasgow commercial interests was that in July 1777 HMS *Arethusa* proceeded to cruise between the Mull of Kintyre and Belfast Lough,[20] but the specific request for an escort vessel (or vessels) for 'the trade of Glasgow' was refused: 'it would be impossible for their lordships to station a ship for the protection of each port, more especially while so great a part of the fleet is stationed in America and the Indies'.[21]

More promising were developments in March 1778 when two out of the eight armed ships fitted out for coastal protection by the Admiralty arrived in the Clyde.[22] Such support was likely to be short-lived, however, as, with the entry of France into the war, the government had to find ships to contain the enemy Channel squadrons and to conduct operations in what was developing into a global conflict. Thus the Clyde was left with a single 'armed ship', HMS *Satisfaction*, one of the two arrivals of 1778. This vessel unfortunately belied her name. She had originally been built as a collier, sailed heavily, and, it was alleged, could hardly keep up with a loaded merchantman. The Lord Provost of Glasgow proclaimed with some anguish how, although the Clyde estuary was 'very much infested with privateers', they had escaped with impunity due to the demonstrable inadequacies of the Clyde's 'guardship'.[23] Only with the despatch of the frigate HMS *Seaford* in April 1781 was naval protection of any validity given to the commerce of the Clyde ports.[24]

Where government defaulted, local initiative would have to fill the gap. This could take various forms. Perhaps the most common of these was the outfitting of privateers and arming of merchantmen. Although no precise figures are available, a recent calculation suggests that throughout the war there were twenty-seven vessels cruising as privateers from the Clyde together with forty-one with a 'letter of marque'.[25] More interesting was an exercise in mercantile co-operation. The merchants of Greenock, Port Glasgow and Glasgow agreed to subscribe £3,000 for the fitting out of three armed ships in the summer of 1777 so that, wrote a contemporary, 'we hope soon to be able to protect our trade without the assistance of government, who it seems, cannot spare us any frigates at present'.[26] So urgently was some form of defence required that the sum was subscribed in two hours.[27] Whatever the psychological benefits which might be derived from showing the flag, the first sortie of the squadron arguably did more harm than good. The picturesquely named *Charming Fanny* had to put back to port while the *Katie* and *Ulysses* set out for an eight-day cruise against the American marauders. The *Katie* sighted a merchant vessel and a brig but did not follow; the *Ulysses* had the embarrassing task of escorting an English ship into Greenock—the master of which, taking her to be an enemy privateer, had thrown his papers overboard. Indeed the one concrete result seems to have been to make confusion worse confounded in the Irish Sea: 'several other brigs, sloops and boats were greatly frightened and almost went ashore to keep from them'.[28] The dénouement of the farce came when the two vessels put into Belfast for information:

> The mayor and aldermen held a council, to take the Captain and the principle officers into custody, under suspicion of their being American privateers, but on finding they were fitted out to protect the trade of Clyde, they desisted from their purpose. On the other hand, when their real designs were made public a mob, instigated by a native of America, had nearly arose to maltreat them....[29]

A third means of defence was the construction of shore batteries: at least this, it was reckoned, would render the anchorages secure. In the autumn of 1778 Lord Frederick Campbell, Commander of the Western Fencibles, quartered in Greenock, was authorised by the town councils of Glasgow and Greenock to establish a battery 'for the defence of shipping belonging to the River Clyde and West Coast'.[30] Twelve cannon were delivered from Carron Ironworks and construction began forthwith, the two town councils being compensated for their expenditure by the government.[31]

By and large, however, the picture presented is one of governmental impotence for long stretches of the war and rather patchy local attempts at creating some sort of deterrent to enemy privateers. The result of this basic situation was that American cruisers were able to rampage almost at will along the Clyde coast, especially in the years 1776-8. The Firth of Clyde, with its two narrow channels, St George's and the North Channel, was a death-trap for Glasgow shipping in these years. In the period 5-14 July 1777, no fewer than nine merchantmen were taken in this area. In the previous June, fourteen had been captured.[32] John Knox insisted (almost certainly with some exaggeration) that 313 vessels 'of various sizes' belonging to Clyde ports were either captured or destroyed by enemy action throughout the war.[33] So great was the panic in the early years of the war that enemy landings were daily expected. In the summer of 1777 the good citizens of Ayr were hastening to remove their 'valuable furniture' farther inland as alarm spread along the west coast.[34]

The West Indian islands were if anything just as hazardous for the merchant in time of war. The late Professor Pares demonstrated that the nature of the inter-island sea routes was such that the privateer was almost invulnerable to Royal Naval control.[35] Line of battle ships were almost useless for everyday cruising among the numerous islands: privateers could escape into refuges where the more unwieldy men-of-war found it impossible to follow. The observations of one Dominican planter must have been fairly typical of the time: he noted that in June 1777 there were operating near the island several American privateers of thirty-six guns and 'an innumerable number of smaller ones' which, he indicated, 'it is very difficult to get hold of, as our ships upon that station are too large and too dull sailors to come up with them'.[36] In addition to the distinct reluctance of the Admiralty to station small vessels in the Caribbean—the traditional arena for fleet confrontations—there is some doubt whether the Royal Navy had any real heart for pursuing privateers. Few were large or heavily armed and the capture of one would mean meagre prize money for officers and men in relation to the trouble involved.[37]

The nature of West India commerce tended to act as a disincentive to the formation of local island-to-island convoys on an ad hoc basis by the merchants concerned. There is no doubt that efforts in this direction were made,[38] but the lack of regular routes or uniform sailing times, and the fact that skippers and supercargoes often had specific instructions on the length of stay in a particular port militated against their success. One gains the impression that Glasgow merchants, many of them fresh to West Indies commerce during the American War, would be at a particular disadvantage. Several were still in the process of making regular contact with planters and could not therefore predict a full freight of sugar, cotton or rum awaiting them when their ships

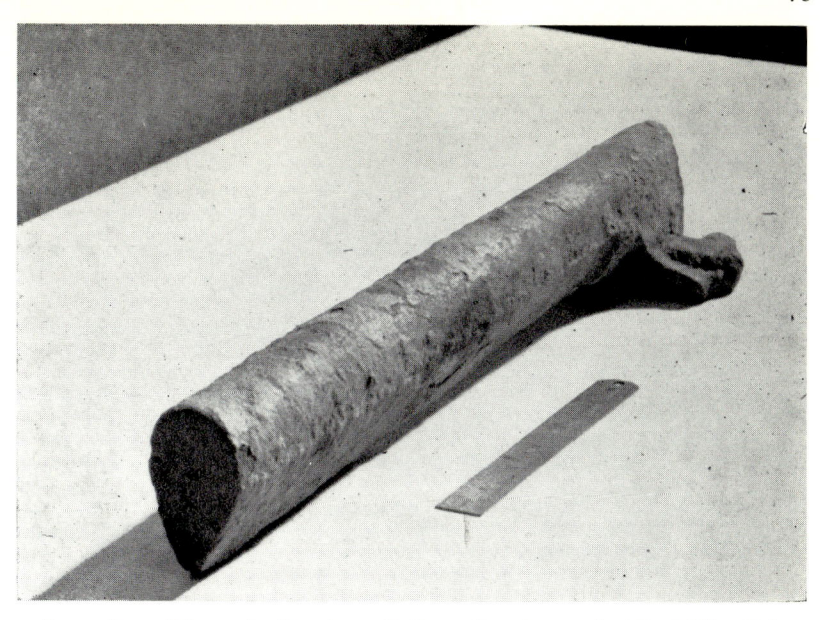

*Part of a rail from the Congleton Railway found near the 'Coal Wharf' in 1967, showing the cross-section at the approximate centre. The 6in rule affords a comparison of size*

*A side view of the same portion of rail (length 16¾in, height 2½in)*
See Hopkins, 'A Fieldwork Note on the Congleton Railway', pp 245–51

274

*A stone sleeper* in situ, *showing clearly the remains of a rail-chair*

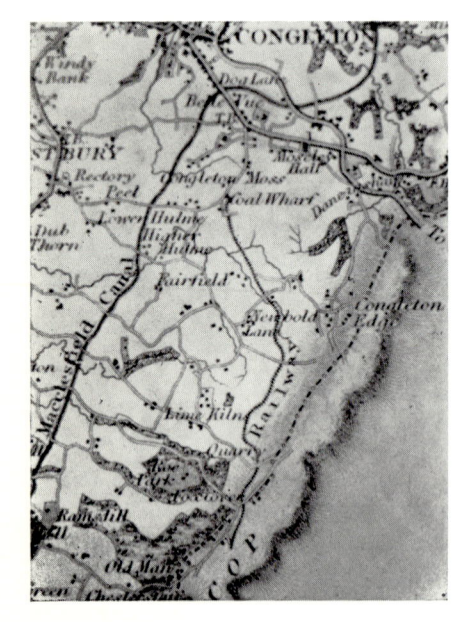

*A portion of Bryant's map of 1831 ($1\frac{1}{4}$in to the mile in the original) showing the Congleton Railway*

See Hopkins, 'A Fieldwork Note on the Congleton Railway', pp 245–51

*A View of Port Glasgow from the South East*

*The Port of Glasgow, founded in 1668. Note the ropewalk in the foreground and the dry dock (the first in Scotland) in the middle distance. From Foulis Academy, Glasgow Views etc 1756–70. (Courtesy: Mitchell Library, Glasgow) See Devine, 'Transport Problems of Glasgow West India Merchants', pp 266–304*

*A View of Greenock*

Greenock in 1768. The customs accounts make it clear that the bulk of the Clyde's West India commerce during the American War was carried on through this port. From Foulis Academy, Glasgow Views etc 1756–70. (*Courtesy: Mitchell Library, Glasgow*)

See Devine, 'Transport Problems of Glasgow West India Merchants', pp 266–304

VIEW FROM THE WINDMILL CROFT LOOKING EASTWARD
FROM A DRAWING EXECUTED ABOUT 1760

*This view gives a fair impression of the depth of the Clyde at Glasgow in 1760; the shallow nature of the river at this point meant that colonial merchants had to load and unload their ocean-going vessels farther down the Clyde at Port Glasgow and Greenock. From Robert Stuart,* Views and Notices of Glasgow in Former Times *(1847). (Courtesy: Mitchell Library, Glasgow)*

See Devine, 'Transport Problems of Glasgow West India Merchants', pp 266–304

*Corris Railway—mixed train at Corris, with locomotive No 2 (Courtesy: Corris Railway Society)*

See 'Notes and News', pp 321–2

Clydesmill No 3 of the Scottish Railway Preservation Society at the society's open day on 22 May 1971. On the right is the Caledonian Railway coach used to give visitors a chance to travel behind a steam locomotive See 'Notes and News', p 323

*PS Lincoln Castle arriving at Hull from New Holland on 5 April 1971*
See 'Notes and News', p 323

*PS* Ludwig Fessler *at Prien-Stock on the Chiemsee, Bavaria, on 13 June 1971*

See 'Notes and News', p 323

put into a particular port. William Dickson, supercargo to Alex Houston & Co, was ordered to proceed to Barbadoes in July 1776; if 'upon enquiry' he found the market suitable, he was to dispose of all or part of his cargo, but if unsatisfied he was directed 'to go on to any other of the British Caribbean islands that you may be advised there be the best chance of sale'.[39] Such instructions meant 'ships swarming about the seas scuttling imprudently from island to island in pursuit of the last halfpenny of profit',[40] and this in turn rendered them easy prey for the lurking privateer.

Once the convoy assembly point was reached there was no guarantee of a safe passage to British waters. The perennial storms of the Caribbean could scatter a convoyed fleet, inadequate liaison between escorting captain and merchantmen might have unfortunate results, and the anticipation of fleet engagements when France entered the war in 1778 could mean that the merchant vessels were stripped of their naval escort.[41]

## II

Enough has been said to demonstrate that although the convoy system did afford some form of defence across the Atlantic sea-routes, at both the Clyde and Caribbean ends of the voyage merchantmen were flung very much on their own resources. The imperfections of the convoy system itself are well known—the recurrent cycle of shortages and gluts with their accompanying price fluctuations which it inflicted on British commodity markets, the delay which was in the logic of any convoy—the speed being that of the slowest vessel in the fleet—the overcrowding in port at the end of a voyage and the stress put on local capital markets as large amounts of cash were required within short time periods to pay customs duties on the imported commodities.[42] For most merchants, however, the system was 'a necessary evil': the marked differential in insurance premium with or without convoy ensured that most would opt for it.[43] There were, however, methods of avoiding or at least of alleviating both its drawbacks and some of the hazards of wartime trading.

The strategic necessity to dispatch a large army to North America and latterly to send troops to the West Indies offered to merchant-shipowners the opportunity of chartering their vessels to the government to act as transports. By so doing the merchant could be sure that his investment would be well protected since such ships rarely sailed without heavy naval escort. On the other hand earnings would be much less than in normal trading activities, although certainly more stable and although owners were cushioned from the high operating costs of wartime by the fact that the government paid wages and offered compensation for damage and loss.[44] In such a period of extreme depression in the West Indies' trade as 1778 the transport service had obvious attractions, as one merchant house noted in that year: 'The large ship . . . which we had purchased we mean to employ in the transport service, which we calculate is much more profitable than any West Indian voyage which we could plan for her.'[45] Glasgow merchants were in a particularly fortunate position in this regard since the Highland regiments left from the Clyde. In January 1776 representatives of the Navy Board arrived in the town to contract for 7,000 tons of shipping for America and by early February the requisite tonnage had been hired.[46] The 31st Regiment left the Clyde in eight transports at the end of that month to be followed in April by the 42nd and 71st Regiments of Highlanders, consisting of 3,466 officers and men, embarked on thirty-three transports. The second substantial exodus was in 1778 when over 6,500 men sailed for North America.[47] The basic drawback in utilising the transport service to offset the risks of wartime trading was that any relief gained tended to be temporary since demand for shipping clustered at certain specific periods. As Professor Syrett has observed, the years 1780–3 were not profitable ones for shipowners who had put their vessels into the transport service.[48]

A more common method of circumventing the problems implicit in the convoy system was to fit out a fast armed merchantman to sail unescorted. Theoretically such ships had considerable advantages: they were able to reach market earlier than convoyed ships and were equally able to gain from the inflexibility of the convoy system itself. Ordinary merchantmen intending to sail in convoy had to be at the assembly point by a precise date; the 'running ship', on the other hand, with no limitations of this sort, could well benefit from late crops or obtain bargain rates from planters desperate to dispose of the remainder of their harvest. As Robert Dunmore & Co's agents in Green Island discovered,

> Now that all the vessels for this fleet are loaded and some goods are shut out that were expected to have gone in them, the proprietors would engage for any market to be sure of getting theirs shipped by next fleet, as we expect no new vessels at Green Island this year.[49]

Yet such activity was hardly less of a gamble than any other form of wartime commerce. The time of arrival of such a ship in the Clyde would determine the profitability of the voyage. If the arrival of the fleet was not far distant, sugar buyers and brokers were likely to refrain from a hasty purchase. Thus the Leith Sugar House Co refused to buy the cargo of the armed ship *Hanover* in the summer of 1778, their manager pointing out that the main West India fleet was expected soon and prices would therefore plummet downwards.[50] In addition the expenses of a 'running ship' were formidable. It demanded a higher complement than the normal merchantman—this too at a time when the war was putting up demand for experienced and inexperienced shipping labour and also creating considerable distortion in the market for such labour.[51] At the same time a more sophisticated armament was required.[52] Innumerable mercantile letters testify to the fact that so great was the outlay on such vessels that a full freight was essential if owners were to make a profit.[53] Even if ships were so armed, such was the saving on insurance premium that they were often urged to take convoy, especially on the return voyage from the Caribbean when holds were likely to be bulging with West Indian produce.[54] Indeed the conclusion must be that, even if heavily armed, 'running it' was very much a last resort. If on *rendezvous* at the convoy assembly point, however, it was found that the fleet had sailed, skippers were usually ordered to proceed without escort, but even then it was preferable to sail in the company of other 'armed ships'.[55]

Investment in privateering might allow the merchant/shipowner to escape the constrictions of regulated convoys and at the same time *benefit* from the incidence of hostilities.

A distinction ought first to be made between what one might call the 'specialised' privateer and the privateer fitted out for battle yet still carrying on the more mundane operations of trade. Captains of the latter vessels were faced with something of a dilemma: the decision whether to aim for the dependable freight or the more elusive but more profitable prize. The difficulties inherent in such a decision are well exemplified in the case of the brig *Hasard* commanded by Captain James Laurie. If the ship was bent on trade with the West Indies, the outward freight from the Clyde, though admittedly much less than the inward cargo, would not allow her to sail 'sufficiently fast to afford hope of success' as a privateer.[56] Similarly Captain Smith of the *Sally* was fortunate enough in 1777 to take a prize off St Kitts, but two days afterwards encountered an American privateer; he had to scuttle his prize and make off since, with the ship's holds already crammed with sugar and rum, his mobility was at a minimum.[57] Clearly the evolution of this hybrid type of vessel was an attempt to cut down the element of gambling in privateering: at least a freight was more or less guaranteed and the privateer might, if luck was in, also make a merchant's fortune with a single capture.

Although a century of endemic warfare had given Glasgow's merchants and shipowners essential experience in the fitting out of these ships, the cost of such outfitting must have been a disincentive to many. A 'letter of marque' for a privateer carrying over 150 men required payment to the Admiralty of £3,000 as bail and security or £1,500 if under that complement.[58] Provisions necessary for a privateer exceeded those for the ordinary merchantman bound for a specific destination within a certain time schedule. The need to stay at sea for as long as possible compelled the privateer's store intake to be above the norm and clearly extra seamen would have to be hired if the vessel was to be transformed into an efficient fighting ship. Not all the profits accrued to the owner since one quarter of the prize money was distributed among the officers and crew and the Crown claimed one-sixth.[59] In view of the risks attached to privateering and the expenses involved, Alderman Creighton of London concluded that a 'letter of marque' was not worth the money, a prize being '... as much a matter of chance as the obtainment of a ten or twenty thousand pounds prize in the lottery'.[60] Nevertheless, privateering exerted a considerable attraction as an investment during the war. It has been calculated that throughout the period of hostilities there were approximately thirty-seven Clyde vessels cruising as privateers and forty-one others with a 'letter of marque'.[61]

The main safeguard against destruction of valuable assets by enemy attack was, of course, insurance. The defeats on the North American mainland, the entry of more powerful enemies into the fray after 1778, and the persistent assaults on shipping assumed visible form in the merchant's accounts in the rise of insurance premium rates.[62] The underwriting system, although in the main satisfactory, did not guarantee speedy compensation for loss of ship or cargo. Innumerable lawsuits took place over whether a shipowner was entitled to the insured sum or whether he had in some way failed to conform to the regulations set out by the underwriters.[63] To this hazard was joined the danger of underwriting bankruptcies. Such failures were commonplace in London to whose underwriters Glasgow merchants were increasingly turning for insurance cover.[64] Alexander Houston & Co spoke of the 'several failures among the underwriters at London' in March 1778 and how as a result they had recovered nothing from the loss of two of their ships.[65] It would appear, indeed, that as the war dragged on even high premiums were insufficient to compensate underwriters for their risks. Thus as early as the summer of 1777 it was reported that most of the Glasgow underwriters had 'given up the trade' and that it was 'difficult to get a large sum done, even at London'.[66] The inter-island trade in the West Indies was regarded as especially unattractive: underwriters were 'very shy of West India risks' and in 1778 they refused to insure craft plying between St Kitts and St Croix.[67] This is scarcely surprising in view of our previous discussion on the extreme vulnerability of commerce within the Caribbean itself.[68] Persons with funds to spare were more likely to invest in government stock which was becoming increasingly lucrative and represented a more secure method of obtaining returns.[69] The recently discovered records of the various concerns in which Alexander Speirs had an interest afford an insight into some of the methods used for getting round these developing difficulties of obtaining insurance and the high premiums to be paid *if* underwriters *were* willing to undertake the risk.[70]

One stratagem was to avoid the Clyde altogether, by simply landing the imported sugar and tobacco at an Irish port, such as Limerick on the south-west coast, pay the duties and then proceed to export the commodities to a Continental market. This meant that the highly vulnerable Irish Sea area and the Clyde estuary would not have to be negotiated; according to Speirs 'the saving in insurance would be marked on such a venture'.[71] There were additional reasons for putting into an Irish port. Speirs, French & Co had increased their interest in the West Indies trade partly because they could gain access to tobacco supplies coming to the neutral islands there from the rebel-held areas in the American colonies. Tobacco duties at home were rising in the last few years of war, particularly in 1781.[72] Utilisation of Irish ports in that year promised a bonus to such Glasgow West India firms as Speirs, French & Co. There was a considerable time-lag in the implementation of the increased levy between Ireland and the mainland. Speirs was of the opinion that the Irish Parliament would not legislate in this regard until 1783 and, as he emphasised to one of his agents in November 1781, the first cargoes from the West Indies in the following year 'should certainly be sold at Ireland to have benefit of the new duty'.[73]

Insurance premiums could also be cut, security for cargo and vessel strengthened and the convoy system avoided by employing neutral ships.[74] Development along these lines had become essential by 1782-3.

In June of 1783 Speirs wrote that such were the pressures on merchants using British ships that 'if war continues one year longer our Trade will be carried in Neutral Bottoms only'.[75] Investment in the latter was a relatively simple matter for the Glasgow company—they had had long-standing links with Rotterdam, Ostend and Hamburg in the tobacco trade and had agents residing in these cities.[76] Inquiries were being made from 'Mr Court at Ostend' in 1782 on the terms he could freight a ship to St Vincent (in French hands since 1779) and concerning duties charged on British-owned produce.[77] The fact that all the Leeward Islands except Antigua were in enemy hands by 1782 lent an urgency to this search for neutral transport since the French had decreed that the produce of captured islands could be sent in neutral bottoms to neutral ports.[78] Inquiries were also made concerning the possibilities of acquiring a merchantman 'under Imperial colours' to take freight from Hamburg to the West Indies. Danish and Venetian vessels were also accounted desirable and Speirs had an agent inside the enemy camp—J. G. Martens, a Danish subject residing in Bordeaux who, it was suggested, might freight goods to San Domingo.[79] By the end of 1782 Speirs, French & Co had two ships trading under 'flags of convenience'.[80]

## III

The threat of enemy action was not the only obstacle to a profitable West Indian voyage during the American War. Operating costs were likely to be boosted upwards because of pressures on ship construction and manpower. Payment for new vessels either sunk or taken by the enemy and outlay on seamen's wages formed the vast bulk of the expenditure on transport of merchant/shipowners. There is little doubt that in 1775-6 there was a surfeit of both ships and men in the Clyde area owing to the interruption of trade with the American colonies.[81] However, the demands of the transport service and the trade boom of 1776-7 to Europe, the West Indies and England soon considerably altered this picture.[82] Replacement of lost tonnage would be much more difficult after 1776 than before. Traditionally Clyde ships had been constructed in the American colonies, sometimes with Glasgow capital and under Glasgow supervision, few areas being able to compete with the colonies' low raw material costs.[83] With this source of supply cut off and with losses accumulating, shipowners had to look elsewhere; for those forced to hire ships there was a dramatic rise in rates. Houstons quoted one example of an arrangement with the owners of the *Nestor* for the hire of the ship for £250 for a voyage to the Caribbean in 1775. By 1777 the rate had rocketed to £600.[84] Relief was sought in various ways, none of them entirely satisfactory. Captured enemy ships were put up for sale and eagerly purchased.[85] The war stimulated the construction of vessels on the Clyde but although contemporaries praised 'the vessels of great burden' constructed upon 'the best principles' and 'of excellent workmanship', only four such ships of a total of 917 tons burden were completed at Port Glasgow in the last year of war. As yet the Clyde was no substitute for America.[86] More exotic sources were explored. Messrs Esdaile & Cathcart sent a representative to Archangel to have a merchantman built there for them, utilising a credit for £1,000 which they held in St Petersburg.[87]

The expansion of the Royal Navy on the outbreak of war and thereafter created difficulties in the labour market. It could well be argued that the merchant was as much at the mercy of naval press-gangs in the safe and rapid delivery of his goods as he was subject to the attention of enemy privateers. Impressment from the merchant service was the only means of augmenting the Navy quickly,[88] and although the surplus in the labour market in 1775–6 alleviated any pressure on shipowners, the approach of war with France in 1778 did impose considerable strain. During the period of hostilities the clauses of the Navigation Acts were relaxed—merchantmen were allowed to carry foreign seamen to the extent of three-quarters of their complement.[89] This facility was used by Glasgow merchants but its effect can only be guessed at: certainly it did not solve the problem of the scarcity and high price of labour.[90] In addition 'protections' purchased from the Admiralty, although very useful, often depended for their effectiveness on the whim of the individual naval commander. In the West Indies and North America, for instance, the distance from central authority encouraged infringement, but even in the Clyde they were no complete guarantee of immunity, particularly at such periods of crisis as the outbreak of war with France in 1778.[91]

Glasgow merchants ran their own system of unofficial exemption. Ships began to anchor in the Fairlie roads off the Ayrshire coast and the crew (except the captain, first mate, ship's carpenter, apprentices bound for three years and boys under eighteen who were all exempt from pressing) left the ship in longboats, heading for the coast. Once there they tended to congregate in the area of Beith. An understanding apparently existed between the farmers and 'smugglers' of Ayrshire and Renfrewshire and the captains of incoming ships which allowed for warnings to be given when the press-gang were in the vicinity.[92] Merchants obviously wanted the best of both worlds—an efficient and vigorously expanding Navy to act as escort to their commerce yet with no diminution in the labour pool available to them. The adopted strategy of paying off and dismissing men before a ship entered port was, however, by no means foolproof. At least one example was found of an escort vessel pressing the merchantmen it had convoyed when they entered the Firth of Clyde and several others were discovered of pressing at sea once the voyage from the West Indies was almost completed.[93]

The first effect of the activities of the press-gang was on the cost and availability of labour. Macpherson calculated that wages in the herring fishery, extensively carried on from ports on the lower Clyde, had risen throughout the period of 1775–83 by something of the order of 400 per cent.[94] The war created an *artificial* scarcity in labour supply: seamen in order to escape the attentions of the press would live in areas while ashore where the shipowner as well as the regulating officer found difficulty in reaching them. The experience of one merchant house's foray into Ayrshire in search of labour is worth quoting here in full. In September 1778 Captain James Troop and Thomas Crawford of Robert Dunmore & Co were scouring the county for seamen. From their base in Largs, they wrote that their journey to Irvine on 21 September had proved 'a very troublesome and unsuccessful expedition'. Only five men had agreed to accept their terms and only two had been 'formally engaged', although the merchantman which they were to crew was at that date clear to sail.[95] Crawford referred to another of the firm's skippers, Captain James McCauslan, who had also been searching for seamen to little avail. 'McCauslan wants yet so many of his complement of men and these are so difficult to be got I am afraid his cruize will be very short.'[96] The following week brought little change in their luck. One of the sailors that Troop had already hired at Irvine sent back his advance pay, having obtained promise of higher earnings for his services elsewhere. McCauslan went to Irvine, Saltcoats and Ayr but 'could not get one man'. As Crawford asked ruefully, 'Is it not very amazing that in Leith, Irvine and Saltcoats, where there are so many sailors, there should be such difficulty in getting so few as we want?'[97] The mechanism of supply and demand was moving favourably towards labour from 1777 onwards and seamen were taking advantage of this fact to bid up wage rates.

The West Indies trade during the American War was so geared to time schedules—the desire to make a convoy and thus save on insurance premium, and the need to arrive in the Caribbean at a suitable period for making effective purchases—that impressment, by interfering with a ship's timetable, could easily render a particular voyage unprofitable; 1778 was a particularly difficult time for those attempting to hire seamen. The approach of war with France meant that they were 'almost all press'd below . . . not a vessel can be got out for want of hands'.[98] Delaying a ship in order to obtain a full complement could be self-defeating as the crew might desert for fear of an approaching press-gang.[99] The *Albion* had been detained at Campbelltown for several weeks 'for want of hands'; by March 1778 she was clear to sail and so her owners bought her cargo of herring; however, the ship then sprang a leak, which, after a lengthy repair delayed her until April. Seamen were so scarce that it was with great difficulty that the captain got her manned: after all this, the majority of his crew were pressed from him in the Fairlie roads.[100] This example illustrates vividly how impressment could form an important addition to the array of 'normal' hazards which faced the merchant in the successful prosecution of his trade.

## IV

The persistent difficulties of rising transport costs could of course be offset if trading returns were at an optimum level during the war. Success in wartime commerce depended on a precarious balance between rising operating costs on the one hand and increasing income from freight rates, West India remittances and prize cargoes on the other. The following table will afford a more precise view of each end of this scale:

| Income | Expenditure |
|---|---|
| (1) Commission on sale of West Indian produce. | (1) Cost of ship and equipment. |
| (2) Freight rates. | (2) Seamen's wages and provisions. |
| (3) Interest on loans to West Indian planters. | (3) Contents of ship. |
| (4) Prize money (if any). | (4) Insurance premiums. |
| (5) Sale of contents of ship in West Indies. | (5) Overheads (agent's salary, upkeep of Glasgow counting house etc). |
|  | (6) Port charges (primage, wharfage, warehouse rental, customs duties, cooperage, weighing expenses). |

Certainly some main elements of income showed marked rises during the war. As Appendix III reveals, there were substantial upward movements in freight rates. To take one example, freight charges 'per cask' for sugar imported from Jamaica, approximately 3s 9d in October 1775, had more than doubled to 8s by November 1778.[101] Although charges from other islands did not reach similar levels, there was a broad picture of consistently upward trends. It might well be argued, therefore, that wartime transport expenses were passed on to the West Indian planter via the medium of freight charges. Again prices of West

Indian commodities, at least for the first two to three years of hostilities, do show (as Appendix IV indicates) an upward climb.[102] In addition to this, there were the windfall gains which might be expected from a successful privateering expedition. Little noteworthy investment in privateering took place until France entered the war in 1778—the expected speedy victory in the colonies and the relatively puny nature of American commerce might have created disincentives for merchants.[103] Clearly rich pickings could be and were made. In the period January–May 1779 alone, four French merchantmen with over 700 hogsheads of clayed sugar in their holds were brought into the Clyde as prizes and it has been suggested that *in toto* forty-four enemy merchant ships were taken throughout the war by Glasgow-owned privateers.[104] Before one puts too much weight on the consequent profit from such activity it must be stressed that the owner of a privateer was as much at the mercy of market forces when he came to sell captured produce as the merchant/shipowner engaged in normal commerce. Prices obtained in an over-supplied market were often insufficient to recoup the owner for the expenses of privateering. Thus Speirs, French & Co lamented in the autumn of 1781 how, although the *Enterprise* had taken two prizes worth 'at least £1200', no profit would be made because of the state of the market and rising costs.[105]

The market for West Indian produce although attractive in 1775–7, as pointed out above, narrowed in the depression of 1778, scarcely recovered in 1779, stagnated in 1780–1 and was again sluggish in 1782 as the poor harvest of that year eroded domestic demand for sugar and cotton and as the prices of these commodities rose in response to inflated freight rates and much augmented customs duties.[106] Rising freight rates were not nearly so beneficial to merchants as one might suppose. It was every exporter's dream to sell for cash or goods in the West Indies and leave no debts behind him, but such a utopian situation did not exist in the harsh world of commercial reality. The West Indian planter's chronic tendency to sink deeper into debt is a well-known phenomenon thanks to the researches of professors Pares, Ragatz and Checkland.[107] That 'malignant organism, a West India debt' had its origin in the fact that crops consigned to a merchant were principally to pay for goods sent out some months before and by the planter's obligations being met by bills of exchange drawn on the trader.[108] The defects of this system from the merchant's point of view were aggravated by planters overdrawing on their accounts, by the delinquency of Caribbean courts over debt actions brought by British merchants, by the overloading of estates with legacies and annuities, and by heavy purchases of slaves.[109]

During the American War the planters' recalcitrance and unwillingness (or inability) to make speedy remittances was likely to be aggravated by the rising cost of his provisions as the flow of bread, flour and fish from the American colonies declined in volume and as Ireland was developed as a substitute source for such stores. All the evidence suggests that food prices in the islands rocketed during the first five years of war to more than 135 to 150 per cent of their pre-war level.[110] On the other hand, the capture of most of the Leeward Islands by France might not necessarily act as a major obstacle to the sending of remittances to Glasgow. The Port Books for Greenock reveal that the city's West Indian trade was by and large oriented towards Jamaica, which was not taken during the war.[111] Even for those firms, such as Alexander Houston & Co, who had close links with Grenada, St Vincent (taken in 1779) and St Kitts (taken in 1782) remittances could still take place through Holland, which was neutral until 1780.[112] Thereafter Ostend, Hamburg and other neutral ports might be utilised.[113] The basic problem remained, however, of an imbalance between remittances and expenditure on transport costs. Merchants involved in the West Indies trade had not only to cope with the latter but also with intense pressure on credit. Relatively plentiful in 1775–7, this became much scarcer in the depression of 1778, with only partial relief in 1779–80, until recession began again in 1781–2. Decreasing confidence in the trade as islands toppled to the French conqueror further narrowed available credit resources, already becoming less fruitful as a result of the increasing attraction of government funds. As one Glasgow merchant house pointed out in 1780,

> ... money is ... very scarce here and not to be borrowed in any security. Many monied people have withdrawn all they had lent here and have gone into the new loan where they have government security and more than 5 per cent.[114]

Amid such stresses extension of commercial interests in the West Indies was a highly risky affair. The correspondence of Messrs Alexander Houston & Co makes plain that from 1778 onward the flow of remittances was not substantial enough to compensate for credit difficulties and rising costs. To their agents in St Vincent in October 1778, they regretfully admitted that 'such was the state of our funds we dare not venture to ship the goods you order'. In 1780 they were 'really very averse to engage further in the West Indies till we see peace established on a solid foundation'.[115] These, it might be added, were the proclaimed policies of what, as is made clear in the customs records, was the largest West India house in Glasgow; it is unlikely that the smaller fry were adopting more positive plans. Figures for importation of West India sugar into Scotland give a similar picture of relative stagnation after 1778: only in two of the seven years of war did gross sugar imports rise above the level of 1775.[116] One must take into account, of course, a likely expansion in the incidence of smuggling as customs duties rose and also the fact that some Glasgow-owned cargoes were landed at London or at Irish ports. Yet the correlation between the evidence of customs and mercantile records is too great to be ignored and it must be concluded that especially in the period 1778–82, Glasgow West India merchants were treading an uneasy and tortuous path between financial disaster, windfall profits (which could be very large) and a continuing, if relatively profitless, solvency. The costs of wartime commerce were not entirely outweighed by the gains and the 'golden age' of the Clyde–Caribbean trade had to await the termination of hostilities and the spectacular rise in demand from West of Scotland industry for 'sea-island' cotton in the later 1780s.

*University of Strathclyde*

## References

1. Tucker's comments are to be found in J. D. Marwick (ed), *Miscellany of Scottish Burgh Records Society*, Edinburgh (1881), 'Report by Thomas Tucker upon the Settlement of the Revenues of Excise and Customs in Scotland, A.D.1656', 26.
2. T. C. Smout, 'The Development and Enterprise of Glasgow, 1556–1707', *Scot Jour Pol Econ*, VII (1960), 207–10; *Scottish Trade on the Eve of Union*, Edinburgh (1963), 80, 175–8.
3. T. C. Smout, 'The Early Scottish Sugar Houses', *Econ Hist Rev*, 2nd ser, XIV (1961), 240–53.
4. A. Brown, *A History of Glasgow*, Glasgow (1800), III. See, for example, J. O. Mitchell, *Old Glasgow Essays*, Glasgow (1903), 37, 332.
5. H. Hamilton, *An Economic History of Scotland in the Eighteenth Century*, Oxford (1963), 270–1; Appendix XI.
6. This was true of Robert Dunmore & Co, Speirs, Bowman & Co, Bogle Scott & Co. See Scottish Record Office (SRO), GD 247/59/Q/2; Glasgow City Archives (GCA), Speirs Papers, Cash Book 1760–1778, TD 131/1; Mitchell Library (ML), Bogle MSS, Bundle 54.
7. SRO, GD 247/59/Q/2.
8. I. S. Harrell, *Loyalism in Virginia*, Durham, North Carolina (1926), 48.
9. GCA, Speirs Papers, Letter Book of Speirs, Bowman & Co, 1781–89, TD 131/9, Speirs, Bowman & Co to Thomas Eden, 20 June 1782. See also GCA, Mitchell Johnston Papers (MJP), Ritchie & Co versus Alexander Houston & Co (1779).
10. For proof of this assertion see Hamilton, op cit, Appendix IX and XI (import figures extracted from Public Record Office (PRO), Customs, 14) and National Library of Scotland (NLS), Papers of Alexander Houston & Co, A. H. & Co, Foreign Letterbook F, 1778–81, MS 8794, A. H. & Co to Archibald Esdaile, 28 Jan 1779.
11. Jacob M. Price, 'The Rise of Glasgow in the Chesapeake Tobacco Trade 1707–1775', *The William and Mary Quarterly*, April 1954, reprinted in P. L. Payne (ed), *Studies in Scottish Business History* (1969), 305.
12. Gomer Williams, *History of the Liverpool Privateers and Letters of Marque with An Account of the Liverpool Slave Trade* (1897, new impression 1966), 181.
13. *Edinburgh Evening Courant*, 21 July 1777.
14. See below, pp 281–3.
15. Ireland gradually replaced the American colonies as the source of West India provisions during the war. Restrictions on trade with West Indies from Ireland removed in 1778 by 18 Geo III, c 55, continued from 1780 by 20 Geo III, c 10. Glasgow–West India merchants kept agents in Cork who maintained those links with provision contractors, SRO GD 247/59/Q/2, William Crawford to Robert Dunmore & Co, 18 August 1778. Cork was also the major depot for shipment of army provisions from Ireland, David Syrett, *Shipping and the American War: A Study of British Transport Organisation* (1970), 44.
16. *Glasgow Mercury*, 22 September 1778.
17. M. K. Barritt, 'The Navy and the Clyde in the American War, 1777–83', *The Mariner's Mirror*, 55 (1969), 33.

18  Sir Herbert Richmond, 'The Navy' in *Johnson's England, An Account of the Life and Manners of his Age*, ed A. S. Turberville, Oxford (1933), I, 40–1.
19  For a sample of these petitions see *Edinburgh Evening Courant*, 23 November 1776, 5 and 26 July 1777; *Caledonian Mercury*, 2 July 1777; GCA, Council Minute Book, 1777–81, C1/1/36/97, 9 Sept 1778.
20  *Edinburgh Evening Courant*, 2 July 1777.
21  Ibid, 26 July 1777, Copy of letter, Phillip Stephens, Secretary to the Admiralty to the Magistrates of Glasgow.
22  *Glasgow Mercury*, 12 March 1778.
23  D. B. Smith, 'Glasgow in 1781', *Scott Hist Rev*, XVI (1919), Hugh Wylie and John Campbell to P. Stephens, 15 Dec 1780; Wylie to John Crawford MP, 1 Dec 1780.
24  *Glasgow Mercury*, 16 November 1780.
25  Barritt, loc cit, 35. This subject is discussed in greater detail below, pp 283-6.
26  *Scots Magazine*, June 1777; *Edinburgh Evening Courant*, 16 July 1777.
27  Ibid.
28  *Edinburgh Evening Courant*, 26 July 1777.
29  Ibid.
30  GCA, Council Minute Book, C1/1/36/97; George Williamson, *Old Greenock*, Paisley (1886), 168.
31  GCA, Council Minute Book, C1/1/37/463.
32  *Edinburgh Evening Courant*, 12 and 19 July 1777; *Caledonian Mercury*, 30 June 1777.
33  John Knox, *A View of the British Empire, more especially Scotland* (3rd edn, 1785), II, 553–4.
34  NLS, Foreign Letter Book E of Alex Houston & Co, MS 8793, A. H. & Co to Captain Daniel Graham, 4 July 1777; *Glasgow Mercury*, 14 July 1777; GCA, Council Minute Book, C1/1/36/29.
35  Richard Pares, *War and Trade in the West Indies 1739–1763*, Oxford (1936), 293.
36  *Edinburgh Evening Courant*, 9 August 1777, 'Extract of a letter from a gentleman at Dominica to his friend at Edinburgh', dated 11 June 1777.
37  Ibid, 20 August 1777, 'Extract of a letter from St Vincent, 10 June 1777'.
38  For an example of such convoys see NLS MS 8793, A. H. & Co to Messrs Turner & Paul, 6 March 1777.
39  NLS MS 8793, A. H. & Co to W. Dickson, 18 July 1776. This is one of several such entries into the company's letterbook for the years 1776–8.
40  Pares, op cit, 288.
41  SRO, GD 247/140, Petition of R. Dunmore & Co to the Rt Hon the Lords and Council of Session, 17 Jan 1786; NLS, Charles Stewart Letterbooks, MS 5031, Thomas Riddoach to Charles Stewart, 20 July 1779; SRO, GD 247/59/Q/2, William Cunninghame to R. Dunmore & Co, 2 July 1778.
42  For a ship captain's views on the drawbacks of the convoy system, see SRO, GD 247/58/P/2, 'Extracts from the Journals of Capt Wright of the ship *Clyde* on her voyage from Jamaica to Clyde in 1778 and 1779'.
43  See Appendix I.
44  David Macpherson, *Annals of Commerce, Manufactures, Fisheries and Navigation* (1805), III, 590; Syrett, op cit, 79–80; Ralph Davis, *The Rise of the English Shipping Industry in the Seventeenth and Eighteenth Centuries* (1962), 330; D. Syrett, 'The West India Merchants and the Conveyance of the King's Troops

to the Caribbean', *Journal of the Society for Army Historical Research*, XLV (1967), 169.
45   NLS, MS 8793, A. H. & Co to Messrs Houston & Paterson, 9 Feb 1778. See also NLS, MS 8759, A. H. & Co to William Crichton, 23 December 1777.
46   *Edinburgh Evening Courant*, 22 and 27 January 1776; 10 and 24 February 1776; SRO, Customs Accounts, Greenock, E 504/15/26, Six ships cleared for transport service; SRO, Customs Accounts, Port Glasgow, E 504/28/15, Seven ships cleared by customs for transport service, February 1776.
47   Syrett, op cit, 201–2, 209–10; SRO, Customs Accounts, Greenock, E 504/15/26. Six ships cleared by customs for transport service, February–March 1778.
48   Ibid, 103–5.
49   SRO, GD 247/139, Notarial copy of Somerville & Noble's letter to R. Dunmore & Co, 23 June 1778.
50   SRO, GD 247/59/Q/2, Charles Cowan to Robert Dunmore & Co, 9 July 1778.
51   GCA, MJP, Thomas Houston Law Papers, Adam Grieve to Messrs Thomas Houston & Co, 14 March 1779. This topic will be given detailed consideration below, pp 288–92.
52   SRO, GD 247/59/P/2; *Glasgow Mercury*, 22 September 1778; 21 October 1779; R. H. Campbell, *Carron Company*, Edinburgh (1961), 191.
53   NLS, MS 8793, Foreign Letter Book E, passim.
54   NLS, MS 8793, A. H. & Co to Captain David Scott, 24 Feb 1779; A. H. & Co to Captain Daniel Graham, 28 Jan 1778.
55   NLS, MS 8793, A. H. & Co to Messrs Turner & Paul, 1 Dec 1778; A. H. & Co to Captain Daniel Graham, 7 Dec 1778; *Caledonian Mercury*, 27 November 1776.
56   SRO, GD 247/58/P/2, Henry King & Co to Robert Dunmore & Co, 7 August 1779.
57   NLS, MS 8793, A. H. & Co to Messrs Turner & Paul, 23 September 1777.
58   *Glasgow Herald*, 13 January 1912.
59   Davis, op cit, 333. For an example of a distribution of prize money see NLS, MS 8794, A. H. & Co to Captain David Scott, 24 Feb 1779.
60   Quoted in Barritt, loc cit, 35.
61   Ibid.
62   See Appendix I.
63   For one example of the kind of tortuous wrangles which could ensue see SRO, GD 247/140, Petition of Robert Dunmore & Co to the Rt Hon the Lords and Council of Session, 17 January 1786.
64   A. H. John, 'The London Assurance Co and the Marine Insurance Market in the Eighteenth Century', *Economica*, new ser, XXV (1958), 127; Parliamentary Papers, Report from the Select Committee on Marine Insurance IV, 1810, 47; SRO, GD 247/140, Insurance Notes; underwriting did continue by local merchants, see Appendix II.
65   NLS, MS 8759, Home Letter-Book H; A. H. & Co to William Crichton, 30 March, 12 June 1778.
66   NLS, MS 8793, A. H. & Co to Messrs Houston & Paterson, 5 June 1777.
67   SRO, GD 247/59/Q/2, Henry Clarke to Robert Dunmore & Co, 17 February 1778; NLS, MS 8794, A. H. & Co to David Macfarlane, 28 January 1778.
68   See above, pp 272, 281.

69 SRO, GD 247/59/Q/2, William Cunninghame to Robert Dunmore, 27 July 1778; T. S. Ashton, *Economic Fluctuations in England 1700–1810*, Oxford (1959); Macpherson, op cit, III, 685.
70 This material is in the possession of Major Crichton-Maitland of Houston House, Houston, Renfrewshire, and is here used from Xerox copies in the custody of the City Archives, Glasgow.
71 GCA, TD 131/9, Letter Book of Speirs, French & Co, 1781–89, S. F. & Co to Thomas Eden, 17 October 1781.
72 ML, Chamber of Commerce MSS, B/6, 'Memorial on behalf of the Importers of Tobacco humbly submitted to the Rt Hon C. J. Fox, June 1783'.
73 GCA, TD 131/9, S. F. & Co to Thomas Eden, 18 November 1781, 20 June 1782, 31 July 1782.
74 Ibid, S. F. & Co to J. G. Martens, 20 May 1782.
75 Ibid, S. F. & Co to Thomas Eden, 20 June 1782.
76 GCA, TD 131/1,3, Cash Book, 1760–1778; Day Book, 1777–82.
77 GCA, TD 131/9, S. F. & Co to Thomas Eden, 3 January 1782.
78 NLS, MS 8794, A. H. & Co to Messrs Houston & Paterson, 5 June 1780.
79 GCA, TD 131/9, S. F. & Co to J. G. Martens, 25 March 1782; S. B. & Co to Mr Anderson, 1 April 1782.
80 Ibid, S. F. & Co to Robert Burton, 2 August 1782.
81 *Caledonian Mercury*, 13 January 1776, 'Glasgow vessels are mostly out of employ', Barritt, loc cit, 33.
82 M. L. Robertson, 'Scottish Commerce and the American War of Independence', *Econ Hist Rev*, 2nd ser, IX (1956), 127; for further details of this loan see *Scots Magazine*, XXXVIII (1776), 393; *Caledonian Mercury*, 15 July, 4 September 1776.
83 Richard Champion, *Considerations on the Present Situation of Great Britain and the U.S.A.* (1784), 14–15; Price, loc cit, 316, n 49.
84 NLS, MS 8793, A. H. & Co to Messrs Houston, Paterson & Co, 1 October 1776.
85 Details of sale of prizes can be found in *Glasgow Mercury*, 1776–83.
86 Brown, op cit, II, 385; James Denholm, *A History of Glasgow*, Glasgow (1804), 532.
87 GCA, TD 131/9, S. F. & Co to Messrs Braumsters, 11 March 1782.
88 For the background to impressment see J. R. Hutchinson, *The Press Gang Afloat and Ashore* (1913); Christopher Lloyd, *The British Seaman* (1968), 115–58. Bounties were as usual tried in the Clyde 1775–7 and found wanting, see GCA, Council Minute Book, C1/1/35/579; C1/1/36/234.
89 16 Geo III, c 20 (1776); renewed 18 Geo III, c 6 (1778), 19 Geo III, c 14 (1779) and 21 Geo III, c 11 (1781).
90 *Edinburgh Evening Courant*, 28 April 1777.
91 Dora Mae Clark, 'The Impressment of Seamen in the American Colonies' in *Essays in Colonial History presented to Charles Maclean Andrews*, Newhaven (1931), 203.
92 SRO, GD 247/59/Q/2, Thomas Crawford to Robert Dunmore & Co, 22 September 1778; *Glasgow Herald*, 14 November 1853, quoted in Senex (J. M. Reid), *Glasgow Past and Present*, Glasgow (1884), II, 139.
93 'Chips from an Old Glasgow Ship's Log, 1777-1823', *Old Glasgow Club Transactions*, III, 102; *Edinburgh Evening Courant*, 9 August 1777.
94 Macpherson, op cit, III, 634.

95 SRO, GD 247/59/Q/2, Thomas Crawford to Robert Dunmore & Co, 22 September 1778.
96 Ibid.
97 Ibid, 26 September 1778. For difficulty in hiring men in New York see SRO, GD 247/58/P/2, H. M. King & Co to Robert Dunmore & Co (nd); one merchant house was of the opinion that since quality of labour was low during wartime—the most experienced men having been pressed—much more seamen were required than in peacetime trading; GCA, MJP, Thomas Houston Law Papers, Adam Grieve to Messrs Thomas Houston & Co, 14 March 1779.
98 NLS, MS 5030, Charles Stewart Letterbooks, John Maclean (Glasgow) to Charles Stewart, 31 March 1778.
99 NLS, MS 8794, A. H. & Co to Messrs Akers & Houston, 14 October 1779.
100 NLS, MS 8759, A. H. & Co to Mrs Milliken, 19 September 1778; A. H. & Co to William McDowall, 1 October 1778.
101 Appendix III, using material extracted from NLS MS 8799.
102 Appendix IV, using material extracted from NLS MSS 8793-4; SRO, GD 247/159.
103 SRO, Customs Accounts, Greenock, April 1779–Oct 1779, E504/15/31. The vast proportion of Glasgow privateers were commissioned in September–October 1778.
104 SRO, Customs Accounts, Greenock, E504/15/31; Barritt, loc cit, 35.
105 GCA, TD 131/9, S. B. & Co to J. G. Martins, 25 October 1781.
106 Robertson, loc cit, 29; NLS, MS 8793-4, passim; GCA, TD 131/9, S. B. & Co to Thomas Eden, 31 July 1782; *Scots Magazine*, XLV, 327; duties stood at 6s $3\frac{9}{10}$d per hogshead of sugar on the outbreak of war; by July 1782 they had reached 12s $3\frac{3}{8}$d—see L. J. Ragatz, *The Decline of the Planter Class in the British Caribbean, 1763–1833*, New York (1928).
107 Richard Pares, *A West India Fortune* (1950), 239-49; Ragatz, op cit; S. G. Checkland, 'Finance for the West Indies, 1780–1815', Econ Hist Rev, 2nd ser, X (1958), 461-9.
108 Pares, op cit, 239.
109 Ibid, 243-9.
110 Macpherson, op cit, III, 618; *Edinburgh Evening Courant*, 30 October 1776; Ragatz, op cit, 153-4.
111 For example, in January–April 1777, of eleven ships freighting for the West Indies, seven were bound for Jamaica, three for St Kitts, Grenada and St Vincent, and one for Antigua (not captured during the war), Customs Accounts, Greenock, E504/15/27.
112 NLS, MS 8794, A. H. & Co to Messrs Turner & Paul, 26 Oct 1779.
113 Ibid, A. H. & Co to Messrs Houston & Paterson, 15 January 1781. Houstons were able to report categorically in 1781 that they 'had not lost materially by the capture of our islands'.
114 Ibid, A. H. & Co to Fergus Paterson, 20 March 1781. That such problems were by no means unique to the West Indies trade is clear from Macpherson, op cit, III, 685.
115 Ibid, A. H. & Co to Messrs Houston, Patterson & Co, 20 July 1778; A. H. & Co to Archibald Esdaile, 28 January 1780.
116 Customs records from PRO, Customs 14, printed in Hamilton, op cit, Appendix XI.

## Acknowledgements

This essay represents an abbreviated version of a more extended paper on 'Problems of Glasgow West India Merchants during the American War of Independence' delivered to the Senior Seminar of the Department of Economic History, University of Strathclyde, in November 1970. I am grateful to all those who contributed to the valuable discussion on that occasion and particularly to my colleagues, John Butt and John Hume, who read an earlier draft and made several useful comments. I am also indebted to the staffs of the Scottish Record Office and National Library of Scotland (Edinburgh), the City Archives and Mitchell Library (Glasgow), for their assistance during the research which went into the preparation of this article.

*For plates, provided by the author, see pp 275-7*

## Appendix I

### A  INSURANCE PREMIUM RATES, CLYDE-WEST INDIES, 1776-80

| Date | Per centage premium | Per centage return for convoy and safe arrival |
|---|---|---|
| Oct 1776 | 7 guineas | No details |
| May 1777 | 10 ,, | ,, |
| June 1777 | 8–10 ,, | 4 guineas |
| Oct 1778 | 20 ,, | 10 ,, |
| April 1779 | 15 ,, | 5–6 ,, |

B  INSURANCE PREMIUM RATES, WEST INDIES–CLYDE, 1777–80

| | | | |
|---|---|---|---|
| June 1777 | 13 guineas | | 5 guineas |
| Dec 1777 | 15 ,, | | 5 ,, |
| March 1778 | 20–25 ,, | | 10 ,, |
| May 1778 | 20 ,, | | 10 ,, |
| Oct 1778 | 25 ,, | | 10 ,, |
| April 1779 | 20 ,, | | 10 ,, |
| August 1780 | 25 ,, | | 10 ,, |
| Oct 1780 | 18 ,, | | 8 ,, |

*Source:* NLS MSS 8793-4, 8759.
SRO GD 241/1, Insurance Notes, 1779.


*Appendix II*

## SUBSCRIPTION TO POLICY OF SHIP *THE FRIENDS* (GREENOCK–DUBLIN–WEST INDIES), 11 DEC 1779

A

| Subscribers | Amount Subscribed |
|---|---|
| John Hamilton | £ 300 st. |
| George Dennistoun | 200 |
| George Crawford | 200 |
| James Johnston | 300 |
| Richard Allan, jun. | 300 |
| John Gordon | 400 |
| John Douglas | 100 |
| Henry Ritchie | 300 |
| Allan Bogle | 200 |
| David Crosse | 200 |
| Alexander Donald | 200 |
| Allan McLean | 100 |
| John Campbell | 100 |
| John Robertson | 200 |
| James Gordon | 300 |

A | Subscribers | Amount Subscribed
--- | --- | ---
| Henry Riddell | 150
| Joseph Scott | 200
| John Laurie | 100
| George Hamilton | 200
| John Hamilton jun. | 50
| Andrew Buchanan jun. | 200
| Archibald Bogle | 100
| James Murdoch | 50
| James McLehose | 200
| David Russell | 50 £4,600

(All merchants resident in Glasgow, Port Glasgow, Greenock)

## SUBSCRIPTION TO POLICY OF SHIP *BLANDFORD* (CLYDE–CORK–JAMAICA), 6 DEC 1779

B | Subscribers | Amount Subscribed
--- | --- | ---
| John Hamilton jun. | £ 300 st.
| Richard Allan | 300
| Hugh Wylie | 100
| John Robertson | 100
| Allan McLean | 100
| George Campbell | 100
| John Campbell sen. | 100
| George Dennistoun | 100
| George Crawford | 100
| David Crosse | 200
| John Alston | 100
| Henry Ritchie | 300
| James Johnston | 100
| John Riddell | 100
| James Gordon | 300
| George Buchanan | 100
| David Elliot | 300
| Thomas Scott | 50
| James McLehose | 150 £3,000

(All merchants resident in Glasgow, Port Glasgow, Greenock)
*Source:* SRO GD 241/1, Insurance Notes, 1779.

*Appendix III*

## ALEX HOUSTON AND COMPANY'S FREIGHT CHARGES FOR SUGAR, 1775-9 (WEST INDIES–GLASGOW)

| Month | Year | Island | Freight Charge 'Per Cask' |
|---|---|---|---|
| October | 1775 | Jamaica | 3s 9d |
| July | 1776 | St Kitts | 3s 6d |
| September | 1776 | ,, | 3s 6d |
| November | ,, | Jamaica | 3s 9d |
| May | 1777 | Grenada | 5s 0d |
| August | ,, | ,, | 5s 0d |
| ,, | ,, | Tobago | 4s 6d |
| September | ,, | ,, | 5s 0d |
| October | ,, | Grenada | 4s 6d |
| ,, | ,, | St Vincent | 4s 6d |
| ,, | ,, | Jamaica | 5s 0d |
| August | 1778 | St Vincent | 5s 0d |
| ,, | ,, | Nevis | 6s 0d |
| September | ,, | St Kitts | 6s 0d |
| November | ,, | Jamaica | 8s 0d |
| March | 1779 | St Kitts | 6s 0d |

*Source:* NLS, MS 8799, Salebook C of Alexander Houston & Co, September 1775–August 1779.

*Appendix IV*

### PRICES OF WEST INDIAN COMMODITIES, 1776-80

| Month | Year | Sugar | Cotton (*per lb*) | Rum (*per gal*) |
|---|---|---|---|---|
| October | 1776 | — | 18d-21d | 2s 2d-2s 3d |
| December | ,, | 38s-48s | ,, | 2s 6d-2s 9d |
| January | 1777 | 42s-50s | — | 2s 9d-3s |
| July | ,, | 37s-40s | 17d-19d | 2s |
| December | ,, | 58s-65s | 16d-19d | 2s 3d-2s 4d |
| January | 1778 | 35s-40s | 'perfectly unsaleable' | — |
| March | ,, | 58s-60s | 'cotton unsaleable' | — |
| April | ,, | — | 13d-15d | — |
| June | ,, | 43s-44s | 13d-15d | — |
| August | ,, | 'Market very dull for all West India produce' | | |
| October | ,, | 40s-45s | 13d-14½d | 'no demand' |
| February | 1780 | 50s | 16d-18d | 2s 6d |
| August | ,, | 50s-54s | 18d-20d | 3s-3s 6d |

*Source:* NLS, MSS 8793-4; SRO, GD 247/159, Dunmore-Cunninghame Correspondence.

# Book Reviews

**The Overtype Steam Road Waggon,** by Maurice A. Kelly, GOOSE & SON, Norwich, 1971, pp 147, ill, diagrams, £3.98.

Take an orthodox steam traction engine, place a cart body in the space normally occupied by footplate and coalbunker and then transfer the driver and fireman to a platform outrigged from the side of the fire box. It was in accordance with this recipe that the British overtype steam waggon was originally evolved.

The idea was first conceived in the 1880s by P. J. Parmiter, a manufacturer of agricultural implements at Tisbury, Wiltshire, and it was later exploited commercially by Mann's Patent Steam Cart & Waggon Company Limited of Leeds who exhibited their first steam cart in 1898.

Mr Kelly's book begins with illustrations showing the original Mann cart of 1898 and an improved one of 1901. Looking at them, one pities the unfortunate driver who was evidently assumed to be a contortionist with a neck like a giraffe. Not only was he expected to drive the vehicle from an off-side platform from which his view of the nearside was totally obscured, but he also had to fire the machine through a small fire door on a level with the calf of his left leg, besides keeping an eye on a water gauge at knee height. Yet this awkward hybrid, believe it or not, was the prototype of a vehicle that became a common sight on British roads until the 1930s when it rapidly died out

Mr Kelly has made a thoroughly researched and magnificently illustrated study of this extinct breed of vehicle which must surely prove definitive. He lists no less than sixteen British makes of overtype waggon and, in those highly individualistic days, the remarkable thing is how closely they resemble each other. They certainly differed in detail, but overall design soon crystallised; radical departures from the orthodox were rare and never proved successful.

Another curious thing is that, although it was widely exported, this should have remained an exclusively British vehicle. The author's exhaustive researches have only disclosed two exceptions to this rule, one French and the other American.

What accounts for its popularity in Britain? Probably its simplicity and accessibility, qualities deriving from its traction engine origin which appealed to a people to whom traction engines had long been familiar. Though later overtypes could boast such refinements as windscreens, Ackermann steering and pneumatic tyres, they failed to compete against the undertype Sentinel in the 1920s, so that even their most celebrated maker, Fodens, was compelled to produce an undertype—the Speed Six—in order to compete with the Sentinel. Although the undertype had a superior performance, the reason for this eclipse in popularity was doubtless the amount of chassis space taken up by the horizontal, locomotive-type boiler as compared with the combination of vertical boiler and under-floor engine. The undertype also obviated the need for over-long chains to transmit the drive from engine to wheels.

Nevertheless, the manufacture of overtype steam waggons was once a considerable industry in this country and this book provides a complete, permanent and most worthy record of it.

*Stanley Pontlarge*                                         L. T. C. Rolt

**Mind the Curve! A History of the Cable Trams,** by John D. Keating, MELBOURNE UNIVERSITY PRESS, Melbourne, 1970, pp xv + 155, ill, $7.50 in Australia; £3.50 in UK, from International Scholarly Book Services Inc, 6A Mill Trading Estate, Acton Lane, London NW 10.

*Mind the Curve!* is the story of Melbourne's extensive but now defunct cable tramways service, which with 46 miles of double track was one of the largest in the world, not excepting either San Francisco or Chicago—an interesting book on an interesting subject. I could be biased, having been 'brought up' with them. Their crews were friendly fellows: one could jump on and off easily under way (for their merits were regularity and frequency, never speed), and the excitement of hanging on round the curves never wore off. You could see it all (except the cable in its slot below the roadway), and feel a part of it—the moustachioed gripman skilfully disengaging the cable after approaching the curve at a furious rate, perhaps up to 13 or 14 knots, with shouts of 'Mind the curve!' and much clanging of his bell—the shout to keep the customers aboard, the bell to warn approaching vehicles and horsemen if any, letting them know that, for the moment at least, the tram was not under command. For cables ran straight and did not round curves: the gripman once round skilfully and rapidly picked up the next, and he had to get round with his way, or stall there. 'Passengers Must Not Talk to the Gripman', said the rules: few bothered about that, except perhaps small boys who were kept in their place then. For the driver stood among his passengers who were seated (or hanging on standing) around the little 'dummy', as the for'ard vehicle was called. The conductor collected his fares without fuss or haste, stepping from car to dummy and back again at full speed with no bother at all, even on the curves. Melbourne's huge sprawl was well suited to a cable tramway service, and for at least two generations the trams were the principal (often the only) means of public transport. Among their merits were regularity, frequency, and quiet. The same cable could haul along as many trams as could hitch on to it.

John Keating, a Melbourne man too, has presented the story thoroughly and well, going into management, finance, relevant Acts of Parliament, personalities and technicalities, combining the whole in lively and readable prose. The many illustrations keep up the same high standard, and the Melbourne University Press has produced an attractive, well-printed and well-bound book.

*Oxford*                                                                    Alan Villiers

**The Nutbrook Canal: Derbyshire,** by Peter Stevenson, DAVID & CHARLES, Newton Abbot, 1970, pp 159, ill, maps and diagrams, £2.25.

Books on industrial archaeology have, so far, dealt with a relatively large area, or a complete industry. Their authors must have regretted being unable to investigate particular topics in depth.

In selecting for study the rise and fall of a now derelict canal, only 4½ miles long, Peter Stevenson has written a book which surely presages a new phase in industrial archaeology. He has shown that research into historical records, combined with a detailed knowledge of the terrain, can produce an eminently readable book. At the same time he has made an important contribution, not only to canal history and to local history, but in addition to the economic history of a much wider area than that immediately involved.

Based as it is on a complex mass of documented information, the book could have been dry reading. Not the least of the author's achievements is that he has produced an account that makes interesting reading. Indeed, Stevenson's feeling for his characters brings them alive, and we begin to know them as people.

The book is meticulously and copiously annotated, and it will be a valuable source of reference to historians of the Midlands.

It is difficult to realise that this is a first book, by one who is neither professional economist nor historian, and we shall look forward eagerly to his next book.

*Duffield*                                                           Frank Nixon

**The Campbeltown & Machrihanish Light Railway,** by Nigel S. C. Macmillan, DAVID & CHARLES, Newton Abbot, 1970, pp 164, ill, maps and diagrams, £2.25.

Mr Macmillan has long been known as an authority on the Campbeltown & Machrihanish Light Railway and, as one would expect, he has produced a very competent history of this little-known Scottish line situated in Kintyre. A 2ft 3in gauge railway which grew from a colliery line, it had the distinction of being completely isolated from any other rail transport. Its history was largely uneventful and it died quietly of bus poisoning in 1932, but it must have been quietly charming in its prime. Smart 0-6-2Ts and long verandaed bogie coaches ran the grandiloquently named 'steamer expresses' and 'golfers' trains', while much more ancient and humble four-coupled machines struggled with the coal traffic. Mr Macmillan has captured its atmosphere well and his handling of facts gives one confidence that they are correct; he has provided detailed drawings even of proposed rolling stock and the appendices are so thorough as to include a chronological list of spare parts ordered for the locomotives!

The book is written in a readable manner, marred only for your reviewer by the author's irritating and rather arch habit of using Scots colloquialisms (eg 'the wee train'). This is a minor point, however. My only real criticism of the book is a regret that, in this day of industrial archaeology, Mr Macmillan has not completed the story. The coalfield and its vicissitudes are chronicled but of the other end of the chain, the shipping of coal and passengers, there is little trace. The locally owned Campbeltown & Carradale Steam Packet Co is dismissed in a paragraph although its best-known vessel the SS *Davaar* appears twice in sketches. If the information is available, it would have been interesting to include some account of the company's activities in connection with the railway.

*Wheathampstead* W. J. K. Davies

**The Golden Arrow,** by A. Hasenson, HOWARD BAKER, London, 1970, pp 208, maps, ill, £3.25.

The Southern Railway, appealing to the would-be plutocrat which it believed to exist within every sensible man and woman, launched in 1929 with appropriate publicity the idea of a train, or rather a combined surface-transport operation, which should symbolise luxury: first-class only, Pullman service, a special ship, a degree of freedom from tiresome entry and exit formalities in nasty customs sheds, and a little more speed than ordinary passengers could get—at £5 single between London and Paris. The name 'Flèche d'Or' had first been used in 1926 on the French side. Some of the glamour so thickly and skilfully spread over what was not a particularly impressive transport performance—the overall time was never quite as good as the 6½ hours of 1913–14—still sticks, and the name 'Golden Arrow—Flèche d'Or' is still found in the railway time-books. But only for two years, from May 1929 to May 1931, did the operation even profess to cater wholly for first-class Pullman passengers, uncontaminated at any point by those of lower grades sharing some part of the train or boat.

Mr Hasenson saw in this one-time glamour train the making of a book. He works up with a chapter on 'The Early Days', outlining the development of the railways and ports concerned to about 1900; then follows 'The First Pullmans', carrying the story to 1926; 'The Golden Arrow' itself, with much information about other continental services, occupies 38 pages. A journey by the train is then described, headed 'Contemporary' but related between Calais and Amiens to steam traction, which ceased in January 1969. Pages 121 to 184 carry a selection of timetables, including Newhaven as well as Dover and Folkestone services, between 1864 and 1962. It is evident that the author has had to cast his net very wide to make up a book, and in the result the text rambles round over a good many slightly related topics; indeed, at one point he disarmingly says: 'We have wandered rather ahead of ourselves and must now get back . . .'.

Timings, connections, and technicalities do not make up a connected story. Ships and locomotives are mentioned, without detailed discussion; but it seems from the loving care with which the fate of individual Pullman cars is traced that these are the author's real love—in fact, whenever one is mentioned its name is printed in capital letters. Figures on the numbers of passengers carried at different dates, which must be available in the railway archives (not cited as a source), would have added depth and point to the story. A good many details

# Book Reviews

are unsurely handled, and even some of the beloved Pullman car names are mis-spelt. There are interesting, though sombrely-printed, photographic illustrations. The maps are excellent.

*London*                                                Michael Robbins

**The Runaway Train,** by J. R. L. Currie, DAVID & CHARLES, Newton Abbot, 1971, pp xii + 148, ill, maps and diagrams, £1.75.

On Wednesday, 12 June 1889, there occurred the most serious disaster in the history of rail transport in Ireland, an accident of such terrible proportions that the memory of it still haunts the minds of Irish railway historians. How did such a major catastrophe occur in the midst of a quiet, rural scene, on a minor branch line carrying light traffic, and in circumstances which by their very nature add poignancy to the fateful event, from beginning to end?

The answers to these questions are given in a new book devoted entirely to the disaster, the first full-length book on any Irish railway accident, and though the recent passing of the last survivors has removed the direct links with that terrible day, the passage of time cannot blur the fearsome impact of such an event on the life of a quiet country town.

Though much has been written on the Armagh disaster—most recently an exhaustive paper by Kevin Murray in the *Journal of the Irish Railway Record Society* for February 1971 (vol 10, no 54)—an event of this nature inevitably attracts a great deal of comment over the years, much of it coloured by close involvement or personal leanings or affiliations of one sort or another. We are indebted to Mr Currie for this summary of the sequence of events leading up to the disaster, of the horrific nature of the collision itself and, less spectacular but none the less important, of the far-reaching consequences which the accident had on the general level of British railway safety.

The events of that fateful day are beyond dispute. On a sustained climb on the hilly Armagh–Markethill–Newry line, close to Hamiltonsbawn, a heavy excursion train out from Armagh, bound for Warrenpoint, ran out of steam. In an attempt to resolve a difficult situation the superintendent in charge of the train decided to separate the rake of fifteen carriages and draw the first five on to Hamiltonsbawn, returning immediately for the remaining ten and clearing the line before the arrival of the regular service working from Armagh to Newry. The rearmost portion of the excursion train, crowded with children on a Sunday School outing, was set in motion and gathering speed at an alarming rate ran backwards down the 1 in 75 slope towards Armagh, colliding violently with the passenger train on a high embankment just outside the town. The death toll amounted to 80, most of them children, and over 260 were injured.

With the perception and clarity of judgement afforded by hindsight, what was the cause of the disastrous accident which overwhelmed this summer excursion on a June morning all these years ago? It appears that there was no single cause but a number of contributory factors, all of them important: the very slight margin of safety when one compares the haulage capacity of the locomotive with the weight of the excursion train in relation to the steep gradients encountered on the hilly terrain of south Armagh (for this blame must be apportioned between the officials at Dundalk who selected a locomotive and driver ill-equipped to handle the heavy excursion special, and the Armagh stationmaster, who failed to notify the railway company of the known increase in the numbers who would be travelling on the train); the misguided judgement of the Dundalk superintendent, who divided the train; the locking of the doors of many of the carriages which turned the small compartments into cells from which escape was impossible; the presence of unauthorised personnel in the rearmost brake van; the inadequate braking system etc. Added to these one must also mention a total breakdown of rational behaviour once the severed portions of the train had begun to move apart, a reaction not altogether surprising in view of the terrible implications already harrowing the minds of the principals involved.

One point which may well hold the key to the entire train of events was that the guard, Thomas Henry, was a relief man, normally a shunter at Dundalk, who had little experience of passenger working or excursion train management. The brake and luggage compartments of his van had a complement of fourteen or fifteen unauthorised persons who might well have prevented him devoting full attention to his duties, even interfering with the handbrake at various times on the journey. It is recorded that to trackside observers the train seemed to be labouring on the incline from quite an early stage. Could it be that Henry had failed to release the van brake properly at the outset (as had been the case leaving Dundalk earlier in the morning) thereby placing an additional strain on the locomotive, sufficient to bring the train to a halt on the bank? Furthermore, if this was the case, whenever Henry tightened the brakes on the van at the rear of the ten carriages moving off down the slope the holding power of the blocks on the tyres would be considerably lessened. This I believe to have been one of the chief factors contributing to the disaster which followed.

While the book affords a comprehensive résumé of events leading up to and resulting from the accident, it adds little to our knowledge of the disaster and may be regarded more as a useful reference work for railway historians from Britain and abroad, recording one of the most fateful days in the history of Irish rail transport.

*Ulster Museum, Belfast*                                W. A. McCutcheon

# Our Contributors

WILLIAM ALBERT is an American who lectures in economic history in the University of East Anglia, Norwich. He gained his London doctorate for a thesis on eighteenth-century roads and previously contributed to *Transport History* in 1968.

J. C. HOPKINS, a member of the Railway and Canal Historical Society, is particularly interested in early waggonways. He lives in Winsford, Cheshire.

R. J. CROFT, MA (Dublin), is a lecturer at Canterbury Technical College and is currently working on various aspects of nineteenth-century railway shipping services from both English and French sources.

T. E. DEVINE is a graduate of the University of Strathclyde where he now lectures in social and economic history. He is presently conducting research for his doctorate on the Glasgow merchant community c 1780–1815.

# Shorter Reviews

**Boats and Boatmen of Pakistan,** by Basil Greenhill, DAVID & CHARLES, Newton Abbot, 1971, pp 191, ill, maps and diagrams, £2.50.

A truly fascinating and original study of the river and seagoing craft of both east and west Pakistan, this book is the product of five years' field-work by Mr Greenhill. As well as defining the different types of vessel, and analysing the constructional techniques used, the author vividly describes the harsh way of life of the boatmen. Seldom has such a major contribution to the history of technology been so pleasantly written.

**LMS Steam,** by O. S. Nock, DAVID & CHARLES, Newton Abbot, 1971, pp 269, ill, £3.15.

This is a companion volume to the same author's *Southern Steam* and *LNER Steam*, and is similar in format and approach. Mr Nock gives a readable and well-illustrated account of the work of pregrouping locomotives under the LMS, and of the evolution of standard types to replace them.

**London & South Western Railway Locomotives,** by H. C. Casserley, IAN ALLAN, London, 1971, pp 184, ill, £3.

Mr Casserley has once again drawn on his magnificent photographic collection in the compilation of this attractive 'miniature pictorial history' of LSWR locomotives. Each class of locomotive is described and illustrated, with tabular information on building and withdrawal. Altogether this is a very pleasing and well-produced volume.

**Met de groeten van Trijn,** by Marie-Anne Asselberghs, BIGOT & VAN ROSSUM NV, Blaricum, Holland, 1971, pp ii + 87, ill, no price stated.

In this pleasant little volume, Mrs Asselberghs, Director of the Railway Museum, Utrecht, has selected eighty-seven commercial postcards of Dutch railway scenes which are reproduced one to a page, and accompanied by short captions and engravings. Most of the cards date from before World War I, and vividly recall the atmosphere of a European system in the great days of the railway. The book's publication coincided with the opening of an exhibition of old picture postcards of Dutch railways.

**Railway Enthusiasts' Handbook 1971-2,** edited by Geoffrey Body, DAVID & CHARLES, Newton Abbot, 1971, pp 169 + xvi, ill, £1.50.

The 1971-2 edition of this useful volume has the same format as the 1970-1 issue. Notes on societies and other bodies concerned with railways, on British Rail developments, on continental railways and on model railway societies are accompanied by some good half-tone illustrations.

**'Twixt Rail & Sea, and The 'King' of Railway Locomotives,** by W. G. Chapman, PATRICK STEPHENS LIMITED, London, 1971, pp 160 each, ill, £1.50 each.

We have already noted Patrick Stephens's reprints of *The 10.30 Limited* and *Caerphilly Castle* (*Transport History*, vol 4, no 2). The latest additions to this publisher's series of reprints of Great Western Railway booklets are similar in style. *'Twixt Rail & Sea* deals with the Great Western Railway's docks in South Wales, and gives a valuable picture of cargo-handling methods in the 1920s. The *'King' of Railway Locomotives* is an account of the evolution of the GWR 'King' class and their construction. Again probably the most interesting aspect of this volume is the account of locomotive building at Swindon in the 1920s.

**GWR Engines: Names, Numbers, Types & Classes,** DAVID & CHARLES REPRINTS, Newton Abbot, 1971, pp 216, ill, £1.75.

Interest in GWR publicity material seems to be intense, as measured by the output of reprints. *GWR Engines* is a reprint of the engine books of 1911, 1928 and 1946, with some pages from the 1938 engine book. The books show how information for enthusiasts became more comprehensive. The 1911 edition is an illustrated list of named engines, the 1928 volume has a note on the evolution of GWR locomotives, and then details of each class, with names where appropriate, illustrated by half-tone side views. The few pages of the 1938 edition reproduced consist of notes on named trains and advertisements, while the 1946 edition has notes on naming, a historical survey, and details of each class, illustrated by half-tones and line drawings. The quality of reproduction is excellent.

**The West Somerset Mineral Railway,** by Roger Sellick, DAVID & CHARLES, Newton Abbot, 1970, pp 128, ill, maps and line drawings, £1.75.

This is the second edition of a book originally published in 1962. The first edition was well received, and indeed this account of iron mining in the Brendon Hills and of the railways called into being to serve the mines is of considerable interest. The way in which the railways' fluctuating fortunes is related to geological and economic conditions is particularly good.

**The Cambrian Railways, Volume I: 1852–1888,** by Rex Christiansen and R. W. Miller, DAVID & CHARLES, Newton Abbot, 1971, ill, maps and diagrams, £2.10.

The first edition of this book, published in 1967, was fully reviewed in *Transport History*, vol 1 (1968), pp 302–4. The second edition embodies some minor corrections, but is otherwise unchanged.

**The Chronicles of Boulton's Siding,** by Alfred Rosling Bennett, DAVID & CHARLES, Newton Abbot, 1971, ill, diagrams, £3.

Some books have a reputation that is almost legendary, and *The Chronicles of Boulton's Siding* is one of these. Published in 1927, when the author was 77, this is a charming history of Isaac Watt Boulton's locomotive business at Ashton-under-Lyne. Boulton was a locomotive dealer, and would buy second-hand locomotives, modify them for industrial use, and sell or hire them. Some very interesting and unusual locomotives passed through his hands, and Mr Bennett wittily describes their origins and vicissitudes. It is indeed good to have a reprint of this delightful volume, which is well illustrated with line drawings and half-tone blocks.

**Miniature Railways, Volume 1—15 Inch Gauge,** by Howard Clayton, Michael Jacot and Robin Butterell, OAKWOOD PRESS, Lingfield, Surrey, 1971, pp 129, ill, maps, £2.

The latest manifestation of the rapidly growing interest in miniature railways, this volume is the most complete account yet published of British 15in gauge lines and their locomotives. The authors, two of whom own locomotives of this gauge, have managed to unearth a great deal of hitherto unpublished material, including photographs. This is a most entertaining book, and includes some intriguing 'detective stories' of the search for the surviving Bassett-Lowke 'Little Giant' class locomotives.

*Papercovered Editions*

David & Charles have issued the following volumes as paperbacks:

**British Railways Shipping and Allied Fleets: The Postwar Period,** by W. Paul Clegg and John S. Styring, (originally published as *British Nationalised Shipping* in 1969), pp 304, ill, £1.50.

**A Century of Traction Engines,** by W. J. Hughes, (originally published in 1959), pp 262, ill, diagrams, £1.25.

**Railways in the Victorian Economy: Studies in Finance and Economic Growth,** by M. C. Reed, (originally published in 1969), pp 231, £1.50.

# Notes and News

*Recent Pamphlets*

Tramways continue to receive detailed attention from authors and publishers, the Tramway Museum Society being to the fore. *Leicester's Trams in Retrospect*, by M. S. W. Pearson, is a very handsomely produced and well-illustrated informal history of the Leicester system. The narrative is enlivened by many personal reminiscences of tramway employees. Price £1, the publication is available from the Tramway Museum, Crich, Matlock, Derbyshire, DE4 5DP. From the same publishers, price 40p, comes *The Crich Mineral Railways*, by 'Dowie'. This is a most attractive account of the two mineral railways built to carry limestone from Crich. The earlier of these, the Butterley Gangroad, was engineered by Benjamin Outram and William Jessop, and was the scene of William Brunton's experiments with his 'steam horse' in 1813. The other line belonged to George Stephenson and was, unusually, of metre gauge. It is on part of this route that the Tramway Museum's line is now constructed.

The London Area of the Light Railway Transport League has followed the successful publication of John Barrie's reminiscences of North London's tramways with a similar booklet entitled *Memories of Glasgow's Tramways 1927-1962*. This nostalgic look at one of Britain's finest systems is nicely illustrated, and costs 30p. Copies are available from F. R. Martin, 32 Church Road West, Farnborough, Hants.

The Light Railway Transport League and the Manx Electric Railway Board have collaborated in the publication of *Snaefell Mountain Railway 1895-1970* by F. K. Pearson. This is a brief illustrated guide to the line and its history. Priced at 13p, copies are available from LRTL Publications (Retail), 130 Coombe Lane, Croydon CR0 5RF.

Not quite railway preservation, and in fact a commercial light railway in a new location, the Lincolnshire Coast Light Railway has not received the attention it deserves. To celebrate the tenth anniversary of the opening of the line, K. E. Hartley has written a booklet *The Lincolnshire Coast Light Railway* which neatly describes the background to the line's construction, the vicissitudes of operation, and the rolling stock used. Very reasonably priced at 12½p, copies may be had from P. Balderston, 46 Cromwell Road, Cleethorpes, Lincolnshire.

Recent Oakwood Press publications include *The Didcot, Newbury & Southampton Railway* by T. B. Sands. The subject of this booklet was originally proposed in 1846, but was not constructed until 1879-91. The line was worked by the Great Western Railway from the start, but not absorbed until 1922. Mr Sands's book is based on a wide range of sources, and is most competently written.

*Railways Round Exmoor* is the title of the latest addition to the Exmoor Press's Microstudy series. Written by Robin Madge, this excellent booklet summarises the history of the numerous lines built and projected in the Exmoor area. Illustrated by some fine maps and sketches, it forms a good introduction to the complex railway history of the area, and is reasonably priced at 50p. Copies are available from The Exmoor Press, Dulverton, Somerset.

To commemorate the diamond jubilee of trolleybus operation in Bradford, the National Trolleybus Association has published an attractive illustrated booklet entitled *60 Years of Bradford Trolleybuses*. Bradford is now the only city in Britain still operating trolleybuses, and was the first to do so. Copies may be had from NTA Publications Dept, 29A Hillfield Park, Muswell Hill, London, N10, price 28p (including postage).

*Archive Teaching Units*
J. T. Ward writes:
Newcastle University Education Department's sixth archive teaching unit, prepared by Messrs C. D. Kilkenny and L. Turnbull, consists of two useful 'background' booklets and 38 well-chosen contemporary documents on *The Northumberland Election, 1826*. The choice of subject to illustrate a pre-Reform county contest is admirable. Northumberland's 3,000 electors were regaled by personal scandals, coach and sea trips, boozy dinners, assorted pamphlets and lampoons, varied slanders and a duel between two partisans. And the candidates were remarkable: T. W. Beaumont (successively Tory, Whig and 'independent' landowner and leadminer); Matthew Bell (Tory squire and coal owner, who inherited the Brandlings' interest); Henry Liddell (Canningite son of the coalmaster-merchant -landowner Lord Ravensworth); and Lord Howick (Whig heir of Earl Grey, hereditary leader of the local aristocratic Whigs). All four had considerable business interests, particularly in mining; all four families were to be involved in aspects of railway history. The immediate interest of this excellent compilation is, however, inevitably political. After 15 days of polling, during which 'beer was plentiful and water was scarce', and after an expenditure of £250,000, Liddell and Bell were returned.

*Periodicals*
We were glad to receive for review a copy of a new journal, *Steam Man*, devoted to all forms of steam engine. Edited by Kenneth Brown, the first of two trial issues includes articles on the Trevithick bicentenary parade, locomotive preservation, and removing boiler tubes, as well as a substantial notes and news section, which contains a 'steam diary'. Copies of this well-produced periodical, price 33p including postage, may be obtained from Steam Man Publications, 66 Neal Street, London WC2, or from the Editorial Office, Stag House, Great Kingshill, High Wycombe, Bucks.

The April 1971 issue of *The Lock Gate*, journal of the Great Ouse Restoration Society, has an interesting note on the problems posed by heavy traffic on the Ouse between Earith and Tempsford, which almost reaches saturation point round St Neots. There is also a fascinating short article on the Danish harbours in Bedfordshire, built as fortified enclosures for longships. The subscription to the society is 50p for 1971–2, and will rise to £1 for 1972–3. The membership secretary is Mr D. W. Simmonds, 47 Park Avenue, Bedford.

As usual, *Railway Philately* manages to publish a wide range of articles. In the June 1971 issue, articles include further instalments of 'Carrier Stamps of the British Isles' and 'Danish Private Railway Stamps', as well as 'France beyond the sea', a note on stamps depicting features of French colonial railways. The annual subscription is

£1.50 with an entrance fee of 25p, the Membership Secretary of the Railway Philatelic Group being A. Violet, 18 Queens Road, Hale, Altrincham, Cheshire. R. A. Kirk of 59A Hartley Road, Kirkby in Ashfield, Nottingham, NG17 8DS, is the indefatigable editor of the journal.

The Summer 1971 number of *Sussex Industrial History* contains a useful article on Dolphin Motors of Shoreham, an early venture of Sir Harry Ricardo, the great internal-combustion engineer. This concern made two-stroke-engined cars for a brief period just before World War I. The Notes and News section also contains material of interest to transport historians. A single issue costs 40p, the annual subscription (for two issues) being 75p. The magazine is obtainable from the publishers, Phillimore & Co Ltd, Shopwyke Hall, Chichester, Sussex.

In *The Industrial Railway Record* for February 1971, there are articles on the railways at the Coronation brickworks, Elstow, Bedfordshire, the locomotives of the La Poveda sugar factory near Madrid, and on narrow-gauge wagons built by W. G. Allen & Sons (Tipton) Ltd. The April issue has notes on the Sundon Cement Works Railway, Bedfordshire, on an 1846 boiler explosion, and on gasworks locomotives. Production is up to the usual high standard, and copies are available from R. V. Mulligan, 41 Egerton Road, Birkenhead, Cheshire, L43 1UJ, price 25p.

*Maritime History*, the new journal devoted to merchant shipping, made its second appearance in September (vol 1, no 2). Among the principal papers are the following important studies which will be of interest to transport historians: 'The Port of Stockton-on-Tees and Its Creeks, 1825-61: A Problem in Port History' by Peter Barton (illustrated); 'Shipping in the Anglo-Russian Grain Trade, to 1870' by Susan Fairlie; and 'Reflections on the Rochdale Inquiry into Shipping' by Derek Aldcroft.

*Maritime History* is published half-yearly by David & Charles at an annual subscription of £1.75 (single copies 90p).

*From the Museums*

*Glasgow.* The Museum of Transport has published another of its useful handbooks. Entitled *Fire Engines*, this deals with the evolution of fire-fighting appliances with particular reference to Glasgow. Though transport only in a narrow sense, there is no doubt of the fascination of fire engines, and the booklet, written by J. L. Wood, Assistant Curator, puts the museum's exhibits neatly into their context. Priced 30p, including postage and packing, copies are available from the Museum of Transport, Albert Drive, Glasgow S1.

*Liverpool.* The City of Liverpool Museums opened a new gallery devoted to the Port of Liverpool on Friday, 16 July. The opening ceremony was performed by Sir John Nicholson, Bart, KBE, CIE, JP. The museums' newsletter in its July 1971 issue contains a note on the shipbuilding activities of the Vulcan Foundry, the well-known locomotive building works. Iron ships were built by the firm on the Irwell at Warrington, and included the fine full-rigged ship *Tayleur* of 1,750 tons. She was lost on her maiden voyage to Australia owing to a false compass reading produced by the iron hull.

*Greenwich.* The National Maritime Museum's new lecture theatre was opened on Wednesday, 14 July, by Sir Hugh Casson. Designed by a team including museum Officers, features include a moving dais, full air-conditioning, remote controlled slide-projectors, lighting dimmers, and first-class tape recording and sound amplification units. The theatre, which seats 120, can be divided by a travelling curtain to provide a smaller room.

*Ironbridge Gorge.* This, the most recent museum of industrial archaeology, has now reached the stage of issuing publications. Those forwarded for review are a guide to Ironbridge Gorge (25p), a smaller guide with a folding map (8p) and an account of the Coalport Tar Tunnel (20p). All are well produced, the first two being illustrated with sketches. In view of the significance of the area as a cradle of rail transport and of iron bridge construction, these publications should be of interest to readers of *Transport History*. The pamphlet on the tar tunnel is particularly interesting, as the tunnel was apparently intended as a canal level, and was in fact used as a railway tunnel linking coal workings with Coalport. As we go to press we learn that Neil Cossons, the able Deputy Director of the City of Liverpool Museums, has been appointed Director of the Ironbridge Gorge Museum. We wish him well.

*News from the Preservation Societies*

*The Yorkshire Derwent.* As promised in our July issue we are now in a position to give readers more details about the campaign to restore the delightful Yorkshire Derwent. The Inland Waterways Association has established a trust (The Yorkshire Derwent Trust Ltd) which has been busily engaged in negotiation with the river authority and others to try to obtain the agreements necessary before actual physical work can be started. We understand that it is likely that work on the lock at Sutton-on-Derwent may be commenced quite soon and that the trust will set up a society, open to public subscription, to support the efforts. At the time of going to press an acting secretary for the future society has not yet been appointed, but we are able to give the name of the trust's secretary who would doubtless be able to supply those interested with more up-to-date information: Dr G. H. Smith, 24 The Moorway, Tranmere Park, Guiseley, Yorkshire.

*The Katie of Padstow Preservation Society.* This society was formed in April 1970 to acquire the Cornish topsail trading schooner *Katie*, to restore her to original condition and to return her to Cornwall. The *Katie* was discovered by Mr Roger Holmes of Liskeard in a dock in Copenhagen under the name *Wiiqouua*. The vessel can be purchased for £500, and £3,000 will be required for immediate repairs. The estimate for complete restoration is about £25,000. The *Katie* was built at Padstow in 1881 by John Cowl & Sons, and was originally engaged in carrying slate to the Continent. She eventually became the last engineless cargo schooner in Europe, and after 1945 was sold to Danish owners for the Baltic trade. Donations to the society should be sent to Dr Frank Argall, 'Katie of Padstow Preservation Society', 36 Bosvean Gardens, Bosvigo, Truro, Cornwall.

*Scottish Inland Waterways Association.* A new society to encourage the use and conservation of inland waterways, particularly canals, in Scotland, was formed in Edinburgh on 8 May 1971. There is growing interest in cleaning and restoring sections of the Union Canal and the Forth & Clyde Canal for various recreational and educational purposes, and the SIWA should act as a catalyst to produce some action. The secretary is J. Howdle, Leith Nautical College, Commercial Road, Leith, Edinburgh.

*The Corris Railway Society* (see p 277). Originally formed in 1966 as The Corris Society, this small but enthusiastic body is establishing a museum at Machynlleth, and eventually proposes to re-lay part of the railway. To raise funds, a good selection of postcard-size prints of Corris Railway scenes is produced for sale, together with a neat reprint of the *Corris Railway Guide of 1895*. This is a charming little booklet, illustrated with engravings, and sells at 12p (including postage). The reprint, and postcards, are available from the Sales Officer, 20 Woodlands Road, Hertford, Herts. Subscription to the society is 80p per annum, plus an entrance fee of 30p, the membership secretary's address being 165 Gynsill Lane, Anstey, Leicester, LE7 7AN.

*Ravenglass & Eskdale Railway*. The railway reports a good start to the 1971 season, with record figures for the Easter holiday period. Four locomotives were in service, though *River Esk* was out of service with valve trouble. The valve chests have since been rebored and new valves fitted. In February a quarter-scale model of a Western class diesel locomotive *Princess Anne* made a trial trip on the line. Built by Severn Lamb for the Lakeside Miniature Railway at Southport, the trip was a complete success. Re-laying of the line with new rail and jarrah sleepers continues, the latest stretch being through Murthwaite, where the opportunity was taken to realign the track.

*Festiniog Railway*. Roy Cunningham writes: With *Merddin Emrys* and *Linda* in top-link condition and three other engines expected to be available for duty, the Festiniog Railway hopes to handle record crowds with efficiency and comfort in 1971. A three-tier fare structure has been introduced, designed to encourage a spread of the load on busy peak-season weekdays.

A great deal of labour has been expended on the development of *Linda's* oil firing, but with results which appear to have vindicated the introduction of this controversial but none the less inevitable feature. Performance now, admittedly under test-train conditions, is generally agreed to be as good as, if not better than, that under coal firing, with a marked absence of the black exhaust and foul odour which attended the early trials in November. The decision has been made to convert *Mountaineer* and *Blanche* as soon as the work can be fitted into the programme. In the case of *Mountaineer* in particular, a considerable amount of work is involved and this will probably be put in hand towards the end of the running season.

Semaphore signalling has been introduced at Portmadoc Harbour Station. A motor-operated 'Up Starter' signal is located a full train's length beyond the King points, enabling all normal shunting movements to take place even when there is a train 'in section'. These shunting movements are protected by a Down Home signal, situated some 200yd beyond the Up Starter, which controls trains approaching the station. The Up Starter, normally in the 'on' position, automatically clears when a staff is withdrawn from the drawlock beside the platform at Harbour Station, and returns to danger when the train passes it. As the Portmadoc Harbour to Minffordd section is one of the most heavily worked on the railway, with, in addition to the regular passenger services, light engines to and from Boston Lodge and the coal traffic between there and Minffordd, the new signalling, in addition to providing an added safeguard against a train inadvertently being taken into the section without having obtained the train staff, will provide greater operating flexibility. Both signals are mounted on SR-type rail-built posts, built from FR rails, and the signals are ex-Great Northern 'somersaults' from Holloway. The colour light signalling at Minffordd is now operational, and a signalling scheme

## Notes and News

for Penrhyn has been approved and is now being installed.

*Scottish Railway Preservation Society.* The society's first open day of the 1971 season was held on 22 May, and was a considerable success. For the first time, two locomotives were in steam—*Clydesmill No 3*, a Barclay 0-4-0 saddle tank, and No 20 of the Wemyss Private Railway, a Barclay 0-6-0 side tank. Visitors were given a chance to ride in a restored Caledonian Railway coach hauled by one of these locomotives (see p 278).

*Dartington Seminar*

As readers will probably know, periodic seminars for those seriously concerned with the study of local history are held at Dartington in Devon. The next one, arranged for the weekend of 12/13 February 1972, will have Charles Hadfield and Peter Kennedy, the Devon County Archivist, among its speakers. Anyone seriously engaged in research in transport history who is interested can write for an invitation to attend. The seminar is a fairly small group and therefore reasonably early application would be advisable. Prospective partici- pants should write direct to Professor W. E. Minchinton, Department of Economic History, University of Exeter, Streatham Court, Rennes Drive, Exeter, EX4 4PU.

*Paddle Steamers*

The few British paddle steamers still in service include three Humber ferries, the *Lincoln Castle* (see p 279), *Tattershall Castle* and *Wingfield Castle*; one Clyde steamer, the *Waverley*; and the Loch Lomond steamer *Maid of the Loch*. Even the Caledonian Steam Packet Company, owners of the *Waverley*, seem to be aware of the ship's value as a rarity, and stress that she is the only sea-going paddle steamer in Europe. Unfortunately 1971 will probably be her last season of operation.

Paddle steamers can still be found on the Continent, and on a recent visit to Germany one of the editors sailed on the *Ludwig Fessler*, the last steamer on the Chiemsee, Bavaria's largest lake. She was built in 1926, and with a capacity of 675 passengers is considerably smaller than most British paddlers—the *Waverley* could take 1,350. Sadly, 1971 will probably, as with the *Waverley*, be her last season (see p 280).

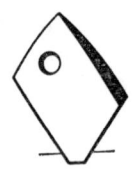

## The Birth of the Great Western Railway

'A railway book out today makes a pleasant change from the endless train locomotive pictures and specifications. "The Birth of the Great Western Railway" comprises extracts from the diary and correspondence of George Henry Gibbs—one of the very few personal records of the work and thoughts of an early railway entrepreneur. The extracts have been edited by Jack Simmons.' MANCHESTER EVENING NEWS. £1.50

## Working to Rule *by Kenneth Hudson*

Railway workshop rules: a study of industrial discipline. 'The collection of working rules drawn up by the railways over a period of 125 years is probably unique in the history of British industrial relations. Mr Hudson deserves to be complimented for assembling this collection in one book.' TIMES LITERARY SUPPLEMENT. £1.80

## Life and Labours of Mr Brassey, 1805–1870

By Arthur Helps. '. . . elegantly reproduced, fortified by an informative introduction from Professor Jack Simmons . . . it contains a great deal of highly interesting information about an astonishingly neglected Victorian giant.' OBSERVER. £2.50

## English Pleasure Carriages *W Bridges Adams*

The classic guide to the horse-drawn carriage, published in 1837. Adams was an inventive engineer who saw transport as a whole and included an interesting discussion on railways. Introduction by Professor Jack Simmons. £3.15

## The Railway Traveller's Handy Book

There is no other book on railway travelling like this one. First published in 1862, it provided 'Hints, Suggestions, and Advice, Before the Journey, On the Journey, and After the Journey.' Illustrated with 15 contemporary engravings, it is the perfect gift for all railway enthusiasts. £1.75

---

**ADAMS & DART** 40 Gay Street Bath Somerset

# RAILWAY AND CANAL HISTORICAL SOCIETY
*Founded 1954*

The Society exists to bring together all those interested in the history of railways and canals and offers a quarterly journal, a lively monthly bulletin, visits to places of interest and local group meetings.

*Details of membership from: Hon Secretary, 174 Station Road, Wylde Green, Sutton Coldfield, Warwickshire.*

The Society also offers the following publications for sale:

**A SHORT HISTORY OF THE LIVERPOOL & MANCHESTER RAILWAY**, by G. O. Holt, (2nd edn, price 38p, post free).

**HOW FFESTINIOG GOT ITS RAILWAY**, by M. J. T. Lewis, (2nd edn, price 63p, post free).

**MAP OF THE KINGTON, LEOMINSTER & STOURPORT CANAL** by R. J. Dean (30 in × 15 in) Scale 1 in to mile 30p.

*Available from Hon Sales Officer, 'Macrae', Stubbs Wood, Amersham, Bucks.*

---

## TRANSPORT HISTORY
Goose publications for industrial archaeologists and transport historians:

**MINOR RAILWAYS OF ENGLAND AND THEIR LOCOMOTIVES, 1900–1939** (new title)
George Woodcock 8¼″ × 5¼″ 188 pages, 77 illustrations
SBN 900404 06 X £2.75

**A SHORT HISTORY OF THE MIDLAND AND GREAT NORTHERN JOINT RAILWAY**
Ronald H. Clark 9¾″ × 7¼″ 224 pages, 111 illustrations, pull-out map
SBN 900404 05 1 £3.75

**THE DEVELOPMENT OF THE ENGLISH STEAM WAGGON**
Ronald H. Clark 9¾″ × 7¼″ 256 pages, 314 illustrations
SBN 900404 02 7 £3.15

**THE OVERTYPE STEAM ROAD WAGGON** (new title)
M. A. Kelly 11″ × 8¼″ 144 pages, 180 illustrations
SBN 900404 07 8 £3.98

**THE VINTAGE YEARS AT BROOKLANDS**
Doctor Joseph Bayley 7¼″ × 9¼″ 272 pages, 136 illustrations
SBN 900404 00 0 £3.75

**BROUGH SUPERIOR**
The Rolls-Royce of Motor Cycles
Ronald H. Clark 8¼″ × 5¼″ 192 pages, 99 illustrations
SBN 900404 03 05 £2.38

**ALWAYS IN THE PICTURE** (new title)
the story of Veloce Limited, Motor-cycle Manufacturers
J. W. Clew and R. W. Burgess
9¾″ × 6″, 250 pages, 114 illustrations
SBN 900404 08 6 £4.50

*In Preparation*
**A TRACTION ENGINE MISCELLANY**
Ronald H. Clark    Publication late 1971

**THE RAILWAY FOUNDRY, LEEDS**
the history of a famous locomotive works by R. N. Redman
Publication late summer 1971

**THE AUTOMOBILES OF CHINA AND THE U.S.S.R.**
Maurice A. Kelly
Probable publication spring 1972

**THE UNDERTYPE STEAM ROAD WAGGON**
the second volume of M. A. Kelly's Complete History of Steam Road Waggon Builders
Publication spring 1972

*From your bookseller or* GOOSE & SON, *publishers, 23 Davey Place, Norwich NOR 38E, Norfolk   Tel: 0603 27241/2*

# The Economics of Tramp Shipping

## B. N. METAXAS

Dr Metaxas draws on his wide practical and academic experience of transport economics to discuss the structure of the industry, its detailed operating costs, opportunities and rewards and to show how it interacts with other maritime industries such as the tanker, bulk carrier and liner fleets. He examines the economic reasons for the fluctuations in freight rates and traces the industry's attempts to institute compensation agreements for the laying up of ships and the stabilization of rates.

0 485 11127 6 £4.50

## The Athlone Press
### UNIVERSITY OF LONDON

---

**ST JOHN THOMAS BOOKSELLERS LTD**

Specialists in Books on Transport History, Industrial History, Social and Economic History. Catalogues of works on these subjects are now available.

**ST JOHN THOMAS BOOKSELLERS LTD**

30 WOBURN PLACE, LONDON WC1H OJR

Telephone 01 580-9449

---

## ALL FORMS OF TRANSPORT

We publish a long illustrated list of books on transport history and allied subjects. Send for our free Transport leaflet which gives details of all our titles on Canals and Waterways, Railways, Road, Steam, Naval and Maritime History.

**David & Charles**
**Newton Abbot**
**Devon**

# NEW from GREENWOOD
## in ECONOMIC HISTORY

**TRANSPORTATION TO THE SEABOARD: The "Communication Revolution" and American Foreign Policy, 1860-1900**
by Howard B. Schonberger, Hampton Institute

Departing from the usual considerations of domestic politics or the growth of the economy, this book puts into historical perspective America's post-Civil War struggle for world power, with full documentation of the dynamic interrelation of transportation, foreign trade, and the emergence of the U.S. as a dominant political and economic force throughout the world.
(Contributions in American History, No. 8)            $10.50

**BUSINESS AND POLITICS IN AMERICA FROM THE AGE OF JACKSON TO THE CIVIL WAR: The Career Biography of W. W. Corcoran**
by Henry Cohen, Loyola University, Chicago

This book deals with the complex combination of factors that shaped the financial and political policies of the U.S. during the 1840s and 1850s, with the focus on the entrepreneur W. W. Corcoran whose intricate web of business-government relationships thrust him into a dominant position of national power and influence.
(Contributions in Economics and Economic, No. 4)          $13.50

**PATERNALISM AND PROTEST: Southern Cotton Mill Workers and Organized Labor, 1875-1905**
by Melton A. McLaurin, University of South Alabama

The evidence offered here refutes the entrenched view that Southern mill operatives rejected the overtures of organized labor during the latter part of the nineteenth-century and shows how management's shrewd use of social, economic, and political pressure ended serious organizational efforts in the South until World War I.
(Contributions in Economics and Economic History, No. 3)        $11.00

**THE DEPRESSION OF THE NINETIES: An Economic History**
by Charles Hoffmann, State University of New York, Stony Brook

A well-documented study that brings into focus the major forces that slowed down the economy in the United States during the 1890s and created one of the most severe depressions in the history of the nation.
(Contributions in Economics and Economic History, No. 2)        $12.00

Order Direct From    **GREENWOOD PUBLISHING COMPANY**
U.S.A.               51 Riverside Ave., Westport, Conn. 06880

# AUTUMN TRANSPORT TITLES

*July*
**The Cambrian Railways: Volume 1 1852-1888.** Rex Christiansen and R W Miller, £2.10 (new edition, *Railway History series*) Vol 2 1889-1968 still available at £2.10
**4-8-0 Tender Locomotives.** D Rock Carling, £2.97 (*David & Charles Locomotive Studies series*)

*September*
**The Great Western Railway in Dean: A History of the Railways of the Forest of Dean—Part Two.** H W Paar, £2.25 (new edition, *Railway History series*). Part One, The Severn & Wye Railway, will be reprinted shortly
**The Railways of Consett and North-West Durham.** G Whittle, £3.45 (*Railway History series*)
**Railways of North Africa: The Railway Systems of the Maghreb.** E D Brant, £3.15 (*Railway Histories of the World series*)

*October*
**Guide to the Great Siberian Railway (1900).** Edited by A I Dmitriev-Mamonov and A F Zdziarski, £5.75 (*David & Charles Reprints*)
**Lost Canals of England and Wales** Ronald Russell, £2.95
**Speed Records on Britain's Railways: A Chronicle of the Steam Era.** O S Nock, £2.75
**Steam Locomotives of the South African Railways: Volume 1 1859-1910.** D F Holland, £3.90 (*David & Charles Locomotive Studies series*)

*November*
**North Eastern Locomotive Sheds.** K Hoole, £2.75
**A Regional History of the Railways of Great Britain Volume 6: Scotland—The Lowlands and the Borders.** John Thomas, £3.50

*January*
**Barging into France.** G W Morgan-Grenville, about £3
**The Lancashire & Yorkshire Railway: Volume 3.** John Marshall, £3.50 (*Railway History series*). Vols 1 and 2 are still available at £2.75 and £3.15 respectively.
**Mountain Moor and Loch: On the Route of the West Highland Railway (1895).** £2.50 (*David & Charles Reprints*)

## DAVID & CHARLES
Newton Abbot . Devon

# Index to Volume 4 of Transport History

(R) indicates a review, bold type an illustration

Agriculture, Board of, and roads, 226
Aircraft, 94–6, 207
Airways, 105
Allen, W. G., & Sons (Tipton), 320
Altrincham, and Manchester, 153
American War of Independence: and Glasgow West India merchants, 266–304; and shipping, 194–6
Anderson, C. W. B., Hull & Barnsley Rlwy dock superintendent, 187
Ardrossan, railway and steamboat services, 3, 9, 10, 12, 13, 17
Armstrong, Joseph, Jr, of GWR, 58
Avonmouth: Dock, 84, 85, 86; pier, 83
Aylesbury, bus service, 28, 29
Ayr, 272, 290; railway and steamboat services, 1–4, 9, 12–13
Ayre, William, canal scourer, 126

Banks, and railway finance, Scotland, 166–8, 177–82
  Aberdeen Bank, 179
  Arbroath Banking Company, 177
  Bank of Scotland, 180
  British Linen Company, 177, 178, 180
  British Trust Company formed, 180
  City of Glasgow Bank, 179
  Clydesdale Bank, 167, 179, 180
  Commercial Bank, 167, 168, 179
  Dundee Banking Company, 180
  and exchange companies, 180–1
  Forbes, Sir W., & Co, 177
  loans to railway companies, 168, 177–9, 182 n 7
  National Bank, 167
  North of Scotland Bank, 178
  railway share holdings, 167–8
  Royal Bank of Scotland, 166, 177, 178, 179, 180
  Union Bank of Scotland, 168
Barges: on Beverley Beck, *170*, *171*; Thames sailing, 210

Barnett & Gale, dock engineers, 84
Barton, James, Hull & Barnsley Rlwy asst accountant, 187
Bedford, bus services, 24–30
Beith area, and press-gangs, 289
Belfast, 271; steamboat services, 8, 12–13
Belvoir Highways Board, 114
Benson, Robert, L & MR director, 153, 156
Beverley: borough finance and Beverley Beck, 121–43
  Beck Fund, 134–5, 138; annuities on, 139
  Beverley Beck Acts (1727 & 1745), 129–31, 133–4, 135, 136
  tolls, 129–32; income and expenditure figures, 131, 143; leasing practice, 131–2; list of lessees, 132, 142
  *See also under* Canals
Bicycling, 106
Birmingham, and Manchester, 155, 156
Birmingham Canals, construction of, *see* Pinkerton, John
Blackwall, railway and steamboat services, 1–8, 14–16, 18
Board of Trade Railway Department, and brakes, 50, 53, 57, 62, 63–4, 73–5
Boase, Charles, banker, 180
Boats and boatmen, Pakistan, 315
Bogle, Scott & Co, 295 n 6
Bolton, and Manchester, 148
Books and pamphlets:
  Abbott, Rowland A. S., *The Fairlie Locomotive* (R), 206
  Abell, P. H., *British Tramways and Preserved Tramcars*, 109
  Albion, Robert Greenhaugh, *The Rise of New York Port (1815–1860)* (R), 211

329

Books and pamphlets—cont.

Anon, *Bicycling 1874: A Textbook for Early Riders* (R), 106
Asselberghs, Marie-Anne, *Met de groeten van Trijn* (R), 315
Atthill, Robin, *The Picture History of the Somerset & Dorset Railway* (R), 212
Bai, Emil G., *Fall! Fall! Fall! öwerall, Berichte über den schleswig-holsteinischen Walfang am Biespiele der Stadt Elmshorn, 1817–1872* (R), 209–10
Ball, E. & P. W., *Holiday Cruising on the Thames* (R), 106
Barnes, E. G., *The Midland Main Line, 1875–1922* (R), 100–1
Bateson, Charles, *The Convict Ships 1787–1868* (R), 210
Bennett, Alfred Rosling, *The Chronicles of Boulton's Siding* (R), 316–17
Bennett, Eric, *The Worshipful Company of Wheelwrights of the City of London 1670–1970* (R), 96–7
Biddle, Gordon, see Hadfield, Charles
Body, Geoffrey (ed), *Railway Enthusiasts' Handbook 1970–71* (R), 106; *Railway Enthusiasts' Handbook 1971–2* (R), 315
Boyd, J. I. C., *Narrow Gauge Railways in Mid-Wales* (R), 212
Brown, G. A., Prideaux, J. D. C., and Radcliffe, H. G., *The Lynton and Barnstaple Railway* (R), 213
Bruce, J. Graeme, *Steam to Silver*, 109
Butterell, Robin, see Clayton, Howard
Caernarvonshire Record Office, Bulletin No 3, 113
Canadian National Historic Sites Service, *Canadian Historic Sites*, 112–13
Cardy, A. A. C., *A History of Modern Road Transport* (R), 211
Casserley, H. C., *London & South Western Railway Locomotives* (R), 315; *Railway History in Pictures: Wales and the Welsh Border Counties* (R), 213
Chapman, W. G., *Caerphilly Castle* (R), 213; *The 'King' of Railway Locomotives* (R), 316; *The 10.30 Limited* (R), 213; *'Twixt Rail & Sea* (R), 316
Chatterton, E. Keble, *The Old East Indiamen* (R), 210–11
Christiansen, Rex, and Miller, R. W., *The Cambrian Railways, Volume I: 1852–1888*, 316
Clayton, Donald C., *Handley Page: An Aircraft Album* (R), 207
Clayton, Howard, Jacot, Michael, and Butterell, Robin, *Miniature Railways, Volume I—15 Inch Gauge* (R), 317
Clegg, W. Paul, and Styring, John S., *British Railways Shipping and Allied Fleets: The Postwar Period*, 317
Corris Railway Society, *Corris Railway Guide of 1895*, 322
Curr, John, *The Coal Viewer, and Engine Builder's Practical Companion* (R), 209
Currie, J. R. L., *The Runaway Train* (R), 311–13
Davies-Shiel, M., see Marshall, J. D.
Davis, Dennis J., *The Thames Sailing Barge: her Gear and Rigging* (R), 210
Doerflinger, Frederic, *Slow Boat through England* (R), 205
'Dowie', *The Crich Mineral Railways* (Tramway Museum Society), 318
Dunstan, John, *The Origins of the Sheffield and Chesterfield Railway*, 214–15
Ellis, C. H., *London Midland & Scottish: a Railway in Retrospect* (R), 208
Essery, R. J., Rowland, D. P., and Steel, W. O., *British Goods Wagons, from 1887 to the Present Day* (R), 107

## Index

Farey, John, *A Treatise on the Steam Engine* (R), 211
Farr, A. D., *The Campbeltown and Machrihanish Railway* (R), 107
Fox, M. J., and King, G. D., *Industrial Steam Album* (R), 205–6
Galton, Francis, *The Art of Travel* (R), 211
Gibson, Cecil, *Commercial Vehicles* (R), 207; *Veteran and Vintage Cars* (R), 207
Giffard, Ann, *see* Greenhill, Basil
Gomm, P. G., *Older Locomotives (1900–42)* (R), 207
Gordon, W. J., *The Horse-World of London (1893)* (R), 209
Great Western Railway, *GWR Engines Names, Numbers, Types & Classes* (R), 316; *Service Timetables, Bristol to Exeter and branches, October 1886* (R), 212
Great Western Society, list of locomotives and rolling stock, 220
Greenhill, Basil, *Boats and Boatmen of Pakistan* (R), 315; and Giffard, Ann, *The Merchant Sailing Ship: A Photographic History* (R), 210
Hadfield, Charles, *Canal Enthusiasts' Handbook, 1970–71* (R), 106; and Biddle, Gordon, *The Canals of North West England* (R), 198–9
Hart, C. A. (ed), *The Railway Theme—A Study of Railways on Stamps* (Railway Philatelic Group), 214
Hartley, K. E., *The Easingwold Railway* (R), 208–9; *The Lincolnshire Coast Light Railway*, 318
Hasenson, A., *The Golden Arrow* (R), 309–11
Hawke, G. R., *Railways and Economic Growth in England and Wales 1840–1870* (R), 189–91
Hibbs, John, *Transport Studies: An Introduction* (R), 196–8
Hughes, W. J., *A Century of Traction Engines*, 317; (ed) *Fowler Steam Road Vehicles—Catalogues and Working Instructions* (R), 205
Hyde, W. G. S., *see* Pearson, F. K.
Industrial Railway Society, *British Industrial Locomotives—National Coal Board Surface Systems 1967–1969* (ed A. R. Etherington), 110; and Narrow Gauge Railway Society, *Preserved Locomotives in the British Isles*, 110
Ironbridge Gorge Museum, pamphlet on the Coalport Tar Tunnel, and guides to Ironbridge Gorge, 321
Jackson, H. T., *The Railway Letter Posts of Great Britain—Part I* (Railway Philatelic Group), 214
Jackson-Stevens, E., *British Electric Tramways* (R), 211
Jacot, Michael, *see* Clayton, Howard
Johnson, W. Branch, *Industrial Archaeology in Hertfordshire* (R), 107
Joy, David, *Railways in the North* (R), 205; *Traction Engines in the North* (R), 205
Joyce, J., *Trams in Colour since 1945* (R), 205
Kalla-Bishop, P. M., *Italian Railways* (R), 212; *Mediterranean Island Railways* (R), 206
Kay, David, *Buses and Trolleybuses 1919 to 1945* (R), 205
Keating, John D., *Mind the Curve! A History of the Cable Cars* (R), 306–7
Kelly, Maurice A., *The Overtype Steam Road Waggon* (R), 305–6
'Kennington', *London County Council Tramways Handbook* (Tramway & Light Railway Society), 109
King, G. D., *see* Fox, M. J.
Kirkaldy, A. W., *British Shipping (1914)* (R), 108
Lee, Charles E., *Seventy Years of the Central*, 109; *The Swansea and Mumbles Railway*, 215
Lewis, M. J. T., *Early Wooden Railways* (R), 191–3

Light Railway Transport League, *Memories of Glasgow's Tramways 1927–1962*, 318; see also Pearson, F. K.
Lipscombe, Commander F. W., *Historic Submarines* (R), 108
McCutcheon, Alan, *Railway History in Pictures, Volume 2* (R), 213
Macmillan, Nigel S. C., *The Campbeltown & Machrihanish Light Railway* (R), 308–9
Madge, Robin, *Railways Round Exmoor*, 318–19
Manx Electric Railway Board, see Pearson, F. K.
March, Edgar J., *Inshore Craft of Britain in the Days of Sail and Oar* (R), 104
Marshall, J. D., and Davies-Shiel, M., *The Industrial Archaeology of the Lake Counties* (R), 104–5
Marshall, John, *The Lancashire & Yorkshire Railway, Volume Two* (R), 101–2
Masé, Armin, see Schneider, Ascario
Mather, F. C., *After the Canal Duke: A Study of the Industrial Estates administered by the Trustees of the Third Duke of Bridgewater in the Age of Railway Building, 1825–72* (R), 200–3
Maxted, Ivan, *The Canterbury & Whitstable Railway*, 215
Midland Counties PSV Restoration Club, set of timetables of independent bus services in Northamptonshire, 214
Miller, R. W., see Christiansen, Rex
Morgan, Bryan, *Railway Relics* (R), 193–4
Munson, Kenneth, *Pictorial History of BOAC and Imperial Airways* (R), 105
Narrow Gauge Railway Society, see Industrial Railway Society
National Trolleybus Association, *60 Years of Bradford Trolleybuses*, 319
Newcastle University Education Department, *The Northumberland Election 1826* (archive teaching unit), 319
Nock, O. S., *The GWR Stars, Castles & Kings, Part 2: 1930–1965* (R), 206; *LMS Steam* (R), 315
Parr, R. B., *An English Country Tramway*, 109
Peacock, Thomas B., *Great Western London Suburban Services* (R), 98–9
Pearson, F. K., *Snaefell Mountain Railway 1895–1970* (Light Railway Transport League and Manx Electric Railway Board), 318; and Hyde, W. G. S., *Isle of Man Tramway Album*, 214
Pearson, M. S. W., *Leicester's Trams in Retrospect* (Tramway Museum Society), 318
Prideaux, J. D. C., see Brown, G. A.
Radcliffe, H. G., see Brown, G. A.
*Railway Clearing House Handbook of Railway Stations (1904), The* (R), 213
*Railway Officials' Directory for 1922* (R), 211–12
Randall, P. E., *Recent Locomotives (1947–70)* (R), 207
Reed, M. C., *Railways in the Victorian Economy: Studies in Finance and Economic Growth*, 317
Rigby, B. L., *The Malta Railway* (R), 206
Rolt, L. T. C., *Talyllyn Adventure* (R), 212; (ed) *Talyllyn Century* (R), 212
Rowland, D. P., see Essery, R. J.
Sands, T. B., *The Didcot, Newbury & Southampton Railway*, 318
Schneider, Ascario, and Masé, Armin, *Railway Accidents of Great Britain and Europe* (R), 206–7
Sellick, Roger, *The West Somerset Mineral Railway* (R), 316
Smith, Peter, *The Turnpike Age* (R), 107
Steel, W. O., see Essery, R. J.
Stevenson, Peter, *The Nutbrook Canal: Derbyshire* (R), 308

*Index* 333

Styring, John S., *see* Clegg, Paul S.
Syrett, David, *Shipping and the American War 1775–83: A Study of British Transport Organisation* (R), 194–6
Thomas, J. M., *Roads before the Railways 1700–1851* (R), 107–8
Tramway & Light Railway Society, *see* 'Kennington'
Tramway Museum Society, *see* 'Dowie' *and* Pearson, M. S. W.
Turner, P. St John, *Handbook of the Vickers Viscount* (R), 94–6
Warren, J. G. H., *A Century of Locomotive Building by Robert Stephenson & Co 1823–1923* (R), 108
Wilson, Roger Burdett, *Go Great Western: A History of GWR Publicity* (R), 98–9
Wood, J. L., *Fire Engines*, 320
Wrottesley, A. J., *The Midland & Great Northern Joint Railway* (R), 207–8
Bough, Mr, Birmingham Canal Navigation superintendent of works, 34–5, 39–40, 43, 44, 46
Boulogne, cross-Channel traffic through (1840–70), 252ff
Boulton, Isaac Watt, locomotive dealer, 316–17
Bradshaw, Robert Haldane, Bridgewater Trust superintendent, 159, 201
Brakes, continuous, and Scottish railways, 50–64, 73–9
Brake systems:
  Clark-Webb Chain Brake, 52, 53–4, 61, 62, 73, 75
  Fay's Mechanical Brake, 52
  Le Chatelier counter-pressure brake system, 78
  Smith's Vacuum Brake, 52ff, 74ff
  Steel McInnes Air Brake, 52–3, 61; system described, 77–8
  Westinghouse Air Brake, 52, 53, 54
  Westinghouse Automatic, 52ff, 73ff
Brake tests, trials, 52–5, 57–8, 59, 60, 63

Bridges, tubular, 110
Bridgewater Trust, trustees, 146–7, 154, 159, 160–1, 200–2
Bridlington, harbour works, 128
Bristol Corporation: outports taken over, 85; resort development at Portishead, 80–1
Bristol docks: City, 83, 84; King Edward, 85. *See also* Avonmouth; Portishead
British Transport Historical Records Office, 114–15, 144
Brittain, George, CR locomotive superintendent, 58, 61
Brunel, I. K.: plans for Portishead, 81–2, 83, 87 n 9; diagrams, 90
Brunswick Wharf, Blackwall, 4, 6, 7, 14–15; landing charges, 19 n 10
Brunton, William, 318
Bryant's Map of Cheshire (1831), 245, 250, **274**
Buckden, Huntingdonshire, bus services, 23–32
Bull, Mr, canal contractor's engineer, 40, 41, 44
Bus companies and operators:
  Aylesbury Bus Company, 28
  Birch Brothers, 30
  Eastern National Omnibus Company, 26, 27, 28
  Gill, A. J., 30
  F. J. Hinsby, 24, 25
  National Omnibus and Transport Company (formerly National Steam Car Co), 25, 26, 28
  Premier Travel, 30
  Tilling Group, 27
  United Counties Omnibus Company, 27, 30
Buses, 25, 205; competitive position (1820–40), 1, 3
Bus services Huntingdonshire–Aylesbury, 23–32; map, 29. *See also* Bus companies and operators
Bus timetables, 23ff, 214
Butler, Joseph, ironmaster, 251
Butterley Company, 114

Cable trams, Melbourne, 306–7

Calais, cross-Channel traffic through (1840–70), 252ff
Campbell, Lord Frederick, Army Commander, 271
Canal cruising, 205
Canals and navigations:
  Aire & Calder Navigation, 33, 184
  Ashby de la Zouch Canal, 251
  Basingstoke Canal, 33, 42, 49 n 40; Greywell Tunnel, 49 n 40
  Barnsley Canal, 33
  Beverley and Barmston Drain, 136, 137, **171**
  Beverley Beck, **169–71**; map, 123; scouring method, 126. See also Beverley
  Billingham embankment and drainage, 33
  Birmingham & Fazeley Canal, 33, 38
  Birmingham Canal, 34, 35, 38; Broadwaters extension, 34, 38. See also Pinkerton, John
  Bridgewater Canal, 159, 160, 161, 200
  Calder & Hebble Navigation, 33, 161
  Coteau du Lac, canal at (St Lawrence River), 112–13
  Cromford Canal, 114
  Coventry Canal (Fazeley–Fradley section), 38
  Derby Canal, 114
  Derwent Navigation, 114
  Driffield Navigation, 33, 137
  Dudley Canal, tunnel, 33, 35–6, 49 n 40
  Erewash Canal, 33, 114
  Fazeley Canal, 34, 39; Curdworth locks, 35, 42; Dunton locks, 42; Dunton tunnel, 35, 41; Minworth–Fazeley section, 35, 39–40. See also Pinkerton, John
  Fradley Canal, 49 n 58
  Gloucester & Berkeley Canal, 33
  Godalming Navigation, 114
  Grand Surrey Canal, 216
  Hedon Navigation (Hedon Haven), 33
  Herefordshire & Gloucestershire Canal, 114
  Lancaster Canal, 33
  Leeds & Liverpool Canal, 148
  Leicester Navigation, 251
  Leicestershire & Northamptonshire Union Canal, proposed extension to Buckby, 114
  Macclesfield Canal, 246, 249
  Manchester, Bolton & Bury Canal, 198
  Market Weighton Navigation & Drainage, 33
  Melton to Stamford Navigation (proposed), 114
  Mersey & Irwell Navigation, 152, 161, 164 n 32, 202
  Nutbrook Canal, 114, 308
  Selby Canal, 33
  Trent & Mersey Canal, 38, 39, 43, 114
  Trent Navigation, 114
  Weaver Navigation, 115
  Wey Navigation, 114
Canals, N W England, 198–9
Canning, Lord, 144
Cardiff, steamboat service, 83
Carlisle, Port of, 113
Car ownership, 30, 31
Carron Ironworks, 271
Cars, veteran and vintage, 207
Castle, M., Bristol & Portishead Pier & Rlwy Co director, 83
Castlefield, 153, 160; canal wharves, 146, 159, 160
Chadwick, Edward, and Poor Law Amendment Act, 237, 240
Chapman, William, drainage works engineer, 136
Chebsey, Staffs, 146, 158
Chester Record Office, 250
Cholmley family, E Yorks, 115–16
Clayton, T. G., MR carriage superintendent, 60
Cleland, James, 2
Clevedon, 80, 82, 86
Clifton Suspension Bridge, 82
Clyde, Firth of, 271, 289
Clyde, River, 269, 286; and merchant shipping, 266ff, **277**, 281, 284–9, 292; ports survey (1656), 267;

# Index

steamboat services, 1–4, 8–13, 16–18; vessel construction on, 20 n 42, 288
Clyde Ship Building and Engineering Co, 186
Cobden-Chevalier Treaty, 263
Conner, Benjamin, CR locomotive superintendent, 52, 61, 62
Collieries:
  Auckland, proposed railways, 114
  Bryn, proposed railway, 114
  Harraton Outside Colliery, 114
  Mow Cop, Staffs, 249
  Sheffield, 209
  Stonetrough, Staffs, 245, 249, 251
  Tower Hill, Staffs, 249
Commercial vehicles, 207
Congleton mineral railway, **273**, **274**; fieldwork to trace route, 245–51
Contributors, notes on, 103, 204, 314
Cook, Captain James, 116
Cook, Thomas, 255–6
Cork, and West India merchants, 269, 295 n 15
Cotton trade (West Indies), 266, 268, 272, 292, 294; prices, 304
Cowan, William, GNSR locomotive engineer, 53, 58, 63, 64
Cowl, John, & Sons, shipbuilders, 321
Crawford, Thomas, of Robert Dunmore & Co, 289–90
Creighton, Alderman, of London, 285
Crewdson family, 152
Crewdson, Isaac, L & MR shareholder, 148, 164 n 51
Crewe, 146, 156, 157, 158
Cropper, Edward, L & MR director, 153
Cropper, John, L & MR director, 148, 153, 164 n 51
Cross-Channel passenger traffic (1840–70), 252–65; class differences, 253–9, 264 n 26; destinations, 259–61; excursions, 254–5, 258–9; fares, 253–5, 263 nn 5, 7; nationalities, 261–3; numbers of passengers, 252, 259, 260, 262, 263 n 3, 264–5; passport restrictions, 256; seasonal variation, 261–2; Thames route, 253
Cross-Channel services, 1, 4, 17

Cubitt, Sir William, civil engineer, 159
Cunninghame, William, tobacco lord, 268

Dadford, Thomas, canal engineer, 36
Danish harbours in Bedfordshire, 319
Dickson, William, supercargo, 281
Dieppe, 252, 253, 256, 264–5
Documents useful to transport historians, 113–15, 216
Dolphin Motors, Shoreham, 320
Doncaster Corporation, and River Don survey, 127
Dover–Calais cross-Channel route, 252ff
Dover–London railway connection, 5
Dover–Ostend cross-Channel route, 256, 261, 264–5
Drake, Francis, historian, 128
Drummond, Dugald, of NBR and CR: and brakes, 53, 54, 56, 57–9, 61
Dublin, steamboat services, 8
Dudley, Lord, 37
Dunmore, Robert, & Co, 268, 283, 289, 295 n 6
Dunoon, steamboat services, 9, 10, 16
Dutton, Thomas, canal sub-contractor etc, 44
Dyson, Thomas, canal contractor, 136, 137

Earle, Hardman, L & MR director, 156, 158
East & West India Dock Company, 4, 14
Egerton family, Oulton Park, 250
Egerton, Lord Francis, 154, 155, 159, 160, 200
Esdaile & Cathcart, merchants, 288
Exchange companies, Scotland, 180–1

Fares, 17, 18
  bus, 25, 26, 27
  rail/boat, 10, 15–16; cross-Channel, 253–5, 263 nn 5, 7
  railway, 6–7, 209, 263 n 5
  steamboat, 10–11, 16, 19 n 15, 21 n 65, 263 n 5

Farey, John, Sr, writer on agriculture, 246, 251
Fazeley, 35, 38, 39, 40
Fenchurch Street station, 22 n 65
Fenton, James, Beverley Beck tolls lessee, 131, 142
Fire engines, 320
Fish, fisheries, 268, 289, 293
Fishbourne, T., shipbuilder, 116
Fleetwood, steamboat services (to Scotland), 8, 13, 17
Folkestone–Boulogne cross-Channel route, 252ff
Ford, Alderman, of Bristol, 83
Fowler, John, & Co, steam road-vehicle manufacturers, 205
Fradley, 38, 40
Franco-Prussian War, and cross-Channel traffic, 256, 265
French Revolution (1848), and cross-Channel traffic, 256, 265
Fry, R., Bristol & Portishead Pier & Rlwy Co director, 83

Gargrave, John, fuller, 124, 125
Garnett, William, L & MR director, 148, 149, 153
Glasgow–London rail-steamer link, 12, 13
Glasgow railways, and steamboat competition, 1–4, 8–13, 16–18
Glasgow West India merchants and the American War of Independence, 266–72, 281–304
  arming of merchantmen, 270, 282–5
  cargoes, see cotton, rum, sugar, tobacco
  charter of vessels to government as transports, 282
  convoys, convoy system, 269–72, 281, 282–4, 286, 289, 290
  customs duties, 281, 292, 294, 299 n 106
  freight charges, 291, 292
  hire of neutral ships, 287–8
  impressment, press-gangs, 299–91, 298 n 88, 299 n 97
  insurance, 285–6; list of subscribers to policies, 301–2; premiums, 281, 283, 285–6, 290, 291, 300–1
  and Ireland, 269, 286, 293, 295 n 15
  labour scarcity, 283, 289–90
  Port Glasgow, 270, **275**, 277, 288
  privateers: British, 270, 284–5, 292, 299 n 103; enemy, 268–9, 270, 271, 272, 281, 284
  and Royal Navy, Admiralty, 269–70, 272, 282, 284, 288–9
Godmanchester, bus services, 24, 25, 28, 29, 30
Gorran Harbour, Cornwall, 113
Gourock, steamboat services, 9, 10
Gravesend, steamboat services, 1, 2, 5–7, 15–16
Greenock: railway and steamboat services, 1–4, 8–12, 16–18, **68**; and West India trade, 270, 271, **276**, 277, 293
Greenwich, railway and steamboat services, 1–8
Gresham & Craven Ltd, 75
Greta Old Bridge, 114

Hamburg, 287, 293
Hansell, J. H., historian, 246
Harrison, T. E., NER engineer, 56
Haswell, James, NER locomotive engineer, 58
Helensburgh, steamboat services, 9, 10, 16
Hertfordshire, industrial archaeology in, 107
Hewitt, Miss Catherine, and Beverley Beck finance, 137, 138
Hodgkiss, William, canal bricklayer, 41
Hodgson, David, L & MR director, 153, 156
Hoggard, Alderman John, of Beverley, 133, 135
Hopwood, Richard, boatbuilder, 133
Hotham, Sir Charles, MP, 129
Hotwells Spa, Bristol, 80, 81, 83
Houghton, John, clerk to Birmingham Canal Navigation, 34, 41, 45–6, 47
Houldsworth, M & LR chairman, 163 n 30
Houston, Alexander, & Co, 281, 285,

## Index

288, 293, 294; freight charges for sugar, 303
Hull, paddle steamer at, **279**
Hull & Barnsley Railway, steamship operation by, 183–8; charter of vessels, 185; and Hull Corporation, 183–4, 185, 187; and NER, 183–4, 185, 187
Hull Bridge, tolls, 132
Hull Corporation, and NER, 183–4, 187
Hull Dock Company, 183
Hull–Liverpool trade by canal, 161
Hull–Rotterdam steamer service, 185, 187
Humber ports, 185
Humphreys, George, arbitrator in canal dispute, 45
Hunslet Engine Company, 111
Huntingdon, bus services, 23–30

Ilfracombe, steamboat service, 83
Inshore craft, 104
Ireland, steamboat services, 1, 3, 8, 10, 12
Irvine, 290

Jessop, William, engineer, 36, 37, 318
Jones, David, HR locomotive superintendent, 64, 73–4
Journals and periodicals:
  *Double Nine* (Pocklington Canal Amenity Society), 215–16
  *Industrial Archaeology*, 116
  *Industrial Archaeology in Wales*, Newsletter No 6, 110
  *Industrial Railway Record*, 110, 215, 320
  *Lincolnshire Transport Review*, 214
  *The Lock Gate* (Great Ouse Restoration Society), 110, 215, 319
  *Maritime History*, 216, 320
  *Railway Philately*, 110, 215, 319–20
  *Steam Man*, 319
  *Sussex Industrial History*, 215, 320
  *Three Banks Review*, 166

Keenan & Froude, bridge builders, **72**, 116

Kilmarnock, railway services, 1–3, 9, 12–13
Kinnear, George, exchange company manager, 180
Knox, John, 271

Lake counties, industrial archaeology of, 104–5
Lancashire & Yorkshire East Coast Steamship Conference (1907), 183
Langham, G. & N., shipbuilders, 116
Langton, Joseph, L & MR director, 153
Largs, steamboat services, 9, 10
Laurie, Captain James, and privateering, 284
Lawrence, Charles, L & MR and GJ chairman, 150, 154, 156, 159, 160
Lawrence, John, arbitrator in canal dispute, 45
Laws, Captain James, M & LR general manager, 151–2, 161
Leeds, and Manchester, 148, 154, 161
Leighton Buzzard, bus service, 28, 29
Leith, and recruitment of seamen, 290
Leith Sugar House Co, 283
Leland, John, 124, 140 n 8
Lelham (or Lellam), William, harbour and canal contractor, 128–9, 141 n 43
Lewin, H. G., railway historian, 159–60
Limerick, 286
Liverpool, and Manchester, 145, 148, 151–2, 154–5, 161, 162
Liverpool–Glasgow steamboat services, 1, 8, 10, 12
Lloyd's Register of Shipping, 185, 186
Local history seminar, Dartington, 323
Loch, George, L & MR director, 149, 153, 155–6, 157, 159, 161, 163–4 n 30, 164 nn 46, 47, 165 n 74
Loch, James, Bridgewater Trust superintendent, 147, 149, 154, 156, 159–61, 165 n 74, 201–2
Lockwood, John, mayor of Beverley, 138
Locomotives:
  *Blanche*, 111, 219, 322
  *Clydesmill No 3*, **278**, 323
  *Earl of Merioneth*, 111, 219

Locomotives—cont.
  Linda, 111, 219, 322
  Lion, **71**
  Merddin Emrys, 111, 219, 322
  Mountaineer, 111, 219, 322
  Princess Anne, 322
  River Esk, 112, 322
  River Irt, 112
  River Mite, **71**, 112, 220
  Shannon, 220
  No 2, Corris Railway, **277**
  Stanier Class 5 4-6-0 No 5025, **176**, 220
  Wemyss Private Railway No 20 (Barclay 0-6-0T), 112, 323
  Borrows well-tank (Cowley Hill Glass Works), 110
  Fairlie and Fairlie-type, 206
  *Jerry M* (Dinorwic Quarries), 113
  *Mole*, 215
  Conner 2-4-0, CR no 92 (1865), 52
  Neilson & Co 0-6-0s (1886), 60
  Paton 0-4-2 (1860), 59
  Stirling 0-4-2s (rebuilt 1885), 60
  Stirling's 4-4-0s (G & SWR), 59, 60
  Wheatley 2-4-0 (1869) (NBR), 59
  Wheatley '420' class (NBR), 57
  Wheatley 4-4-0, second class, no 421 (NBR), 57
  '8' class 2-4-0s, 60
  '71' class 2-4-0s, 60
  '119' class 4-4-0s, 60
  '157' class 2-4-0s, 60
  '187' class 0-4-2s, 60
  '221' class 0-4-2s, 60
Locomotives, industrial, 205–6; gasworks, 320; glass works, 110; NCB surface, 110
Locomotives, main line, 207; GWR, 206, 213, 316; LMS, 315; LSWR, 315
Locomotives, preserved, 110; list, Great Western Society, 220
London: bus link with Bedford, 30; Exhibitions, 262, 265; rail-steamer link with Glasgow, 12, 13; railway connections with Manchester, 155, 157–8, 160, 162; railways and steamboat competition, 1–8, 14–18; wheelwrights, 96–7; working horses, 209

*See also* Turnpike Trusts, London
London Bridge, 1, 7
Londonderry, steamboat service, 8, 13
London–Paris passenger traffic, 253ff
Lowther, Lord, and turnpike trusts, 229, 236

McAdam, James, 239
McAdam, John Loudon, roadmaker, and turnpike trusts, 227–9, 231, 236–7, 239–41, 243 n 63
McCauslan, Captain James, Robert Dunmore & Co skipper, 290
Macclesfield, 146, 158
MacNeill, Sir John: Portishead pier plan, 81; diagram, 91
Manchester, railway junction proposals, 144–65
  and canal interests, 146, 159–61
  Hunts Bank scheme, 146ff, 164 n 6
  map, 151
  stations: Central, 163 n 3, Irwell St, Salford, 145, 147; Liverpool Road, 145, **172**, **173**; St George's St, Oldham Road, 145, 146, 148, 150; Store St, London Road, 145, 148, 150, 153–4, 158, 162; Victoria, 146, **174**, **175**
Manson, James, locomotive engineer, 60, 64
Margate, and London, 5
Marindin, Major, inquiry by, 62
Martens, J. G., trading company agent, 287
Massey, W. A., Hull & Barnsley Rlwy director, 185, 186
Mathieson, James, G & SWR superintendent, 58
Metropolis Roads Commission, 228, 237, 239, 240
Middleton, Alderman William, of Beverley, 137
Midgeley, Alderman Jonathan, of Beverley, 135
Milliken, James, & Co, 267
Millport, steamboat services, 9, 10
Milton Keynes, 217–18
Miniature railways, 317

# Index

Moncrieff, J. Mitchell, bridge designer, 72, 116
Moon, Sir Richard, L & NWR chairman, 62
Moss, John, L & MR deputy chairman, 149–50, 153, 155–8, 164 n 46
Municipal Corporations Act (1835), 238
Museums:
    City of Lincoln Libraries, Museum and Art Gallery, 215
    Crich Tramway Museum, 318
    Crystal Palace (proposed) transport museum, 216
    Great Western Railway Museum, Swindon, 112
    Ironbridge Gorge industrial archaeology museum, 321
    Liverpool City Museum, **69–71**, 112, 320
    Museum of Transport, Glasgow, 320
    National Maritime Museum, 112, 216, 320–1
Mylne, William C., Portishead pier proposal, 81

Narrow Gauge Railways of Wales Joint Marketing Panel, 219–20
NUR, Rowsley branch, 114
Navigation Acts, 267, 288
Neale, W. R.: Portishead plan, 82–3
Nelson, Alderman William, of Beverley, 130, 133
Newall, East Lancs Rlwy engineer, 50
Newhaven–Dieppe: cross-Channel route, 252, 253, 256, 257, 264–5; ferry, 115
New York port, 211

Oakley, Henry, GNR general manager, 56
Osborne, Robert, borough recorder, 136
Ostend, 256, 261, 264–5, 287, 293
Outram, Benjamin, engineer, 318

Paddle steamers, 323
    *Favorite*, 215
    *Lincoln Castle*, **279**, 323
    *Ludwig Fessler* (Germany), **280**, 323
    *Maid of the Loch*, 323
    *Tattershall Castle*, 323
    *Waverley*, 323
    *Wingfield Castle*, 323
Paisley, railways, 1–3, 8–13
Palmer, William, waterways surveyor, 128
Paris Exhibitions (1855 and 1867), 254, 255, 259, 265
Paris–London passenger traffic, 253ff
Paton, William, locomotive engineer, 51
Perry, John, waterways engineer, 128
Pickernell, Francis, lighthouse builder etc, 72, 116
Pickfords, carriers, 161
Pinkerton, George, 37, 39, 40
Pinkerton, John, canal contractor, and Birmingham Canals, 33–49
    and Broadwaters extension, 34, 38
    contracts, 33
    and Dudley Tunnel, 35–7
    and Fazeley Canal, 34–5, 39ff
    legal proceedings against, 43–7
Plimsoll, Samuel, 216
Poor Law Amendment Act (1834), and roads, 237, 238, 240
Porthcawl Harbour, 114
Portishead development, 80–93
    docks, dock projects, **65**, **66**, 82–6
    leisure industry, estate development, 80–4, 85–6; diagrams, 89–93
    piers, pier schemes, **67**, **68**, 80–3
    Royal Hotel, **67**, 80–3
    tidal harbour plan, 82
    tide mill, **67**
Postal services, railway, 214
Post Office, and roads, 226
Post Office steam packets, 216
Post offices, travelling, 110
Poyton, Richard, arbitrator in canal dispute, 45
Prattman, John, of Beverley, 137
Preservation groups:
    Corris Railway Society, 277, 321–2
    Douglas Cable Car Group, 214
    Festiniog Railway, 111–12, 218–19, 322–3

Preservation groups—*cont.*
  *Katie* of Padstow Preservation Society, 321
  Keighley & Worth Valley Railway, 220; train, **176**
  Ravenglass & Eskdale Railway, 112, 220, 322; locomotive, **71**
  Scottish Inland Waterways Association, 321
  Scottish Railway Preservation Society, 112, 220, 278, 323
  Talyllyn Preservation Society, 212, 219
  Yorkshire Derwent Trust, 220, 321
Pullman trains, 59, 310
Pybus, Anthony, and Beverley Beck finance, 133

Railway accidents, 206–7; and brakes, 52, 56, 62; Armagh, 56, 311–13; Lockerbie, 62; Royal Commission on, 63
Railway companies and lines (actual and projected):
  Arbroath & Forfar, 177, 178
  Ardrossan, 3, 12
  Ashbourne–Wirksworth, 113
  Avon–Evesham line, 114
  Ayrshire & Wigtownshire, 60
  Birmingham & Derby line, 157
  Bolton & Leigh line (L & MR), 148
  Bristol & Exeter, 82, 83, 99
  Bristol & Portishead Pier & Railway Company, 83, 84
  Bristol Port Railway & Pier Company, 83
  Burton & Ashby Light Railway, 109
  Butterley Gangroad (limestone), 318
  Caledonian: and brakes, 52, 53–4, 58, 60–3, 75; coach of, **278**; and steamboat services, 12, 17
  Cambrian Railways, 316
  Campbeltown & Machrihanish Light Railway, 107, 308–9
  Canterbury & Whitstable, 215
  Central London (tube), 109
  Churnet Valley line (L & MR), 158, 160
  City of Glasgow Union, 60
  Congleton mineral railway, *see* separate entry
  Cromford & High Peak, 113, 114
  Devon & Cornwall, 113
  Didcot, Newbury & Southampton, 318
  Duffryn, Llynir & Porthcawl, 114
  Easingwold (private), 208–9
  Eastern Counties, 8
  East Lancashire, 50
  Edinburgh & Glasgow, 51
  Edinburgh–Glasgow line, 53, 56, 57–8
  Edinburgh, Perth & Dundee, 179
  Fairbourne, 220
  Glasgow & South Western, 53, 54, 58, 59, 60, 64, 75, 77
  Glasgow–Carlisle line (G & SWR), 54, 59
  Glasgow, Paisley & Greenock, 1–4, 8–12, 16–18, 22 n 65
  Glasgow, Paisley, Kilmarnock & Ayr: and brakes, 51; and steamboat services, 1–3, 9, 10, 12–13, 17
  Grand Junction, 146, 152, 155–8
  Great Central, 185
  Great Eastern, 17, 187, 255
  Great Northern, 114; and brakes, 52, 56, 76–7
  Great North of Scotland, 178, 179; and brakes, 53, 57, 58, 63–4, 75
  Great Western, 84, 115, 318; and brakes, 58; London suburban services, 98–9; publicity, publications, 98–9, 212, 213, 316
  Hay, 113
  Heseper Peat Railway, West Germany, 110
  Highland, and brakes, 51, 53, 57, 64, 73–5, 78–9
  Hull & Barnsley, *see* separate entry
  Hull & Selby, 19 n 1
  Hull, Barnsley & West Riding Junction Railway & Dock Company, 183
  Joint:
    East Coast Joint Stock, 56, 76–7
    Midland & Great Northern Joint, 207–8

# Index

Midland-Scottish Joint Stock Agreement, 77
West Coast Joint Stock, 54
Lancashire & Yorkshire, 101–2, 115, 185; and brakes, 52, 58
Lincolnshire Coast Light Railway, 318
Liverpool & Manchester, 145, 146, 147–62, 164 nn 46, 47; list of directors in 1839, 156
London & Birmingham, 158
London & Blackwall, 1–8, 14–16, 18, 19 n 9, 22 n 65
London & Greenwich, 1–3, 18
London & North Eastern, 26, 115
London & North Western, 114, 184; and brakes, 52–3, 54, 62–3, 64, 73, 74
London–Bedford line, 114
London, Brighton & South Coast, 252, 253, 255, 258
London, Chatham & Dover, 252, 254, 255–6, 263 n 5
London Midland & Scottish, 26, 208
Lynton & Barnstaple, 213
Manchester & Birmingham, 145, 146, 148–56, 158, 160
Manchester & Bolton, 145
Manchester & Cheshire Junction, 146, 157
Manchester & Leeds, 145, 146–57, 161, 162, 164 nn 46, 47
Manchester & South Union, 157
Manchester, Bolton & Bury, 146, 147, 149, 153–4, 155, 165 n 75
Manchester–Chebsey line (M & BR), 146, 158
Manchester Connection, 146
Manchester, Sheffield & Lincolnshire, 17, 56, 185
Manchester, South Junction & Altrincham, 154, 164 n 47
Manx Electric Railway, as postal carrier, 215
Midland, 84, 100–1, 115, 215; and brakes, 52, 56, 57, 60, 63, 77
Midland Great Western, Ireland, 78
Nord, France, 254, 260, 263 n 7

North British, 178; and brakes, 53, 54ff, 75, 76–7
North Eastern, 183–5, 187–8; and brakes, 56, 58, 60
Ouest, France, 252, 253, 255, 258
Preston & Wyre, 13
Portpatrick & Wigtownshire, 75
Rumney, 113
Settle & Carlisle, 115
Sheffield & Chesterfield, 214–15
Sheffield, Ashton-under-Lyne & Manchester, 145, 148, 149, 151, 153–4
Slammannan, 179
Snaefell Mountain Railway, 318
Snowdon Mountain Railway, 78, 220
Somerset & Dorset, 212
South Eastern, 252, 254–6, 263 n 3, 264 n 26
Southern: Golden Arrow, 309–11
Stockton & Darlington, stamps issued by, 215
Sundon Cement Works Railway, 320
Swansea & Mumbles, 215
Vale of Rheidol, 220
Welshpool & Llanfair, 220
West Somerset mineral railway, 316
Weymouth & Abbotsbury, 114
Whittonstall (colliery line), 110
Wigton–Penrith light railway, 113
Wishaw & Coltness, 178
Worcester–Hereford line, 114
Railway companies, cross-Channel shipping services of, 252ff
Railway finance, Scotland, 166–8, 177–82
Railway goods wagons, 107
*Railway Magazine*, 185
Railway relics, 193–4
Railway Returns (Continuous Brakes) Act (1878), 56
Railways, and economic growth, 189–91
Railways, and steamboat competition, 1–22; Glasgow, 1–4, 8–13, 16–18; London, 1–8, 14–18
  charter of boats, 6, 10, 13, 16

Railways, & steamboat competition—*cont.*
  fares, 6–7, 10–11, 15–18, 21 n 65
  maps, 5, 9
  profitability, 12, 14–18
  purchase of boats, 6, 12, 13
  railway steamboat co, 10–12, 17
  size of boats, 19 nn 7, 15
Railway scenes on postcards, 315
Railways, Exmoor, 318–19
Railways, Ireland, 213
Railways, Italian, 212
Railways, Mediterranean islands, 206
Railways, northern, 205
Railway stations handbook (1904), 213
Railways, Wales and Welsh border, 212, 213
Railways, wooden, 191–3
*Railway Times*, 263
Ramage & Ferguson, shipbuilders, 186
Ramsgate, 5
Rathbone, Theodore W., 153, 156
Regulation of Railways Act (1889), 56–7
Reviewers:
  Aldcroft, Derek H., 105, 196–8
  Brooks, Peter W., 94–6
  Davies, W. J. K., 308–9
  Devine, T. M., 194–6
  Duckham, Baron F., 104
  Ellis, Hamilton, 100–1
  Gordon, D. I., 207–8
  Hall, J. A., 193–4
  Lee, Charles E., 191–3
  Lythe, S. G. E., 96–7
  McCutcheon, W. A., 311–13
  Musson, A. E., 104–5
  Nixon, Frank, 308
  Pollins, Harold, 189–91
  Reed, Malcolm, 208
  Rees, Paul T. L., 101–2
  Robbins, Michael, 98–9, 309–11
  Rolt, L. T. C., 305–6
  Storer, J. D., 207
  Villiers, Alan, 306–7
  Ward, J. T., 200–3, 209
  Willan, T. S., 198–9
Ricardo, Sir Harry, internal-combustion engineer, 320

Rivers: *see also* Canals and navigations
  Avon (Bristol), 80, 82, 86
  Clyde, *see* separate entry
  Don, 127, 128
  Esk (N Yorks), 116
  Frome, 80
  Hull, 121, 124, 128, 130, 132–3, 136, 139 n 2, 170
  Humber, 21 n 63, 121
  Irwell, 145, 146, 147, 152, 160, **175**, 320
  Ouse (Yorkshire), 21 n 63, 127, 128
  Severn, 89 (map)
  Thames: holiday cruising, 106; steamboat services, 1–8, 14–18
  Wear, 114
Roads, pre-railway, 107–8
Roads, repair of, 225–9, 231, 234, 239
Road transport history, 211
Robertson, Provost, of Dundee, 61
Robertson, Thomas, HR line superintendent, 53
Robinson, Alderman, of Bristol, 83
Robinson, Peter, locomotive engineer, 51
Rochdale, 145, 148
Rothesay, steamboat services, 9, 10, 16, 17
Rotterdam, 185–7, 287
Royal Albert Bridge, Cornwall, 113
Rugby, and Manchester, 155, 158
Rum trade (West Indies), 266, 272, 284; prices, 304
Rushworth, John, stonemason, 137–8
Rye Harbour Commissioners, 115

St Ives, bus services, 24–9
St Neots, bus services, 23–30
Salford, 145–7, 149, 150, 153, 154
Saltcoats, 290
Sandars, Joseph, L & MR director, 150, 153, 156
Sanders, MR locomotive engineer, 60
Savage, George, millwright, 132–3
Scotland, *see* Banks, and railway finance; brakes, continuous; Glasgow West India merchants
Scott, Walter, 177
Seven Years War, 268

## Index

Shardlow Boat Company, 114
Sharp, CR director, 61
Shaw, MR canal surveyor, 41–2
Sheasby, Thomas, canal engineer, 35, 40, 43
Sheffield Company of Cutlers, 127
Shipping, 320; and American War of Independence, 194–6, 266–72, 281–94
Ships: convict, 210; East Indiamen, 210–11; merchant sailing, 210; and shipping industry, 108
Sinclair, Sir John, and Bd of Agriculture, 226
Skidby Drainage Act (1785), 135
Sligo, steamboat service, 8
Smellie, 60
Smith, Mr, brake designer, 58
Smith, Captain, and privateering, 284
Smith, George, canal repairer, 137, 138
Smithells, James, CR general manager, 58, 61
Smyth, Sir Greville, 83
Society of Merchant Venturers, 87
*Somerset Herald*, 127
Southwark Bridge Company, 216
Speirs, Alexander, W India merchant, 286, 287
Speirs, Bowman & Co, 295 n 6
Speirs, French & Co, 286, 287, 292
Stafford Record Office, 249, 250
Staffordshire County Council, 41
Stage-coaches, 241
Stamps, railway, 215, 319; Danish, 110, 215, 319
Stamps, railways on, 214, 319
Statutory Requirements for Railways (1862 ed), 51
Steamboat, steamship companies:
  Burns, J. & G., 12, 13
  Bute Steampacket Company, 10, 11
  Caledonian Steam Packet Co, 323
  Castle Steamboat Company, 10, 11
  Diamond Steampacket Company, 5, 7, 19 n 15
  Dumbarton Steamboat Co, 10
  General Steam Navigation Co, 252–3
  Helensburgh & Gareloch Steamboat Company, 10
  Hull & Netherlands Steamship Company, 187
  John O'Groat Steam Shipping Co, 186
  Largs, Millport & Arran Steamboat Company, 10
  Pyman Steam Ship Co, 185
  Railway Steampacket Company, 11, 12, 16, 17
  Rasona Steam Ship Co, 186
  Sons of the Thames Co, 19 n 15
  Star Company, 7, 19 n 15
  Waterman's Company, 6
  Woolwich Steam Packet Company, 5, 6, 19 n 10
Steamboats, Kent coast, 1, 4, 19 n 7
Steam engines, 211
Steam road waggons, 305–6
Stephenson, George, 318
Stephenson, Robert, & Co, 108
Stevens, William, & Sons, barge-owners, 114
Stirling, James, G & SWR locomotive superintendent, 58, 59
Stirling, Patrick, of GNR, 56, 77
Stockport, and Manchester, 145
Stockton-on-Tees, port of, 320
Stone, Staffs, 158
Stranraer, steamboat service, 3, 13
Submarines, 108
Sugar trade (West Indies), 266, 267, 268, 272, 283, 284, 286, 294; duties, 299 n 106; freight charges, 291, 303; prices, 304; and privateers, 292
Sutherland, dukes of: archives, 144; railway interests, 153. *See also* Bridgewater Trust
Sutherland, First Duke of, 147, 159–61, 200–1
Sutherland, Third Duke of, 64, 74

Tamworth, and Manchester, 157
Thomas, C. F., Portishead plan of, 82–3
Thompson, James, Beverley Beck tolls lessee, 132, 142
Thompson, Matthew W., NBR and MR chairman, 60, 64
Tide mill, Portishead, **67**, 92

*Times, The*, 228, 233, 234, 235, 254
Tipton, 35
Tobacco trade, 267, 268, 287; duties, 286
Traction engines, 205
Tramway companies, and LCC, 109
Tramways, tramroads, 109, 205, 211, 318; Derbyshire, 113; Herefordshire, 113; Isle of Man, 214; Somerset, 115; Wantage Tramway, 220
Transport Act (1947), 27
Transport systems, 196–8
Transport Teachers, Guild of (proposed), 216
Travel agents, 255–6
Travel, Continental, 253–6, 259–61
Treaty of Union (1707), 267
Trolleybuses, 205, 319
Troop, Captain James, Robert Dunmore & Co skipper, 289–90
Trotter, Charles, Hull & Barnsley Rlwy chairman, 184, 186
Truro harbour and river, 113
Tucker, Thomas, C & E Commissioner, 267
Turnpike Acts, 226, 242 n 8
Turnpike roads, 107–8, 113, 114, 115
Turnpike system, and railways, 241
Turnpike Trusts, 113; Bristol, 227; Essex, 231; Middlesex, 230, 232; North Wales, 228
Turnpike Trusts, London, 225–44
finance, 229–32, 239
legislation (incl Bills), 226, 229, 231–4, 237–8, 242 n 8
Metropolis Roads Commission, 228, 237, 239, 240
reform efforts, 226–9, 232ff
repair of roads, 225–9, 231, 234, 239
trusts: Archway-Kentish Town, 230, 232; Brentford, 233, 235, 236; Commercial, East India Docks, 230, 231, 232; Kilburn, 234; Kilburn Bridge, 237; New Cross, 232, 233; Poplar–Greenwich Ferry, 230, 232; Southwark–Highgate, 232; Whitechapel–Shenfield, 233
*See also* McAdam, John Loudon

Union Bank of Scotland, 13, 168
Upwey Station, 114

Vincent, William, engineer, 133, 141 n 43
Vulcan Foundry, 320

Wages: canal contract, 36; canal construction workers', 44; herring fishery, 289; seamen's, 287, 290, 291; wage costs in transport, 198
Wales Tourist Board, 220
Warburton, John: plan for Beverley Beck, 127–8, 140 n 25
Warton, Sir Ralph, 141 n 31
Warton family, E Yorkshire, 126
Waterways, West Surrey, 114
Watkin, Sir Edward, railway magnate, 56, 185
Watt, James, 35
Watt, Smeaton, canal surveyor, 39
Webbs, the, and turnpike trusts, 230, 237
Weel Enclosure Act (1785), 135
Wells, C., historian, 85
Westinghouse, George, 51–2, 58, 60
Westinghouse Air Brake Co, 61, 63
Weston-super-Mare, 80, 82, 86
Whaling, 116, 209–10
Wheelwrights, London, 96–7
Whitby harbour, 72, 115–16
Wildgoose, John, canal surveyor, 36
Wilson, Thomas, & Co, 184, 185
Wolstanton, 245, 249, 251
Wolverton, railway town, 216–18
Woods, Edward, L & MR engineer, 149
Woolwich, steamboat services, 1, 5–7, 16
Workington harbour, 113
Wright, Barton, L & YR locomotive superintendent, 58
Wright, W. S., Hull & Barnsley Rlwy chairman, 186
Wrightson, Thomas, Beverley Beck tolls lessee, 134, 142
Wyatt, Benjamin, 251

York Corporation, and River Ouse navigation, 127